Shojo Beat

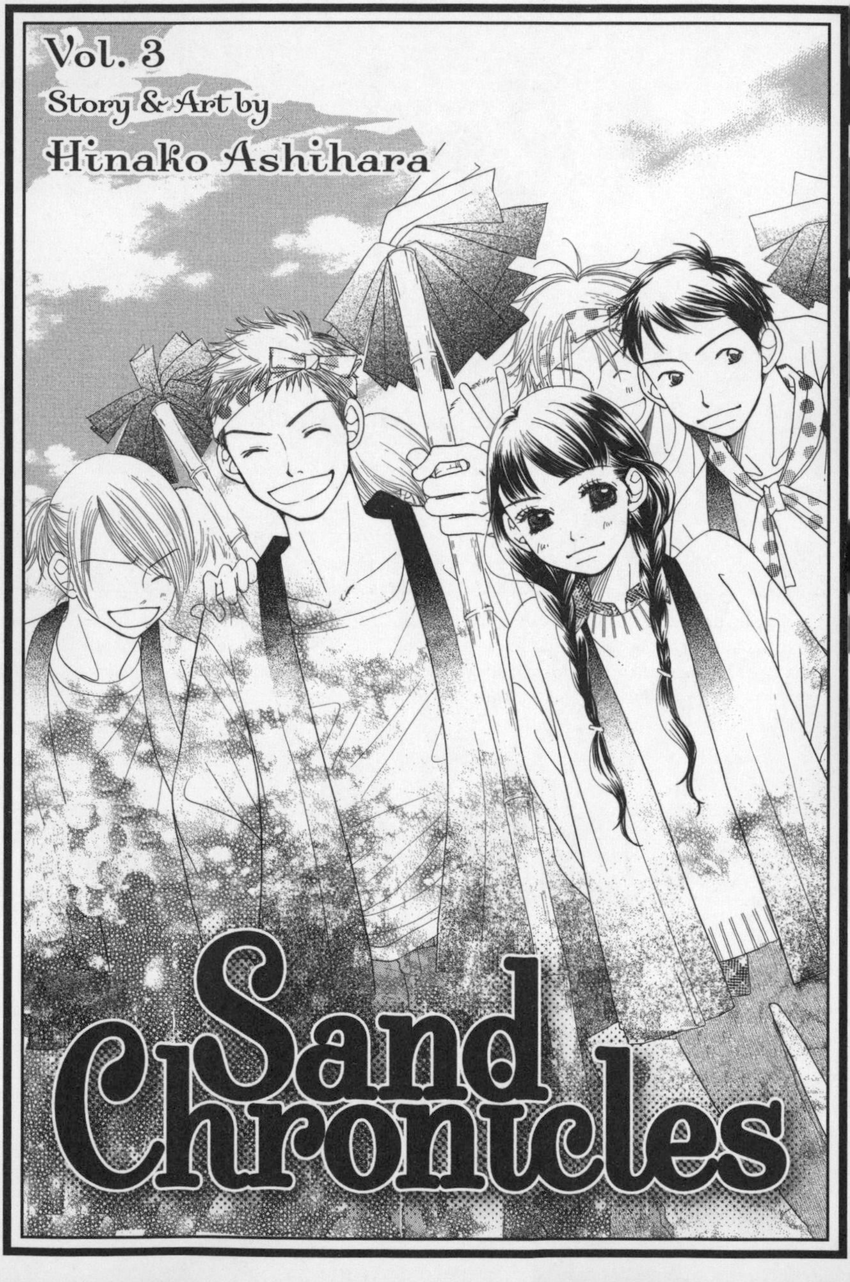
Vol. 3
Story & Art by
Hinako Ashihara
Sand Chronicles

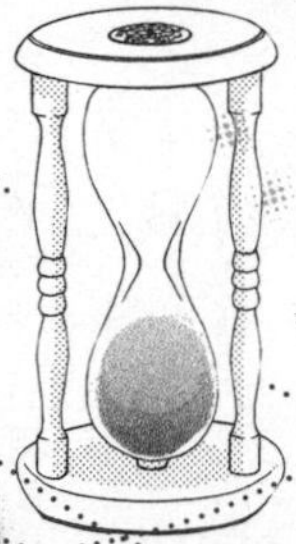

# Sand Chronicles

## Volume 3

## Contents

Summer, Age 16: The House of the Moon—5

Autumn, Age 16: Cicada Shells —107

Glossary—188

### Story thus far...

After her parents' divorce, Ann moved to Shimane with her mother. At first Ann didn't like living in the country, but then she met Daigo and other kids her age and found a place for herself. After her mother's suicide, her friends became her surrogate family. But then her father asked her to move back to Tokyo to be with him. Now she and Daigo struggle to maintain a long-distance relationship...

### Main characters

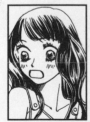 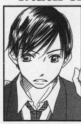 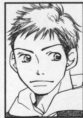 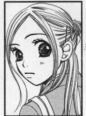

**Shika Tsukishima**
Fuji's younger sister. Soft-spoken and popular with boys.

**Fuji Tsukishima**
The son of an important family. Uncomfortable in groups.

**Daigo Kitamura**
Boyish and rough but also kind.

**Ann Uekusa**
Strong-willed but sensitive like her mother.

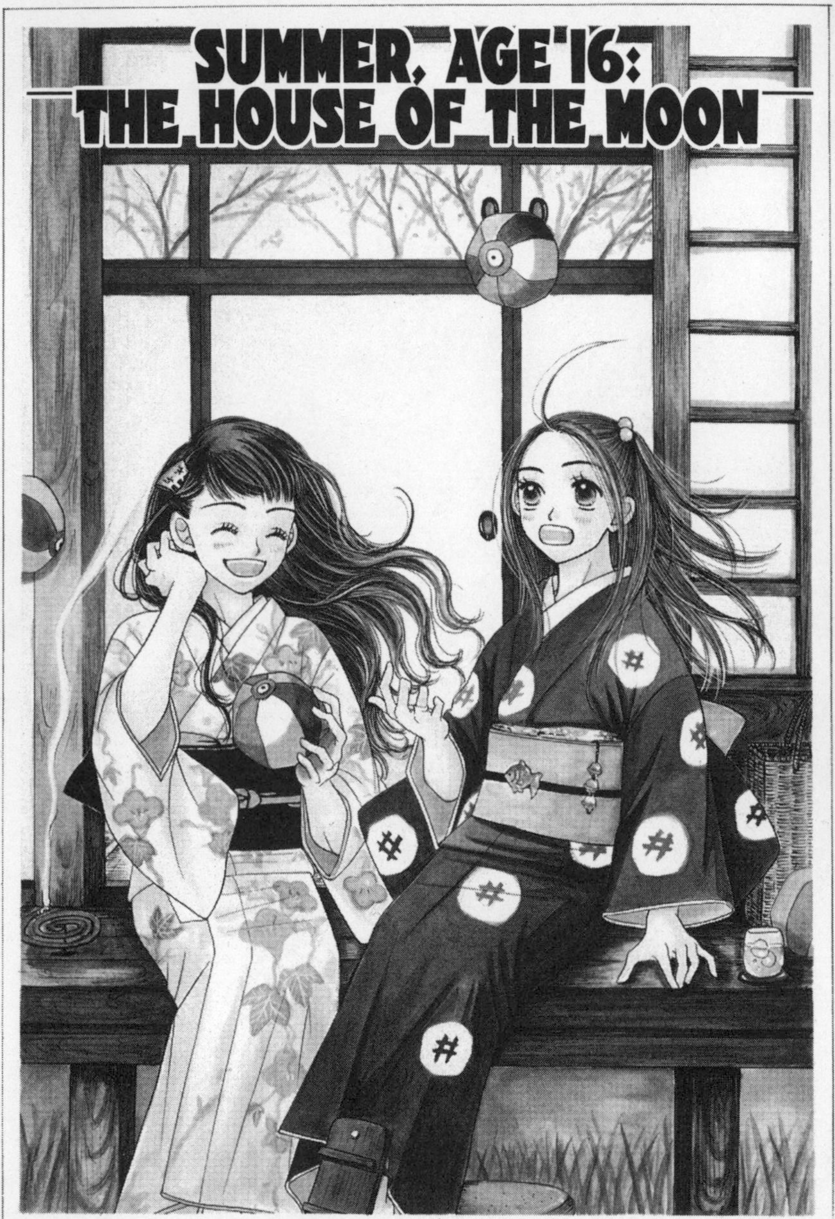
SUMMER, AGE 16:
THE HOUSE OF THE MOON

## Sand Chronicles

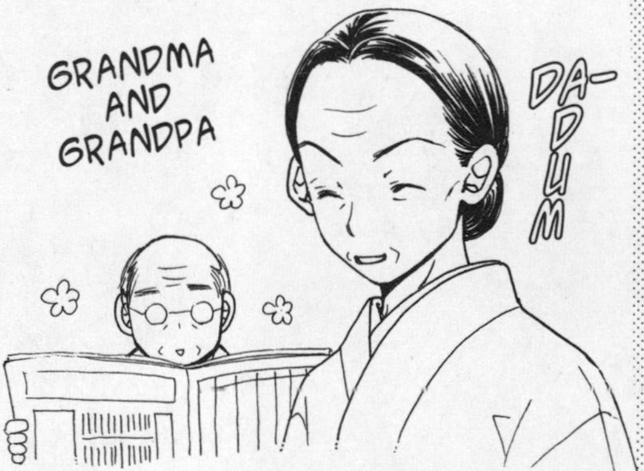
DA-DUM
GRANDMA AND GRANDPA

"Really? Ann has a grandfather?"
I often get this reaction from my assistants.
I guess Grandma makes a stronger impression.

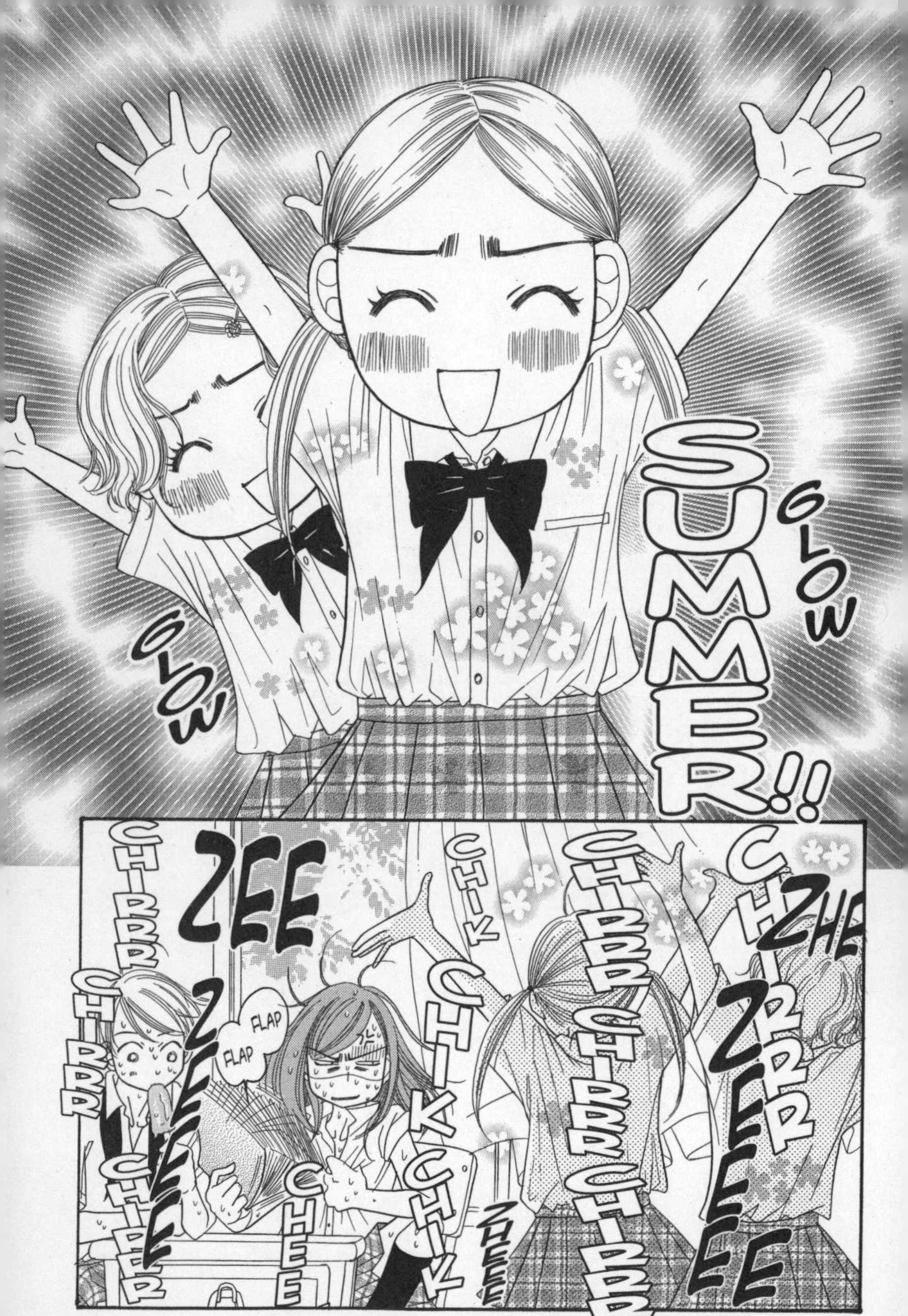
GLOW
SUMMER!!
GLOW
CHIRRR
ZHE
ZEEEEE
CHIRR CHIRR CHIRR
CHIK
CHIK CHIK CHIK
ZHEEE
CHEE
FLAP
FLAP
ZEE
ZEEEEE
CHIRR CHIRR
CHIRR CHIRR CHIRR

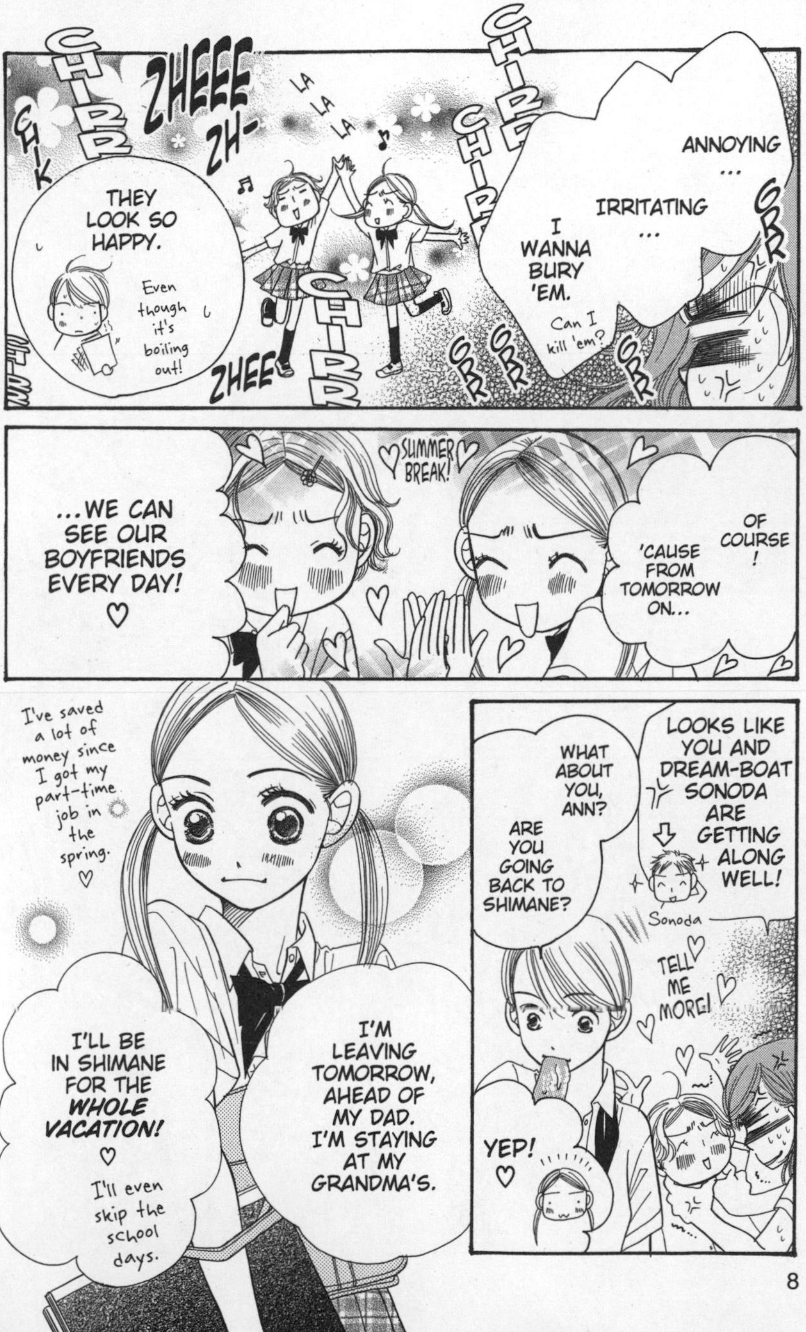

ANNOYING...
IRRITATING...
I WANNA BURY 'EM.
Can I kill 'em?
GRR GRR GRR GRR
CHIRP CHIRP CHIRP
ZHEEE ZH-
LA LA LA
CHIRP CHIK
THEY LOOK SO HAPPY.
Even though it's boiling out!
ZHEE
OF COURSE!
'CAUSE FROM TOMORROW ON...
SUMMER BREAK!
...WE CAN SEE OUR BOYFRIENDS EVERY DAY! ♡
LOOKS LIKE YOU AND DREAM-BOAT SONODA ARE GETTING ALONG WELL!
Sonoda
TELL ME MORE!
WHAT ABOUT YOU, ANN? ARE YOU GOING BACK TO SHIMANE?
YEP! ♡
I'M LEAVING TOMORROW, AHEAD OF MY DAD. I'M STAYING AT MY GRANDMA'S.
I'LL BE IN SHIMANE FOR THE *WHOLE VACATION!* ♡
I'll even skip the school days.
I've saved a lot of money since I got my part-time job in the spring. ♡

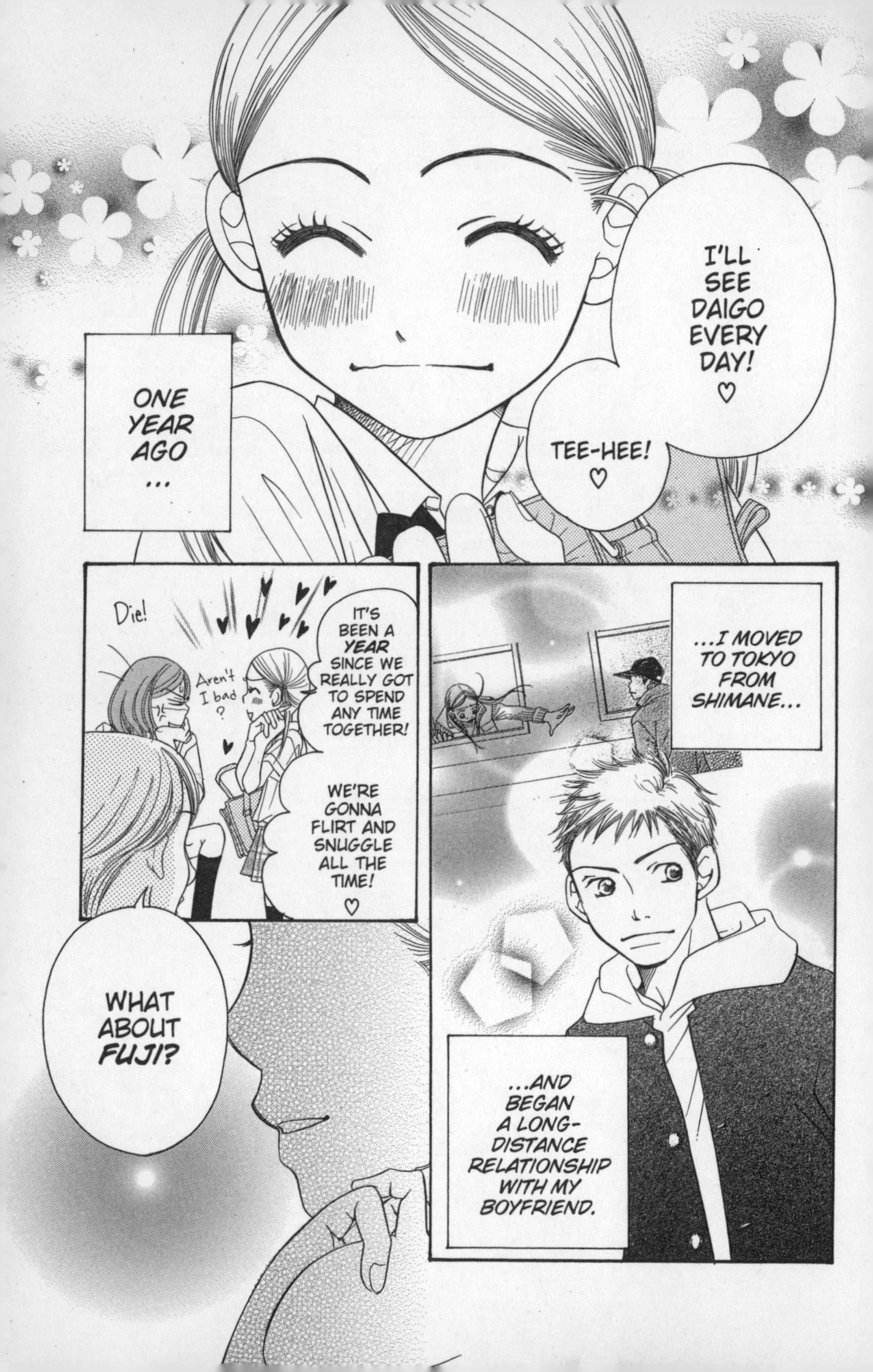

I'LL SEE DAIGO EVERY DAY! ♡
TEE-HEE! ♡
ONE YEAR AGO ...
...I MOVED TO TOKYO FROM SHIMANE...
...AND BEGAN A LONG-DISTANCE RELATIONSHIP WITH MY BOYFRIEND.
IT'S BEEN A YEAR SINCE WE REALLY GOT TO SPEND ANY TIME TOGETHER!
WE'RE GONNA FLIRT AND SNUGGLE ALL THE TIME! ♡
Aren't I bad?
Die!
WHAT ABOUT FUJI?

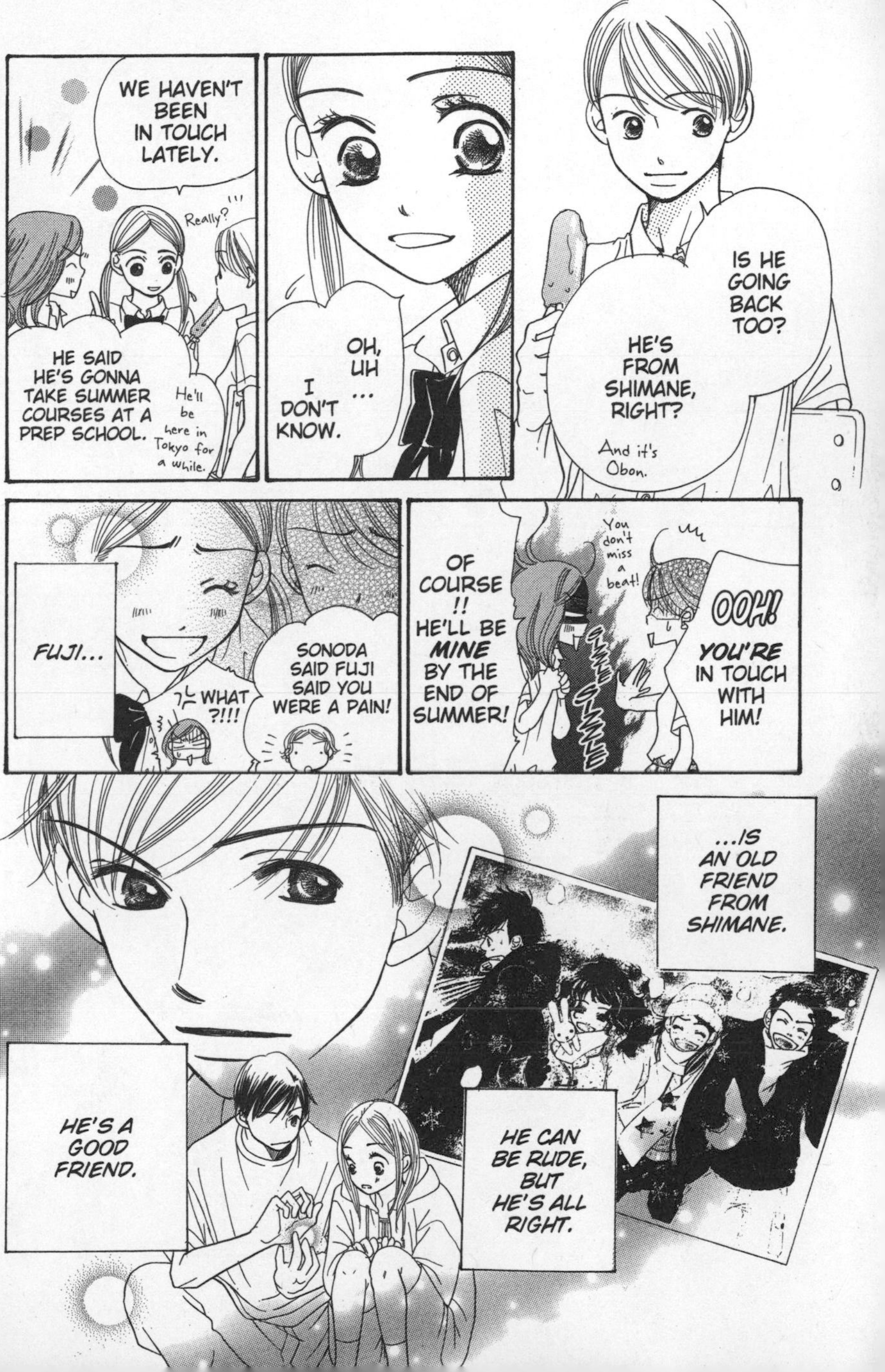
IS HE GOING BACK TOO?
HE'S FROM SHIMANE, RIGHT?
And it's Obon.
OH, UH ...
I DON'T KNOW.
WE HAVEN'T BEEN IN TOUCH LATELY.
Really?
HE SAID HE'S GONNA TAKE SUMMER COURSES AT A PREP SCHOOL.
He'll be here in Tokyo for a while.
OOH!
YOU'RE IN TOUCH WITH HIM!
You don't miss a beat!
SIZZLE SIZZLE
OF COURSE !! HE'LL BE MINE BY THE END OF SUMMER!
FUJI...
SONODA SAID FUJI SAID YOU WERE A PAIN!
WHAT ?!!!
...IS AN OLD FRIEND FROM SHIMANE.
HE CAN BE RUDE, BUT HE'S ALL RIGHT.
HE'S A GOOD FRIEND.

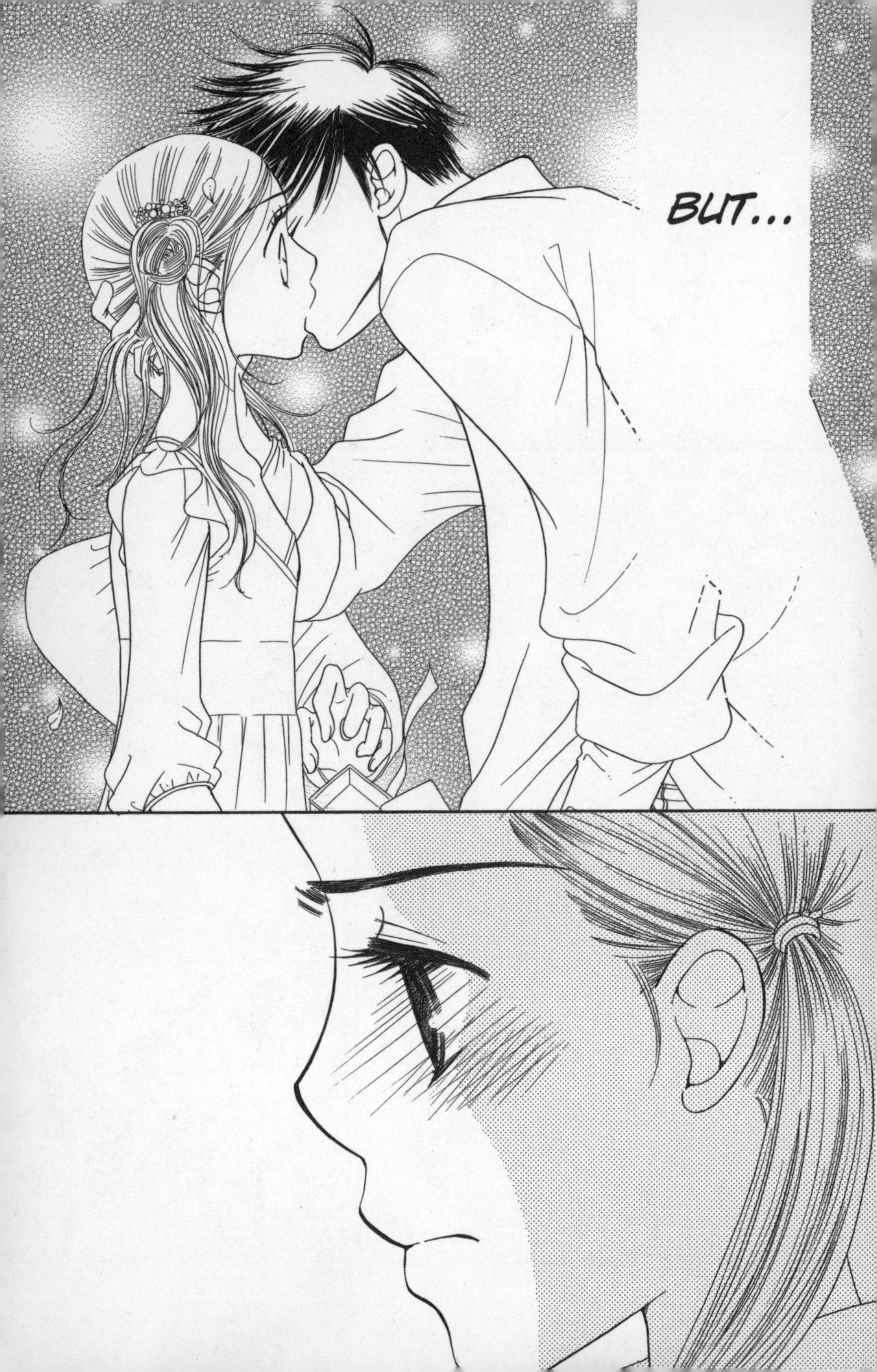
BUT...

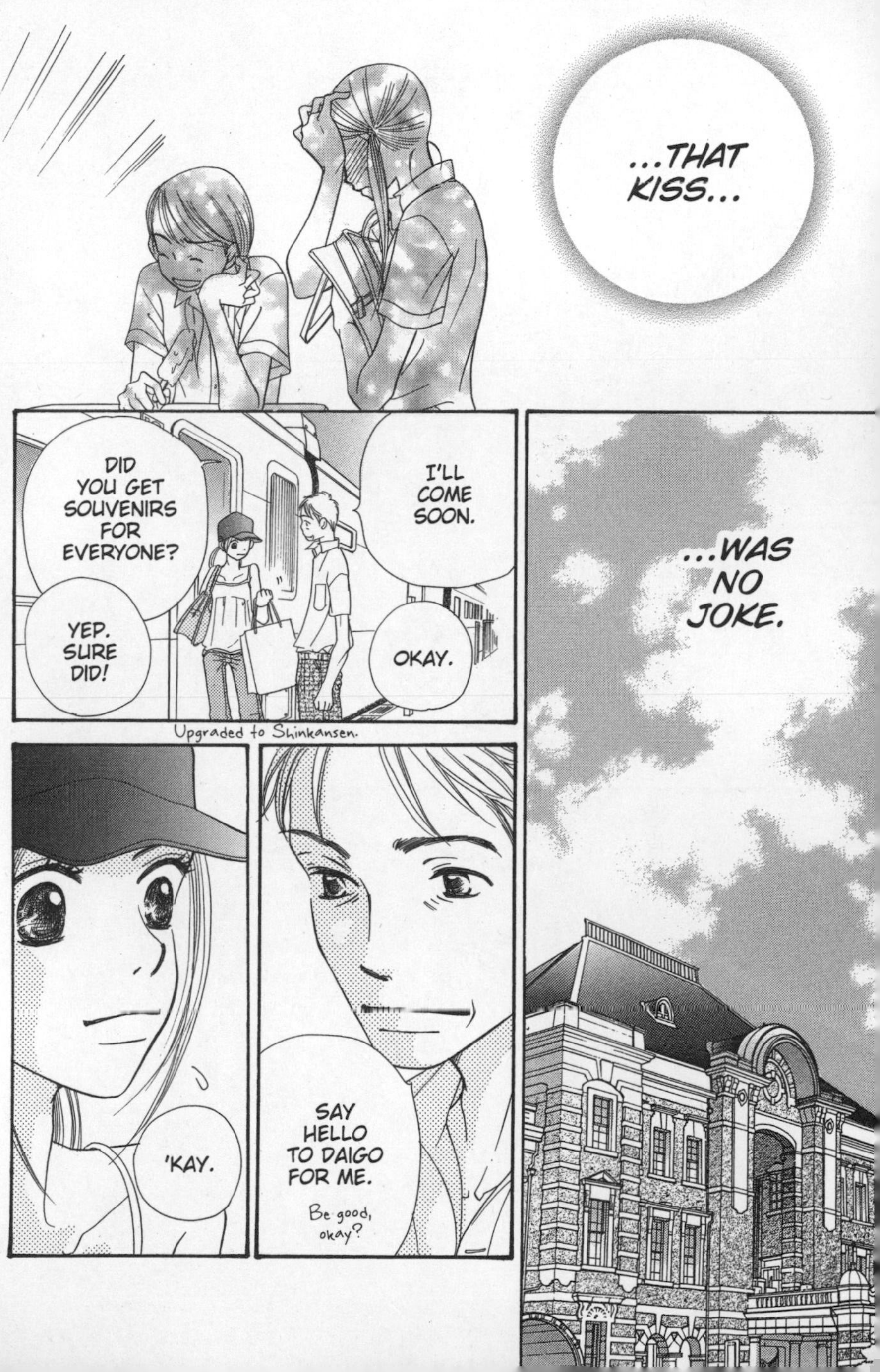
...THAT KISS...
...WAS NO JOKE.
I'LL COME SOON.
DID YOU GET SOUVENIRS FOR EVERYONE?
OKAY.
YEP. SURE DID!
Upgraded to Shinkansen.
SAY HELLO TO DAIGO FOR ME.
Be good, okay?
'KAY.

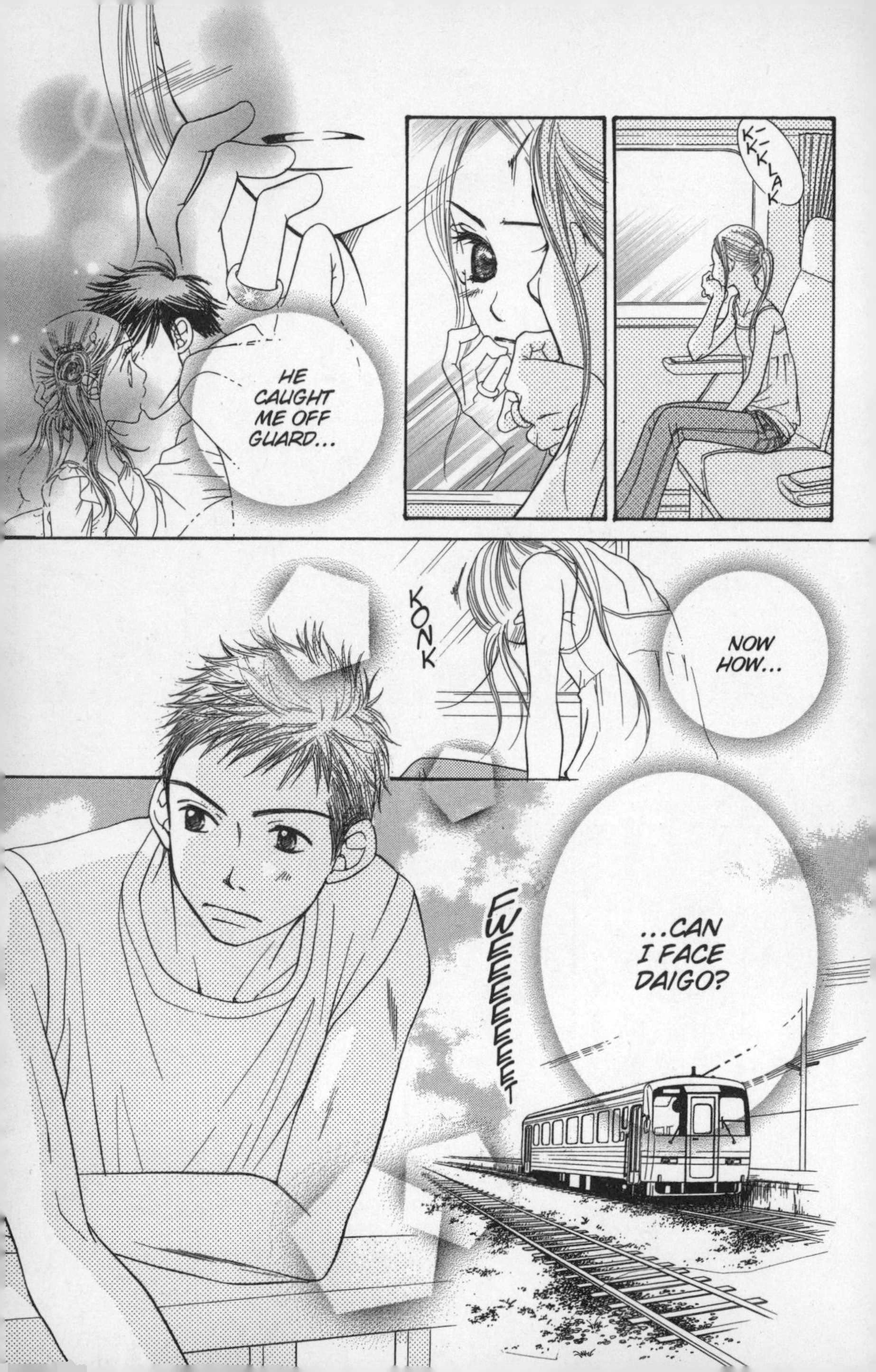
K-K-KKLAK
HE CAUGHT ME OFF GUARD...
KONK
NOW HOW...
...CAN I FACE DAIGO?
FWEEEEEEET

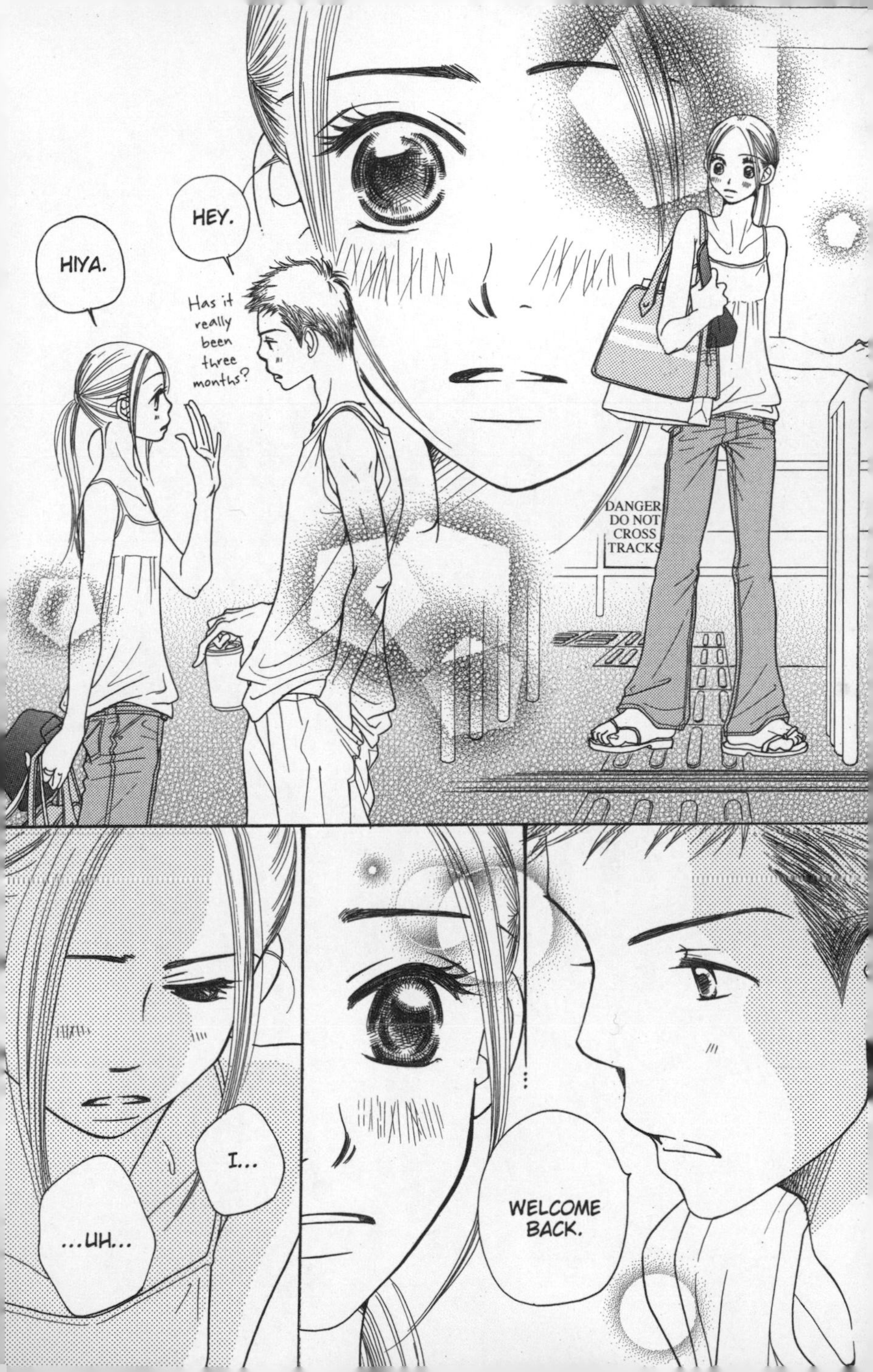
DANGER DO NOT CROSS TRACKS
HEY.
HIYA.
Has it really been three months?
WELCOME BACK.
I...
...UH...

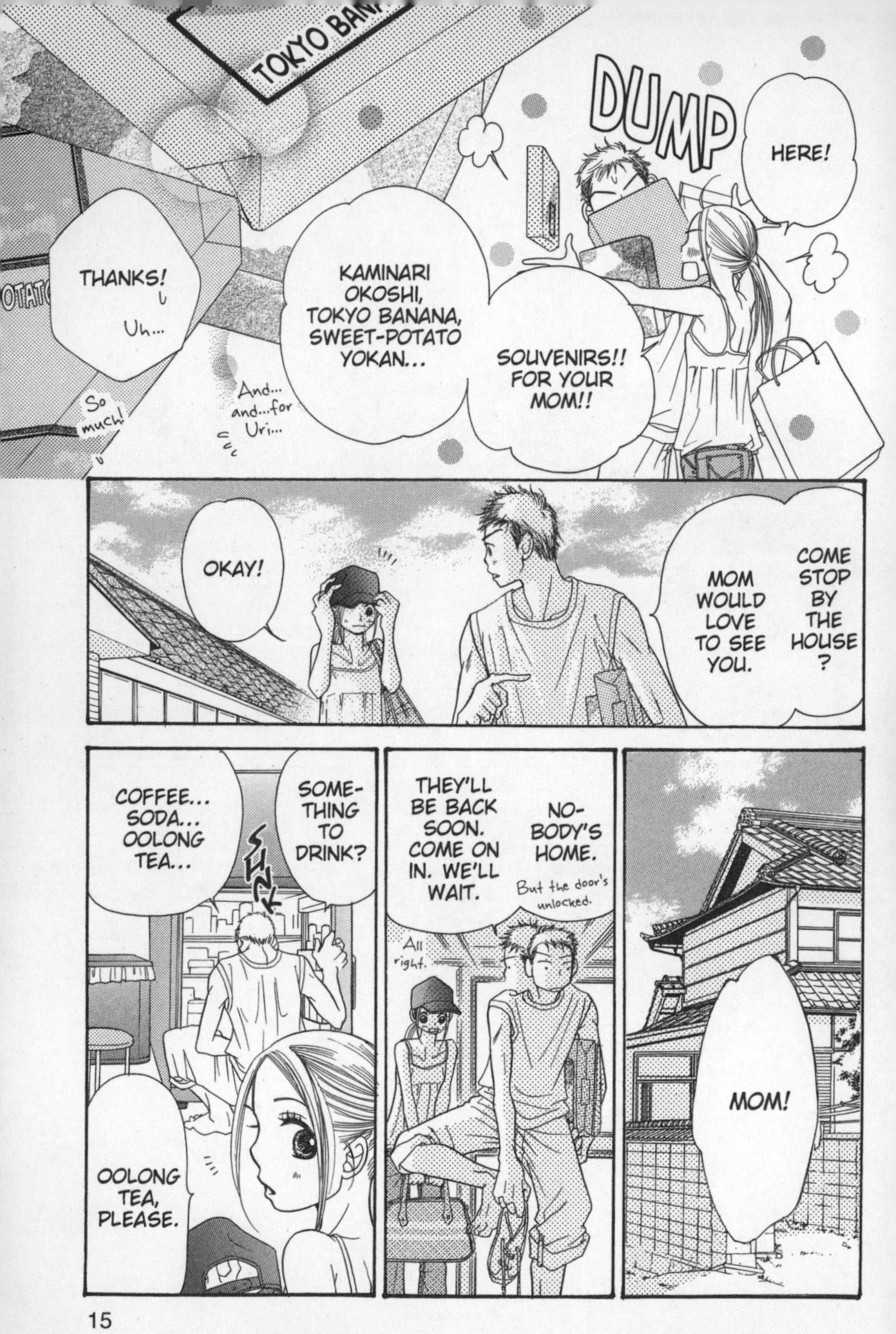
DUMP
HERE!
SOUVENIRS!! FOR YOUR MOM!!
KAMINARI OKOSHI, TOKYO BANANA, SWEET-POTATO YOKAN...
THANKS!
Uh...
And... and...for Uri...
So much!
COME STOP BY THE HOUSE?
MOM WOULD LOVE TO SEE YOU.
OKAY!
MOM!
NO-BODY'S HOME.
But the door's unlocked.
THEY'LL BE BACK SOON. COME ON IN. WE'LL WAIT.
All right.
SOME-THING TO DRINK?
SHUNK
COFFEE... SODA... OOLONG TEA...
OOLONG TEA, PLEASE.

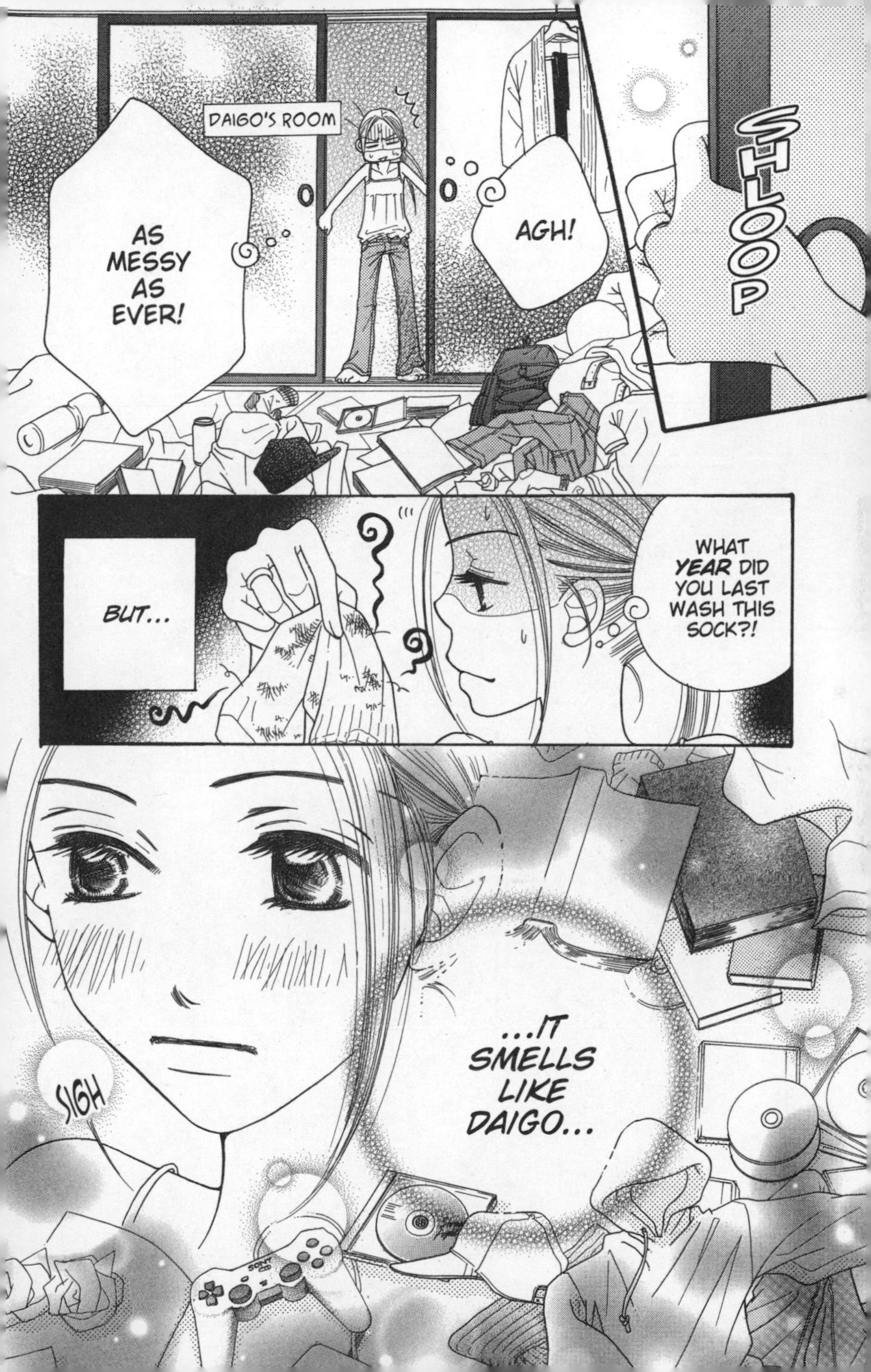
SHLOOP
AGH!
DAIGO'S ROOM
AS MESSY AS EVER!
WHAT YEAR DID YOU LAST WASH THIS SOCK?!
BUT...
...IT SMELLS LIKE DAIGO...
SIGH

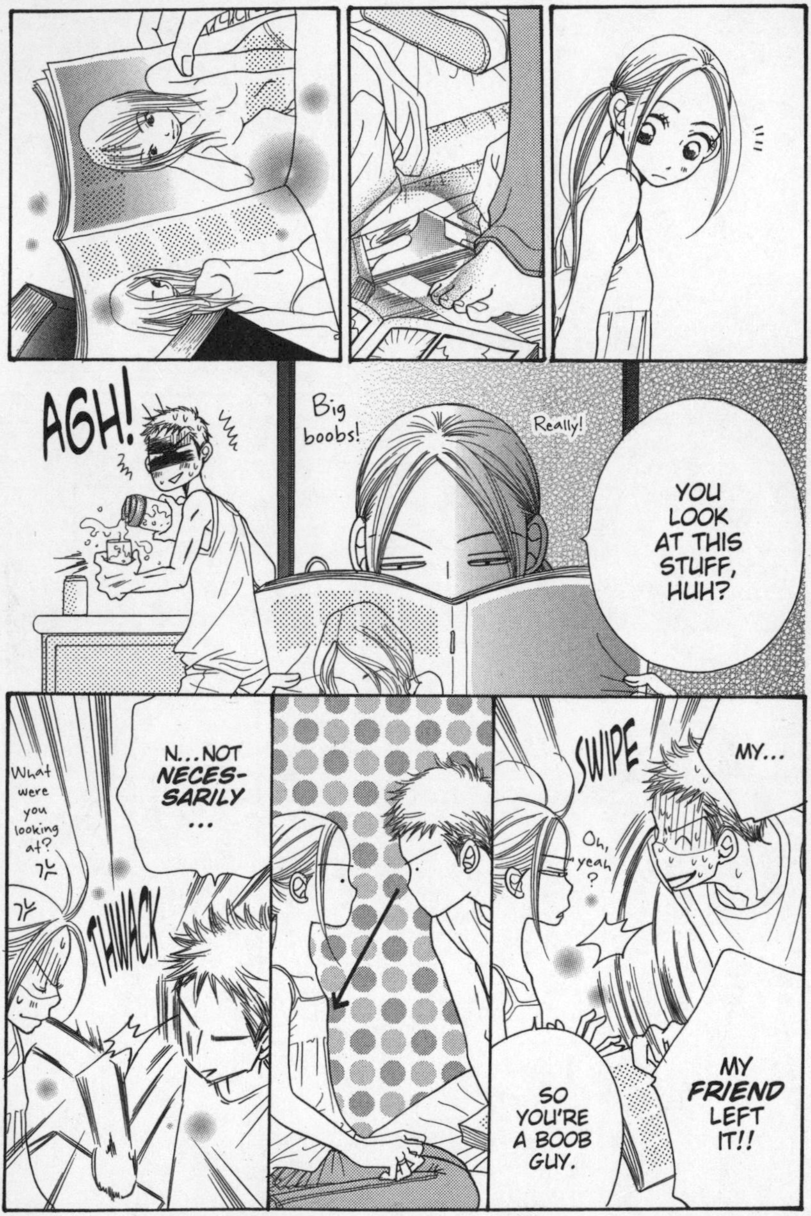
YOU LOOK AT THIS STUFF, HUH?
Really!
Big boobs!
AGH!
MY...
SWIPE
Oh, yeah?
MY FRIEND LEFT IT!!
SO YOU'RE A BOOB GUY.
N...NOT NECES-SARILY...
What were you looking at?
THWACK

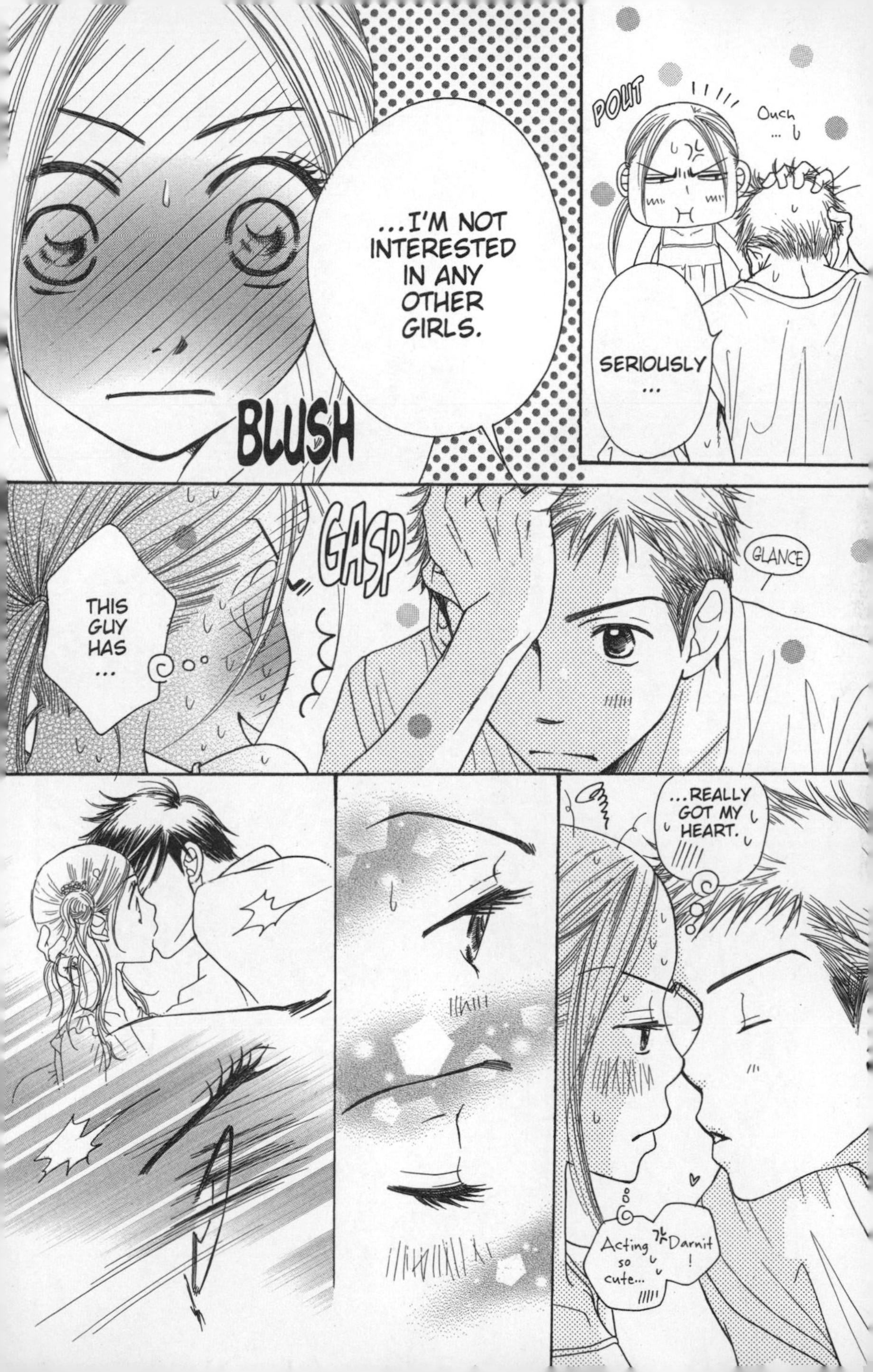
POUT
Ouch ...
SERIOUSLY ...
...I'M NOT INTERESTED IN ANY OTHER GIRLS.
BLUSH
GLANCE
GASP
THIS GUY HAS ...
...REALLY GOT MY HEART.
Darnit!
Acting so cute...

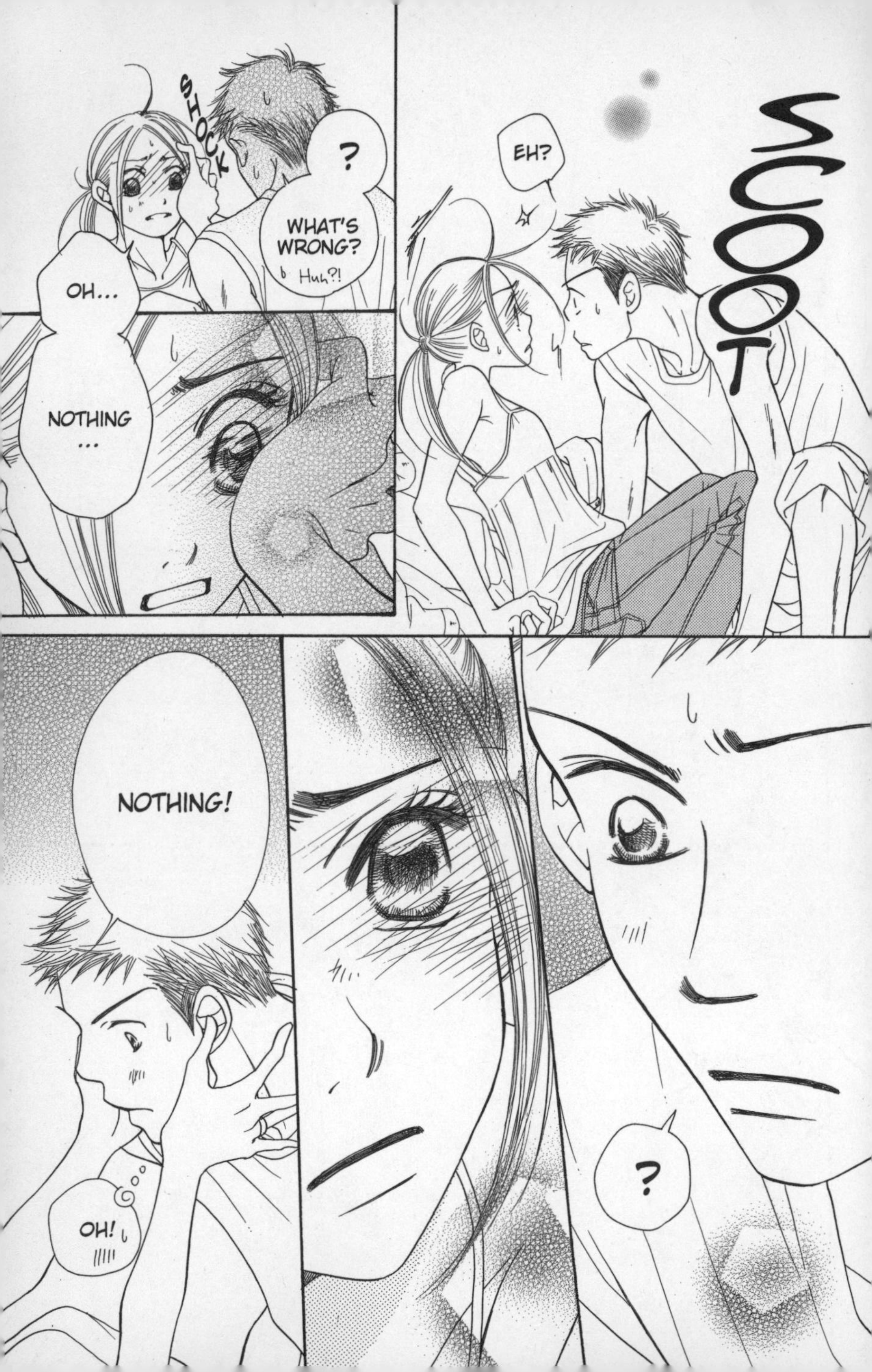
SCOOT
EH?
?
WHAT'S WRONG?
Huh?!
SHOCK
OH...
NOTHING ...
?
NOTHING!
OH!

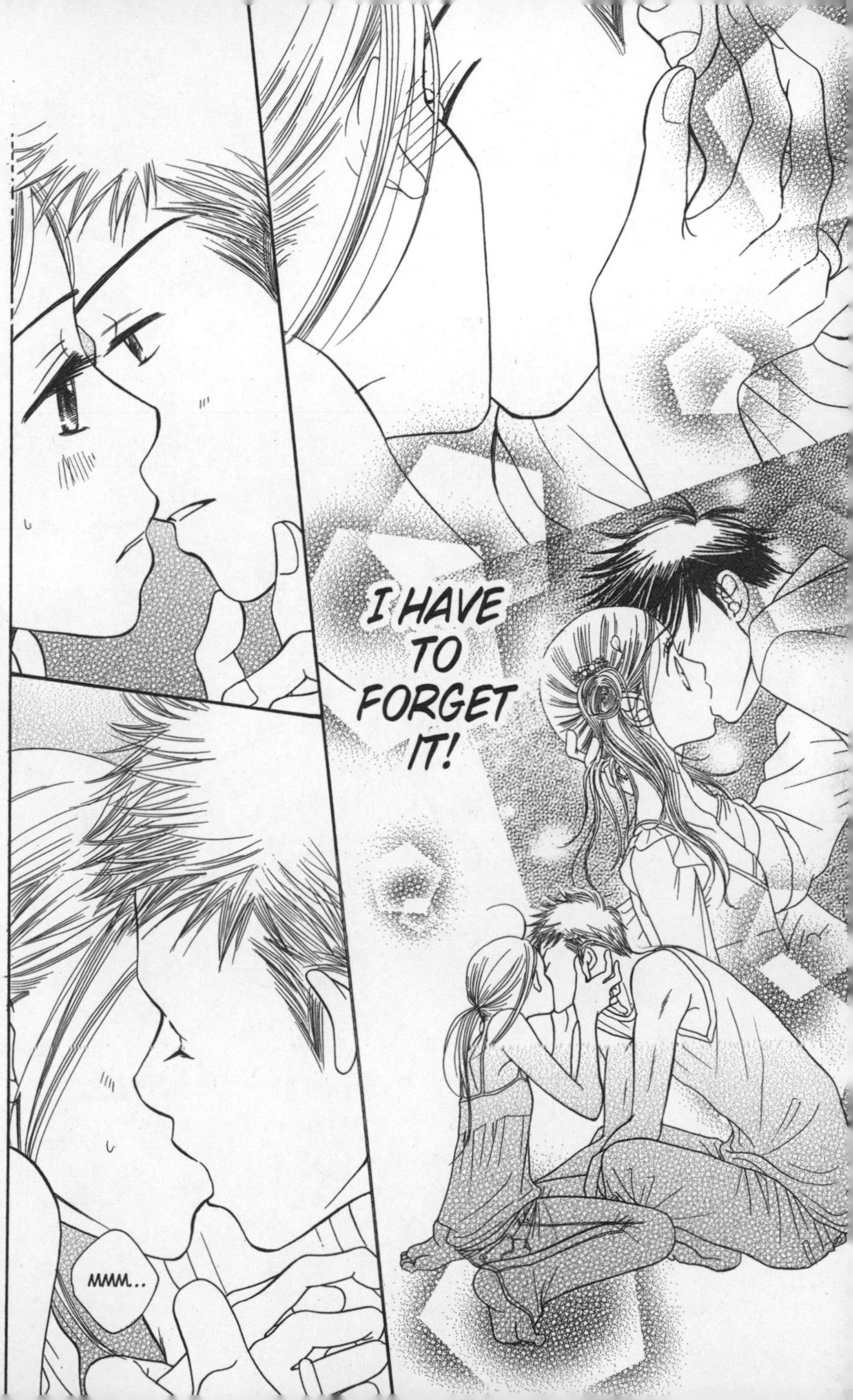
I HAVE TO FORGET IT!
MMM...

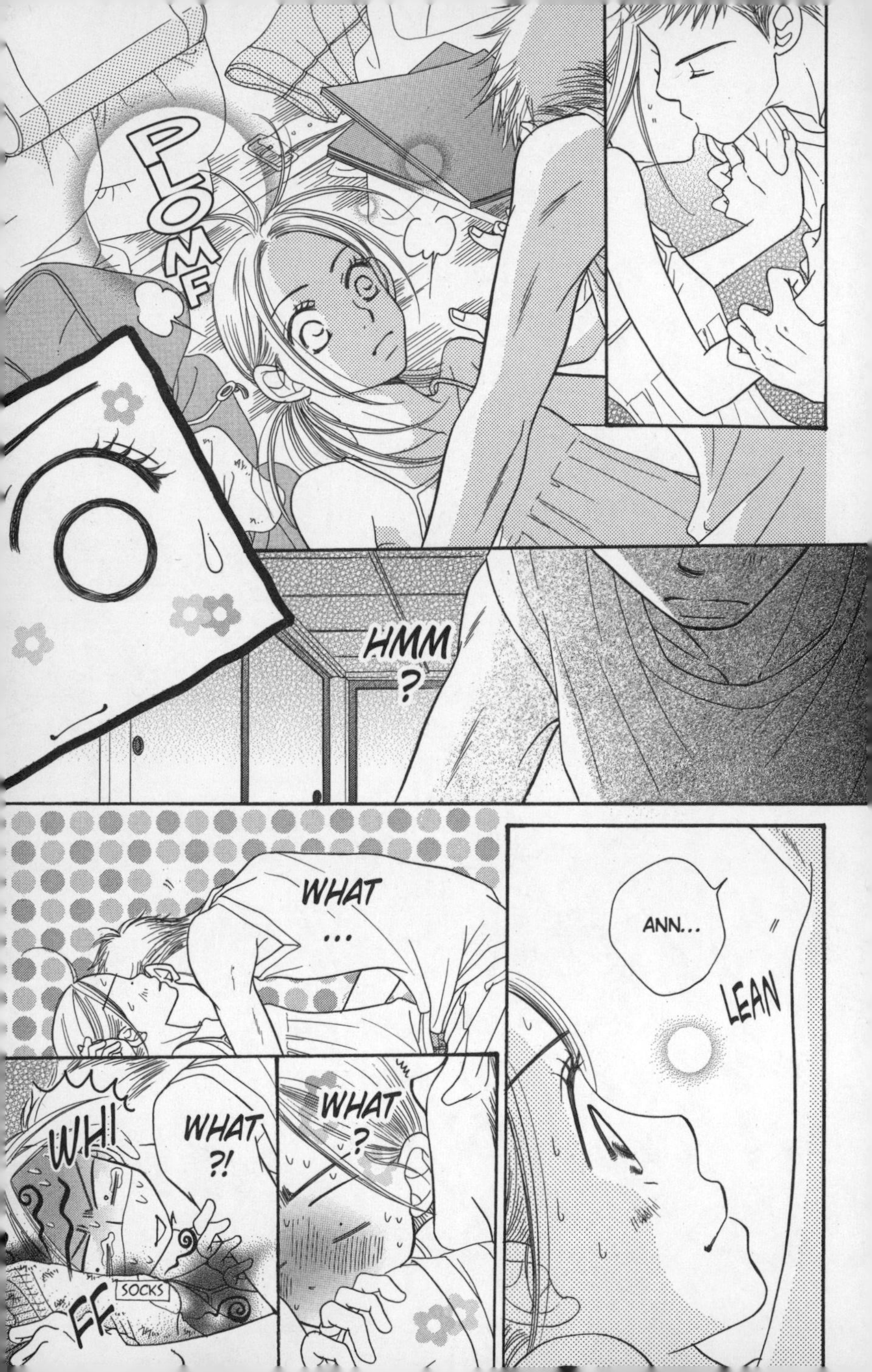
PLOMF
HMM ?
ANN...
LEAN
WHAT ...
WHAT ?
WHAT ?!
WHI
FF
SOCKS

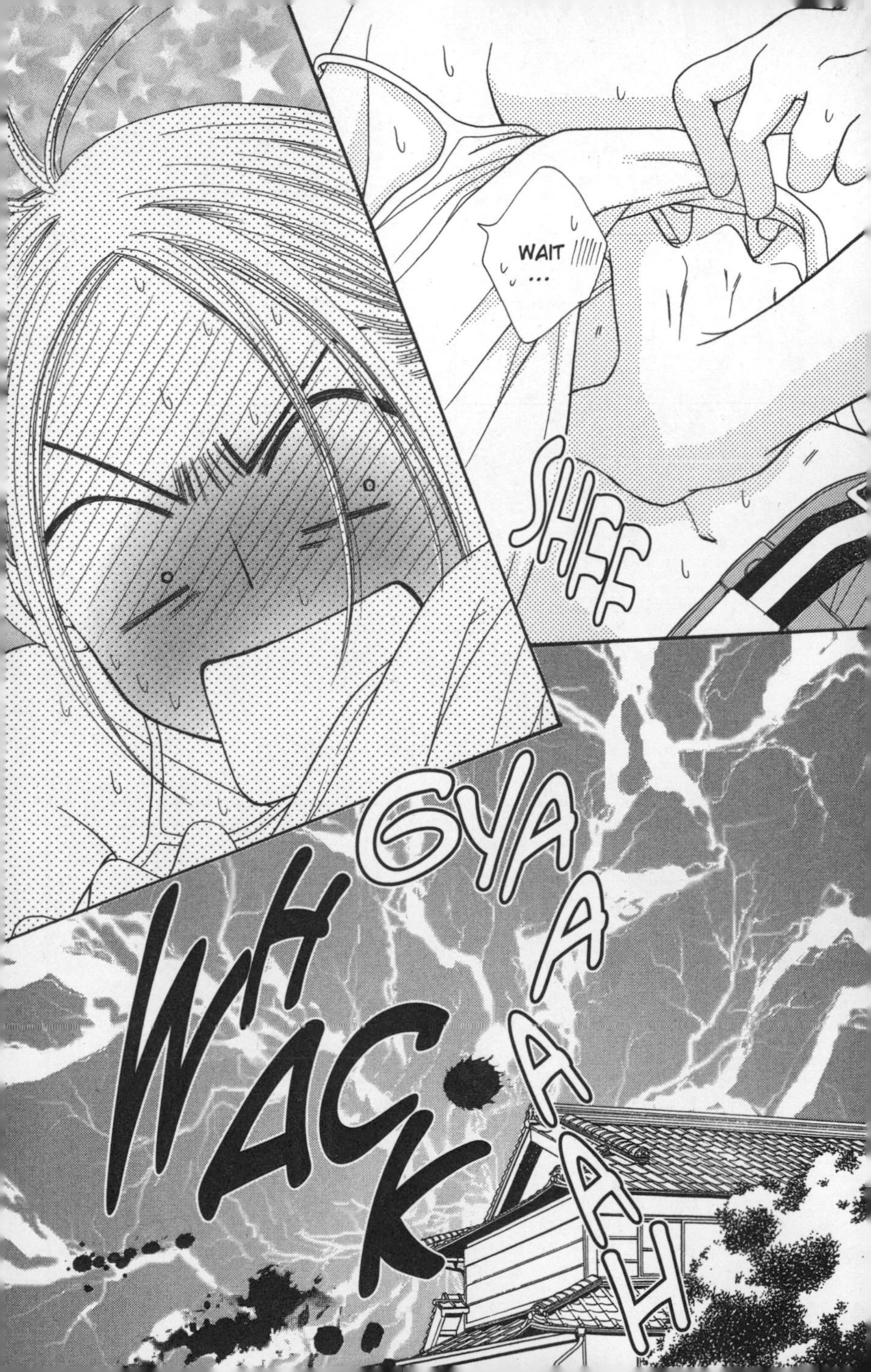
WAIT ...
SHFF
GYAAAAH
WHACK

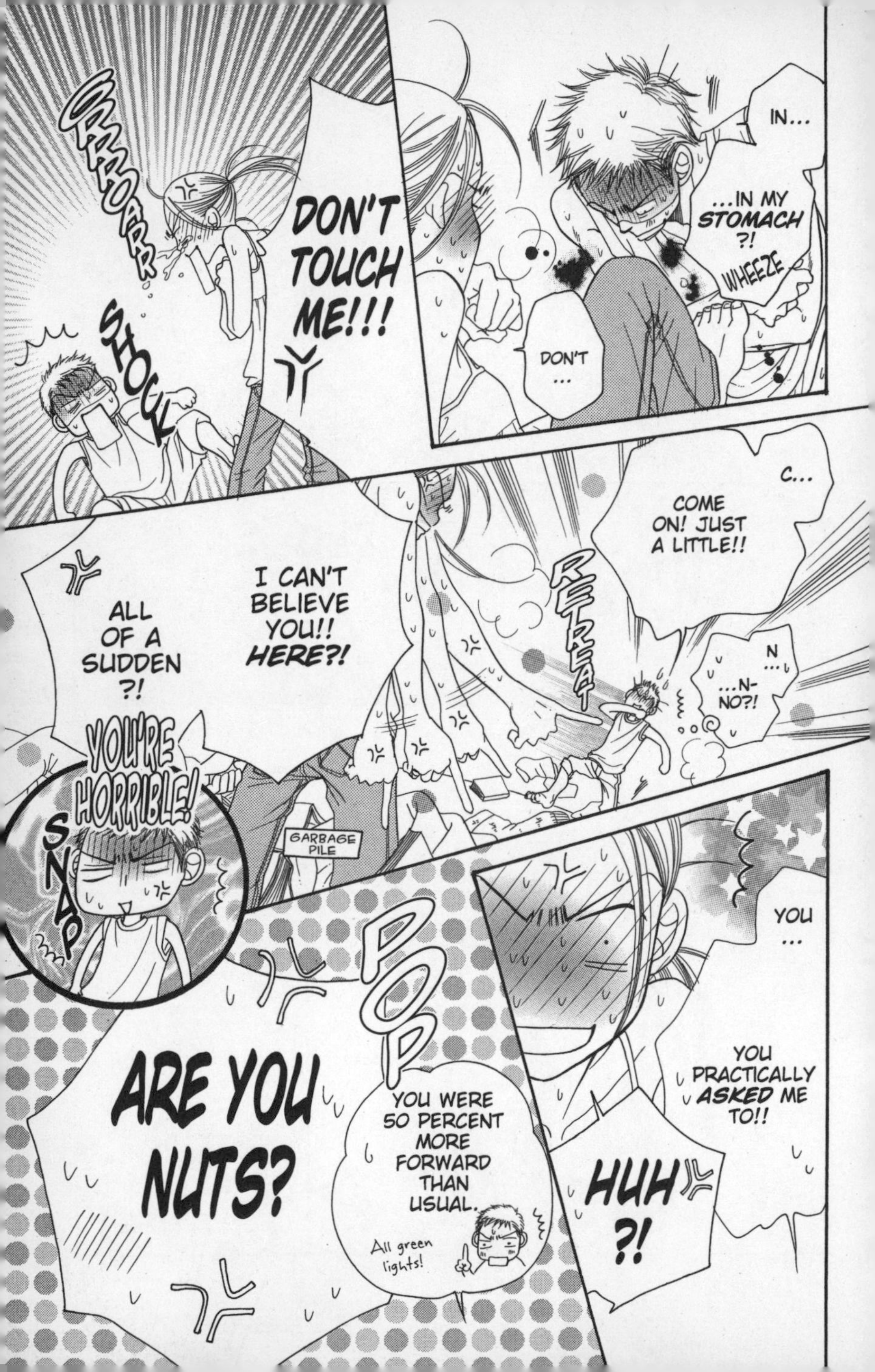
IN...
...IN MY STOMACH ?!
WHEEZE
DON'T ...
GRRROARR
DON'T TOUCH ME!!!
SHOCK
C...
COME ON! JUST A LITTLE!!
RETREAT
N... ...N-NO?!
I CAN'T BELIEVE YOU!! HERE?!
ALL OF A SUDDEN ?!
YOU'RE HORRIBLE!
SNAP
GARBAGE PILE
YOU ...
YOU PRACTICALLY ASKED ME TO!!
HUH ?!
POP
YOU WERE 50 PERCENT MORE FORWARD THAN USUAL.
All green lights!
ARE YOU NUTS?

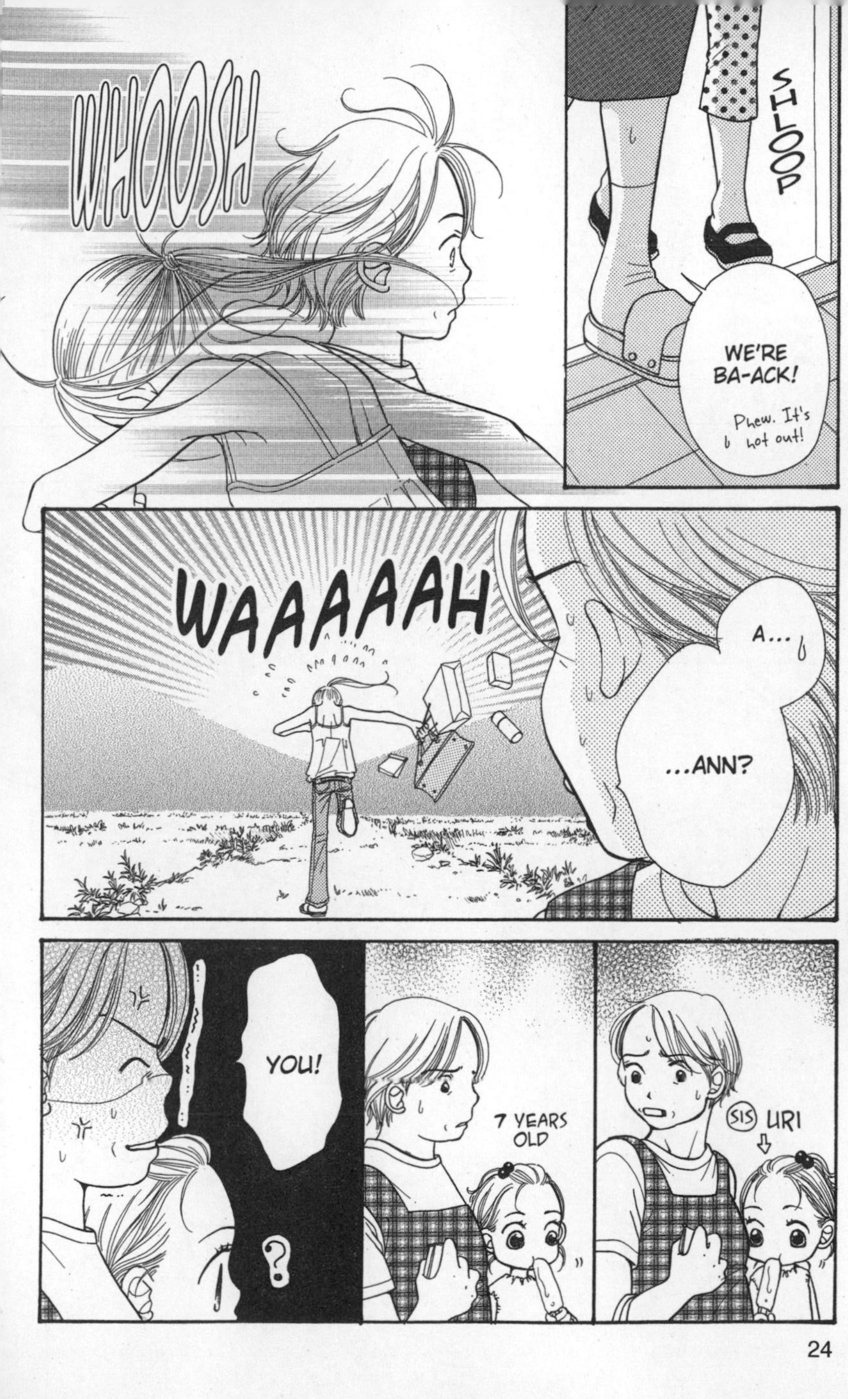
SHLOOP
WE'RE BA-ACK!
Phew. It's hot out!
WHOOSH
A...
...ANN?
WAAAAAH
SIS URI
7 YEARS OLD
YOU!
?

YOU PUT THE MOVES ON HER, DIDN'T YOU?!
KRAK KRAK
CRINGE
HORRIBLE!
HORRIBLE!
HORRIBLE!!
DAIGO IS SUCH A BIG JERK!
WHAT HAPPENED? JUST BACK AND YOU'RE ALREADY IN A SULK!
WE HAD A FIGHT...
After being apart for so long!
DING DONG
SOB SOB SOB
SLUMP

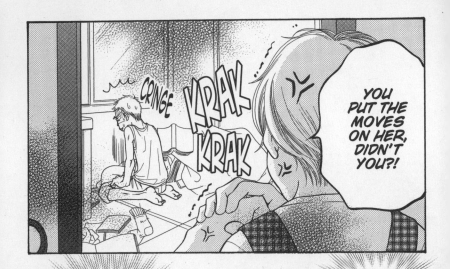

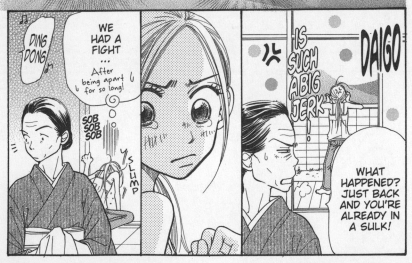

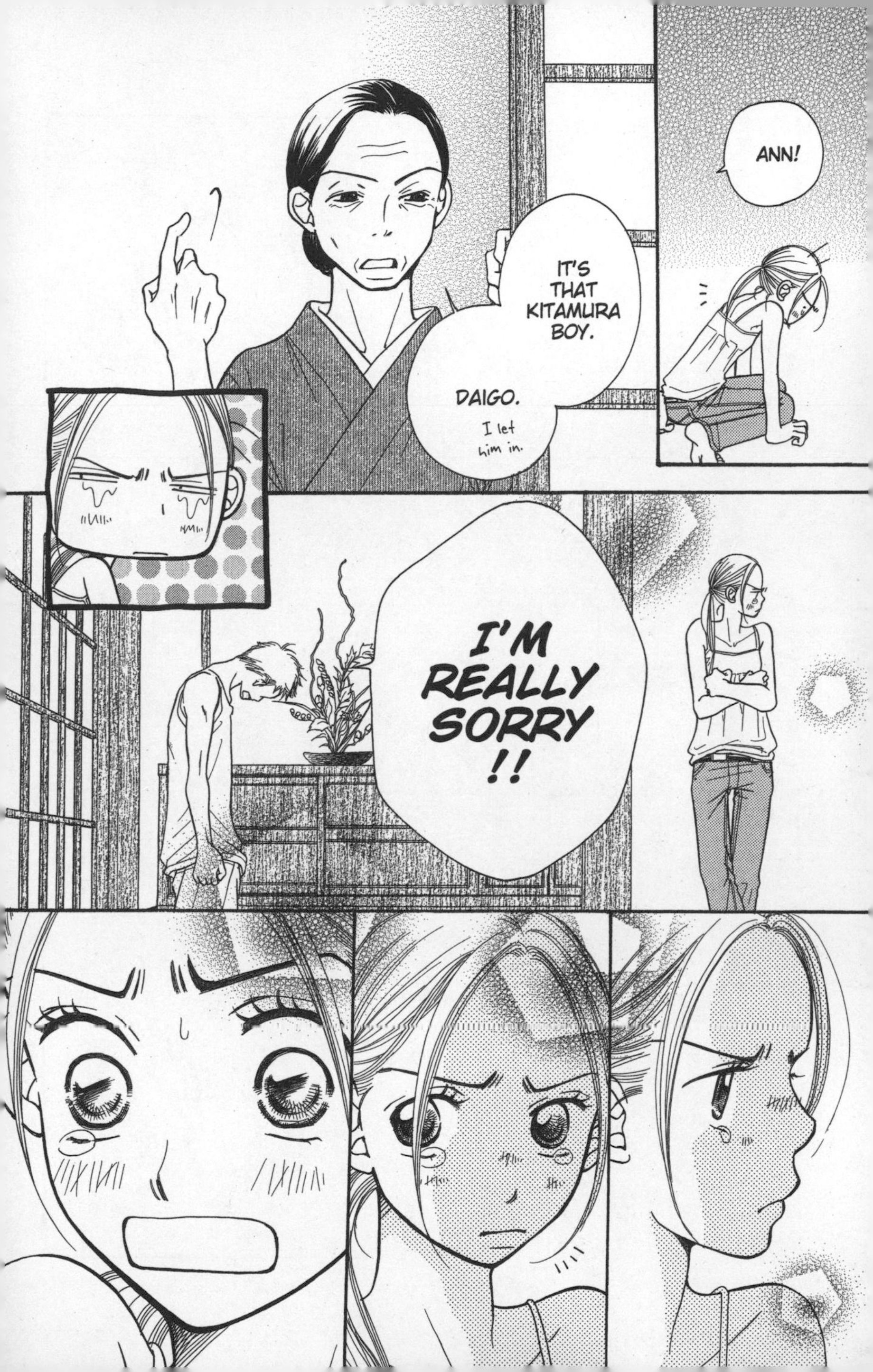
ANN!
IT'S THAT KITAMURA BOY.
DAIGO.
I let him in.
I'M REALLY SORRY!!

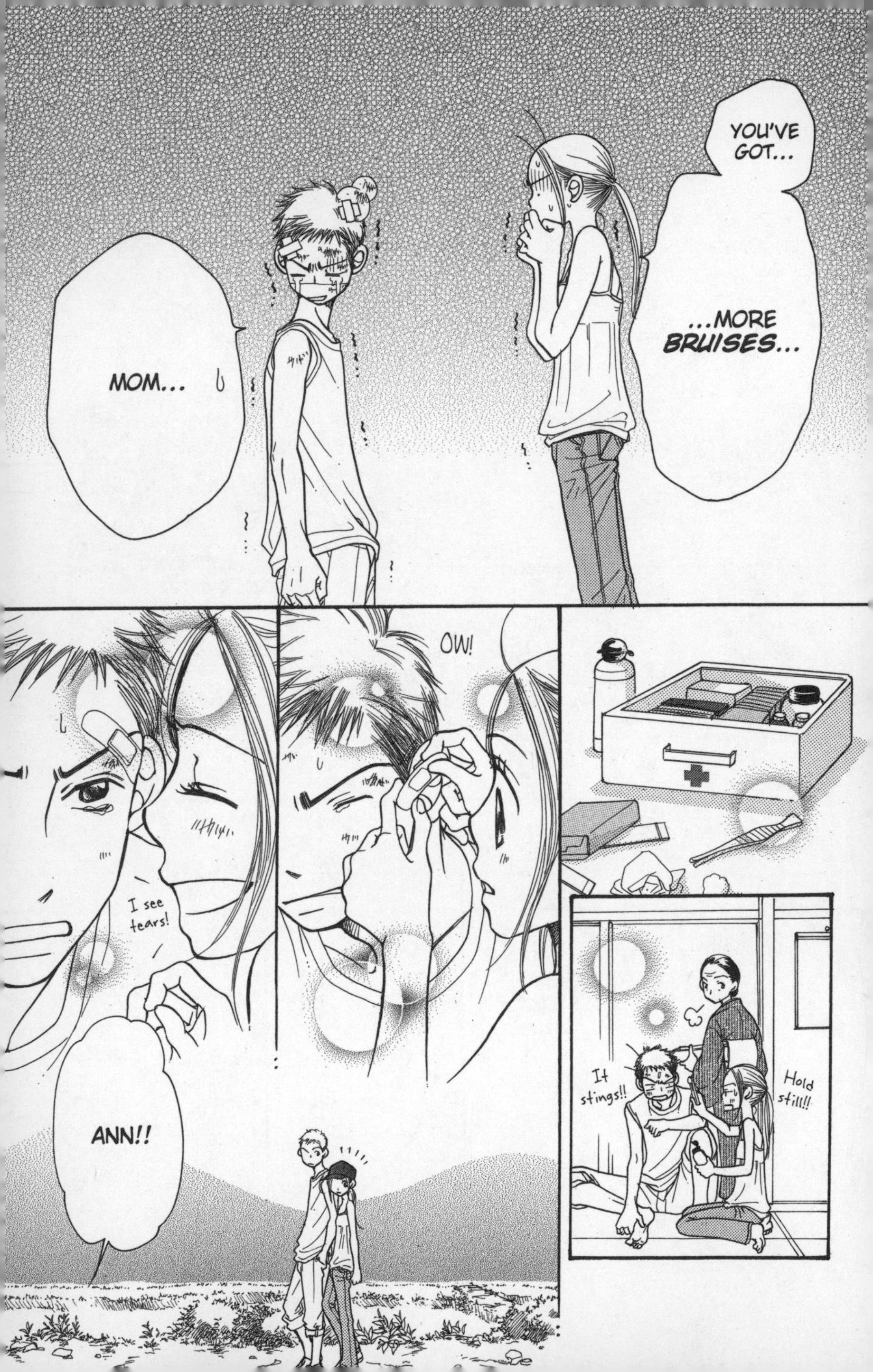
YOU'VE GOT...
...MORE BRUISES...
MOM...
Hold still!!
It stings!!
OW!
I see tears!
ANN!!

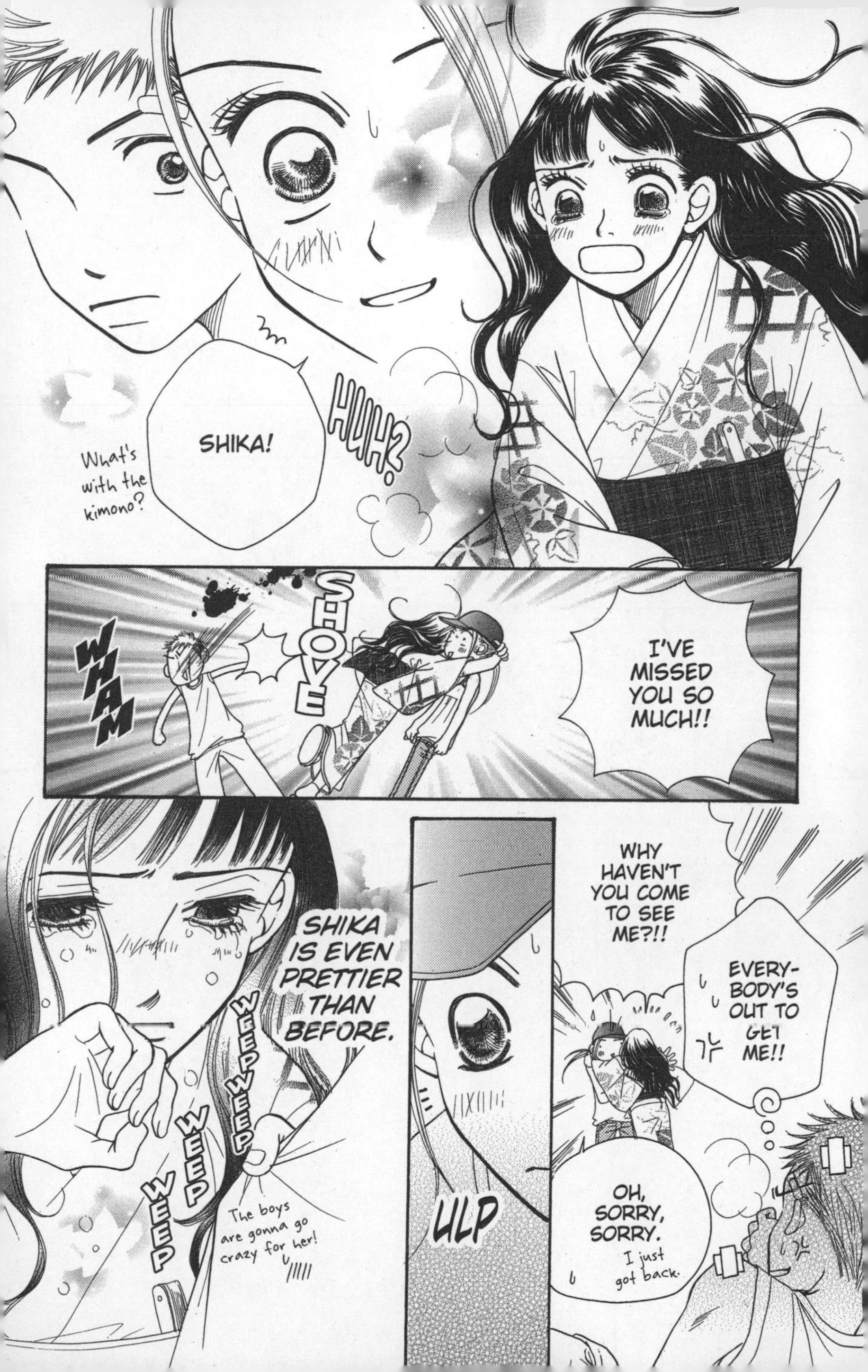
HUH?
SHIKA!
What's with the kimono?
I'VE MISSED YOU SO MUCH!!
SHOVE
WHAM
WHY HAVEN'T YOU COME TO SEE ME?!!
EVERY-BODY'S OUT TO GET ME!!
OH, SORRY, SORRY.
I just got back.
ULP
SHIKA IS EVEN PRETTIER THAN BEFORE.
WEEP WEEP
WEEP
WEEP
The boys are gonna go crazy for her!

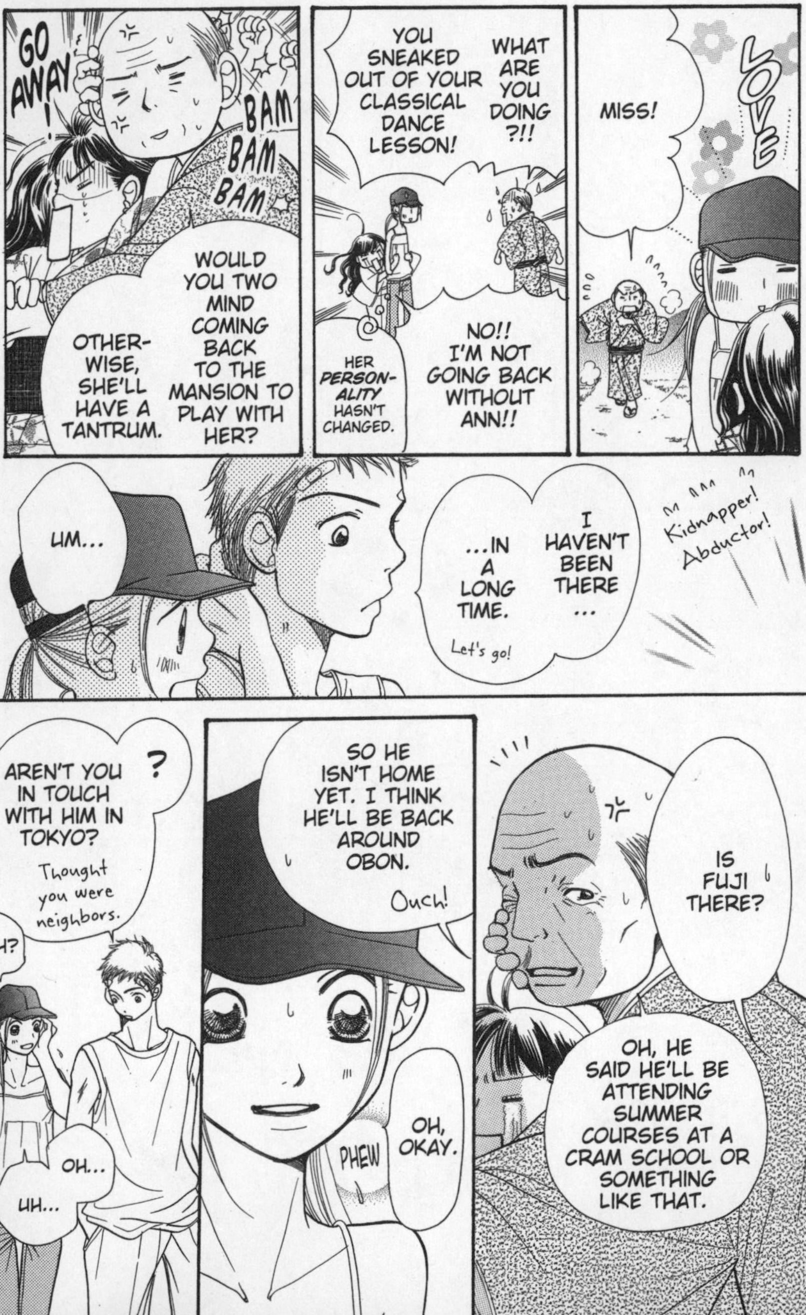
LOVE
MISS!
WHAT ARE YOU DOING?!!
YOU SNEAKED OUT OF YOUR CLASSICAL DANCE LESSON!
NO!! I'M NOT GOING BACK WITHOUT ANN!!
HER PERSONALITY HASN'T CHANGED.
BAM BAM BAM
GO AWAY!
WOULD YOU TWO MIND COMING BACK TO THE MANSION TO PLAY WITH HER?
OTHER-WISE, SHE'LL HAVE A TANTRUM.
Kidnapper! Abductor!
I HAVEN'T BEEN THERE...
...IN A LONG TIME.
Let's go!
UM...
IS FUJI THERE?
OH, HE SAID HE'LL BE ATTENDING SUMMER COURSES AT A CRAM SCHOOL OR SOMETHING LIKE THAT.
SO HE ISN'T HOME YET. I THINK HE'LL BE BACK AROUND OBON.
Ouch!
OH, OKAY.
PHEW
AREN'T YOU IN TOUCH WITH HIM IN TOKYO?
?
Thought you were neighbors.
HUH?
OH...
UH...

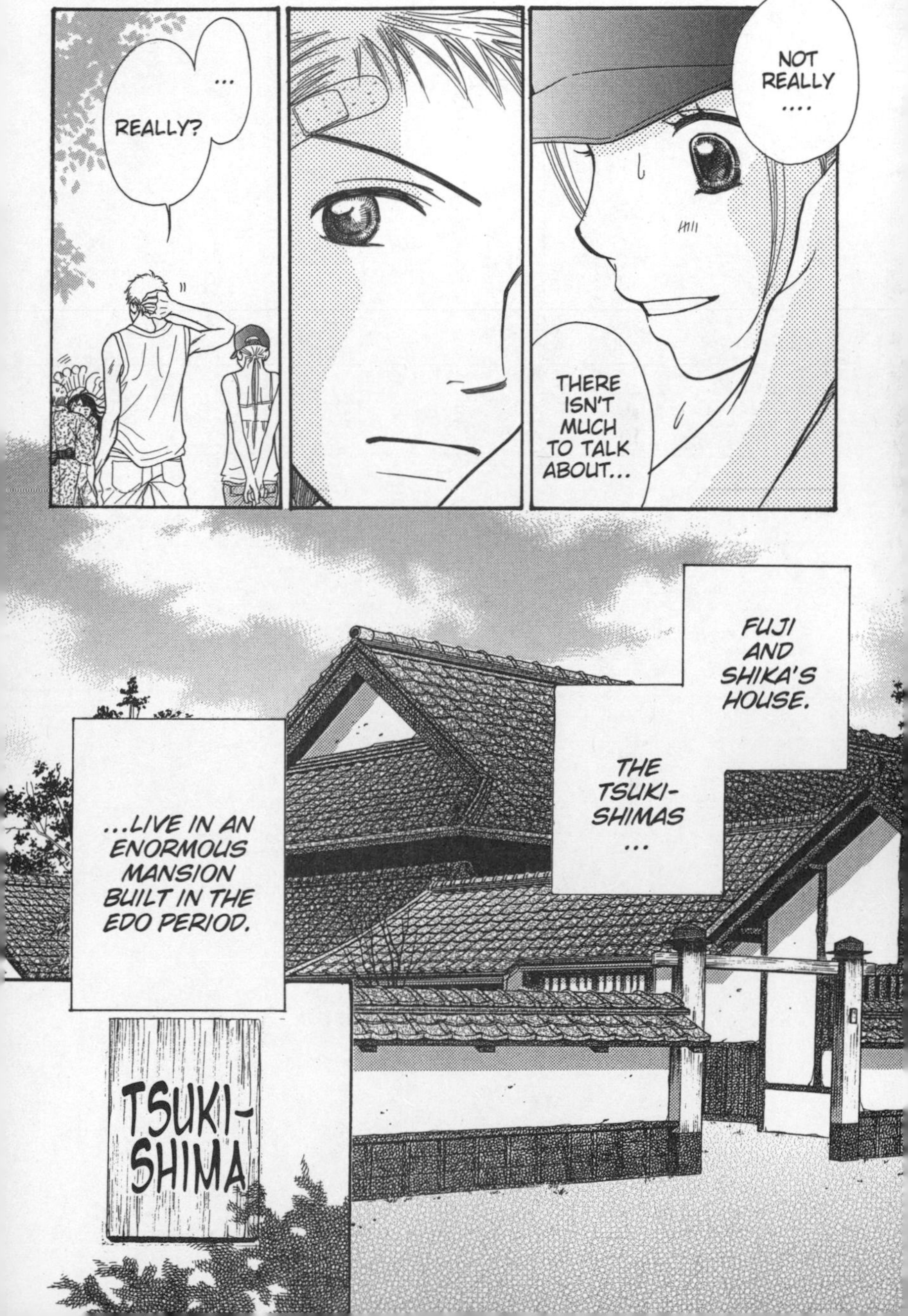
NOT REALLY ....
THERE ISN'T MUCH TO TALK ABOUT...
... REALLY?
FUJI AND SHIKA'S HOUSE.
THE TSUKI-SHIMAS ...
...LIVE IN AN ENORMOUS MANSION BUILT IN THE EDO PERIOD.
TSUKI-SHIMA

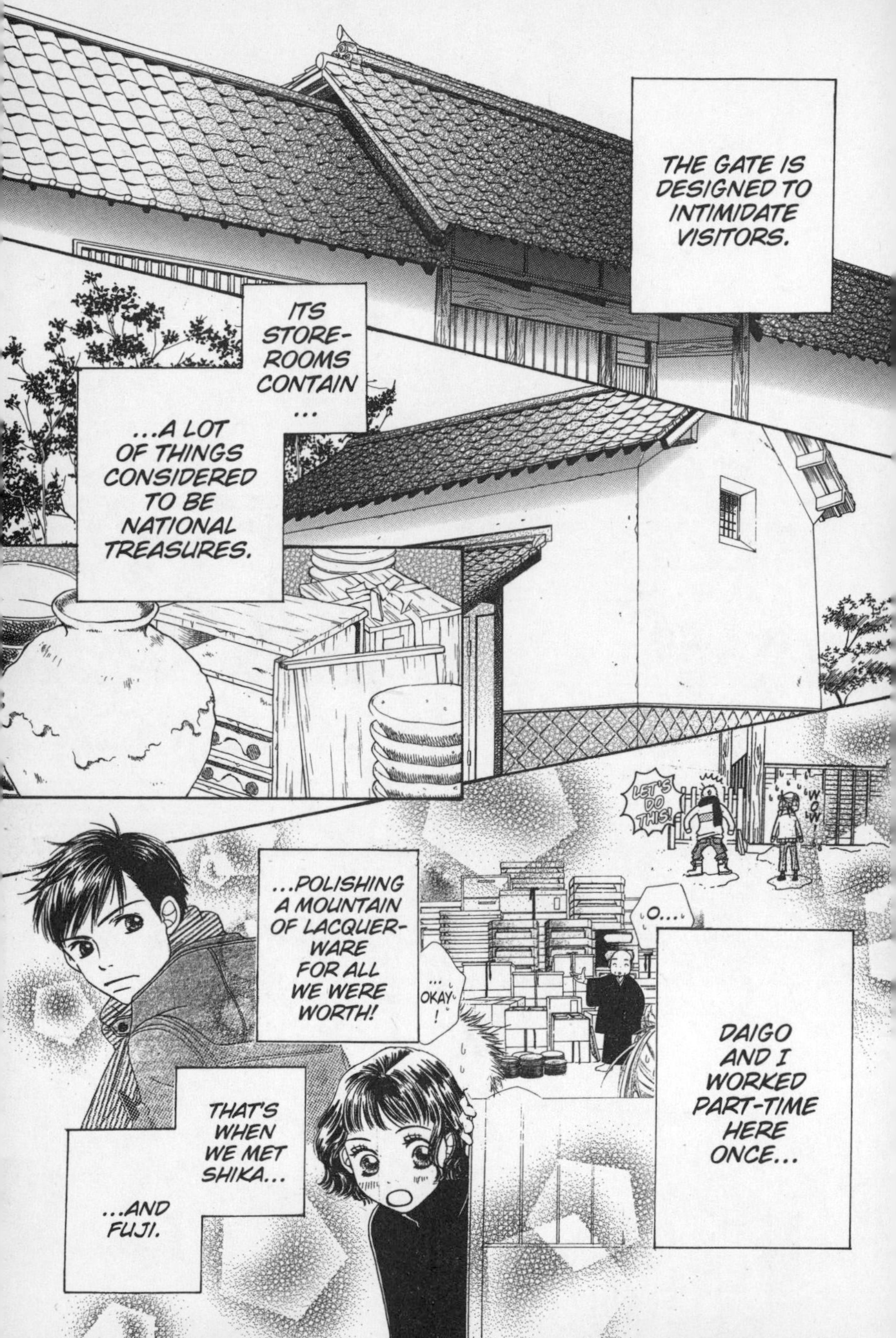
THE GATE IS DESIGNED TO INTIMIDATE VISITORS.
ITS STOREROOMS CONTAIN...
...A LOT OF THINGS CONSIDERED TO BE NATIONAL TREASURES.
WOW
LET'S DO THIS!
DAIGO AND I WORKED PART-TIME HERE ONCE...
O....
...OKAY!
...POLISHING A MOUNTAIN OF LACQUERWARE FOR ALL WE WERE WORTH!
THAT'S WHEN WE MET SHIKA...
...AND FUJI.

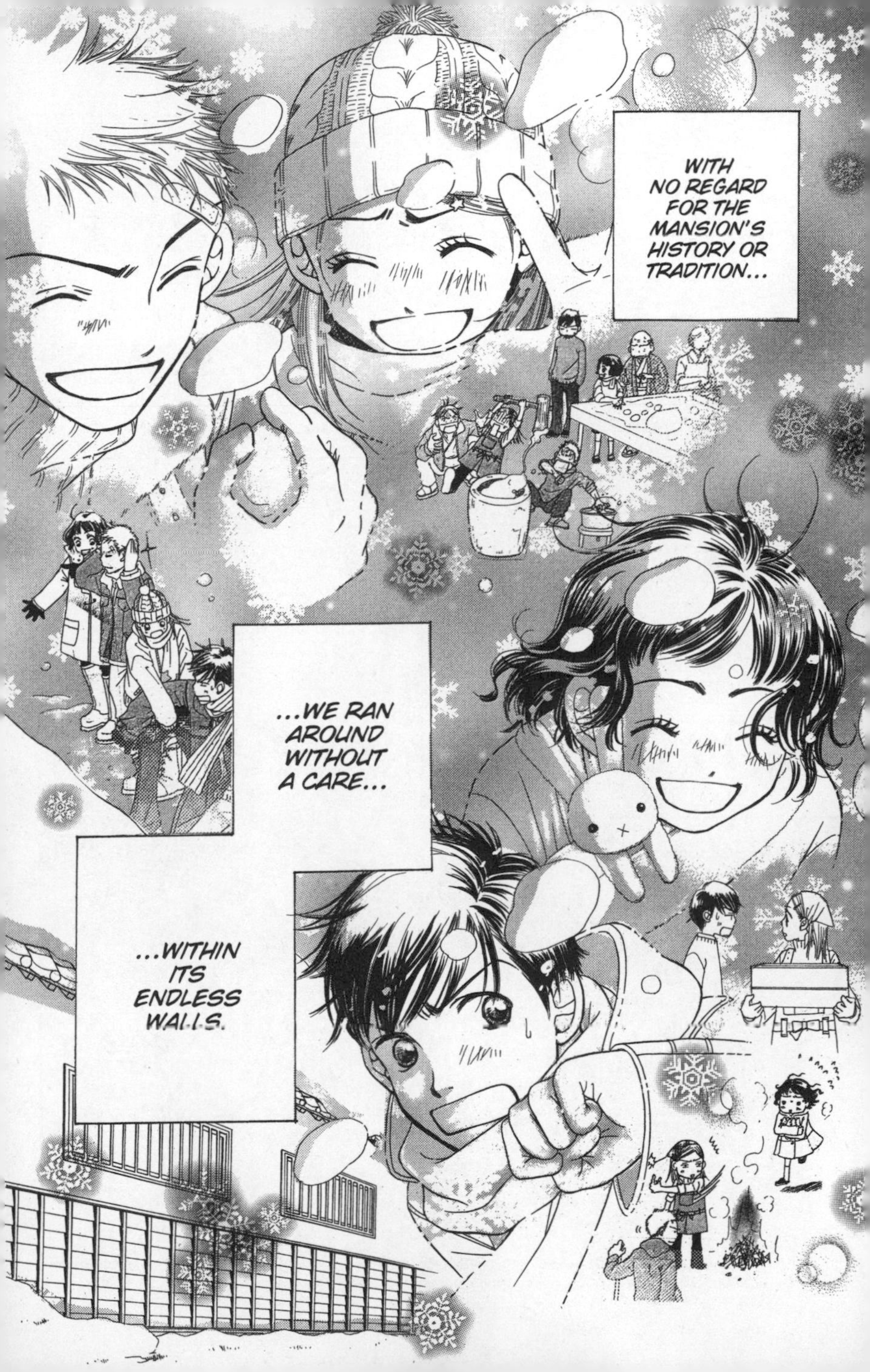
WITH NO REGARD FOR THE MANSION'S HISTORY OR TRADITION...
...WE RAN AROUND WITHOUT A CARE...
...WITHIN ITS ENDLESS WALLS.

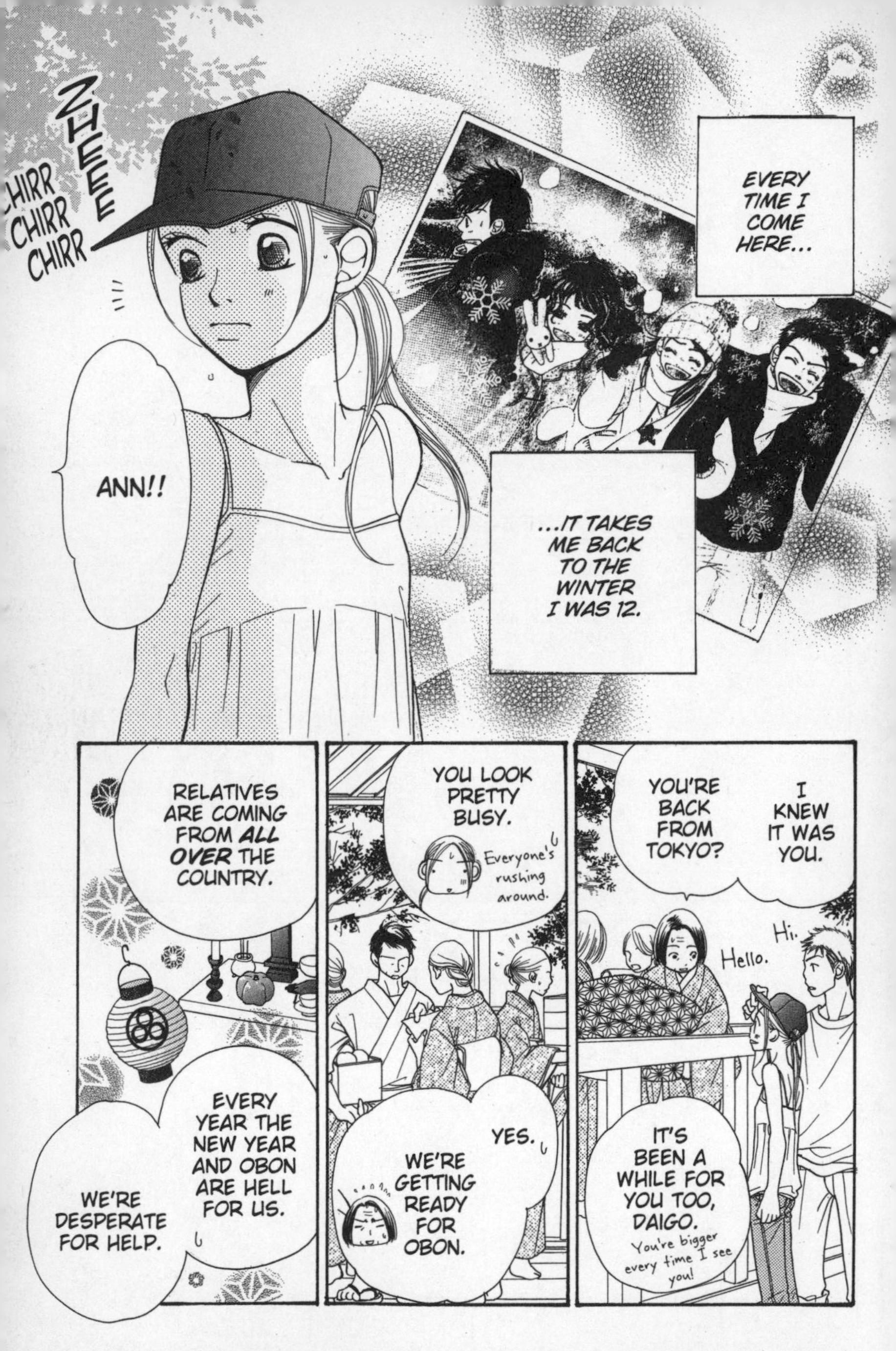
EVERY TIME I COME HERE...
...IT TAKES ME BACK TO THE WINTER I WAS 12.
ZHEEEE
CHIRR CHIRR CHIRR
ANN!!
I KNEW IT WAS YOU.
YOU'RE BACK FROM TOKYO?
Hi.
Hello.
IT'S BEEN A WHILE FOR YOU TOO, DAIGO.
You're bigger every time I see you!
YOU LOOK PRETTY BUSY.
Everyone's rushing around.
YES.
WE'RE GETTING READY FOR OBON.
RELATIVES ARE COMING FROM ALL OVER THE COUNTRY.
EVERY YEAR THE NEW YEAR AND OBON ARE HELL FOR US.
WE'RE DESPERATE FOR HELP.

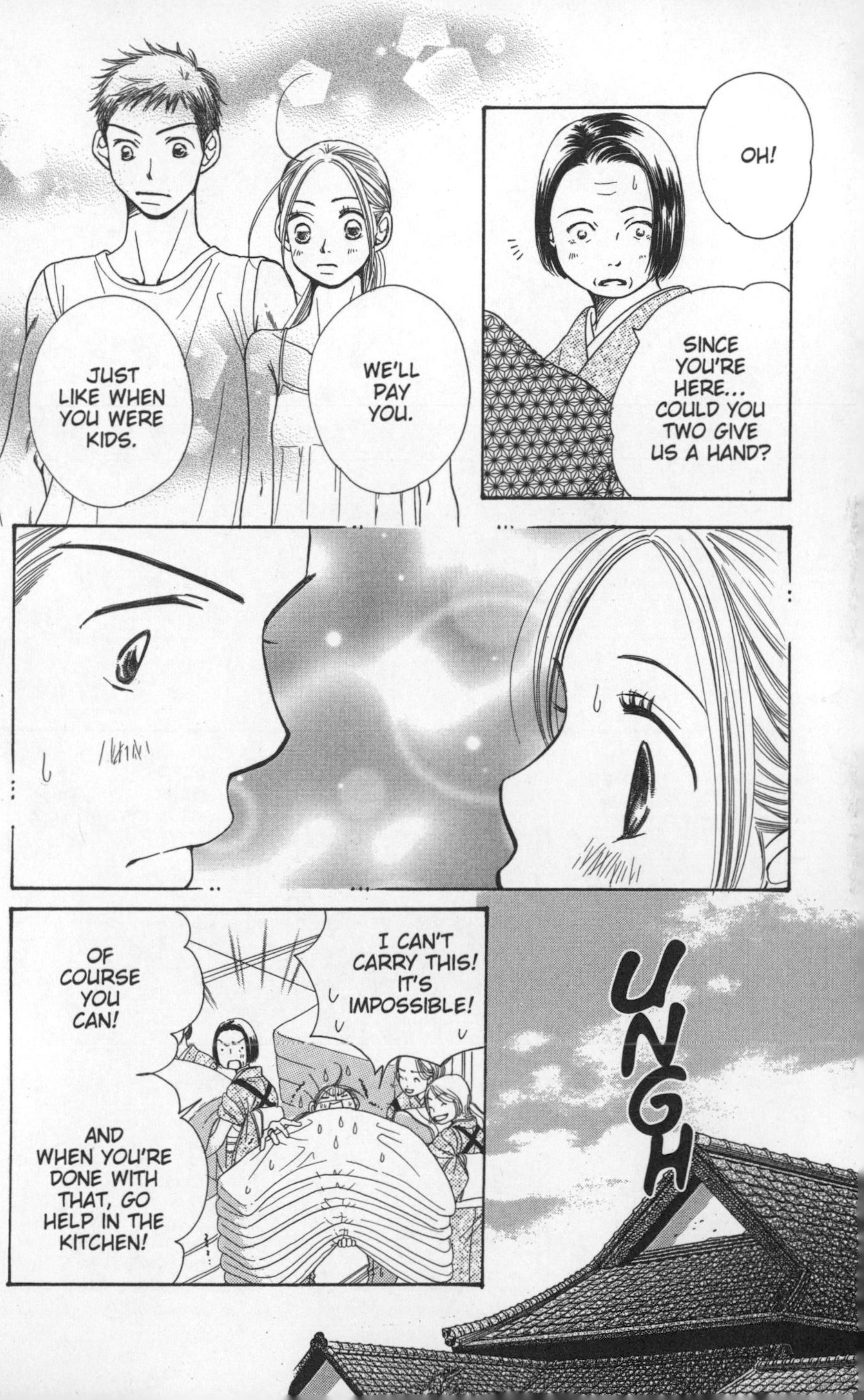
OH!
SINCE YOU'RE HERE... COULD YOU TWO GIVE US A HAND?
WE'LL PAY YOU.
JUST LIKE WHEN YOU WERE KIDS.
UNGH
I CAN'T CARRY THIS! IT'S IMPOSSIBLE!
OF COURSE YOU CAN!
AND WHEN YOU'RE DONE WITH THAT, GO HELP IN THE KITCHEN!

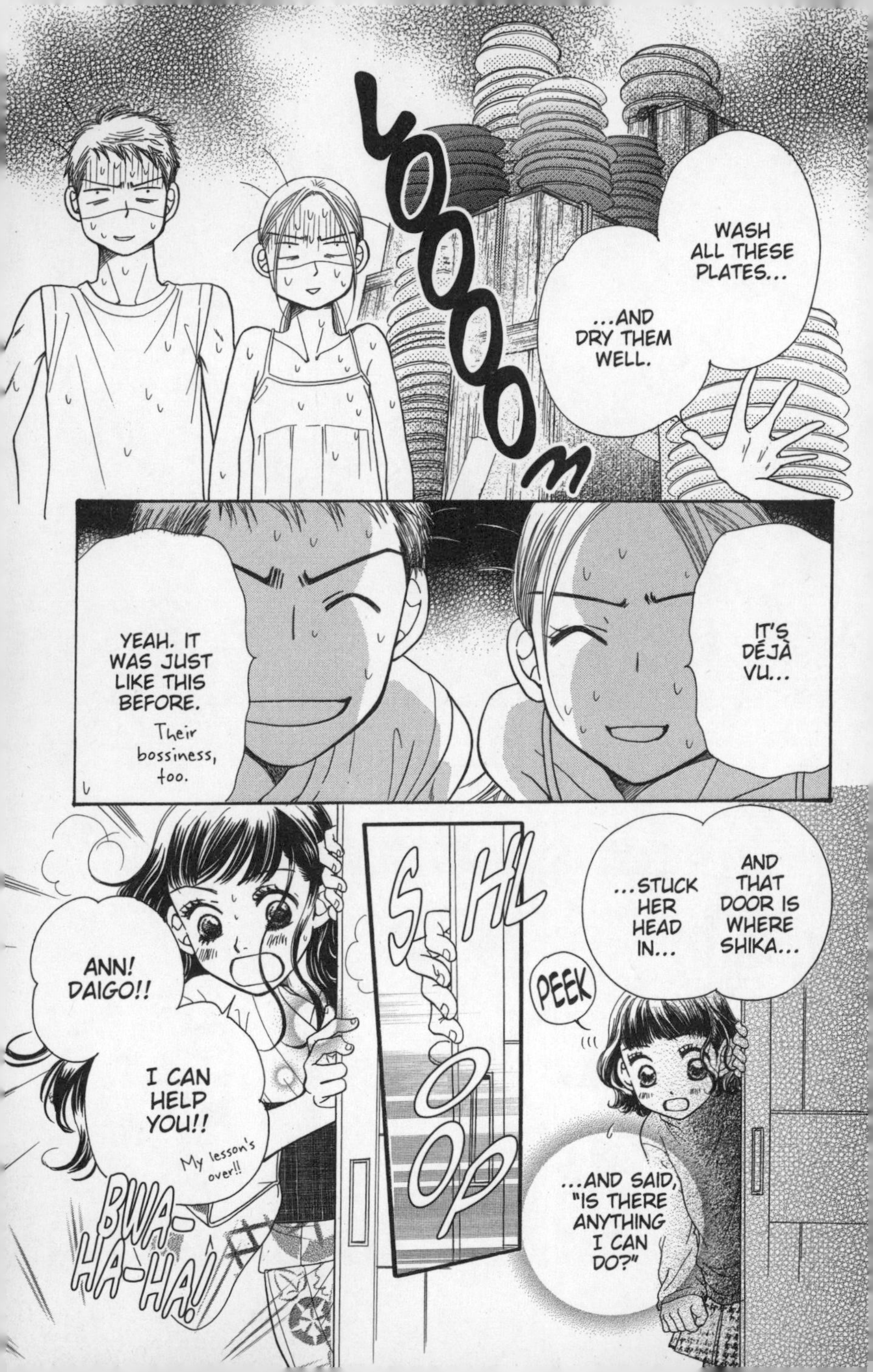
VOOOOOm
WASH ALL THESE PLATES...
...AND DRY THEM WELL.
IT'S DÉJÀ VU...
YEAH. IT WAS JUST LIKE THIS BEFORE.
Their bossiness, too.
AND THAT DOOR IS WHERE SHIKA...
...STUCK HER HEAD IN...
PEEK
...AND SAID, "IS THERE ANYTHING I CAN DO?"
SHLOOP
ANN! DAIGO!!
I CAN HELP YOU!!
My lesson's over!!
BWA-HA-HA!

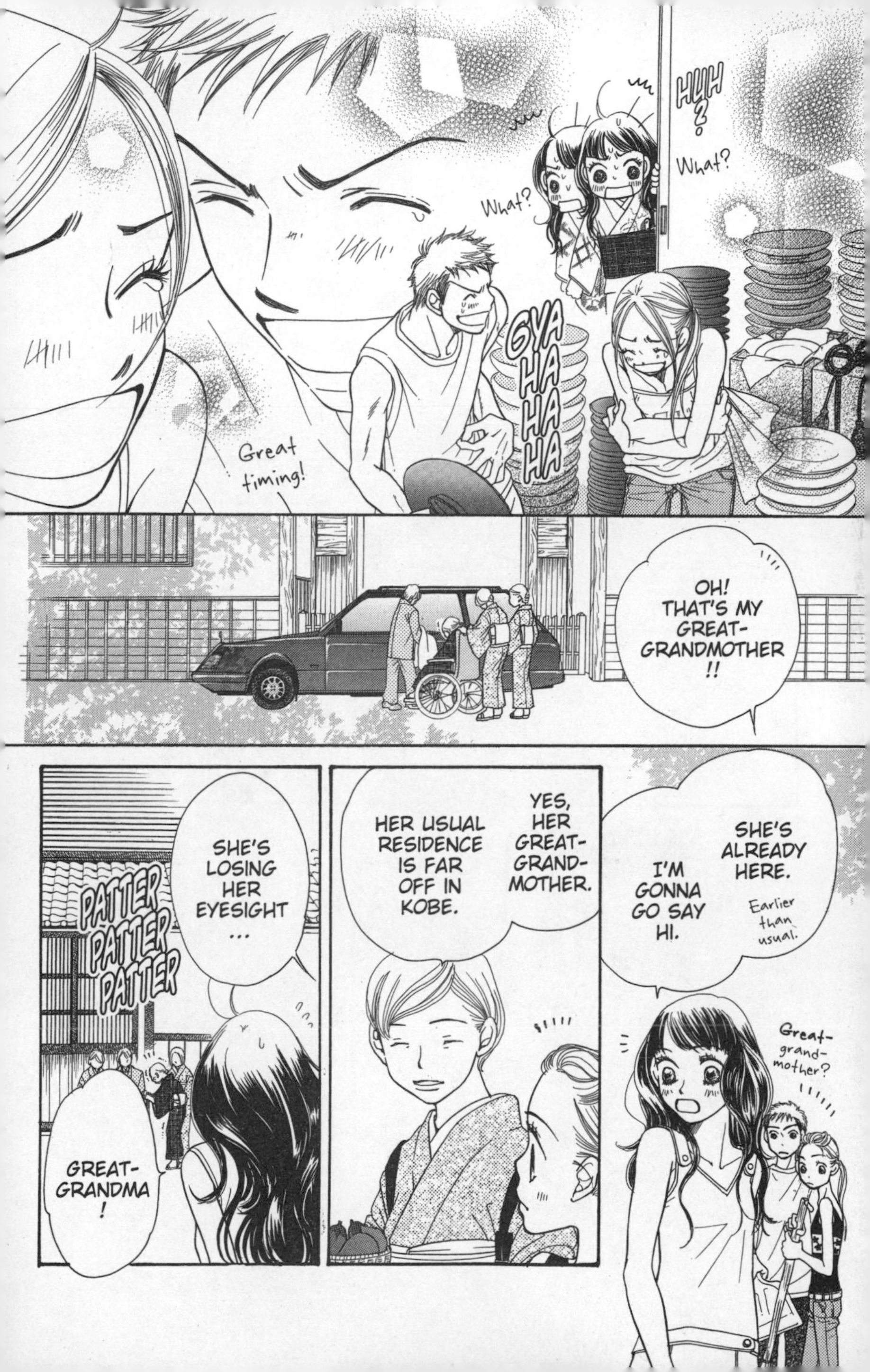
HUH?
What?
What?
GYA HA HA HA HA
Great timing!
OH! THAT'S MY GREAT-GRANDMOTHER!!
SHE'S ALREADY HERE.
Earlier than usual.
I'M GONNA GO SAY HI.
Great-grandmother?
YES, HER GREAT-GRANDMOTHER.
HER USUAL RESIDENCE IS FAR OFF IN KOBE.
SHE'S LOSING HER EYESIGHT...
PATTER PATTER PATTER
GREAT-GRANDMA!

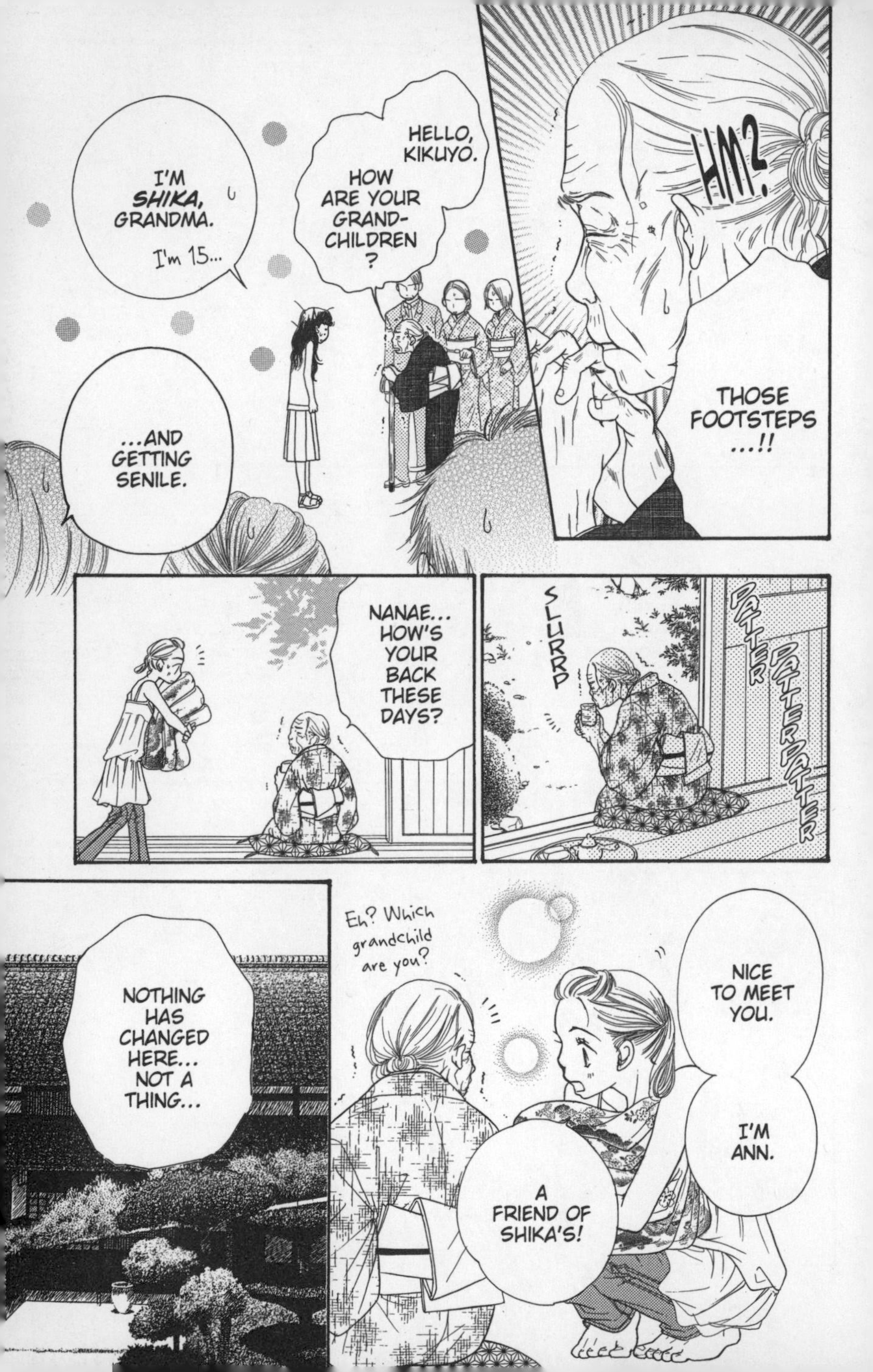
HM?
THOSE FOOTSTEPS ...!!
HELLO, KIKUYO.
HOW ARE YOUR GRANDCHILDREN?
I'M SHIKA, GRANDMA.
I'm 15...
...AND GETTING SENILE.
PATTER PATTER
SLURRP
NANAE... HOW'S YOUR BACK THESE DAYS?
NICE TO MEET YOU.
I'M ANN.
A FRIEND OF SHIKA'S!
Eh? Which grandchild are you?
NOTHING HAS CHANGED HERE... NOT A THING...

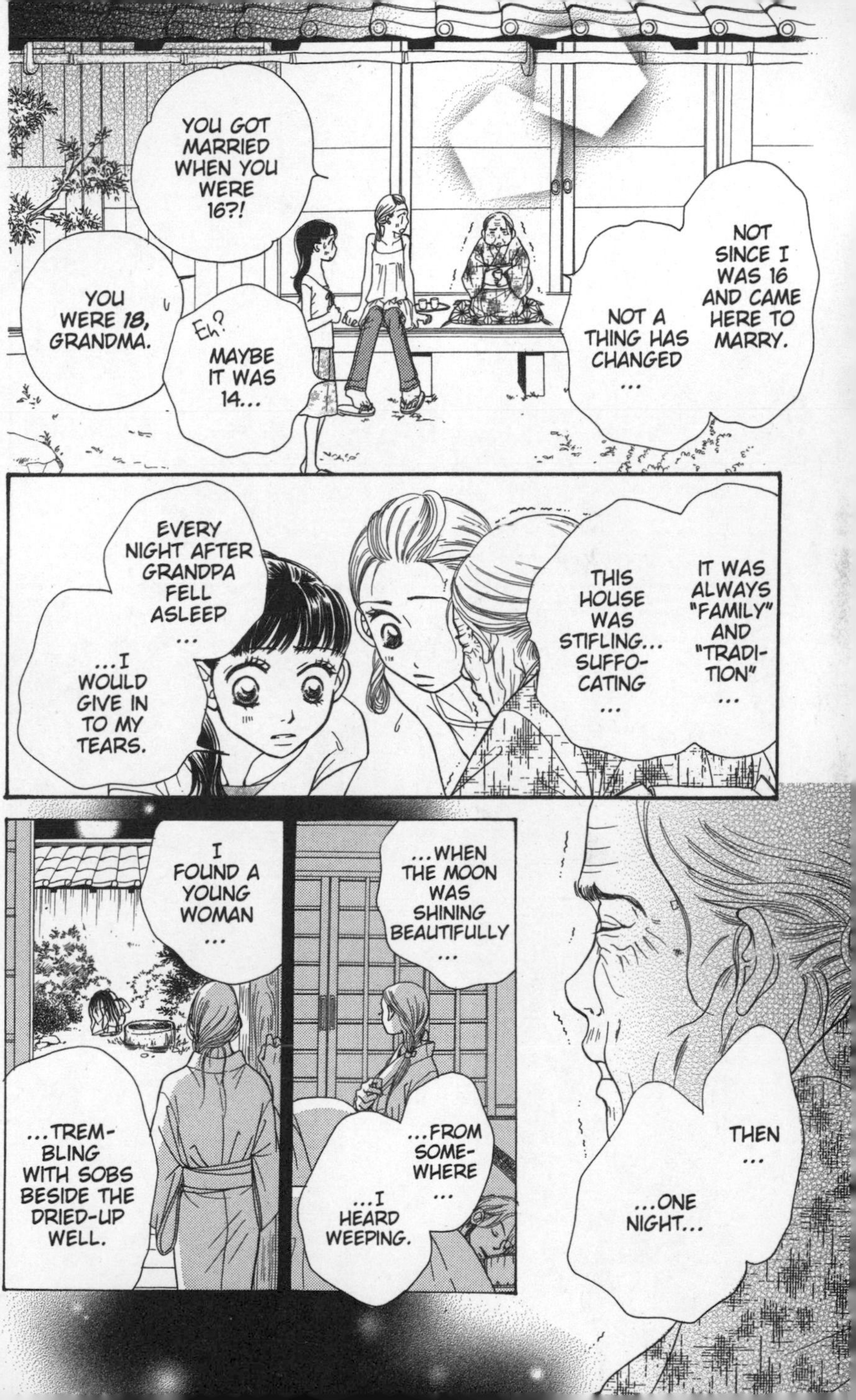
NOT SINCE I WAS 16 AND CAME HERE TO MARRY.
NOT A THING HAS CHANGED ...
YOU GOT MARRIED WHEN YOU WERE 16?!
Eh?
MAYBE IT WAS 14...
YOU WERE 18, GRANDMA.
IT WAS ALWAYS "FAMILY" AND "TRADITION" ...
THIS HOUSE WAS STIFLING... SUFFOCATING ...
EVERY NIGHT AFTER GRANDPA FELL ASLEEP ...
...I WOULD GIVE IN TO MY TEARS.
THEN ...
...ONE NIGHT...
...WHEN THE MOON WAS SHINING BEAUTIFULLY ...
...FROM SOMEWHERE ...
...I HEARD WEEPING.
I FOUND A YOUNG WOMAN ...
...TREMBLING WITH SOBS BESIDE THE DRIED-UP WELL.

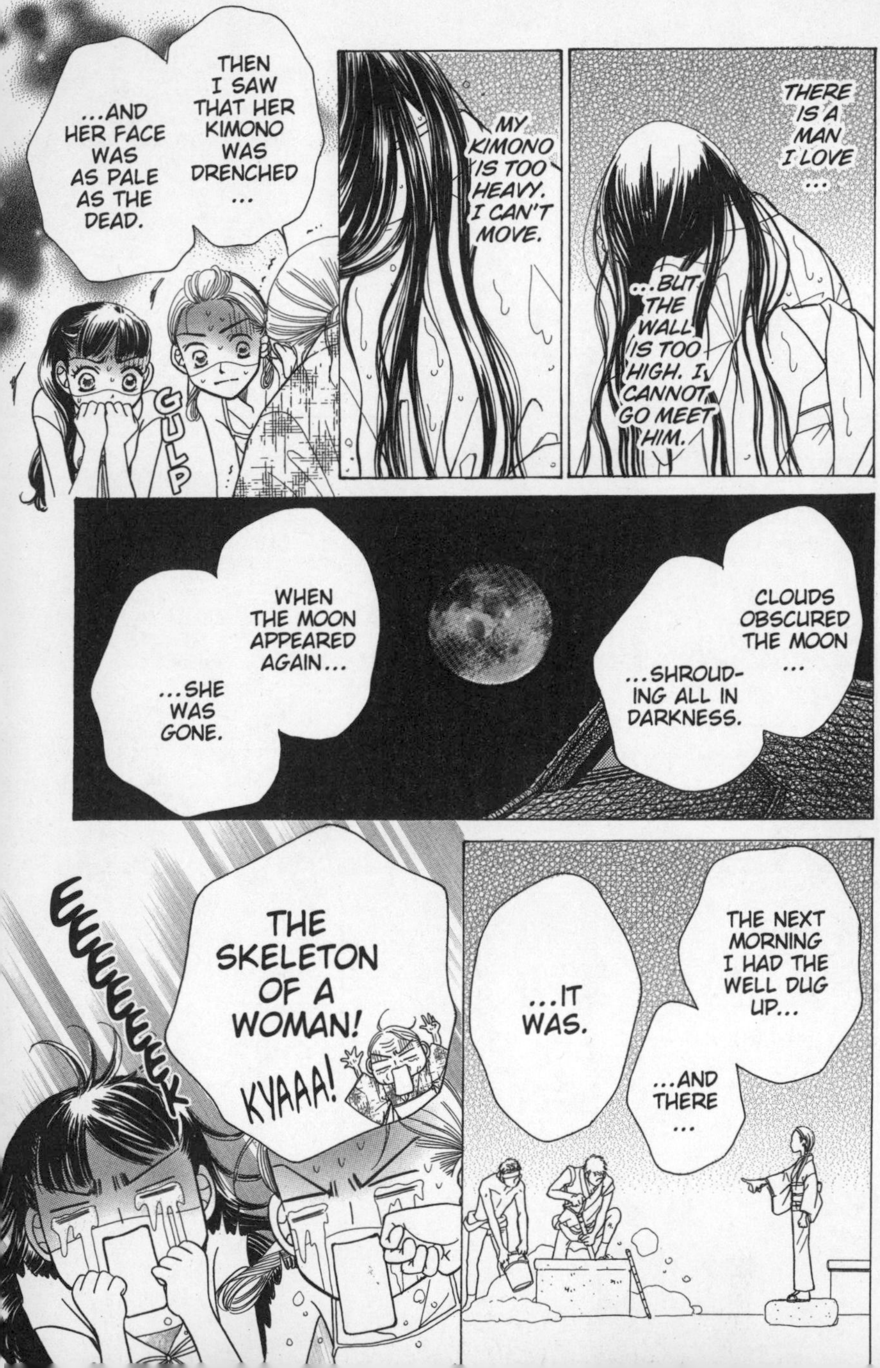
THERE IS A MAN I LOVE ...
...BUT THE WALL IS TOO HIGH. I CANNOT GO MEET HIM.
MY KIMONO IS TOO HEAVY. I CAN'T MOVE.
THEN I SAW THAT HER KIMONO WAS DRENCHED ...
...AND HER FACE WAS AS PALE AS THE DEAD.
GULP
CLOUDS OBSCURED THE MOON ...
...SHROUDING ALL IN DARKNESS.
WHEN THE MOON APPEARED AGAIN...
...SHE WAS GONE.
THE NEXT MORNING I HAD THE WELL DUG UP...
...AND THERE ...
...IT WAS.
THE SKELETON OF A WOMAN!
KYAAA!

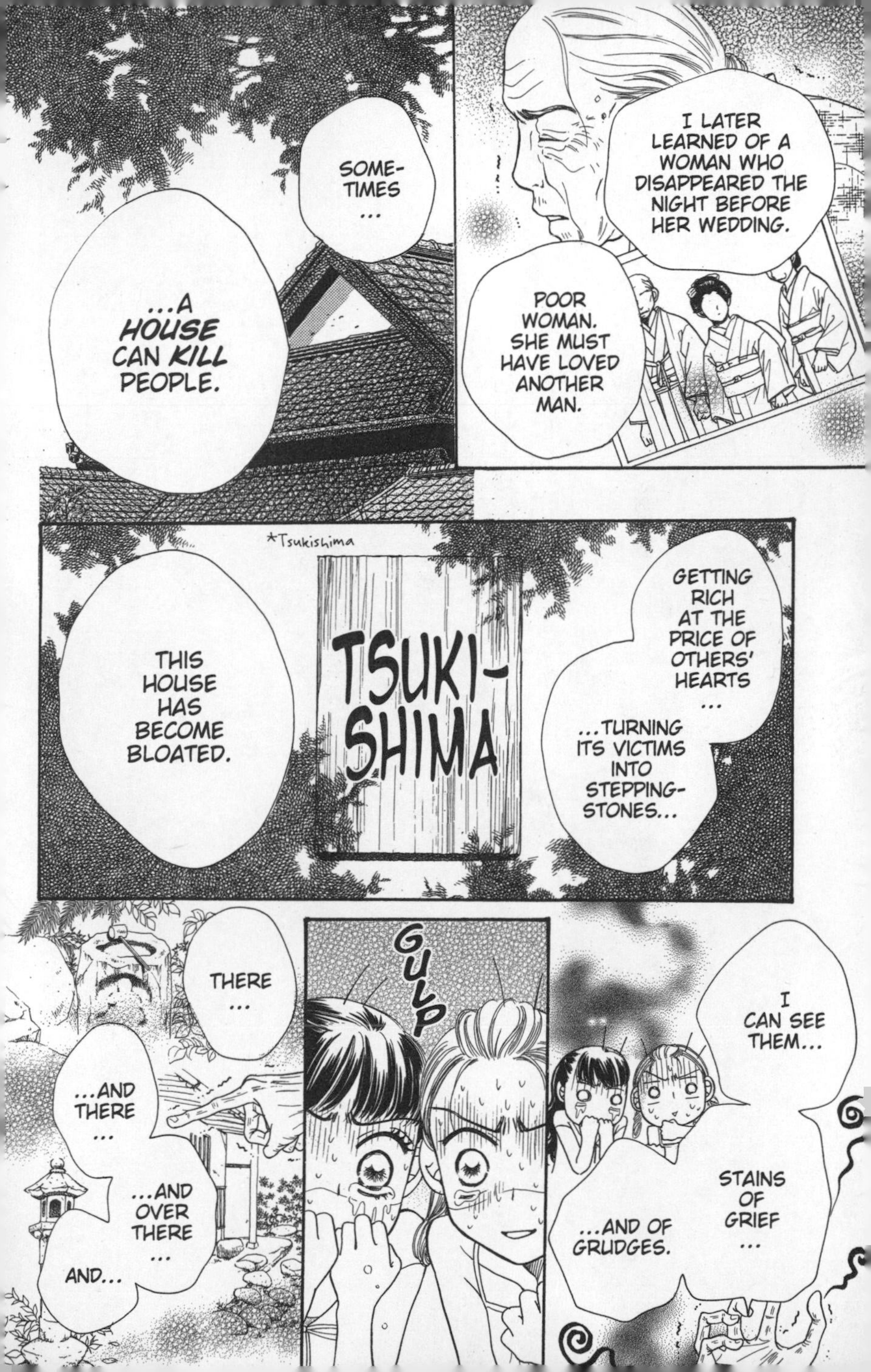
I LATER LEARNED OF A WOMAN WHO DISAPPEARED THE NIGHT BEFORE HER WEDDING.
POOR WOMAN. SHE MUST HAVE LOVED ANOTHER MAN.
SOME-TIMES ...
...A HOUSE CAN KILL PEOPLE.
GETTING RICH AT THE PRICE OF OTHERS' HEARTS ...
...TURNING ITS VICTIMS INTO STEPPING-STONES...
TSUKI-SHIMA
*Tsukishima
THIS HOUSE HAS BECOME BLOATED.
I CAN SEE THEM...
STAINS OF GRIEF ...
...AND OF GRUDGES.
GULP
THERE ...
...AND THERE ...
...AND OVER THERE ...
AND...

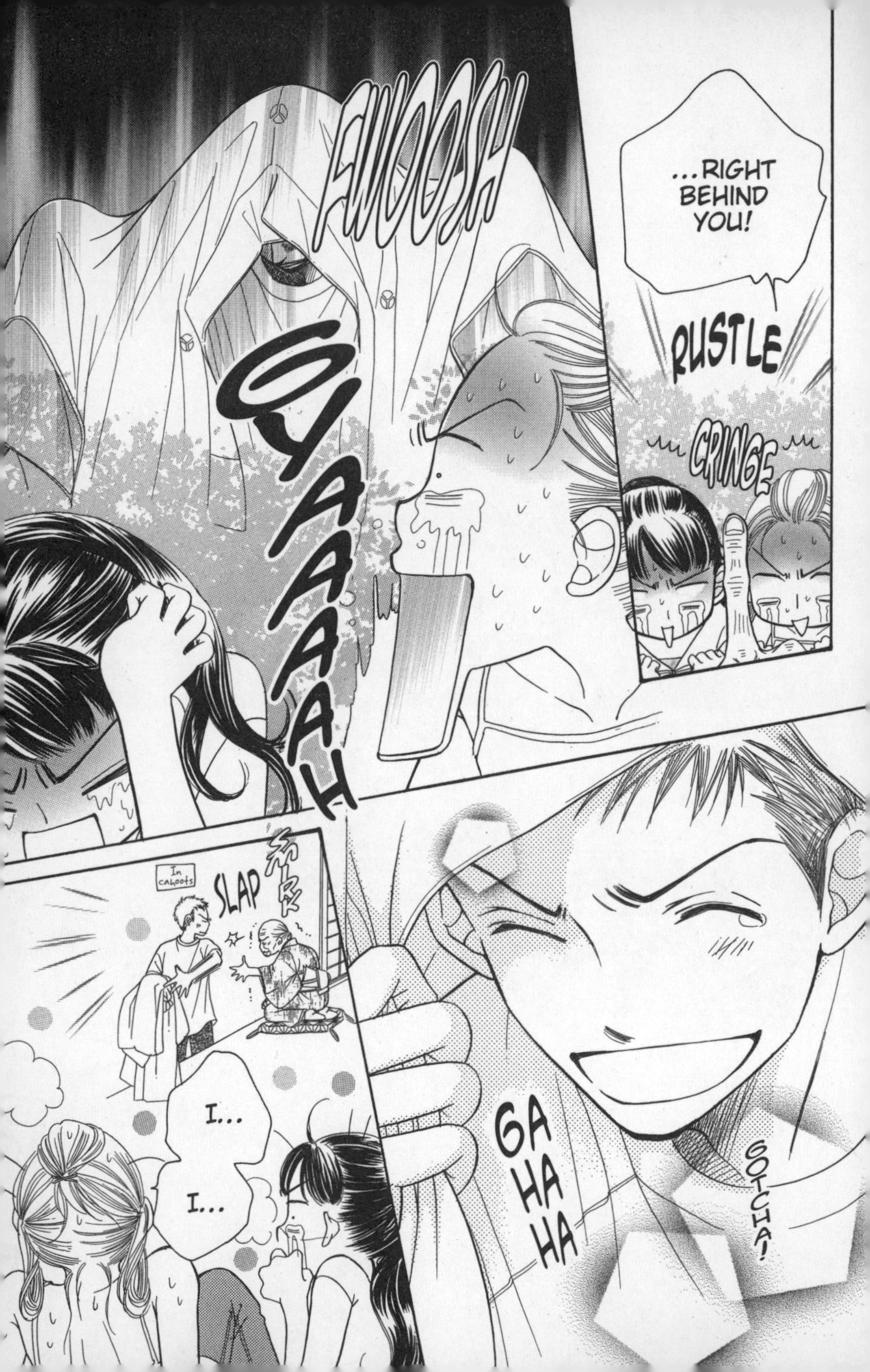
...RIGHT BEHIND YOU!
RUSTLE
CRINGE
FWOOSH
GYAAAAAAH
GAHAHAHA
GOTCHA!
In cahoots
SLAP
SMIRK
I...
I...

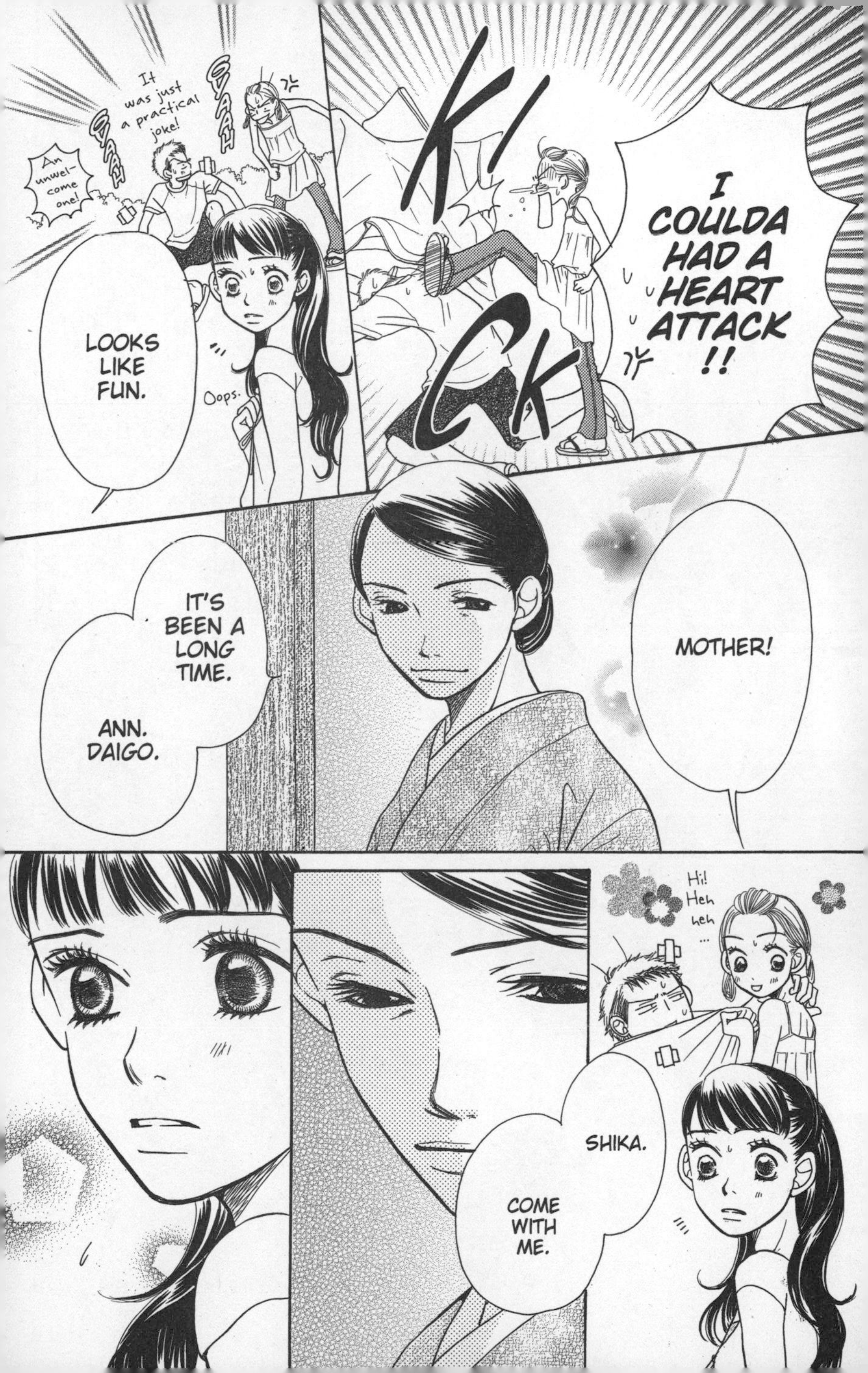
I COULDA HAD A HEART ATTACK!!
It was just a practical joke!
An unwelcome one!
LOOKS LIKE FUN.
Oops.
MOTHER!
IT'S BEEN A LONG TIME.
ANN. DAIGO.
Hi! Heh heh ...
SHIKA.
COME WITH ME.

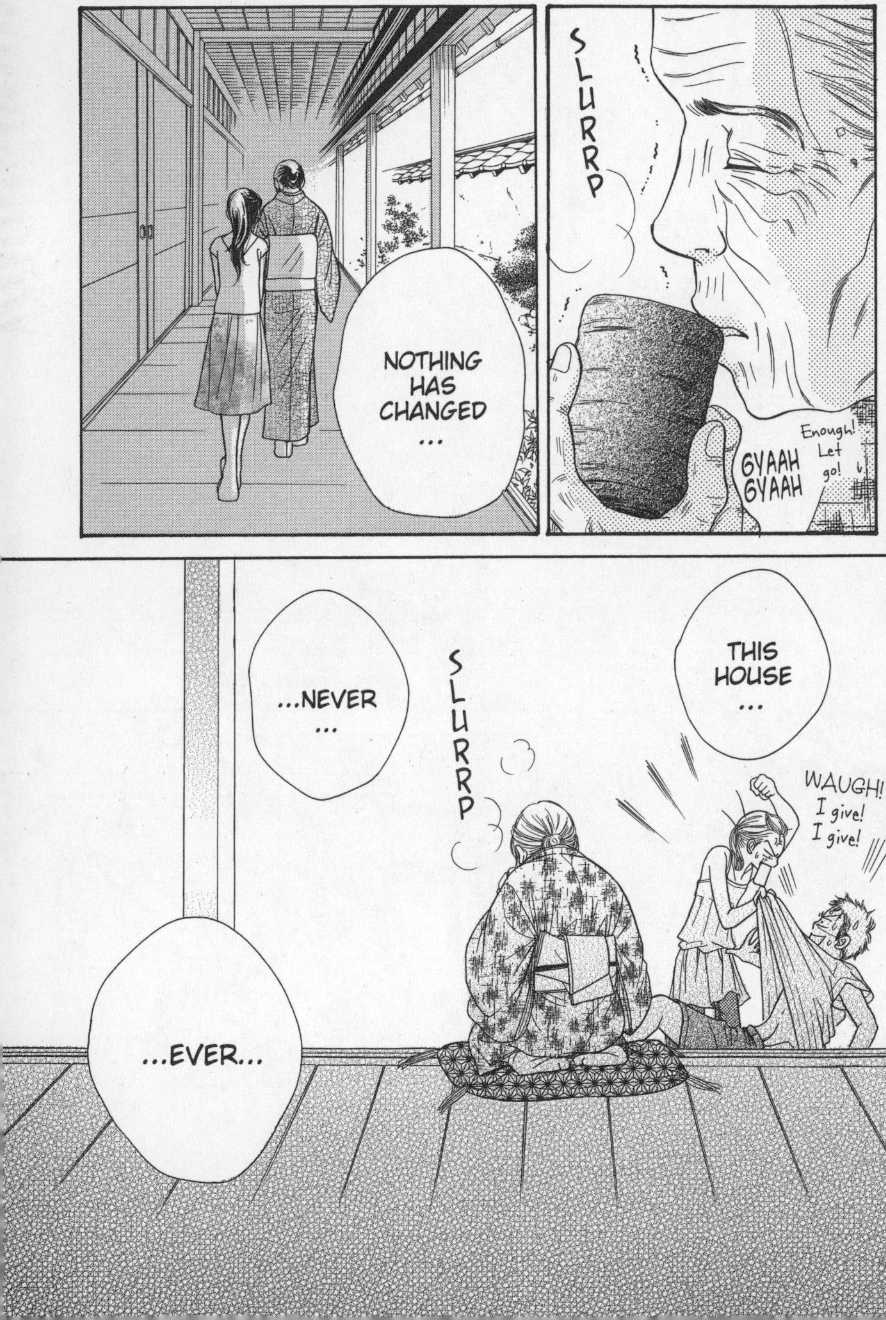
SLURRP
GYAAH GYAAH
Enough! Let go!
NOTHING HAS CHANGED ...
THIS HOUSE ...
WAUGH! I give! I give!
SLURRP
...NEVER ...
...EVER...

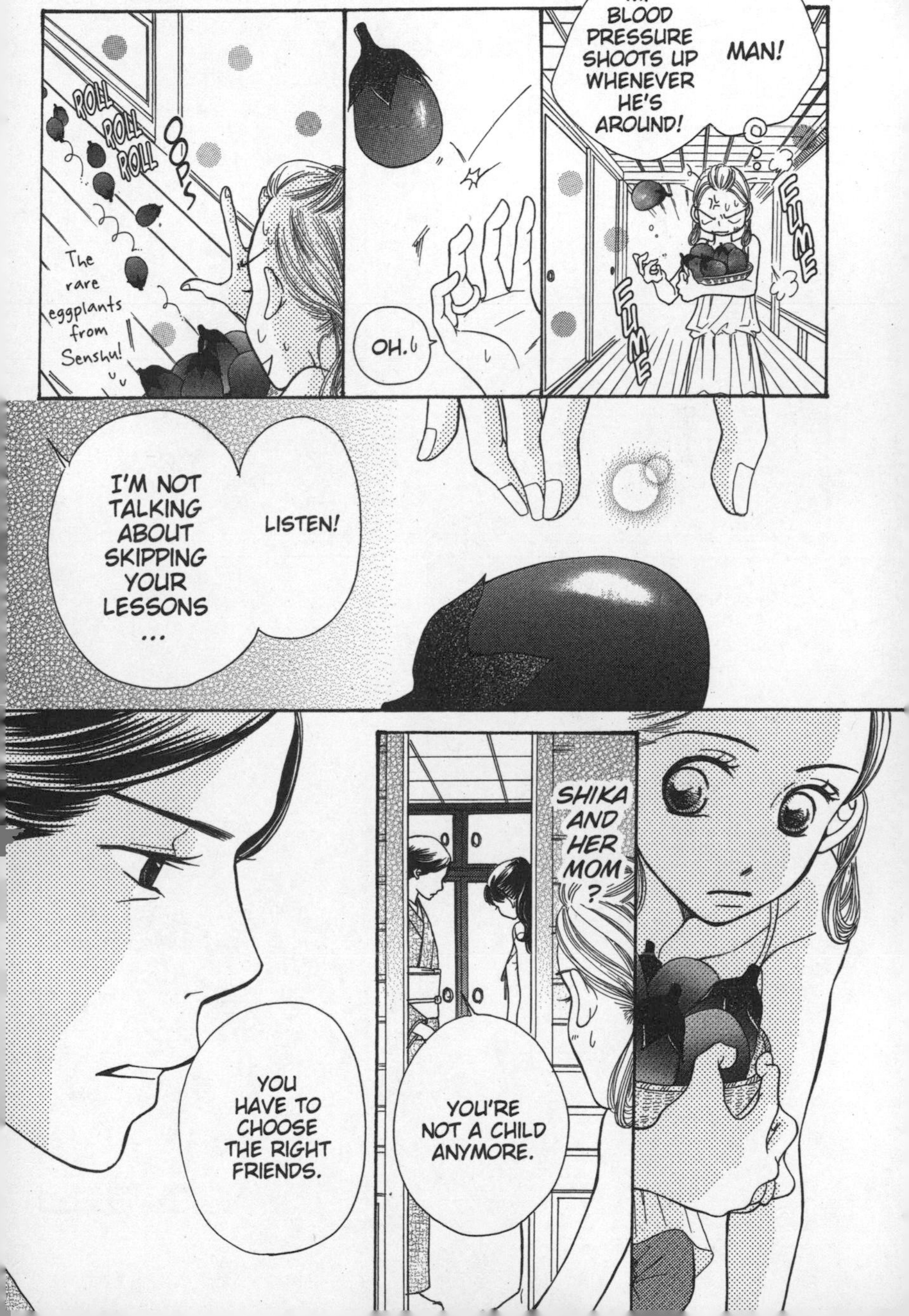
MAN!
MY BLOOD PRESSURE SHOOTS UP WHENEVER HE'S AROUND!
FUME
FUME
OH.
ROLL ROLL ROLL
OOPS
The rare eggplants from Senshu!
LISTEN!
I'M NOT TALKING ABOUT SKIPPING YOUR LESSONS ...
SHIKA AND HER MOM?
YOU'RE NOT A CHILD ANYMORE.
YOU HAVE TO CHOOSE THE RIGHT FRIENDS.

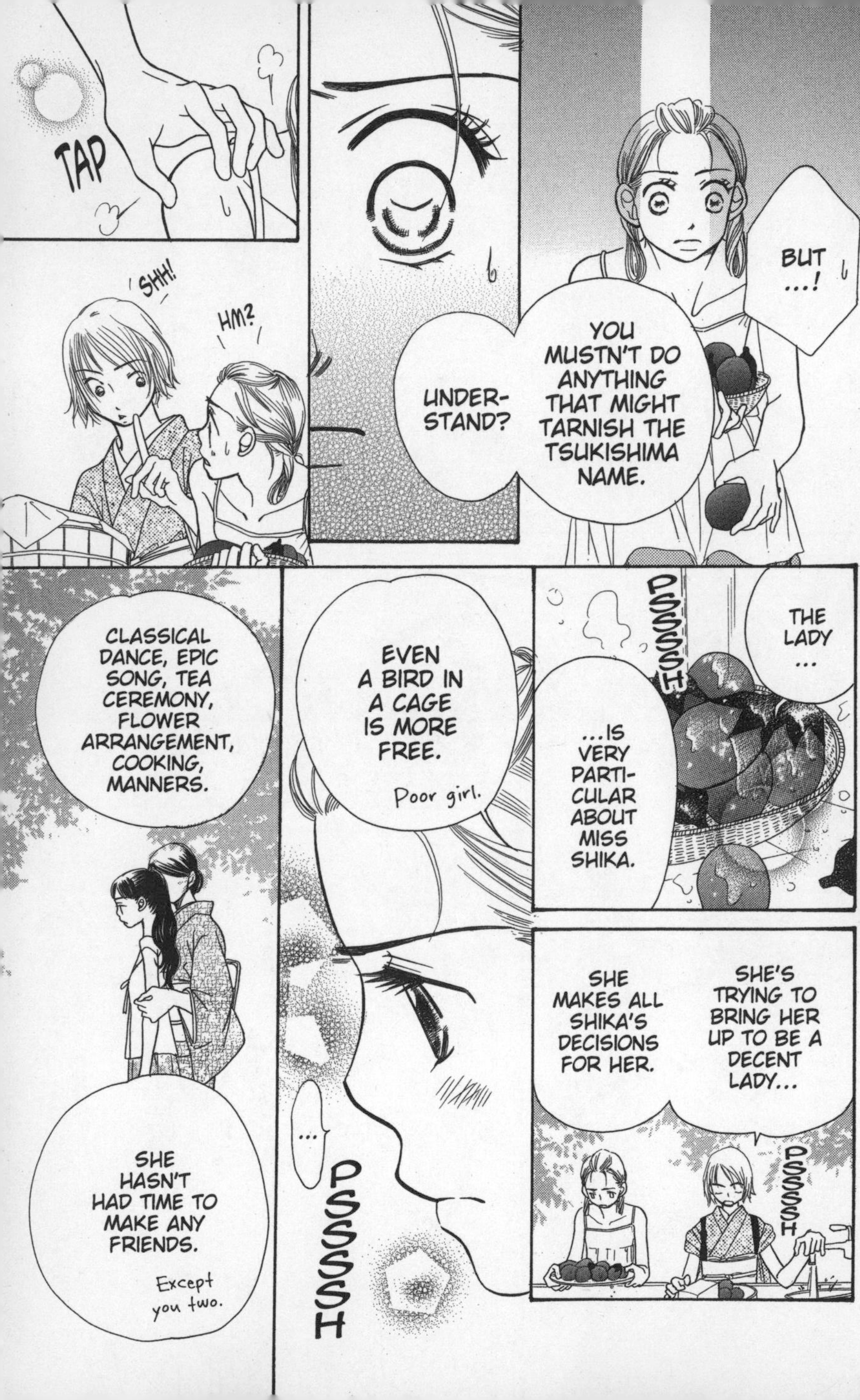

BUT ...!
YOU MUSTN'T DO ANYTHING THAT MIGHT TARNISH THE TSUKISHIMA NAME. UNDER-STAND?
TAP
SHH!
HM?
THE LADY ...
...IS VERY PARTI-CULAR ABOUT MISS SHIKA.
PSSSSH
SHE'S TRYING TO BRING HER UP TO BE A DECENT LADY...
SHE MAKES ALL SHIKA'S DECISIONS FOR HER.
PSSSSH
EVEN A BIRD IN A CAGE IS MORE FREE.
Poor girl.
...
PSSSSH
CLASSICAL DANCE, EPIC SONG, TEA CEREMONY, FLOWER ARRANGEMENT, COOKING, MANNERS.
SHE HASN'T HAD TIME TO MAKE ANY FRIENDS.
Except you two.

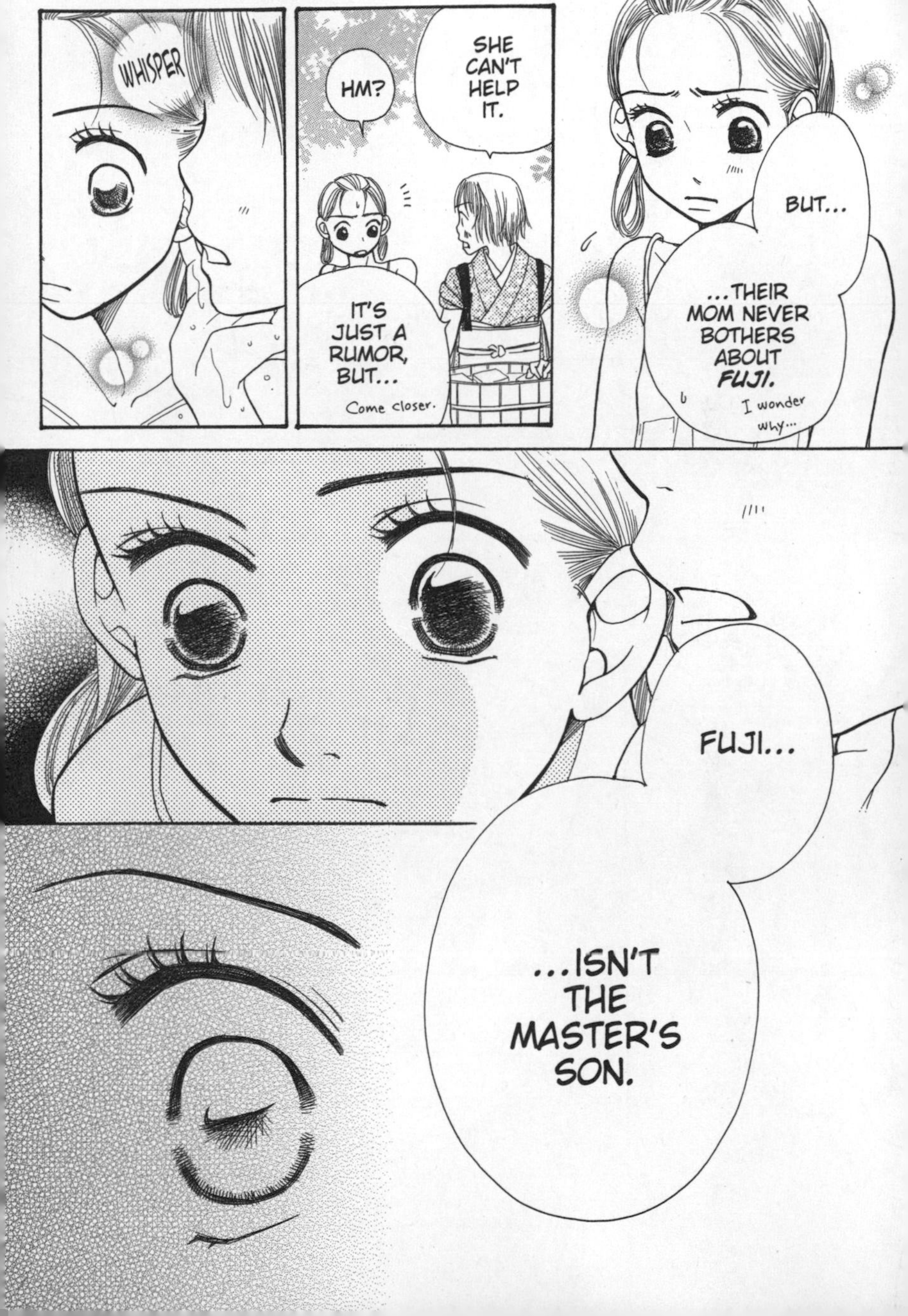
BUT...
...THEIR MOM NEVER BOTHERS ABOUT *FUJI.*
I wonder why...
SHE CAN'T HELP IT.
HM?
IT'S JUST A RUMOR, BUT...
Come closer.
WHISPER
FUJI...
...ISN'T THE MASTER'S SON.

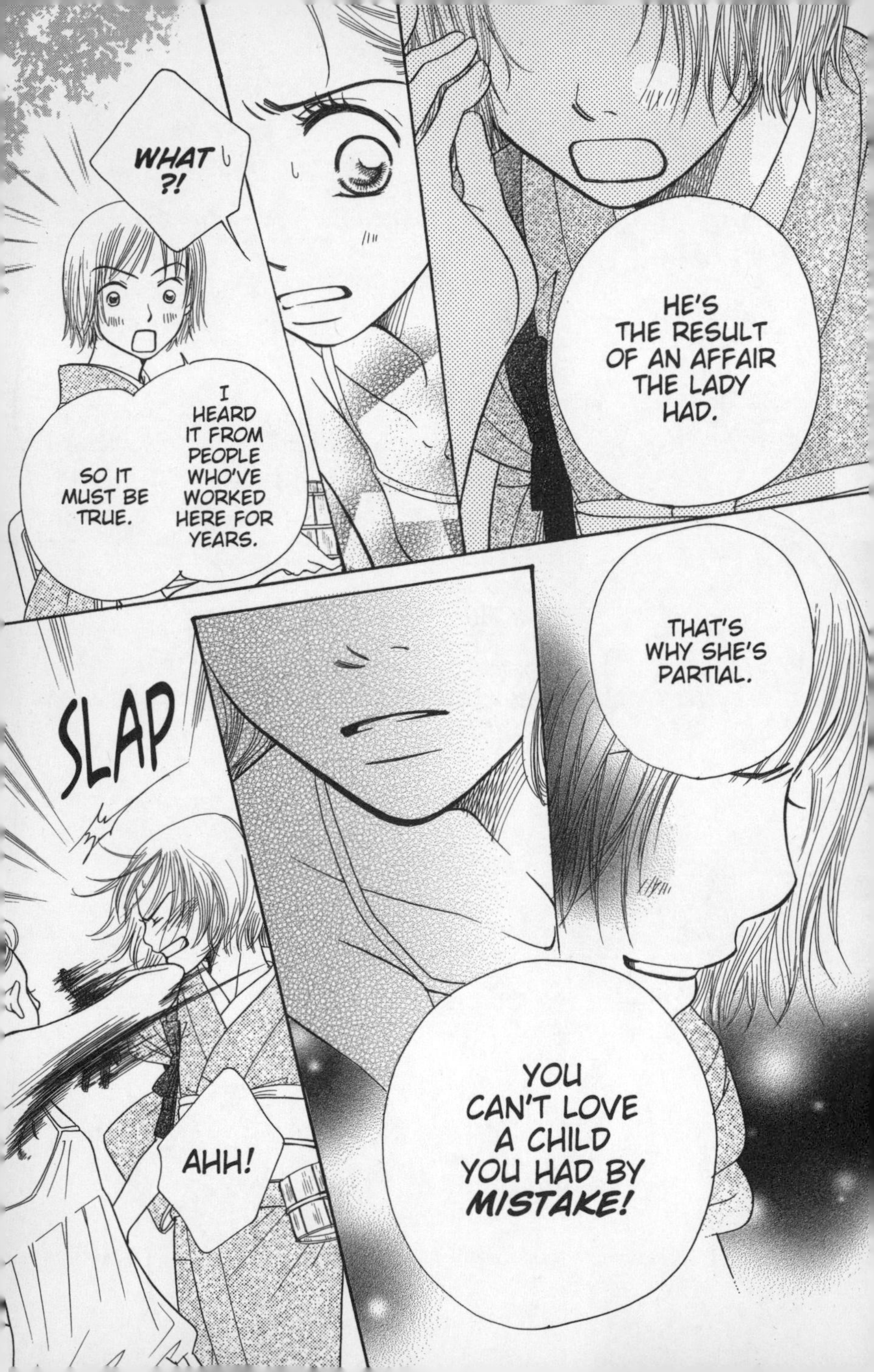
HE'S THE RESULT OF AN AFFAIR THE LADY HAD.
WHAT ?!
I HEARD IT FROM PEOPLE WHO'VE WORKED HERE FOR YEARS.
SO IT MUST BE TRUE.
THAT'S WHY SHE'S PARTIAL.
YOU CAN'T LOVE A CHILD YOU HAD BY MISTAKE!
SLAP
AHH!

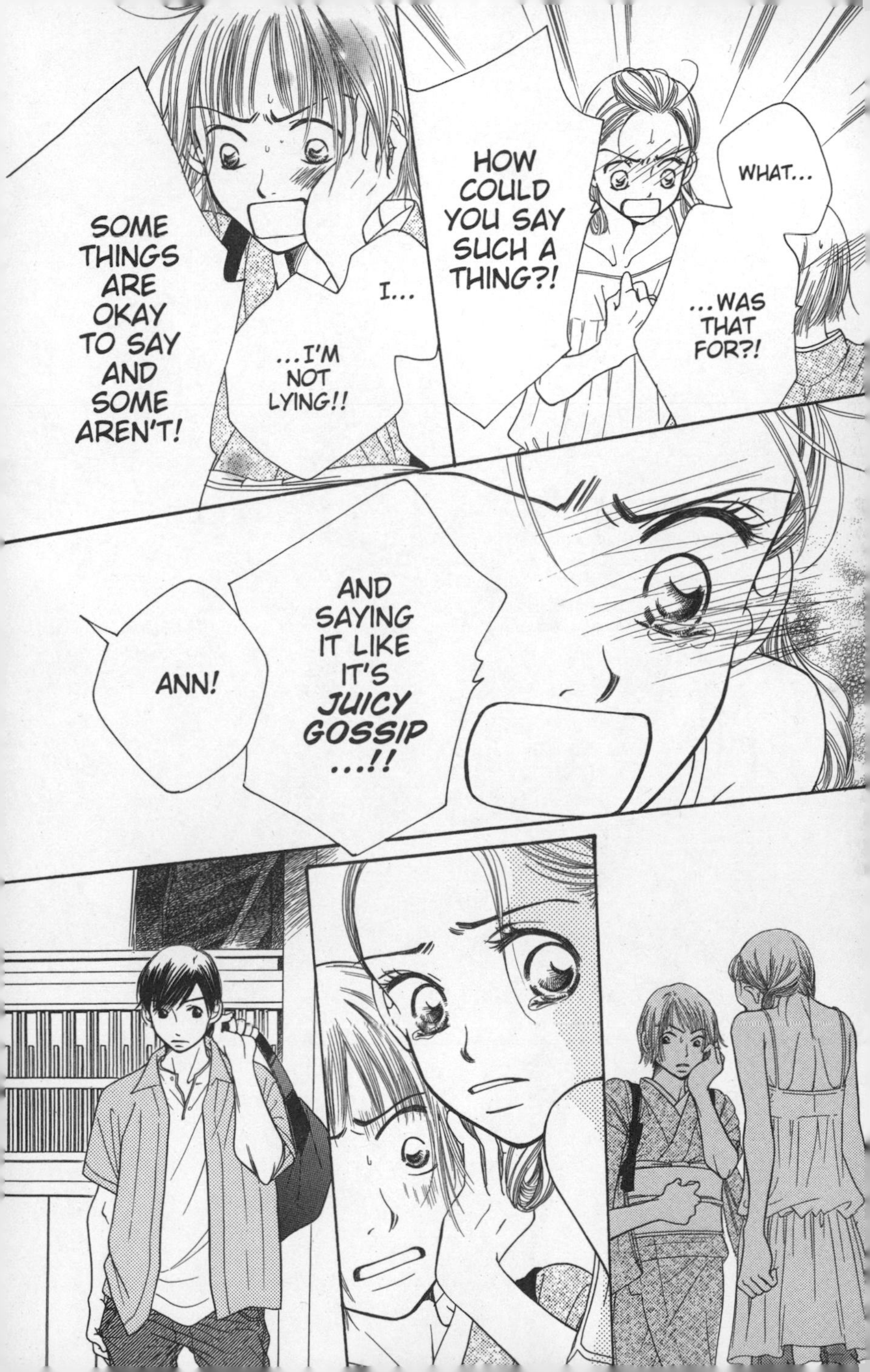
WHAT...
...WAS THAT FOR?!
HOW COULD YOU SAY SUCH A THING?!
I...
...I'M NOT LYING!!
SOME THINGS ARE OKAY TO SAY AND SOME AREN'T!
AND SAYING IT LIKE IT'S *JUICY GOSSIP*...!!
ANN!

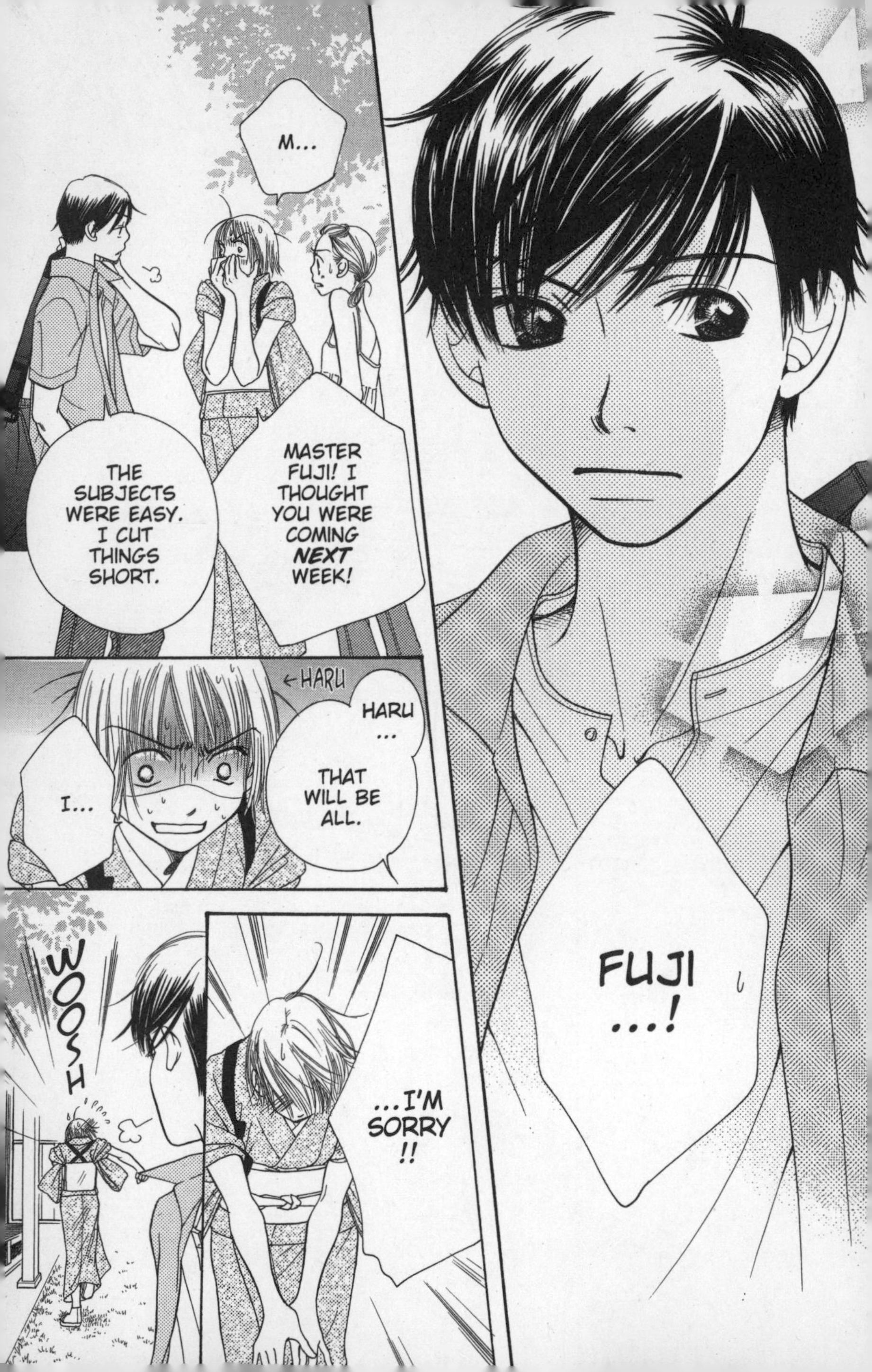
FUJI ...!
M...
MASTER FUJI! I THOUGHT YOU WERE COMING *NEXT* WEEK!
THE SUBJECTS WERE EASY. I CUT THINGS SHORT.
← HARU
HARU ... THAT WILL BE ALL.
I...
...I'M SORRY !!
WOOSH

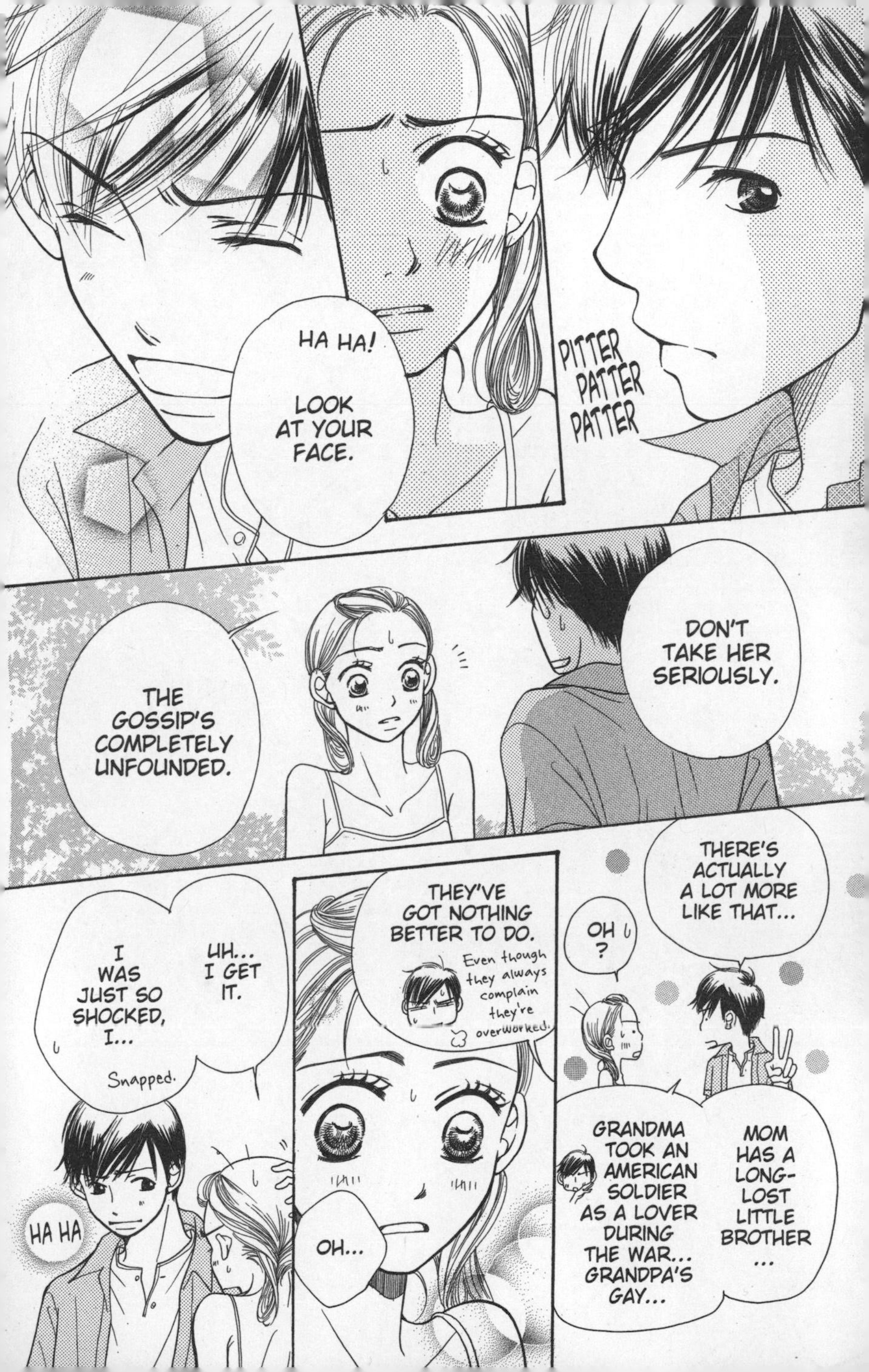
PITTER PATTER PATTER
HA HA!
LOOK AT YOUR FACE.
DON'T TAKE HER SERIOUSLY.
THE GOSSIP'S COMPLETELY UNFOUNDED.
THERE'S ACTUALLY A LOT MORE LIKE THAT...
OH ?
MOM HAS A LONG-LOST LITTLE BROTHER...
GRANDMA TOOK AN AMERICAN SOLDIER AS A LOVER DURING THE WAR... GRANDPA'S GAY...
THEY'VE GOT NOTHING BETTER TO DO.
Even though they always complain they're overworked.
OH...
UH... I GET IT.
I WAS JUST SO SHOCKED, I...
Snapped.
HA HA

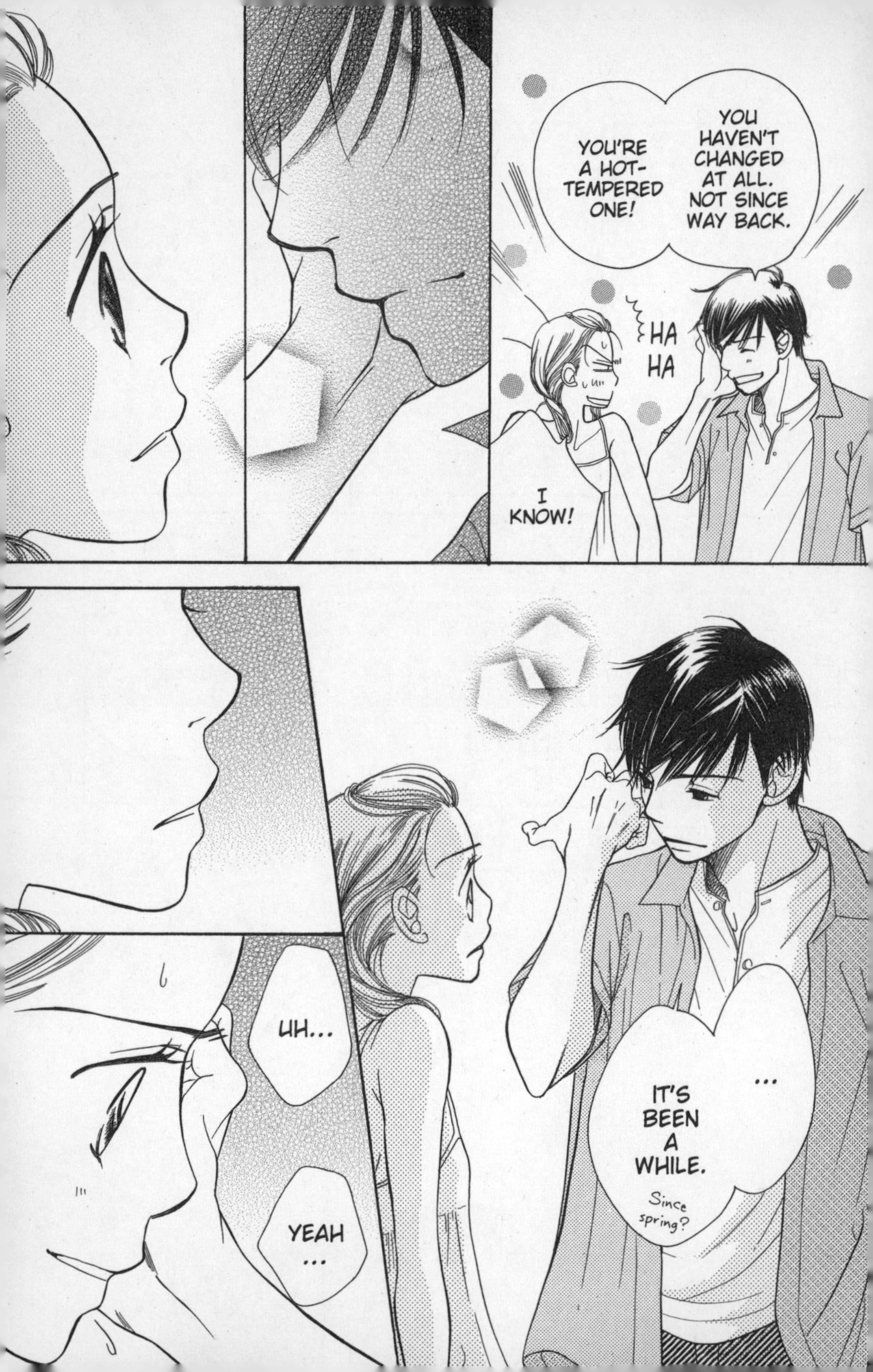
YOU HAVEN'T CHANGED AT ALL. NOT SINCE WAY BACK.
YOU'RE A HOT-TEMPERED ONE!
HA HA
I KNOW!
...
IT'S BEEN A WHILE.
Since spring?
UH...
YEAH...

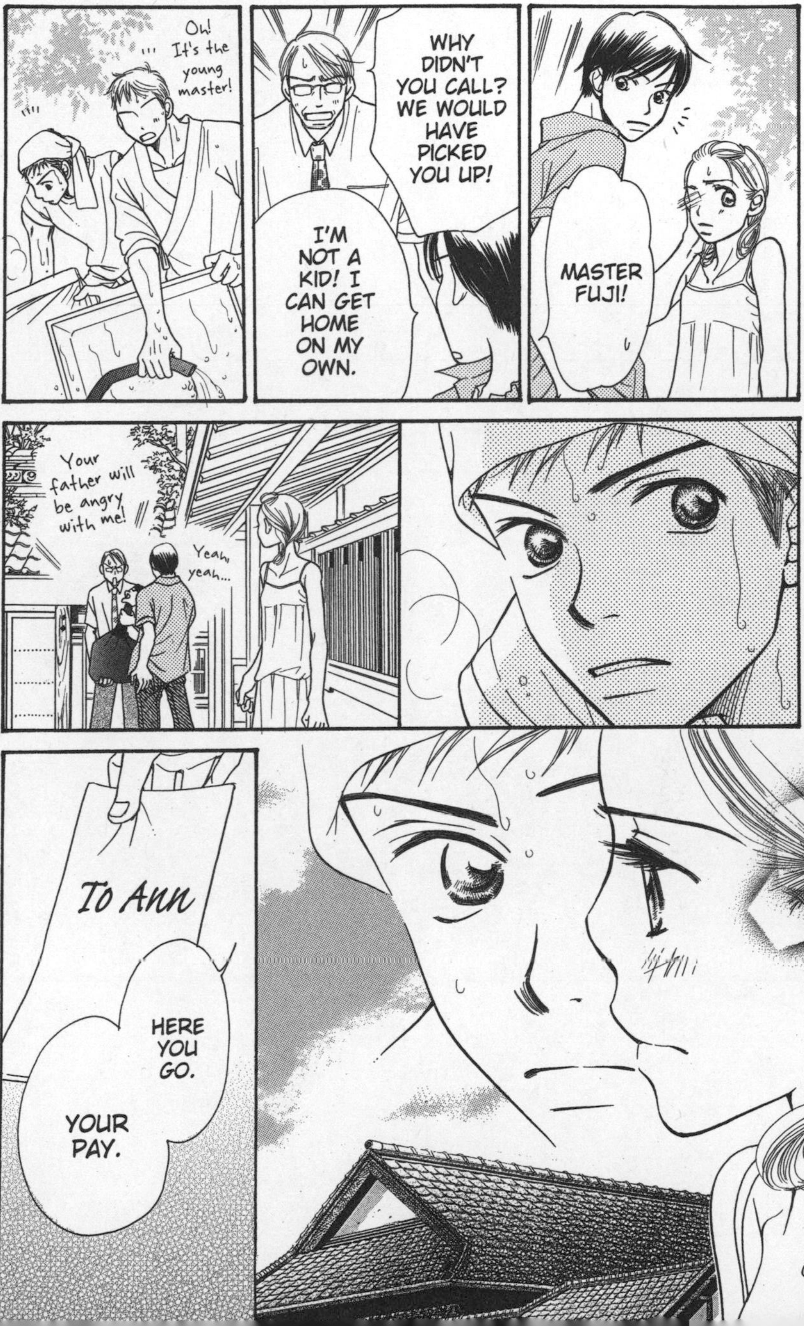
MASTER FUJI!
WHY DIDN'T YOU CALL? WE WOULD HAVE PICKED YOU UP!
I'M NOT A KID! I CAN GET HOME ON MY OWN.
Oh! It's the young master!
Your father will be angry with me!
Yeah yeah...
To Ann
HERE YOU GO.
YOUR PAY.

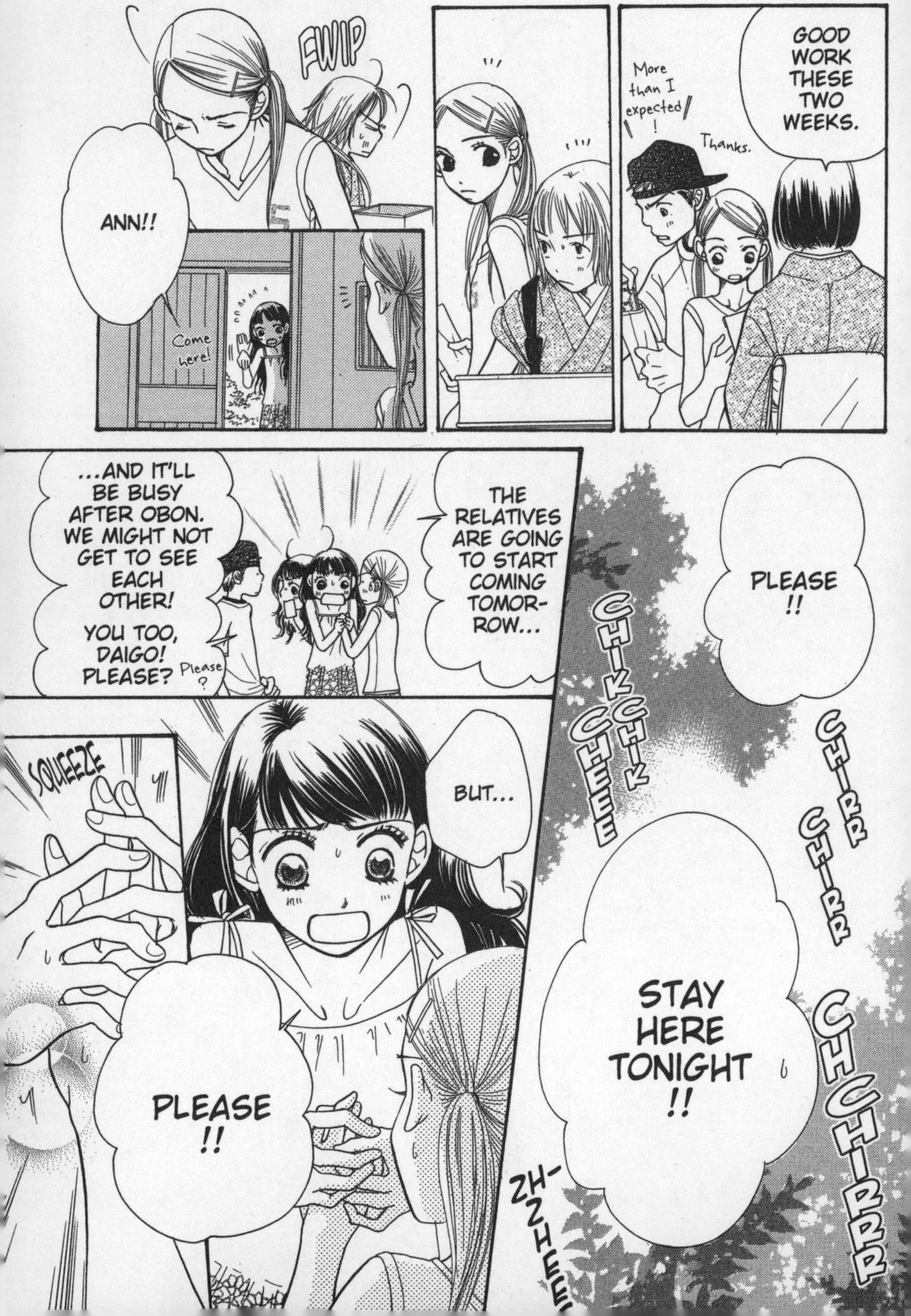
GOOD WORK THESE TWO WEEKS.
More than I expected!
Thanks.
FWIP
ANN!!
Come here!
PLEASE!!
CHIRR CHIRR
CHIK CHIK CHEEE
STAY HERE TONIGHT!!
CHCHIRRR
ZH-ZHEEE
THE RELATIVES ARE GOING TO START COMING TOMORROW...
...AND IT'LL BE BUSY AFTER OBON. WE MIGHT NOT GET TO SEE EACH OTHER!
YOU TOO, DAIGO! PLEASE?
Please?
BUT...
SQUEEZE
PLEASE!!

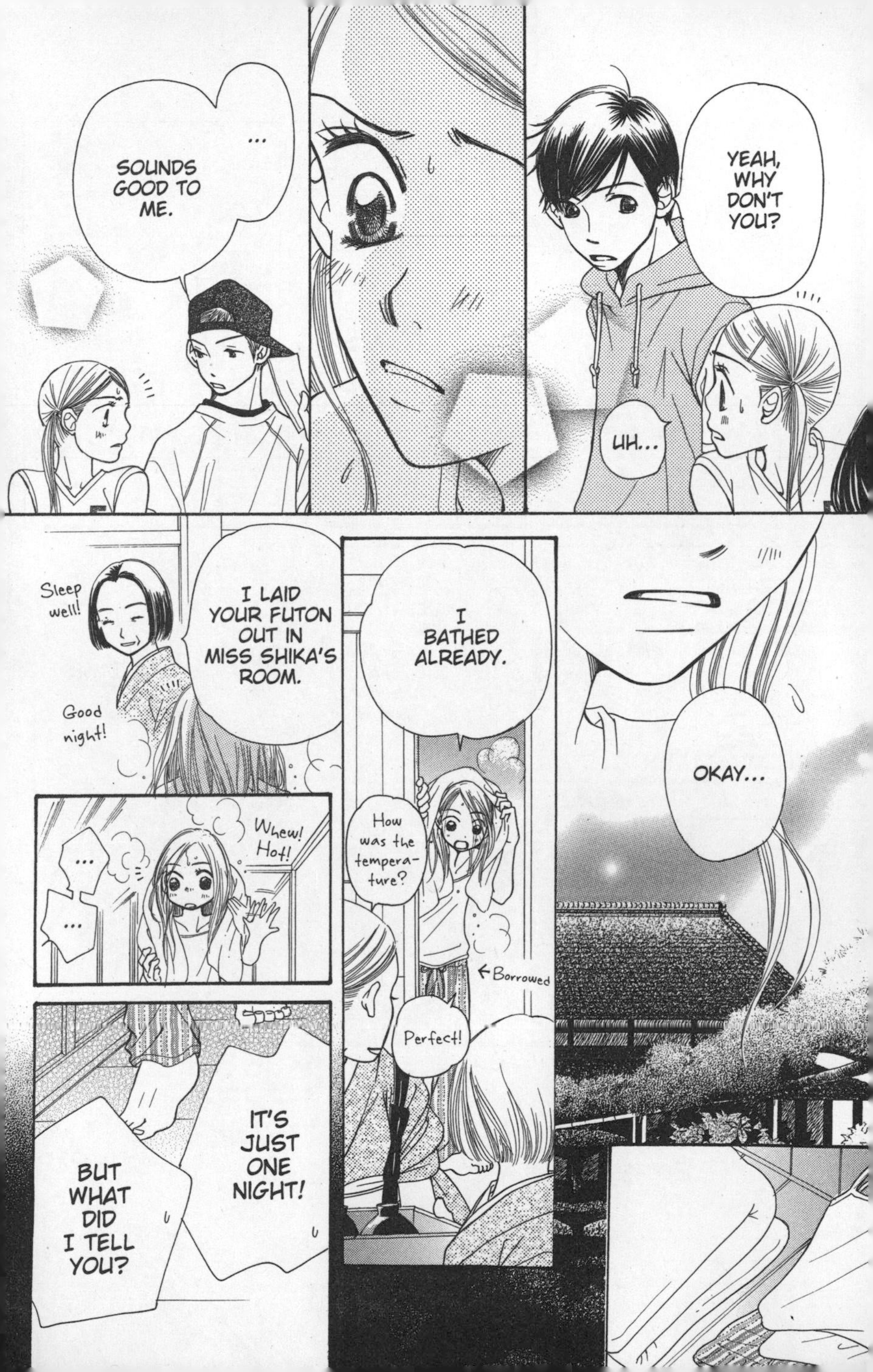
YEAH, WHY DON'T YOU?
UH...
... SOUNDS GOOD TO ME.
OKAY...
I BATHED ALREADY.
How was the tempera-ture?
← Borrowed
Perfect!
I LAID YOUR FUTON OUT IN MISS SHIKA'S ROOM.
Sleep well!
Good night!
Whew! Hot!
...
...
IT'S JUST ONE NIGHT!
BUT WHAT DID I TELL YOU?

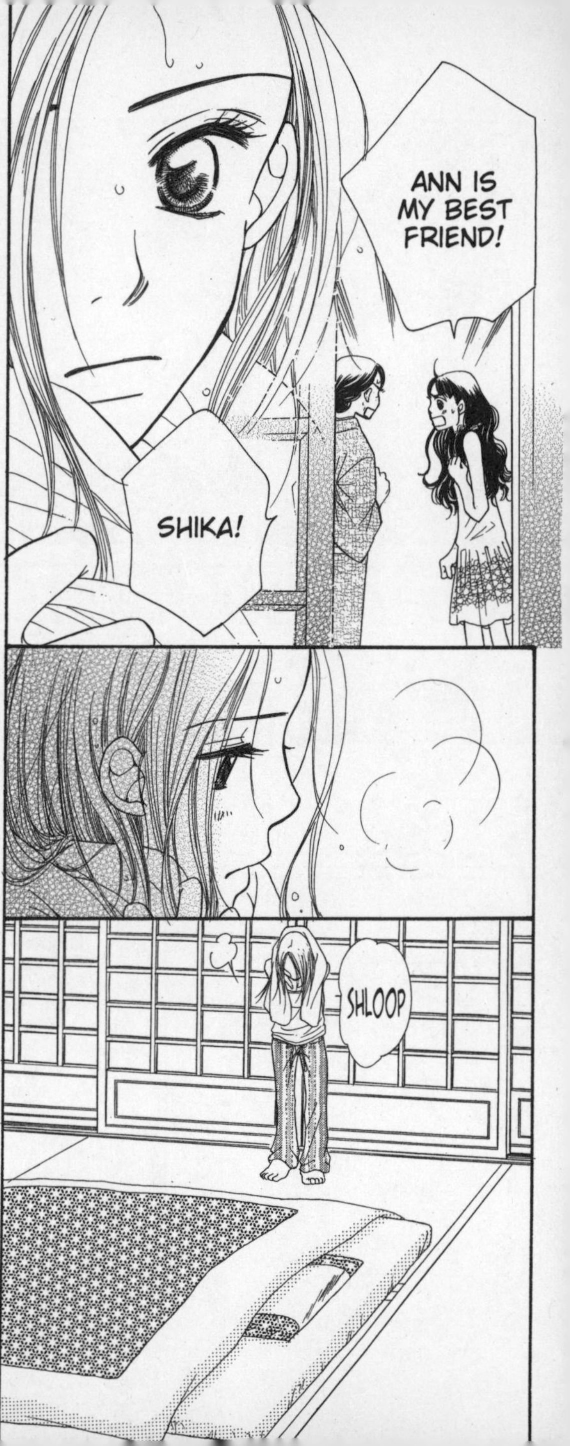
ANN IS MY BEST FRIEND!
SHIKA!
SHLOOP

Summer, Age 16: The House of the Moon

This is volume 3! Thank you for reading. This continues the story of Ann and the others at age 16.

The House of the Moon...

Old Japanese houses... I love them, but they can be scary at night. When I was a kid, the outhouse at my grandma's house in the country was terrifying. I could almost see a hand creeping up out of the hole! I could never muster the courage to go alone. We sold it, and now a pretty new house stands there. I can really sense all the years that have passed.

My assistants undertook the time-consuming task of drawing lots of old Japanese houses! As always, thanks!

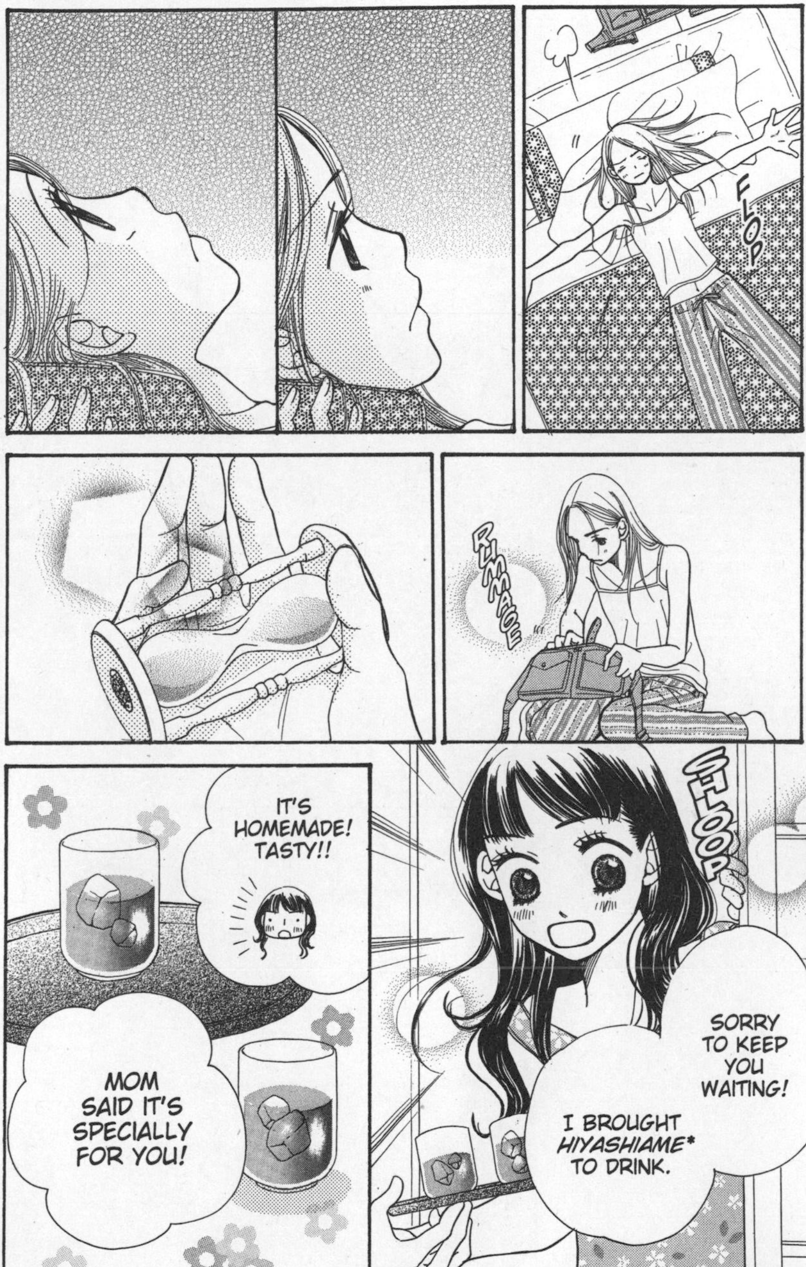
FLOP
RUMMAGE
SHLOOP
SORRY TO KEEP YOU WAITING!
I BROUGHT *HIYASHIAME** TO DRINK.
IT'S HOMEMADE! TASTY!!
MOM SAID IT'S SPECIALLY FOR YOU!
*malt ginger drink

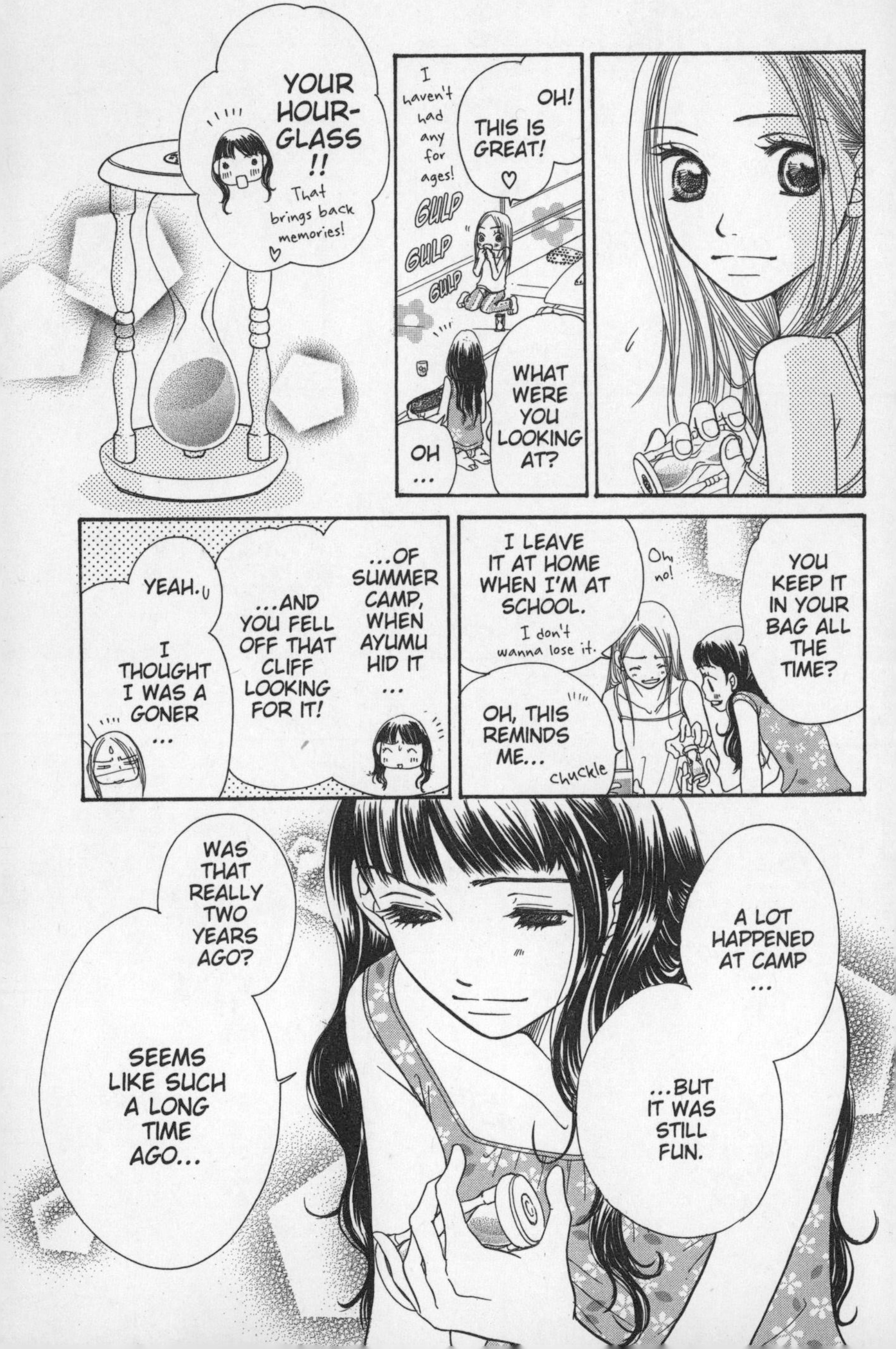
OH! THIS IS GREAT!
I haven't had any for ages!
GULP
GULP
GULP
WHAT WERE YOU LOOKING AT?
OH ...
YOUR HOUR-GLASS!!
That brings back memories!
YOU KEEP IT IN YOUR BAG ALL THE TIME?
Oh no!
I LEAVE IT AT HOME WHEN I'M AT SCHOOL.
I don't wanna lose it.
OH, THIS REMINDS ME...
chuckle
...OF SUMMER CAMP, WHEN AYUMU HID IT ...
...AND YOU FELL OFF THAT CLIFF LOOKING FOR IT!
YEAH.
I THOUGHT I WAS A GONER ...
A LOT HAPPENED AT CAMP ...
...BUT IT WAS STILL FUN.
WAS THAT REALLY TWO YEARS AGO?
SEEMS LIKE SUCH A LONG TIME AGO...

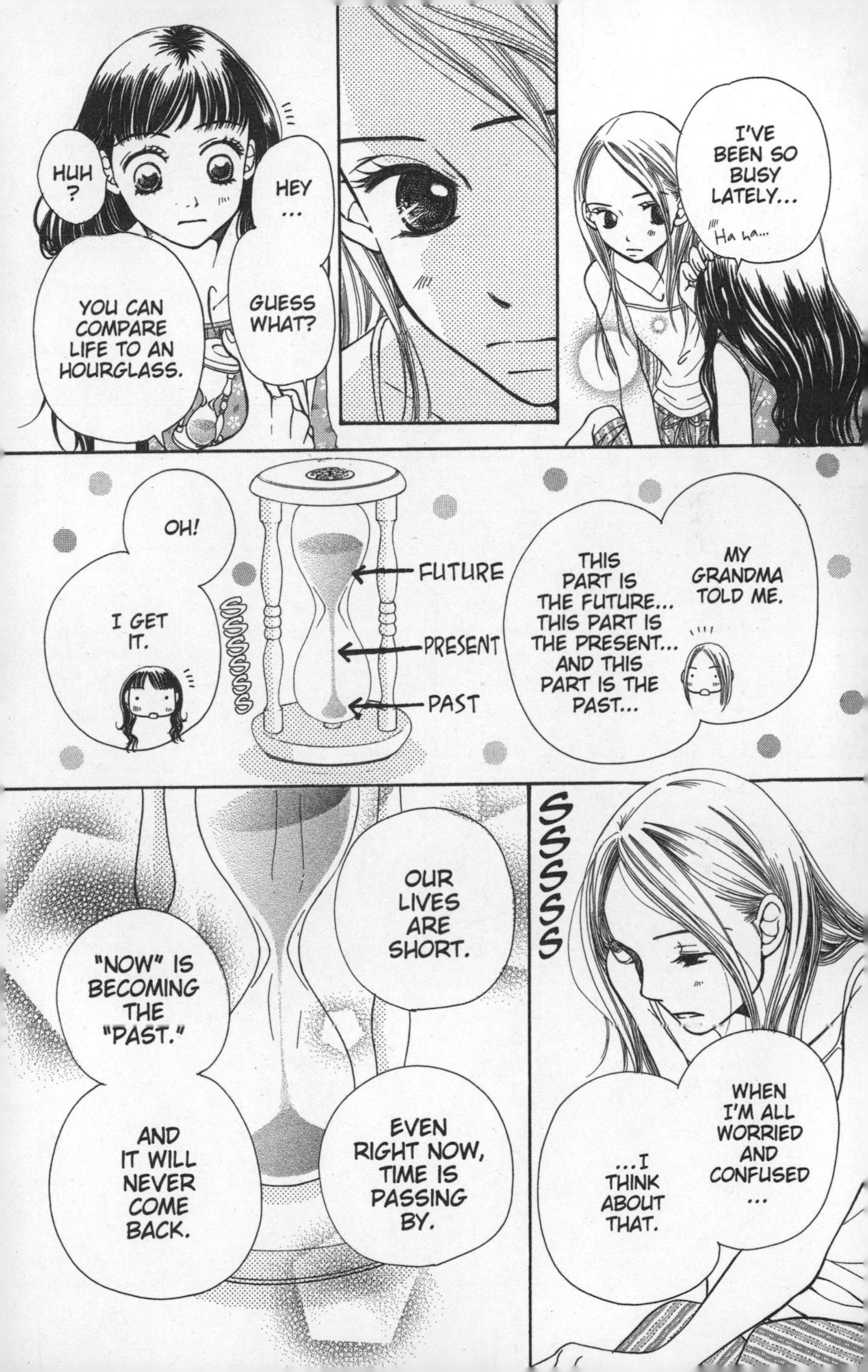
I'VE BEEN SO BUSY LATELY...
Ha ha...
HEY ...
GUESS WHAT?
HUH ?
YOU CAN COMPARE LIFE TO AN HOURGLASS.
MY GRANDMA TOLD ME.
THIS PART IS THE FUTURE... THIS PART IS THE PRESENT... AND THIS PART IS THE PAST...
FUTURE
PRESENT
PAST
SSSSSS
OH!
I GET IT.
SSSSS
WHEN I'M ALL WORRIED AND CONFUSED ...
...I THINK ABOUT THAT.
OUR LIVES ARE SHORT.
EVEN RIGHT NOW, TIME IS PASSING BY.
"NOW" IS BECOMING THE "PAST."
AND IT WILL NEVER COME BACK.

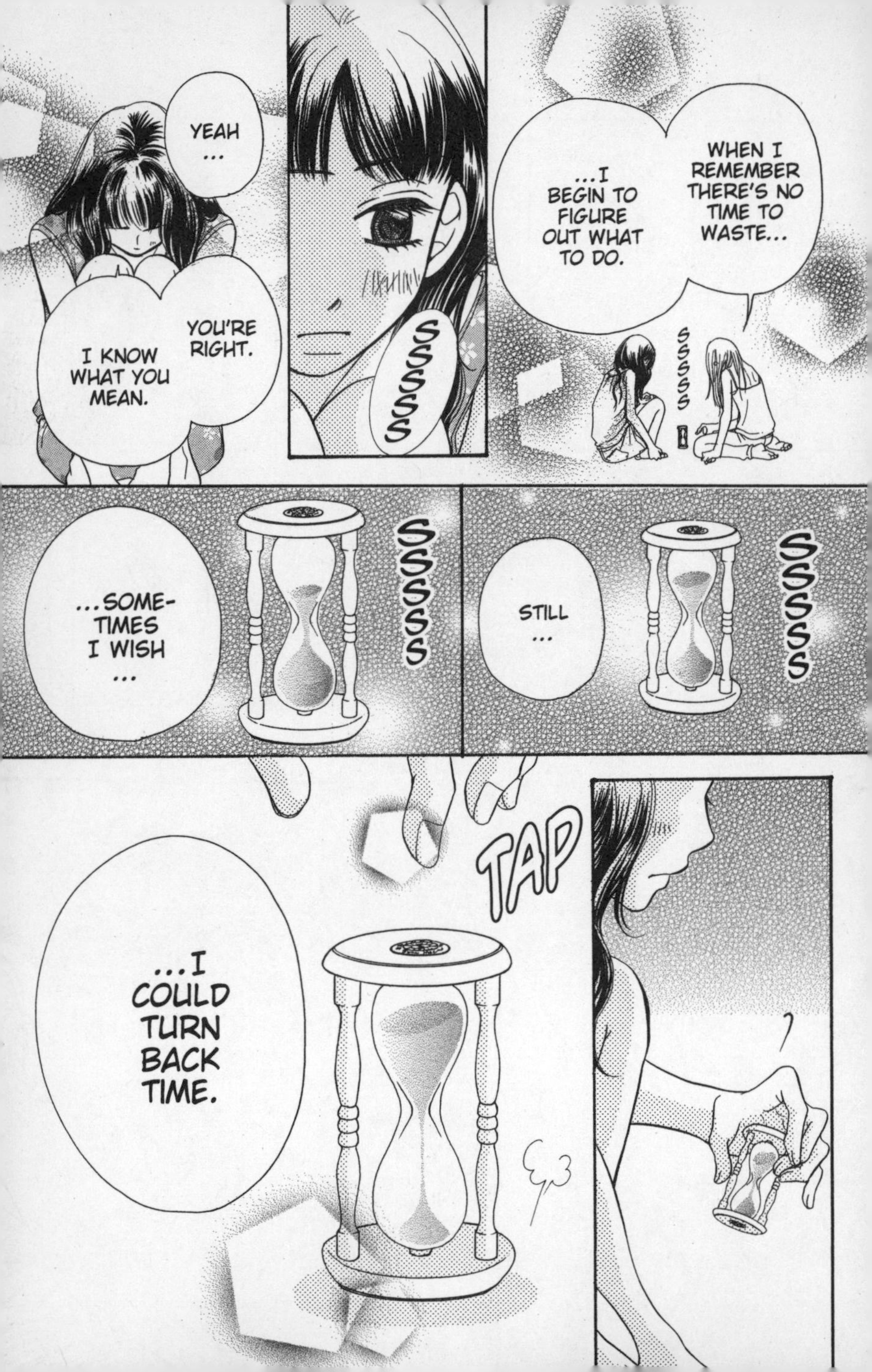
WHEN I REMEMBER THERE'S NO TIME TO WASTE...
...I BEGIN TO FIGURE OUT WHAT TO DO.
SSSSS
SSSSS
YEAH ...
YOU'RE RIGHT.
I KNOW WHAT YOU MEAN.
SSSSS
STILL ...
SSSSS
...SOME-TIMES I WISH ...
TAP
...I COULD TURN BACK TIME.

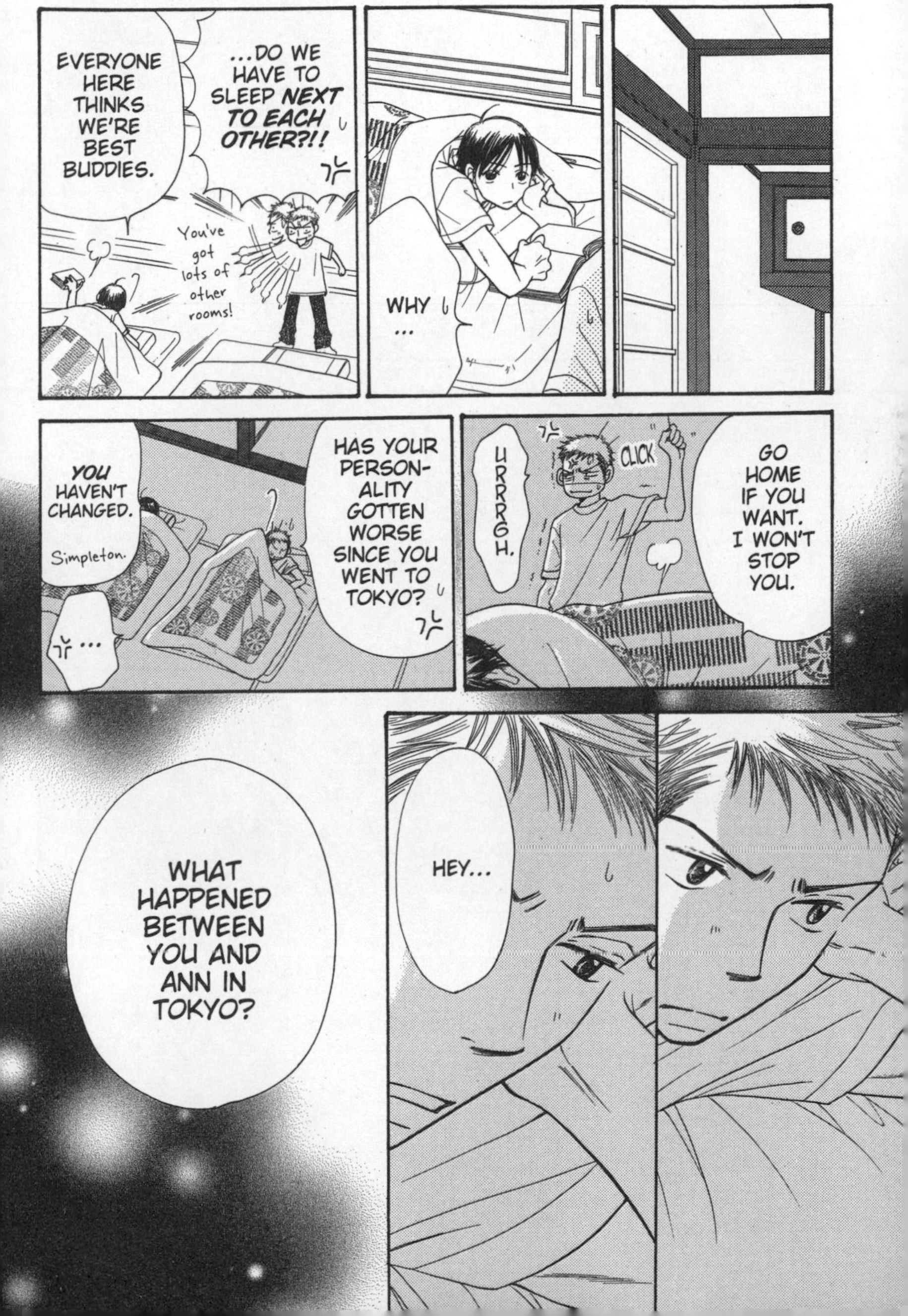
WHY...
...DO WE HAVE TO SLEEP ***NEXT TO EACH OTHER?!!***
EVERYONE HERE THINKS WE'RE BEST BUDDIES.
You've got lots of other rooms!
GO HOME IF YOU WANT. I WON'T STOP YOU.
CLICK
URRRGH.
HAS YOUR PERSONALITY GOTTEN WORSE SINCE YOU WENT TO TOKYO?
***YOU*** HAVEN'T CHANGED.
Simpleton.
...
HEY...
WHAT HAPPENED BETWEEN YOU AND ANN IN TOKYO?

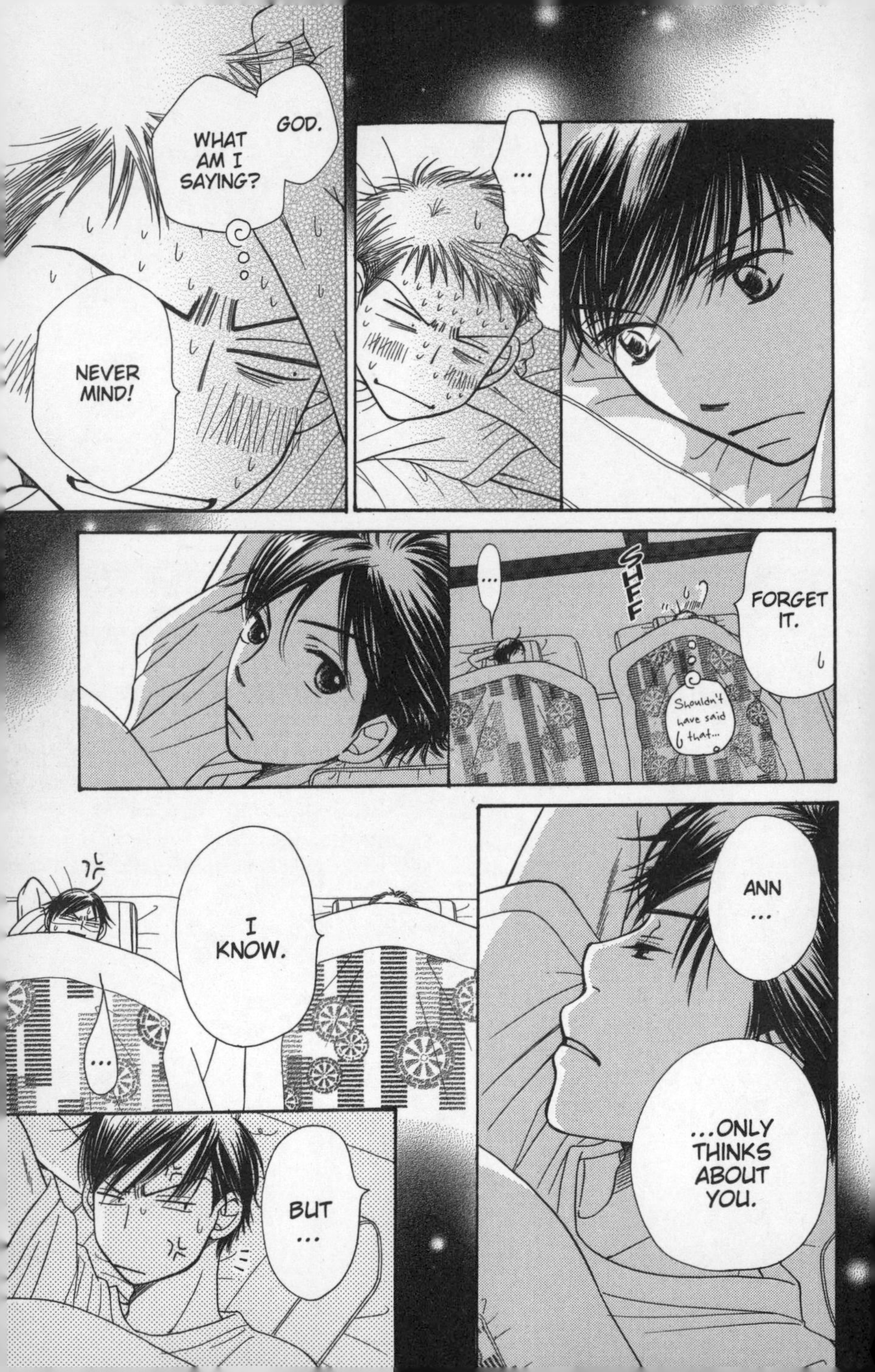
...
GOD.
WHAT AM I SAYING?
NEVER MIND!
FORGET IT.
Shouldn't have said that...
SHFF
...
ANN ...
...ONLY THINKS ABOUT YOU.
I KNOW.
...
BUT ...

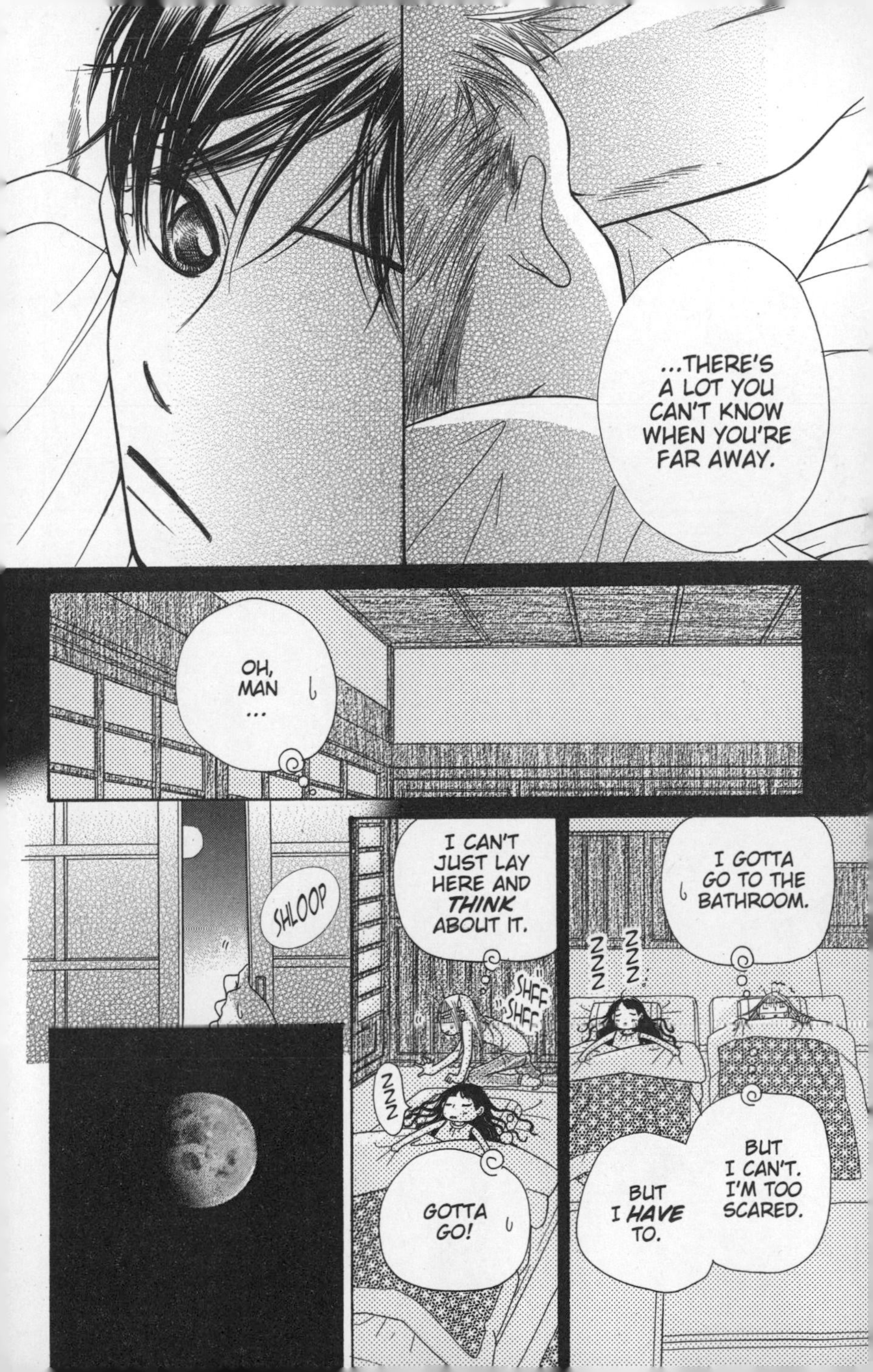
...THERE'S A LOT YOU CAN'T KNOW WHEN YOU'RE FAR AWAY.
OH, MAN ...
I GOTTA GO TO THE BATHROOM.
ZZZ
ZZZ
BUT I CAN'T. I'M TOO SCARED.
BUT I *HAVE* TO.
I CAN'T JUST LAY HERE AND *THINK* ABOUT IT.
SHFF SHFF
ZZZ
GOTTA GO!
SHLOOP

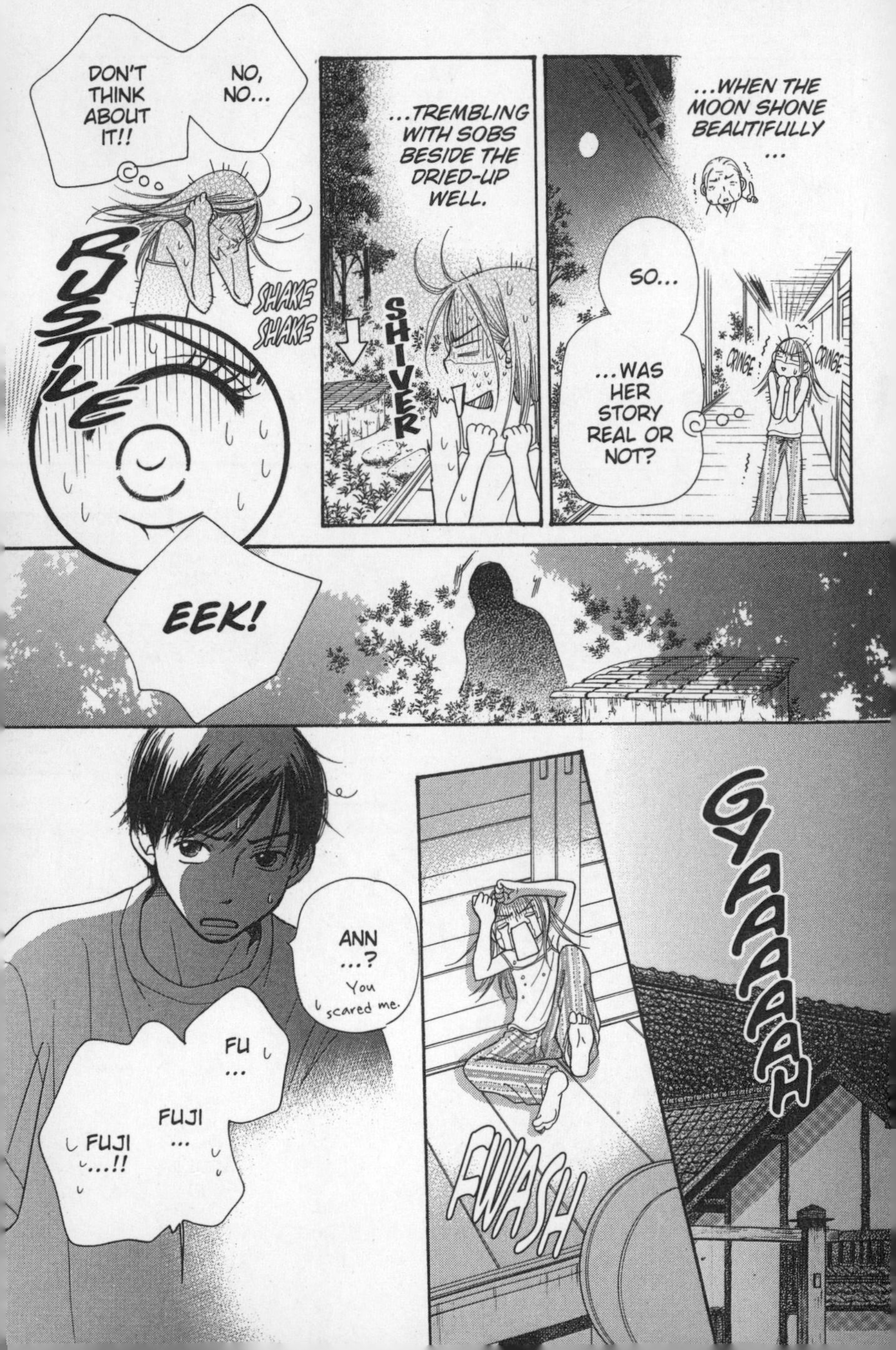
...WHEN THE MOON SHONE BEAUTIFULLY ...
SO...
...WAS HER STORY REAL OR NOT?
CRINGE
CRINGE
...TREMBLING WITH SOBS BESIDE THE DRIED-UP WELL.
SHIVER
NO, NO...
DON'T THINK ABOUT IT!!
SHAKE SHAKE
RUSTLE
EEK!
GYAAAAAAH
FWASH
ANN ...?
You scared me.
FU ...
FUJI ...
FUJI ...!!

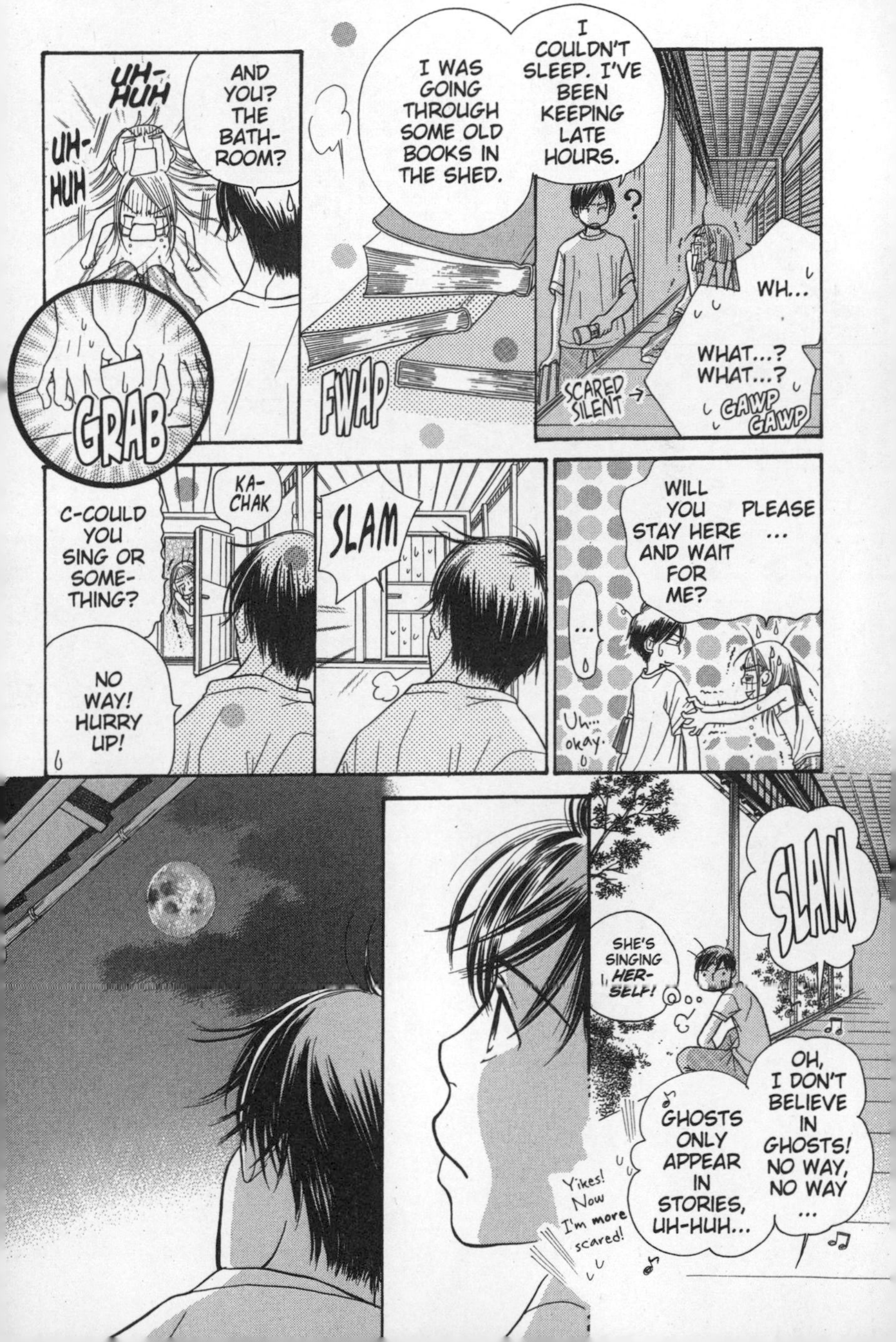
I COULDN'T SLEEP. I'VE BEEN KEEPING LATE HOURS.
WH...
WHAT...? WHAT...?
GAWP GAWP
SCARED SILENT
I WAS GOING THROUGH SOME OLD BOOKS IN THE SHED.
FWAP
AND YOU? THE BATH-ROOM?
UH-HUH
UH-HUH
GRAB
WILL YOU PLEASE ... STAY HERE AND WAIT FOR ME?
...
Uh... okay.
SLAM
KA-CHAK
C-COULD YOU SING OR SOME-THING?
NO WAY! HURRY UP!
SLAM
SHE'S SINGING HERSELF!
OH, I DON'T BELIEVE IN GHOSTS! NO WAY, NO WAY ...
GHOSTS ONLY APPEAR IN STORIES, UH-HUH...
Yikes! Now I'm more scared!

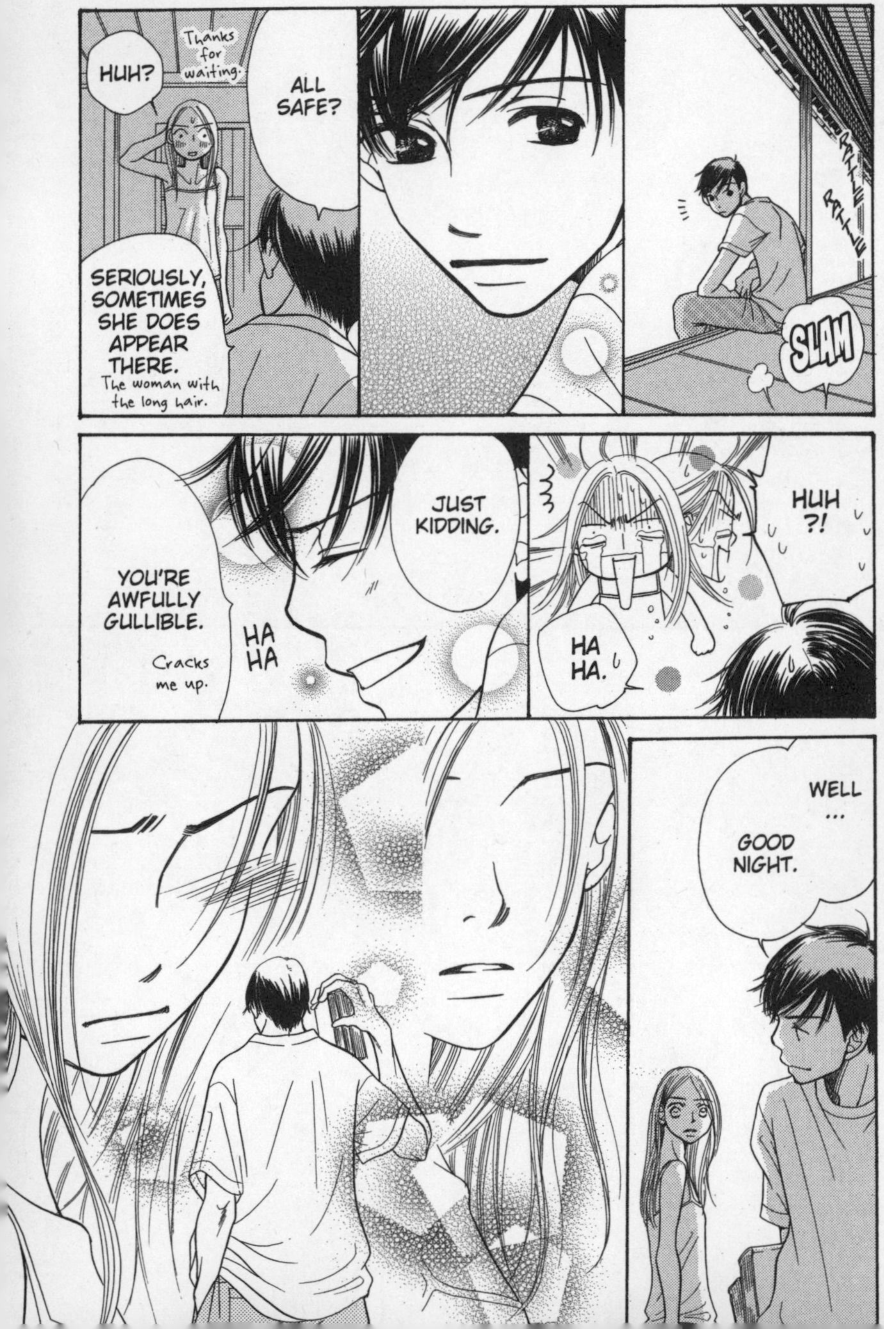
RATTLE RATTLE
SLAM
ALL SAFE?
Thanks for waiting.
HUH?
SERIOUSLY, SOMETIMES SHE DOES APPEAR THERE.
The woman with the long hair.
HUH ?!
HA HA.
JUST KIDDING.
YOU'RE AWFULLY GULLIBLE.
HA HA
Cracks me up.
WELL ... GOOD NIGHT.

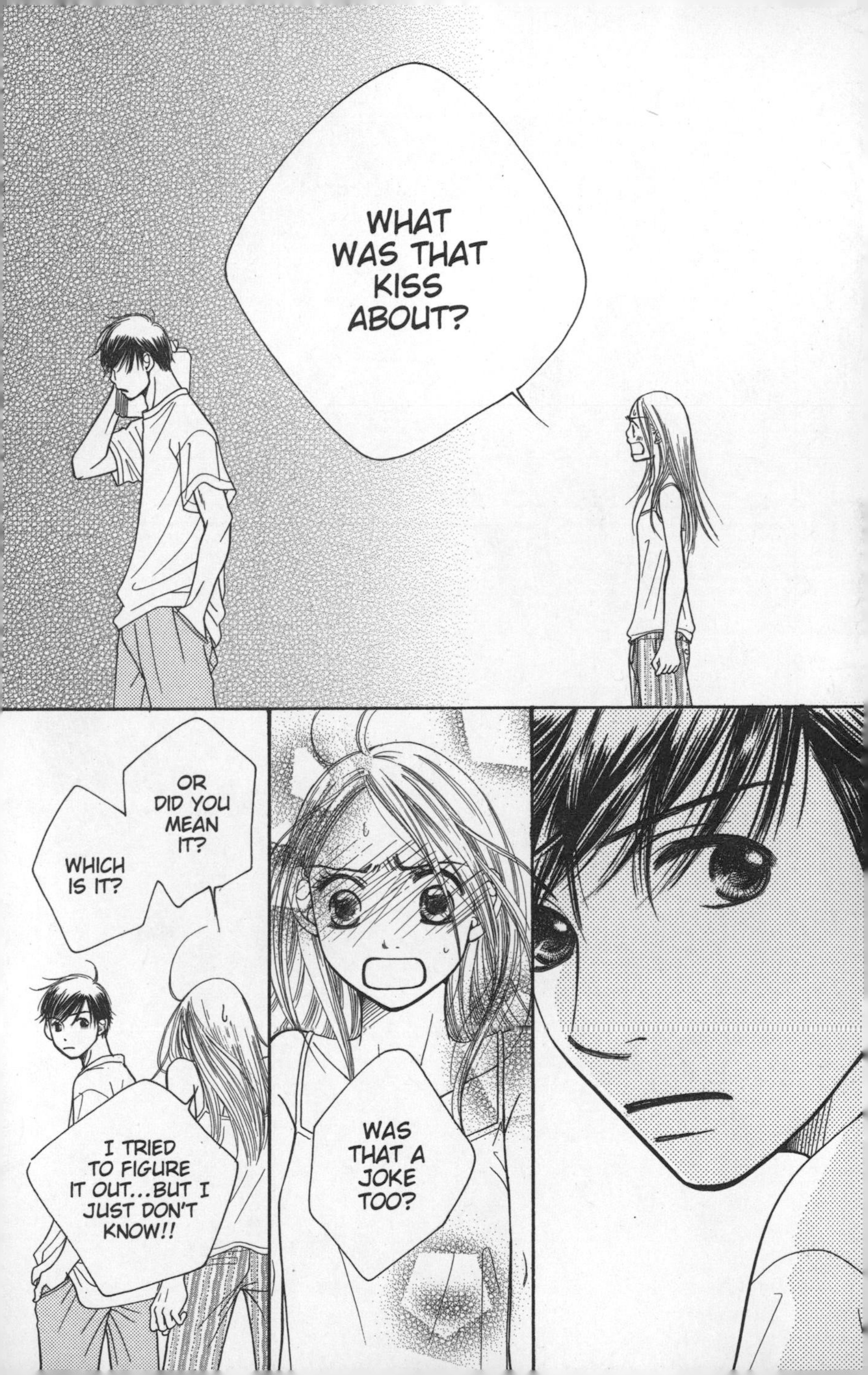
WHAT WAS THAT KISS ABOUT?
WAS THAT A JOKE TOO?
OR DID YOU MEAN IT?
WHICH IS IT?
I TRIED TO FIGURE IT OUT...BUT I JUST DON'T KNOW!!

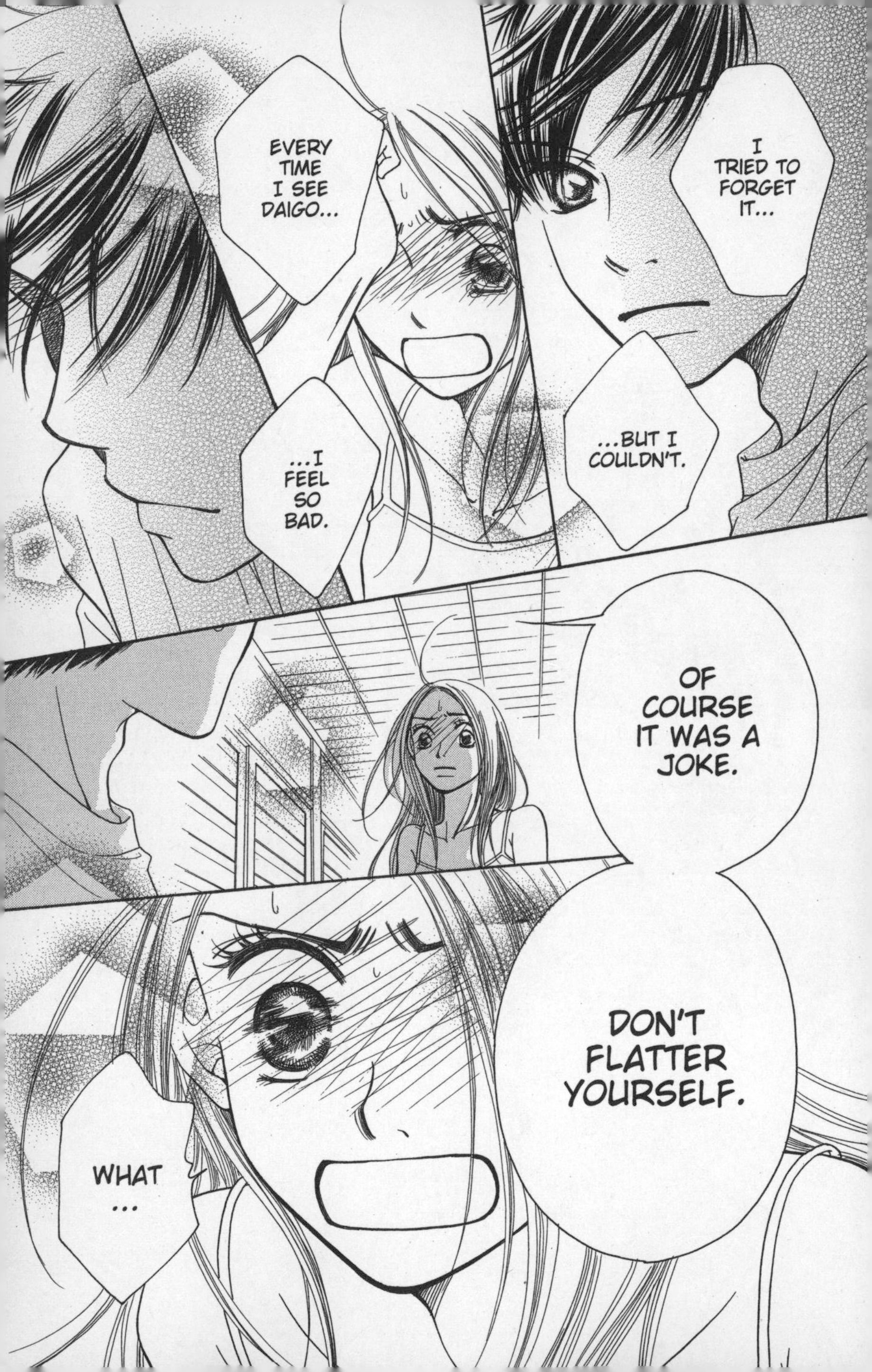
I TRIED TO FORGET IT...
...BUT I COULDN'T.
EVERY TIME I SEE DAIGO...
...I FEEL SO BAD.
OF COURSE IT WAS A JOKE.
DON'T FLATTER YOURSELF.
WHAT...

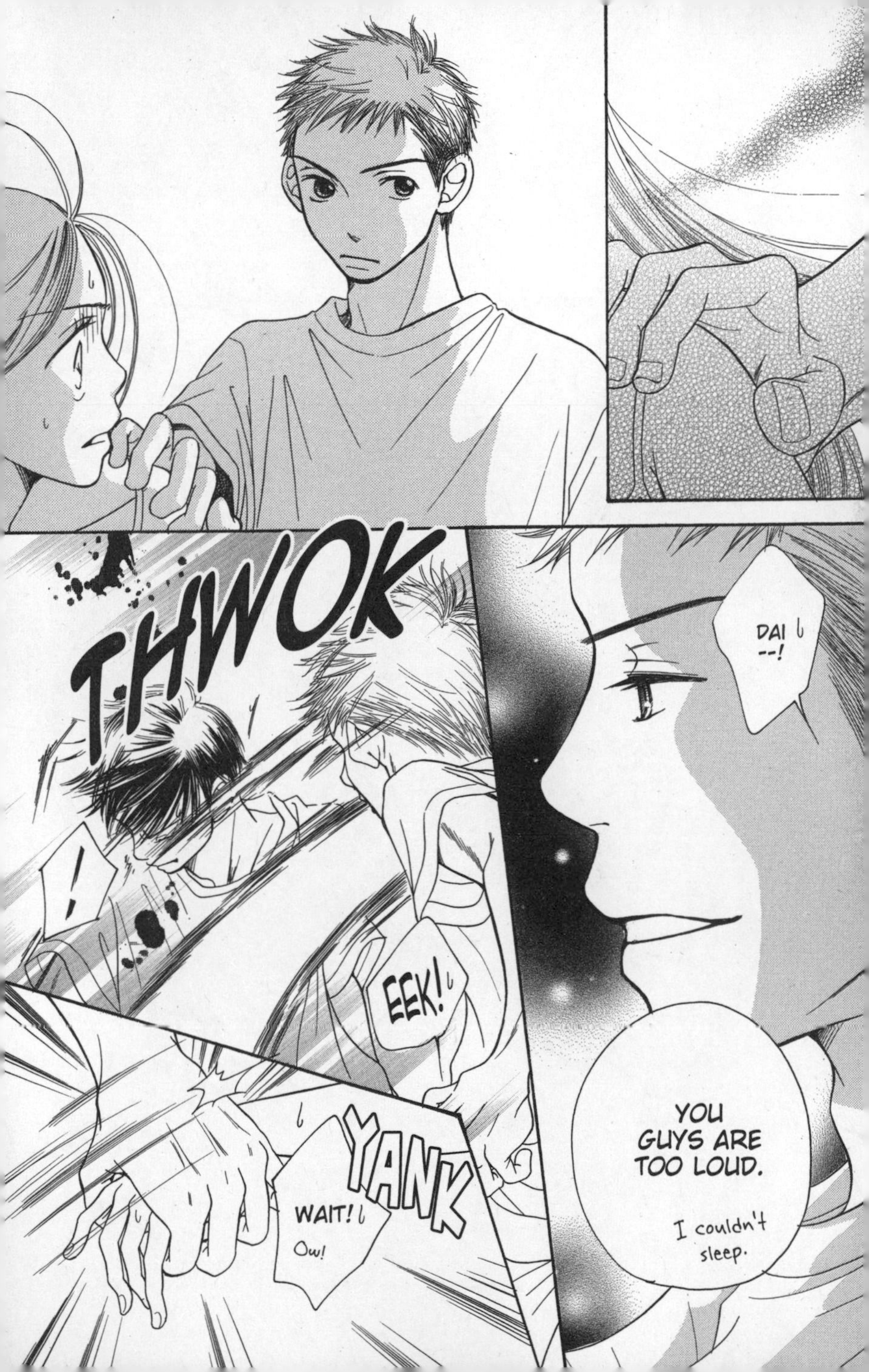
DAI --!
YOU GUYS ARE TOO LOUD.
I couldn't sleep.
THWOK
!
EEK!
YANK
WAIT!
Ow!

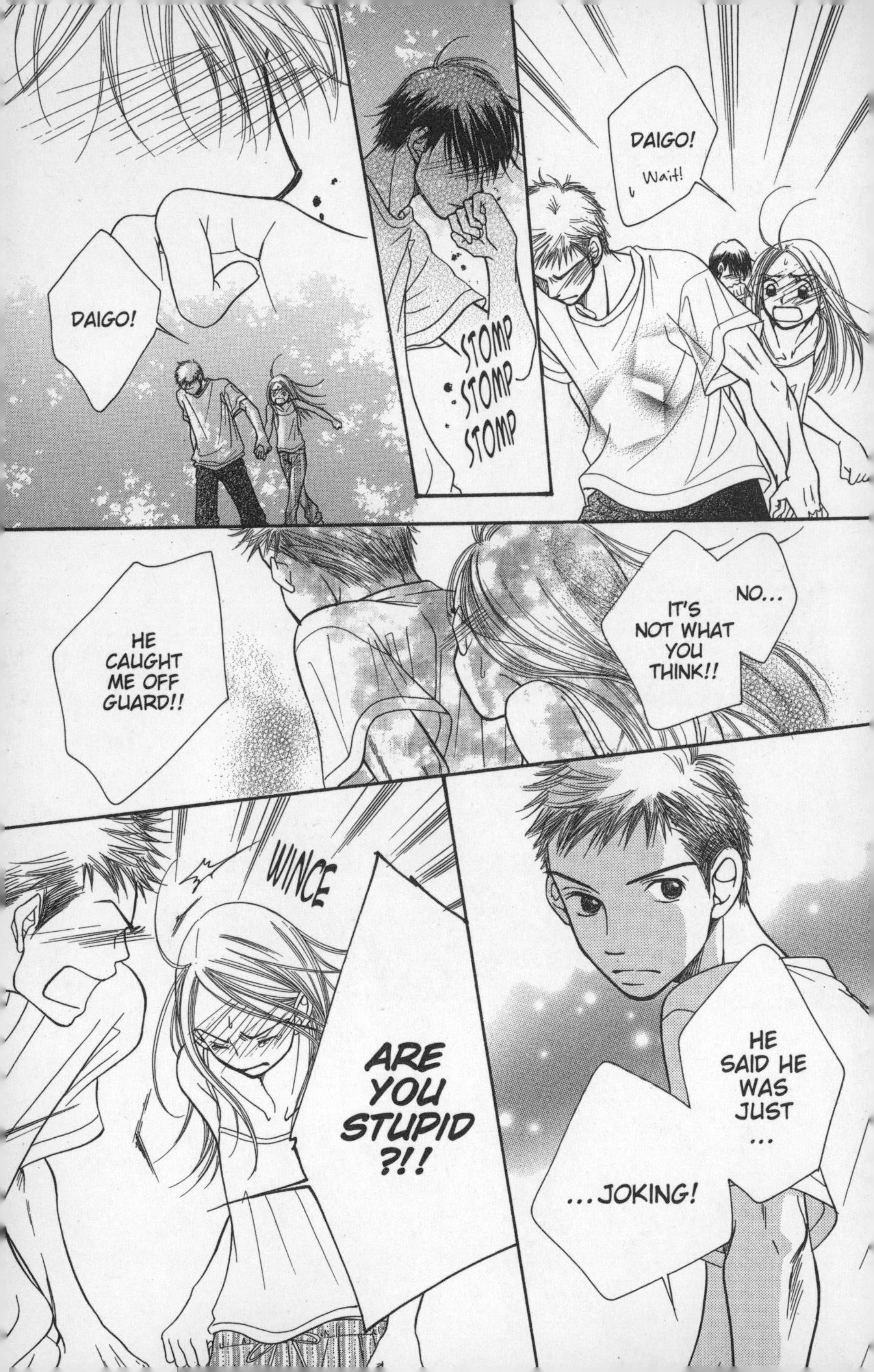
DAIGO!
Wait!
STOMP STOMP STOMP
DAIGO!
NO... IT'S NOT WHAT YOU THINK!!
HE CAUGHT ME OFF GUARD!!
HE SAID HE WAS JUST ...
...JOKING!
WINCE
ARE YOU STUPID ?!!

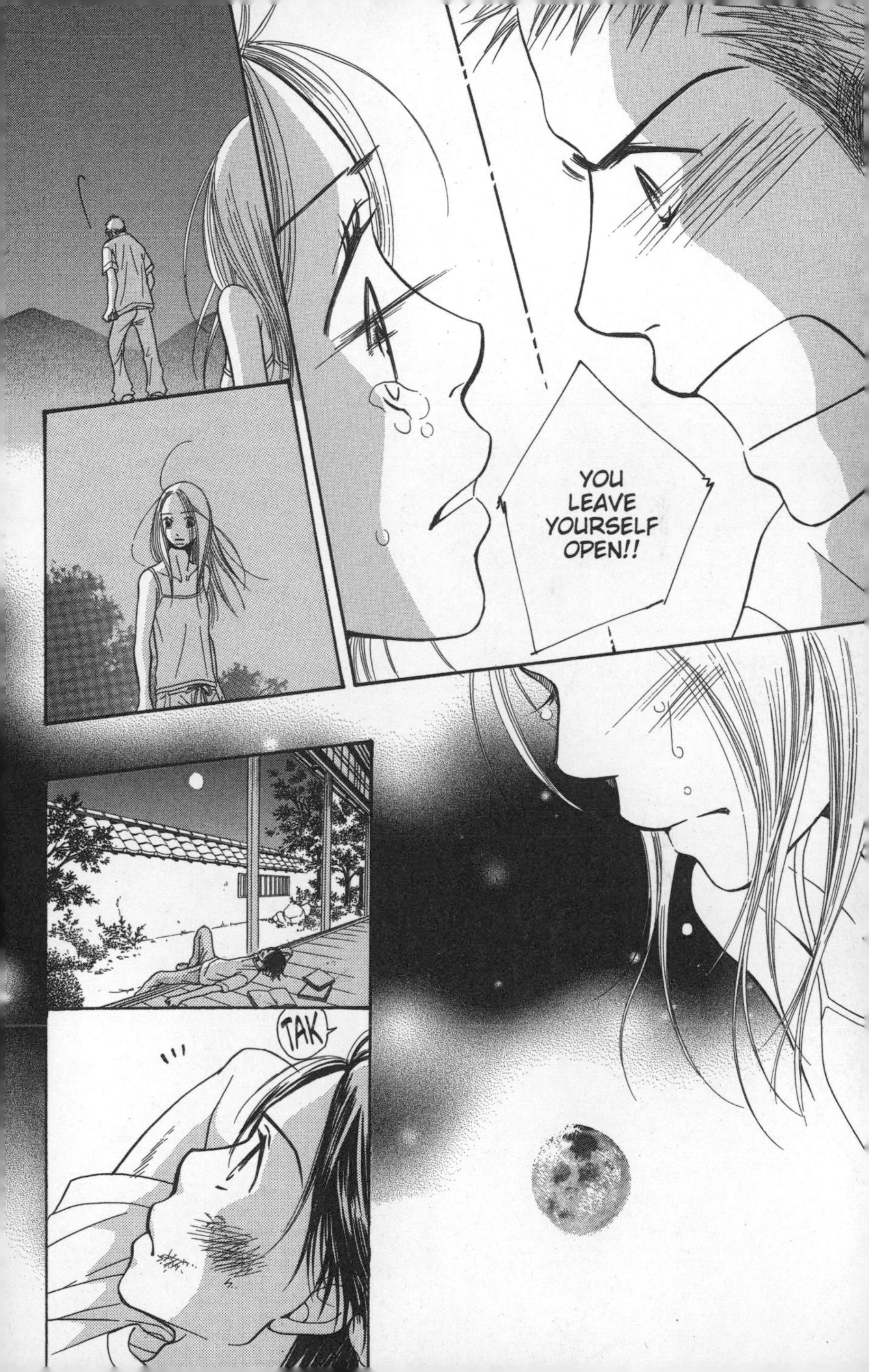
YOU LEAVE YOURSELF OPEN!!
TAK

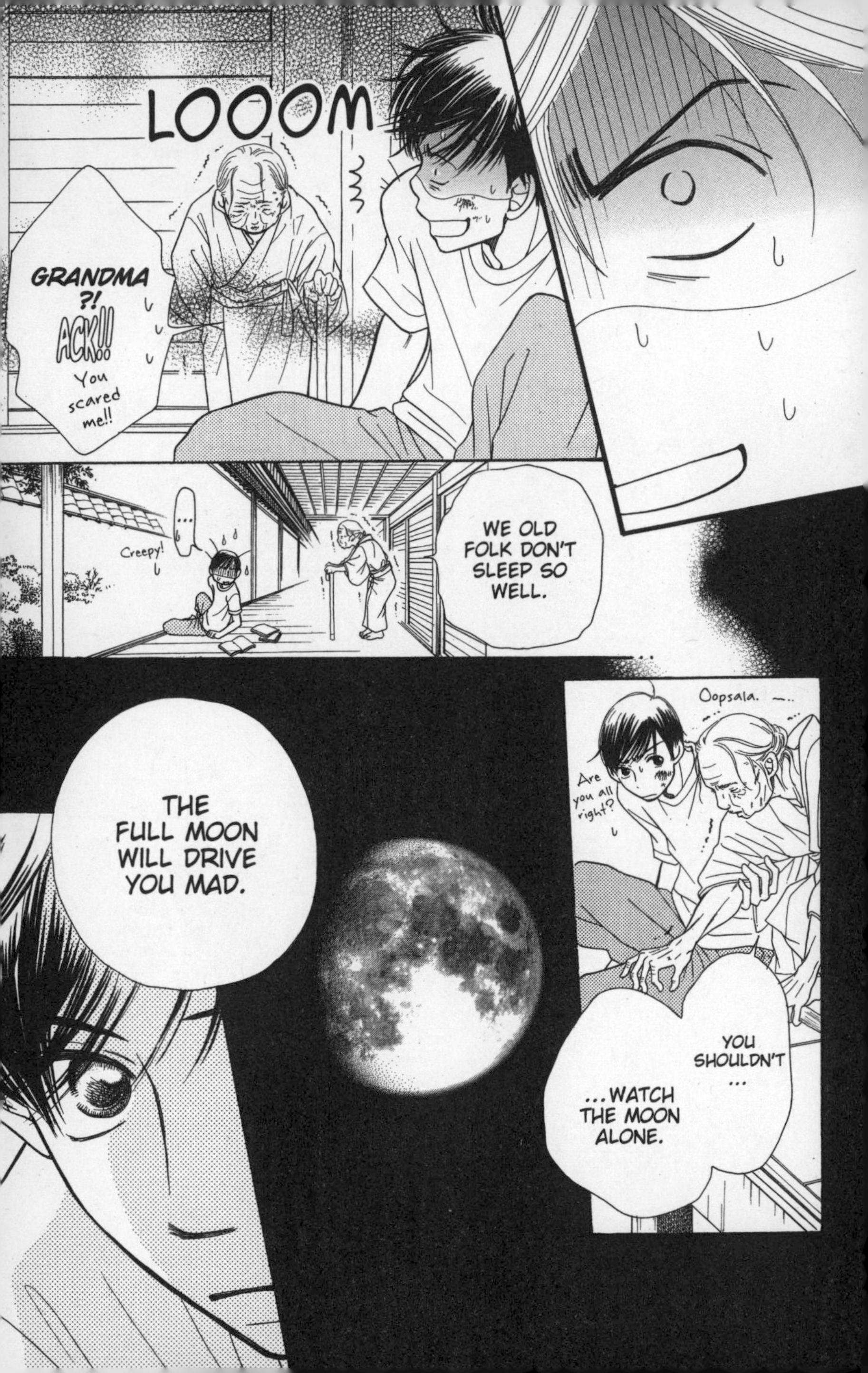
LOOOM
GRANDMA?! ACK!! You scared me!!
WE OLD FOLK DON'T SLEEP SO WELL.
...
Creepy!
Oopsala.
Are you all right?
YOU SHOULDN'T...
...WATCH THE MOON ALONE.
THE FULL MOON WILL DRIVE YOU MAD.

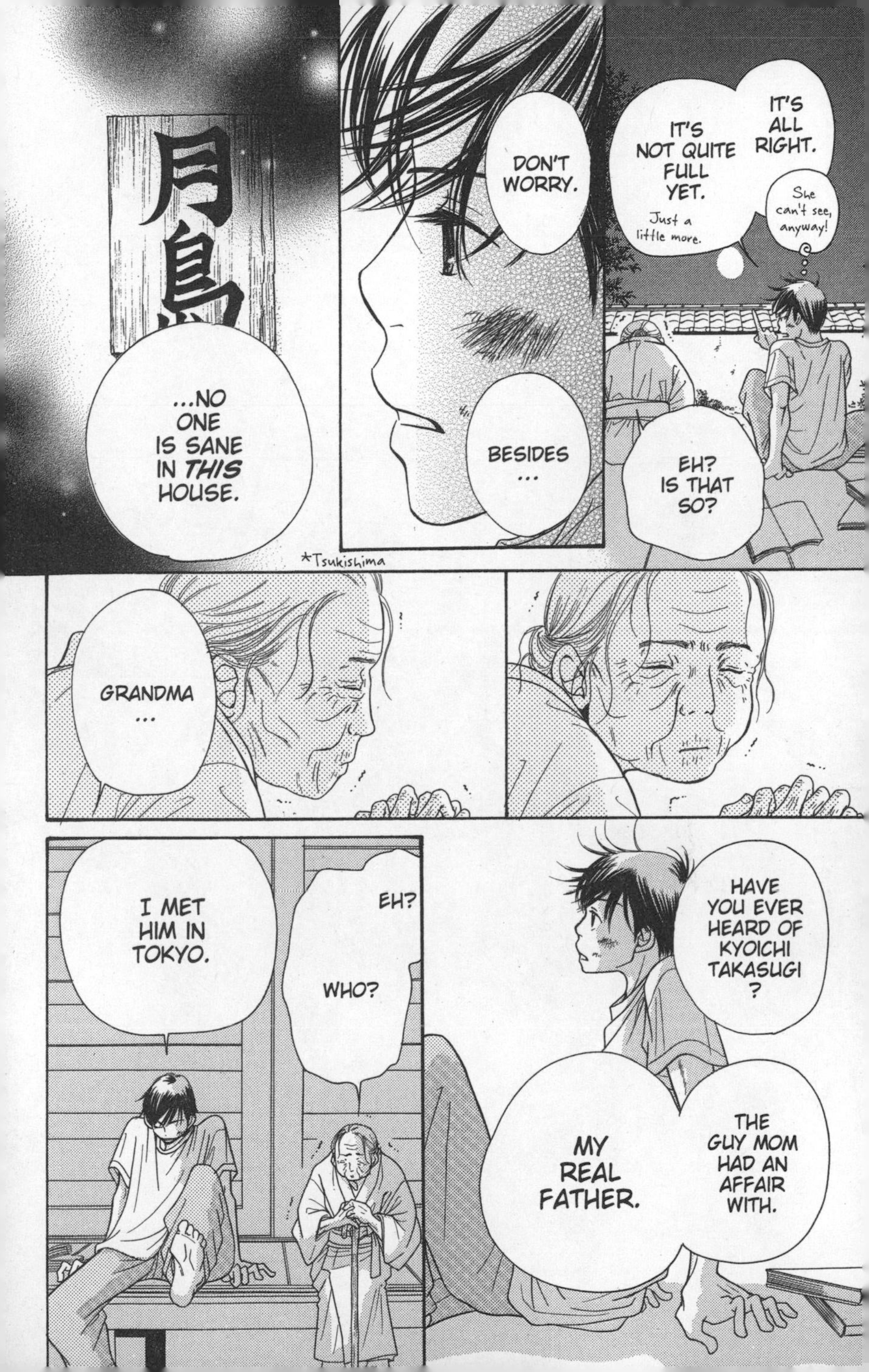
IT'S ALL RIGHT.
IT'S NOT QUITE FULL YET.
Just a little more.
She can't see, anyway!
EH? IS THAT SO?
DON'T WORRY.
BESIDES...
月島
...NO ONE IS SANE IN *THIS* HOUSE.
*Tsukishima
GRANDMA...
HAVE YOU EVER HEARD OF KYOICHI TAKASUGI?
THE GUY MOM HAD AN AFFAIR WITH.
MY REAL FATHER.
EH?
WHO?
I MET HIM IN TOKYO.

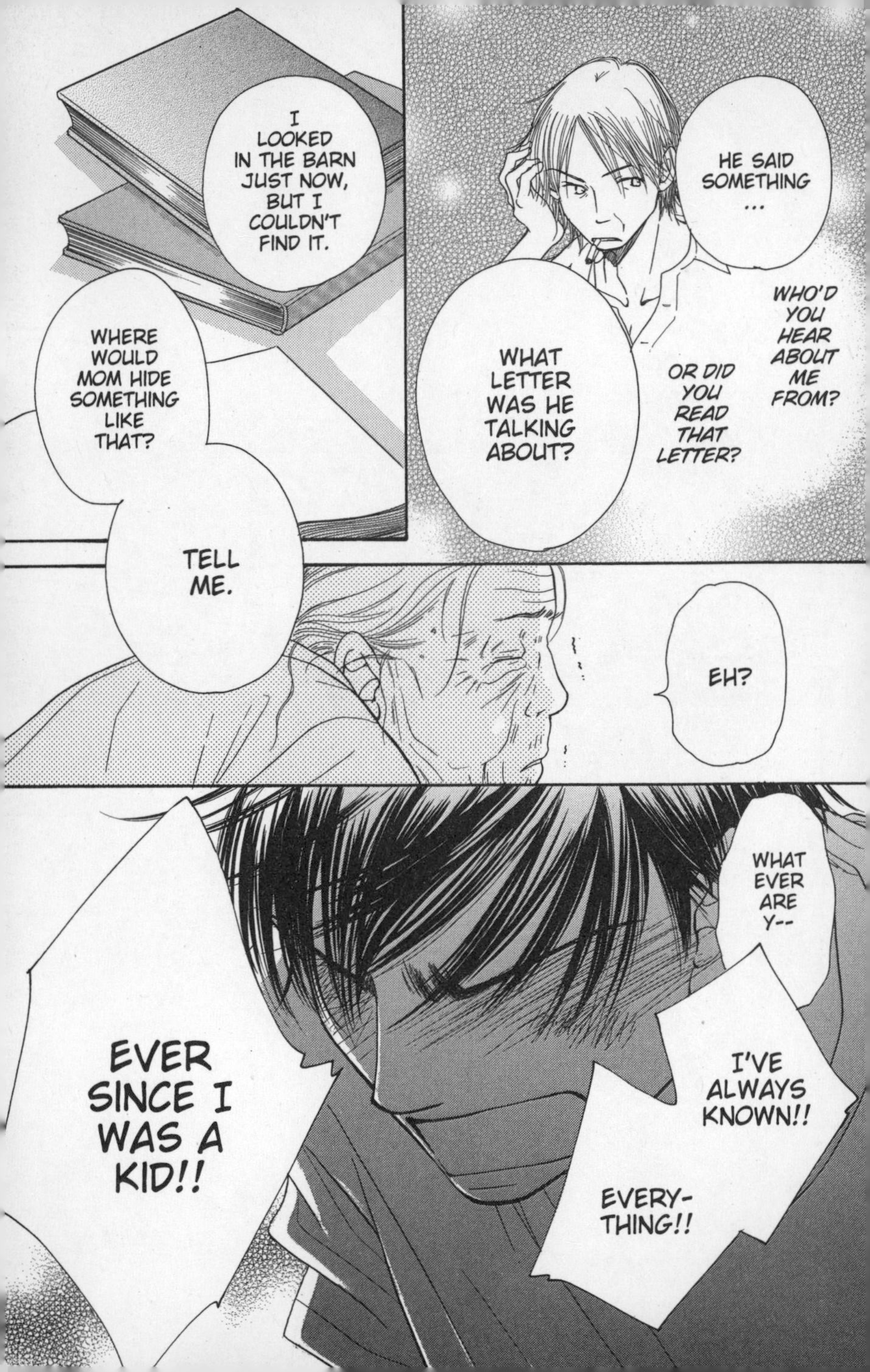
HE SAID SOMETHING ...
WHO'D YOU HEAR ABOUT ME FROM?
OR DID YOU READ THAT LETTER?
WHAT LETTER WAS HE TALKING ABOUT?
I LOOKED IN THE BARN JUST NOW, BUT I COULDN'T FIND IT.
WHERE WOULD MOM HIDE SOMETHING LIKE THAT?
TELL ME.
EH?
WHAT EVER ARE Y--
I'VE ALWAYS KNOWN!!
EVERY-THING!!
EVER SINCE I WAS A KID!!

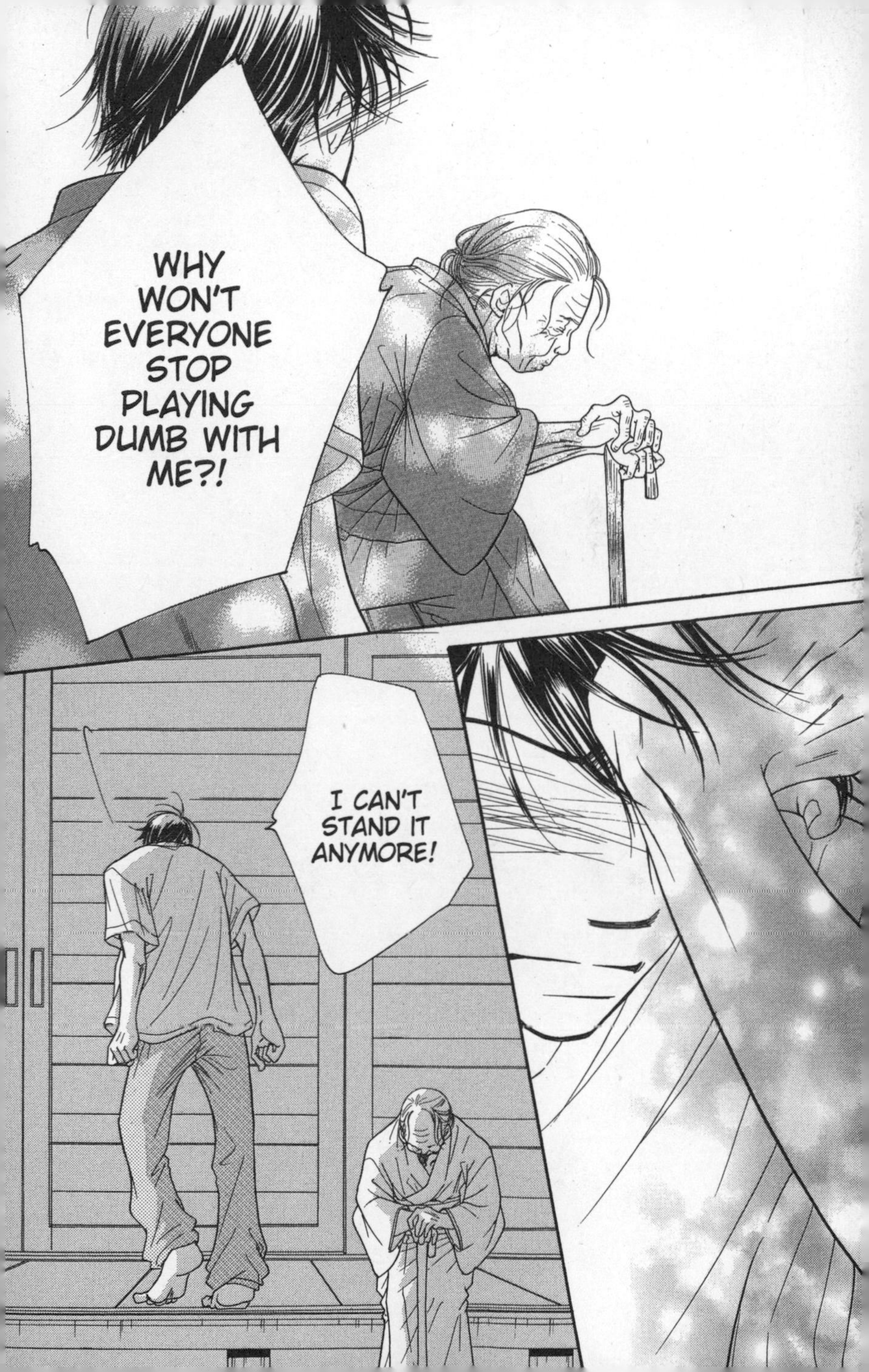
WHY WON'T EVERYONE STOP PLAYING DUMB WITH ME?!
I CAN'T STAND IT ANYMORE!

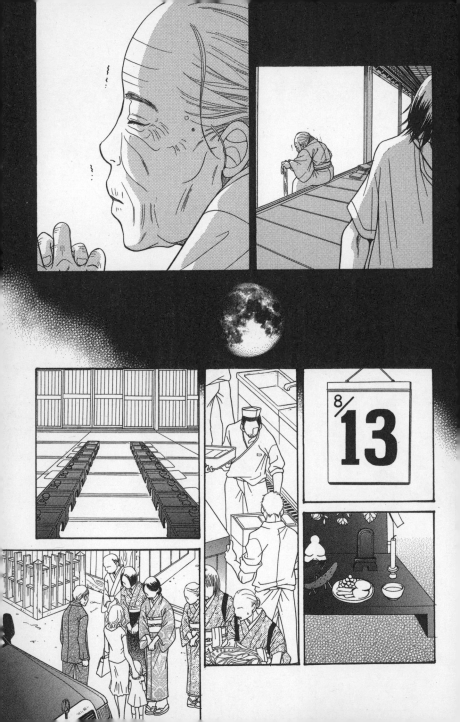

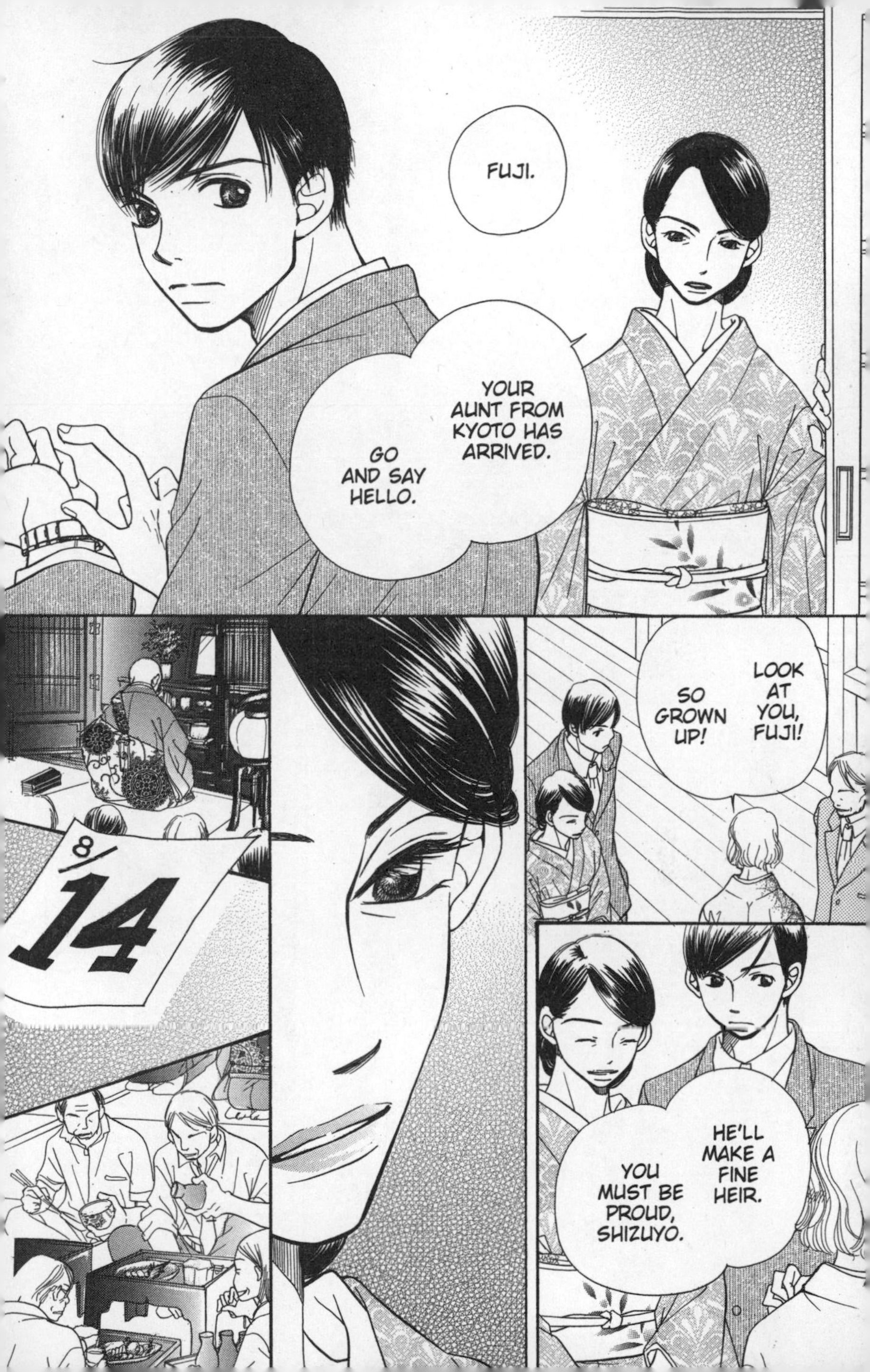
FUJI.
YOUR AUNT FROM KYOTO HAS ARRIVED.
GO AND SAY HELLO.
LOOK AT YOU, FUJI!
SO GROWN UP!
HE'LL MAKE A FINE HEIR.
YOU MUST BE PROUD, SHIZUYO.
8/14

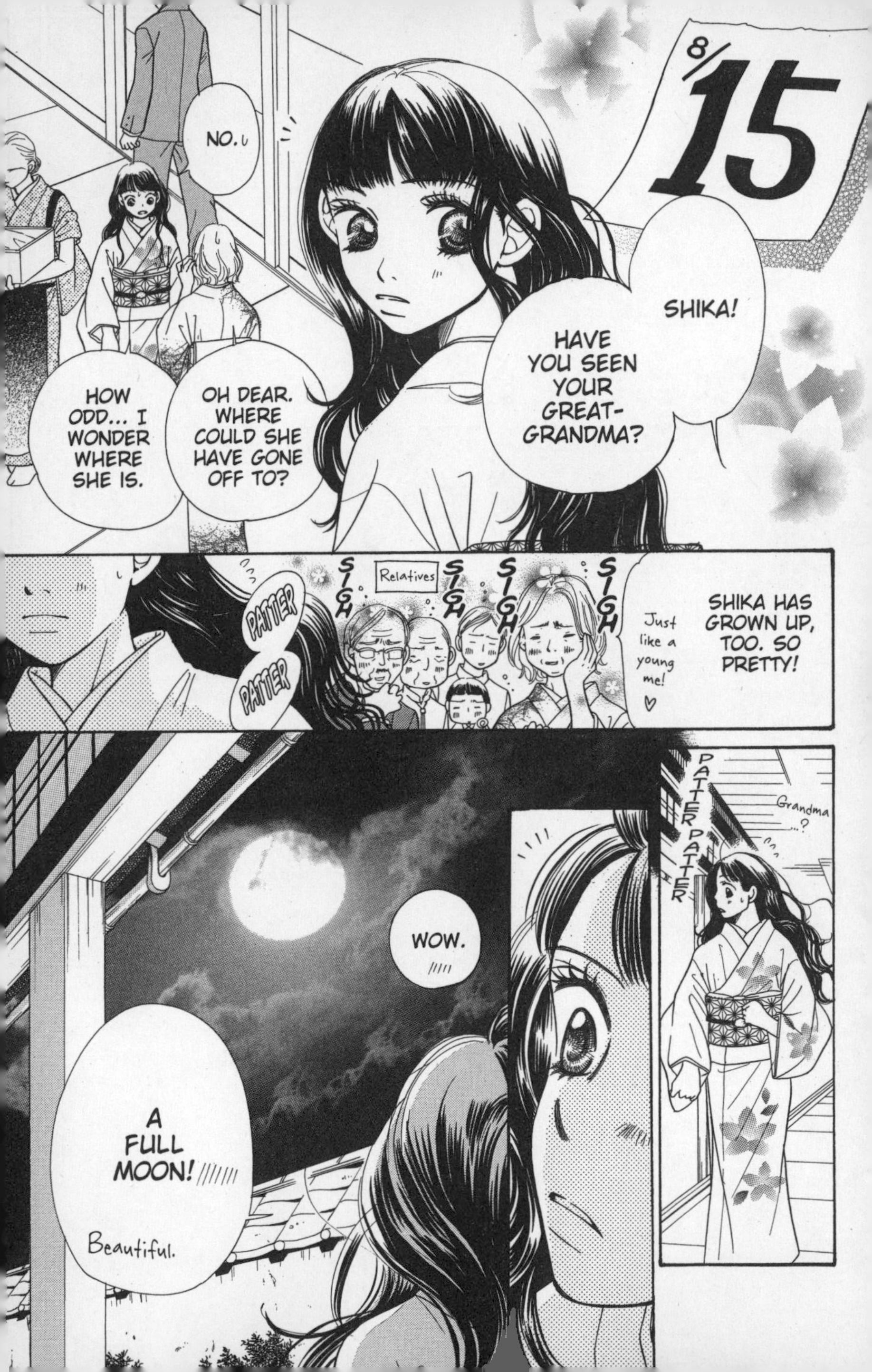
8/15
SHIKA!
HAVE YOU SEEN YOUR GREAT-GRANDMA?
NO.
OH DEAR. WHERE COULD SHE HAVE GONE OFF TO?
HOW ODD... I WONDER WHERE SHE IS.
SHIKA HAS GROWN UP, TOO. SO PRETTY!
Just like a young me! ♥
SIGH
SIGH
SIGH
Relatives
SIGH
PATTER
PATTER
PATTER PATTER PATTER
Grandma...?
WOW.
A FULL MOON!
Beautiful.

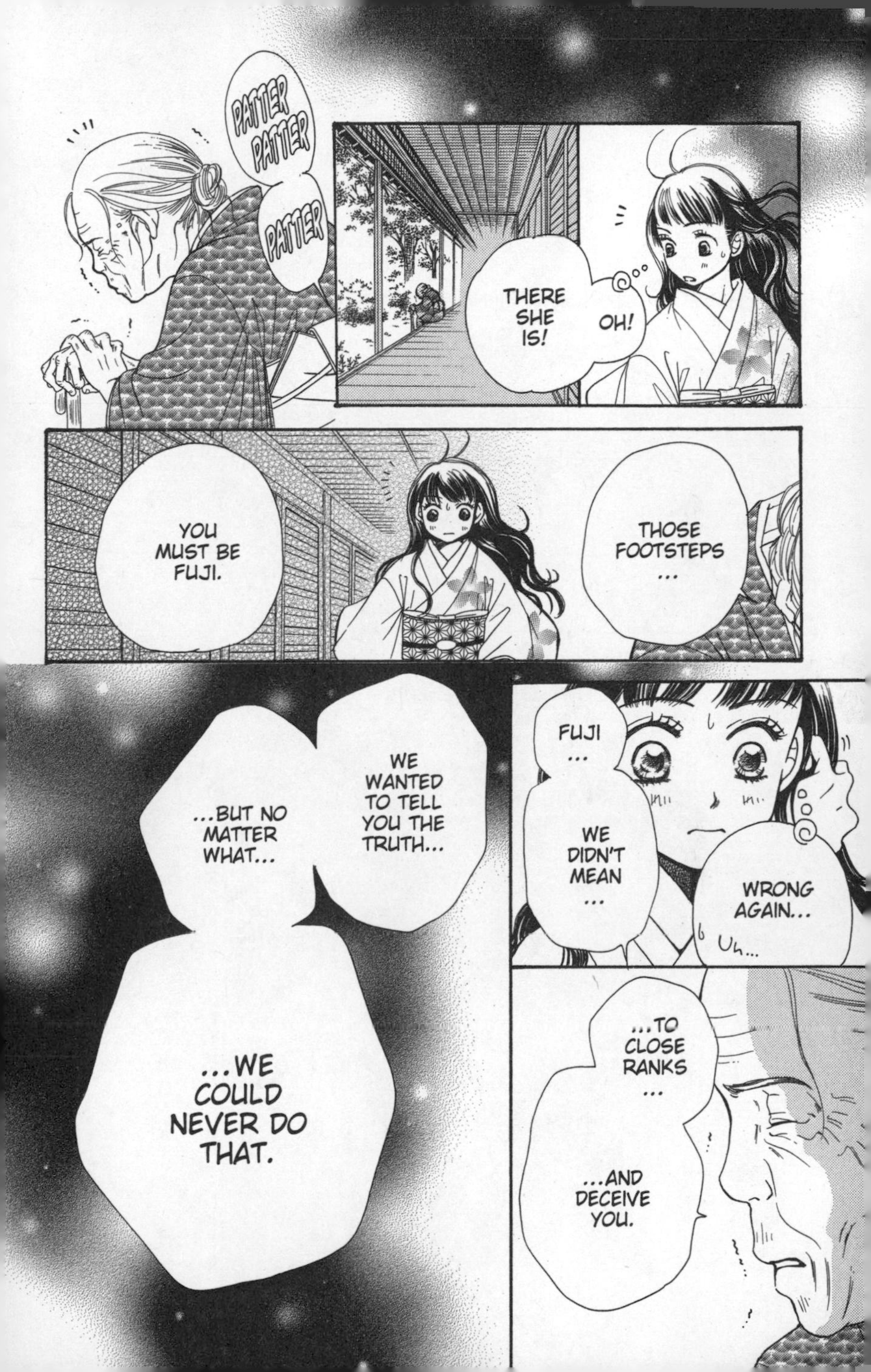
OH!
THERE SHE IS!
PATTER PATTER
PATTER
THOSE FOOTSTEPS...
YOU MUST BE FUJI.
FUJI...
WE DIDN'T MEAN...
WRONG AGAIN...
Uh...
...TO CLOSE RANKS...
...AND DECEIVE YOU.
WE WANTED TO TELL YOU THE TRUTH...
...BUT NO MATTER WHAT...
...WE COULD NEVER DO THAT.

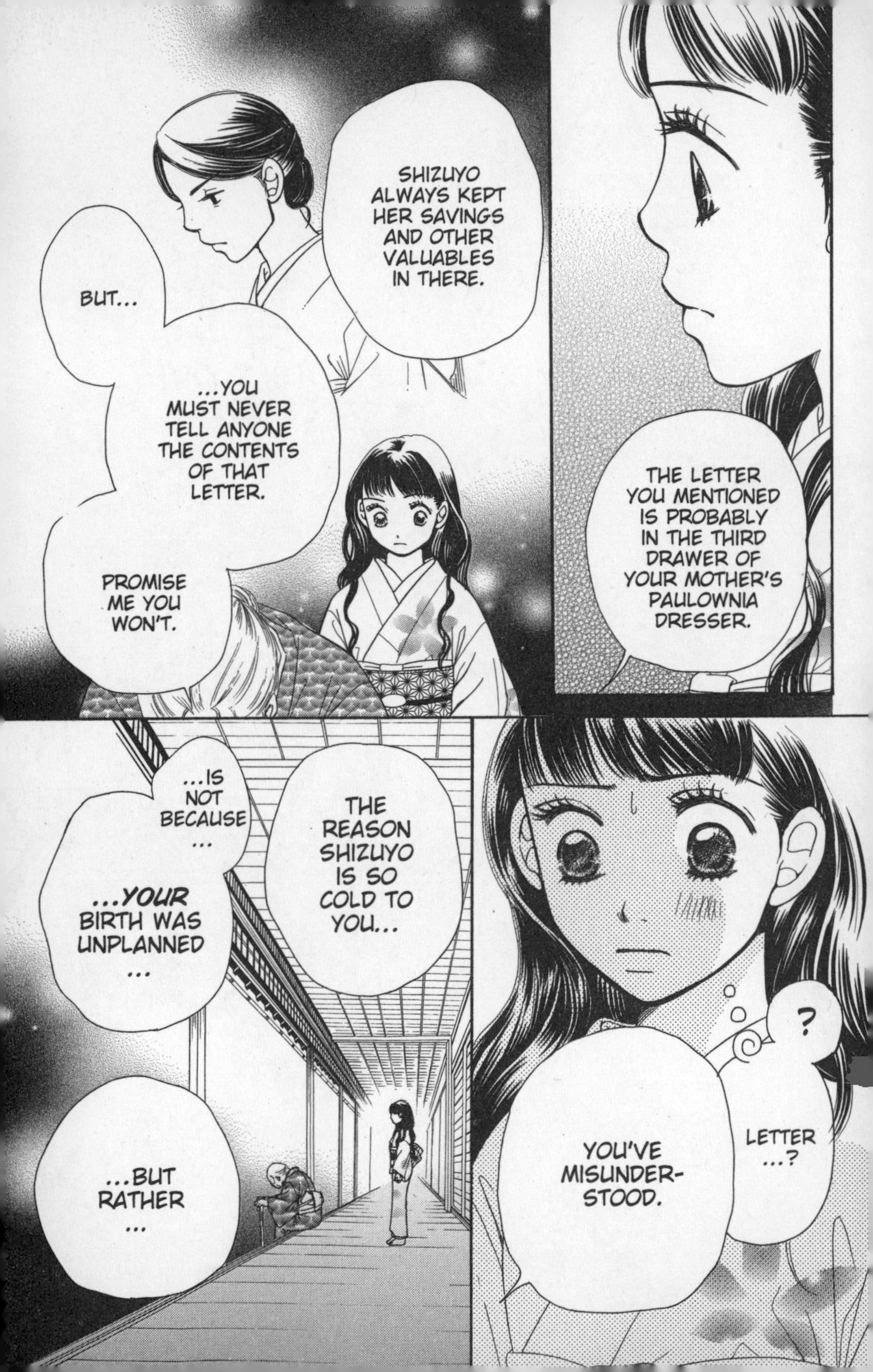
THE LETTER YOU MENTIONED IS PROBABLY IN THE THIRD DRAWER OF YOUR MOTHER'S PAULOWNIA DRESSER.
SHIZUYO ALWAYS KEPT HER SAVINGS AND OTHER VALUABLES IN THERE.
BUT...
...YOU MUST NEVER TELL ANYONE THE CONTENTS OF THAT LETTER.
PROMISE ME YOU WON'T.
?
LETTER ...?
YOU'VE MISUNDER-STOOD.
THE REASON SHIZUYO IS SO COLD TO YOU...
...IS NOT BECAUSE ...
...*YOUR* BIRTH WAS UNPLANNED ...
...BUT RATHER ...

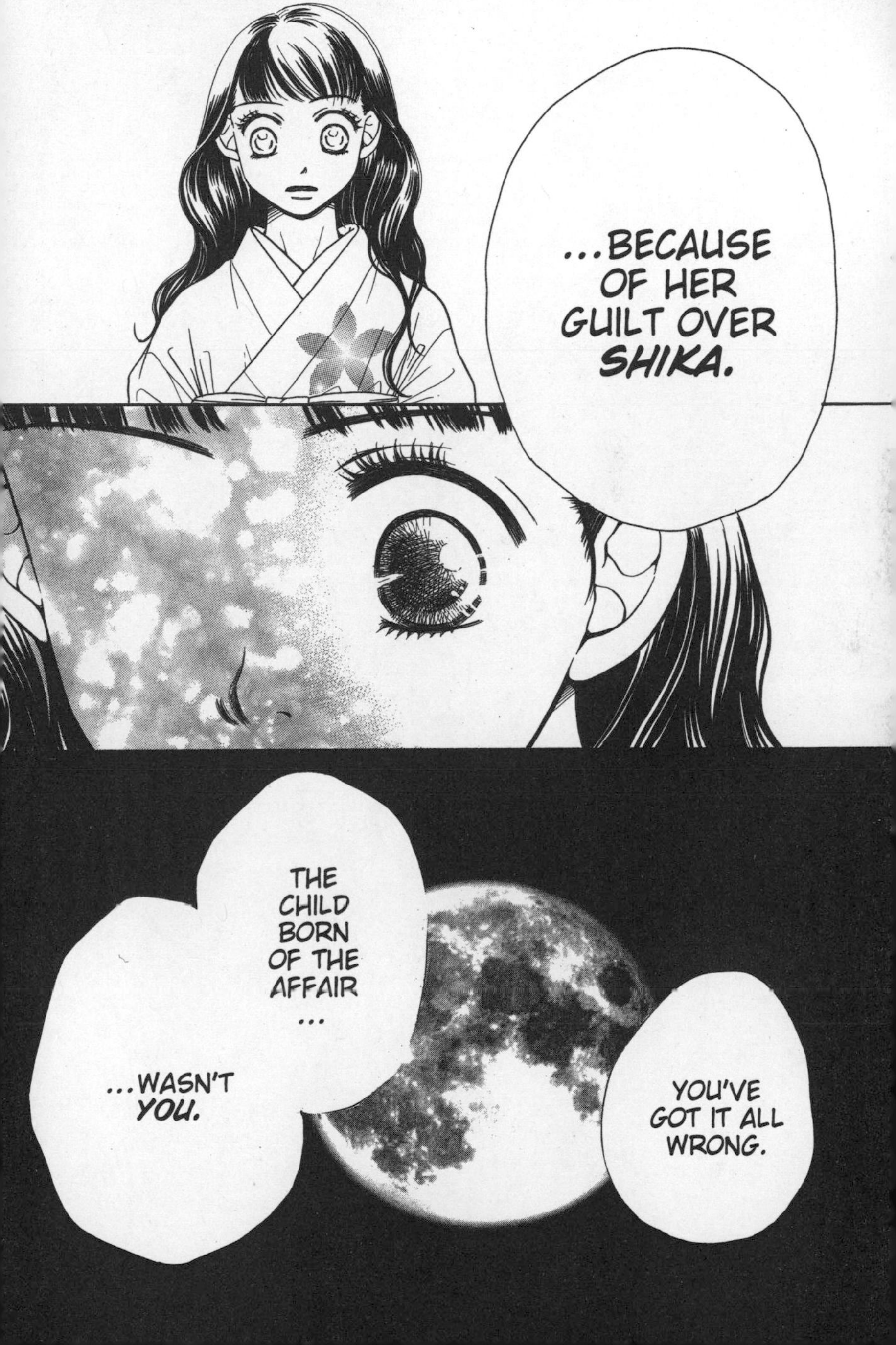
...BECAUSE OF HER GUILT OVER SHIKA.
YOU'VE GOT IT ALL WRONG.
THE CHILD BORN OF THE AFFAIR ...
...WASN'T YOU.

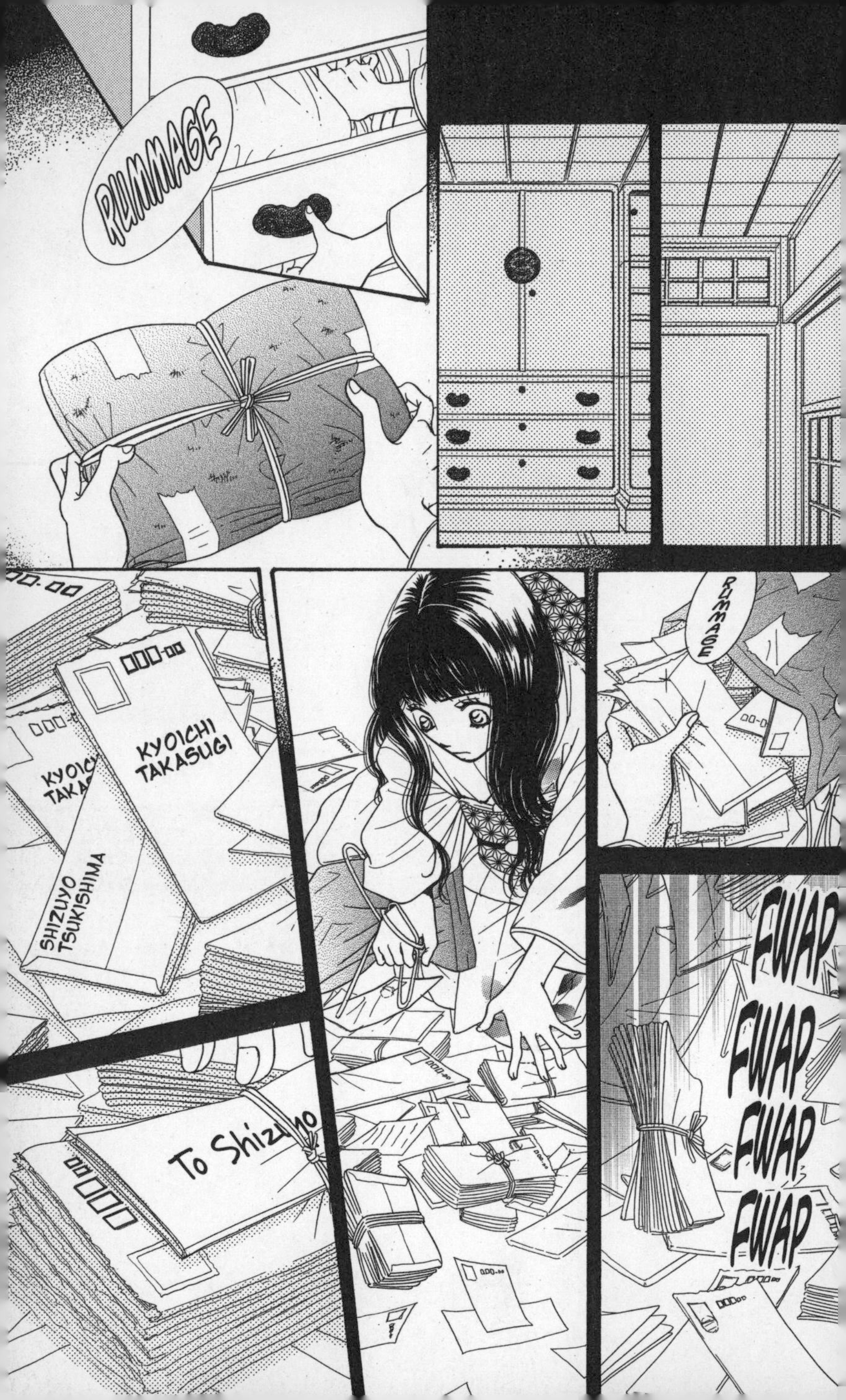
RUMMAGE
RUMMAGE
FWAP FWAP FWAP FWAP
KYOICHI TAKASUGI
KYOICHI TAKA
SHIZUYO TSUKISHIMA
To Shizu

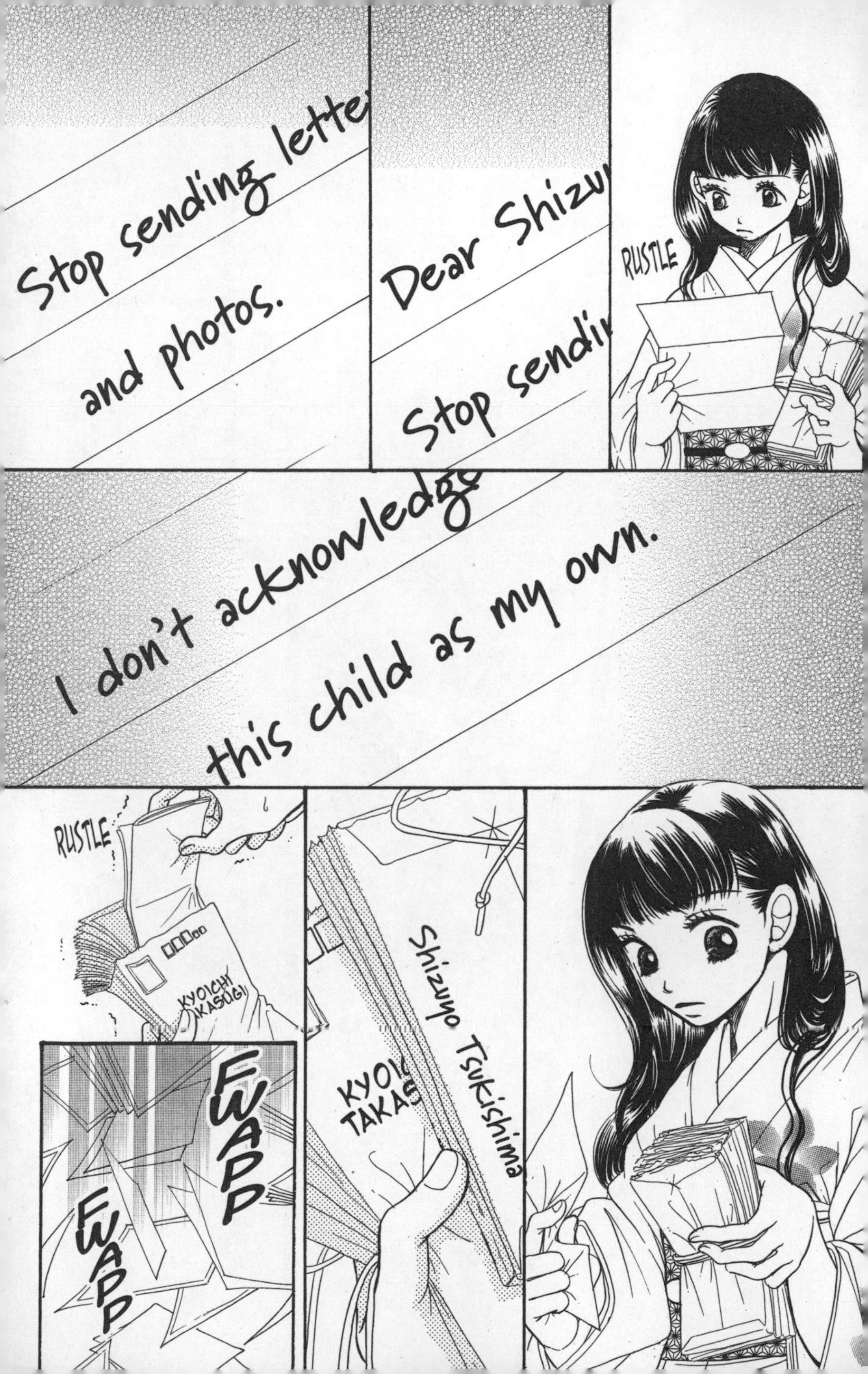
RUSTLE
Dear Shizu
Stop sendi
Stop sending lette
and photos.
I don't acknowledge
this child as my own.
Shizuyo Tsukishima
KYOIC
TAKAS
RUSTLE
KYOICHI
TAKASUGI
FWAPP
FWAPP

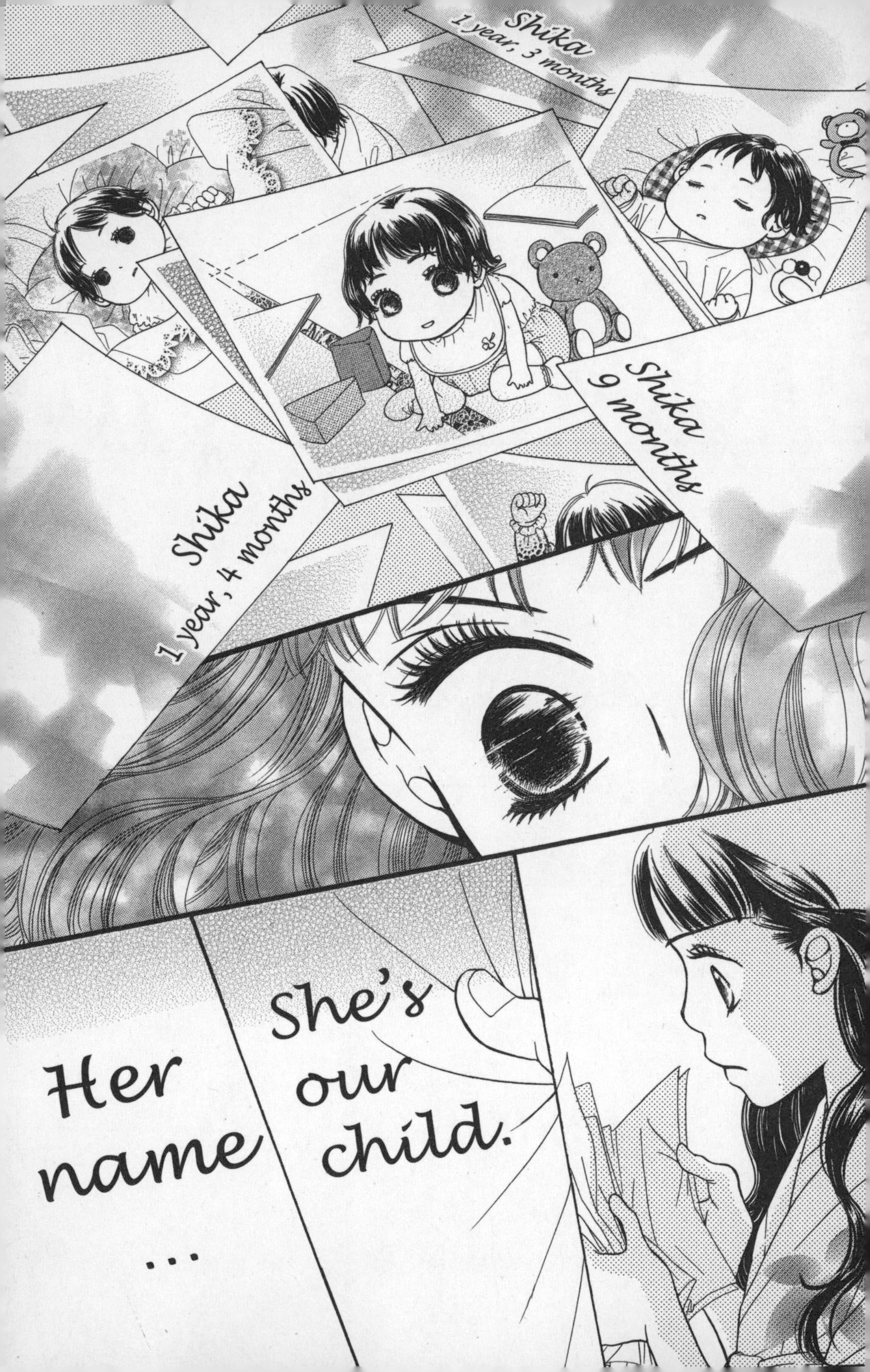
Shika
1 year, 3 months
Shika
9 months
Shika
1 year, 4 months
She's our child.
Her name
...

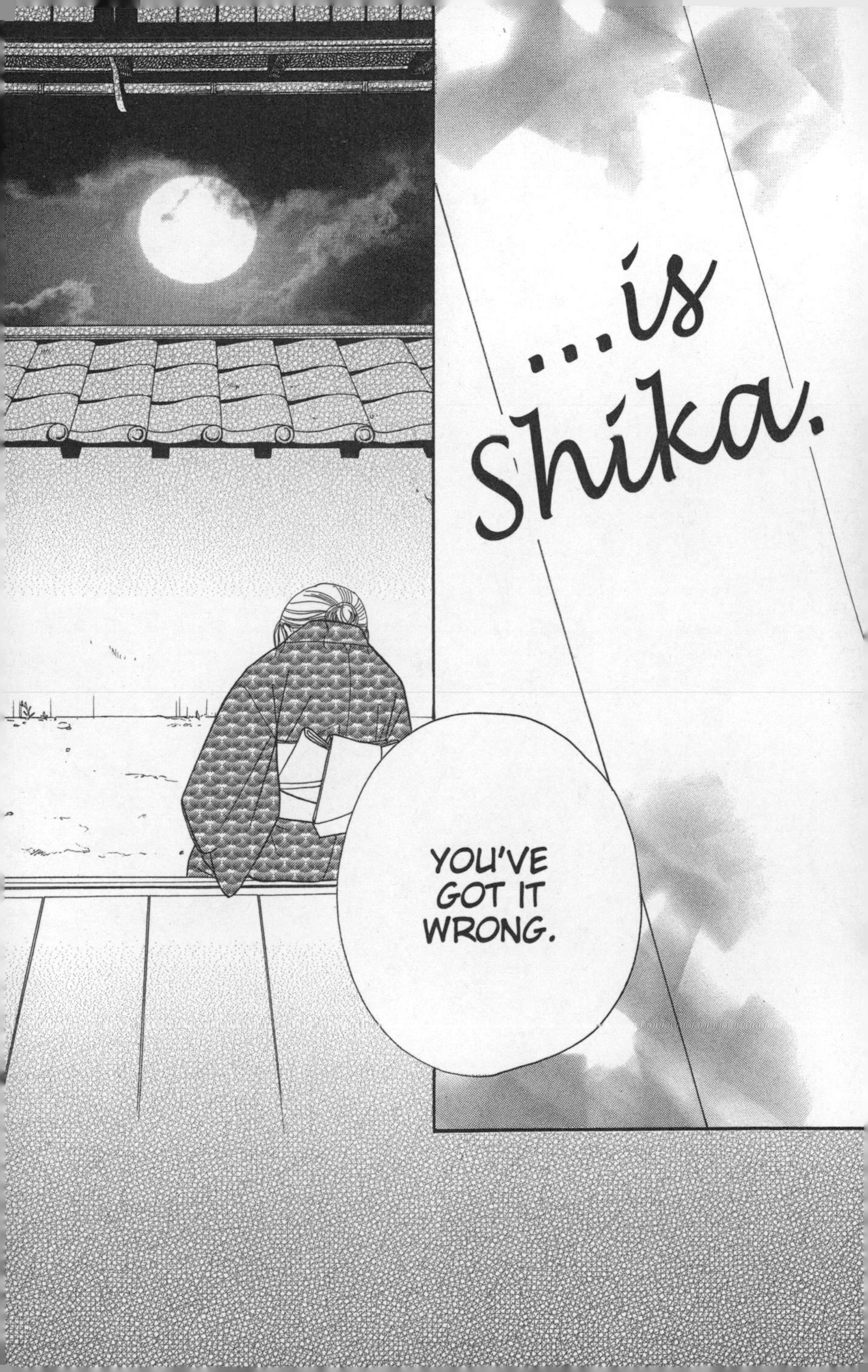
...is Shika.
YOU'VE GOT IT WRONG.

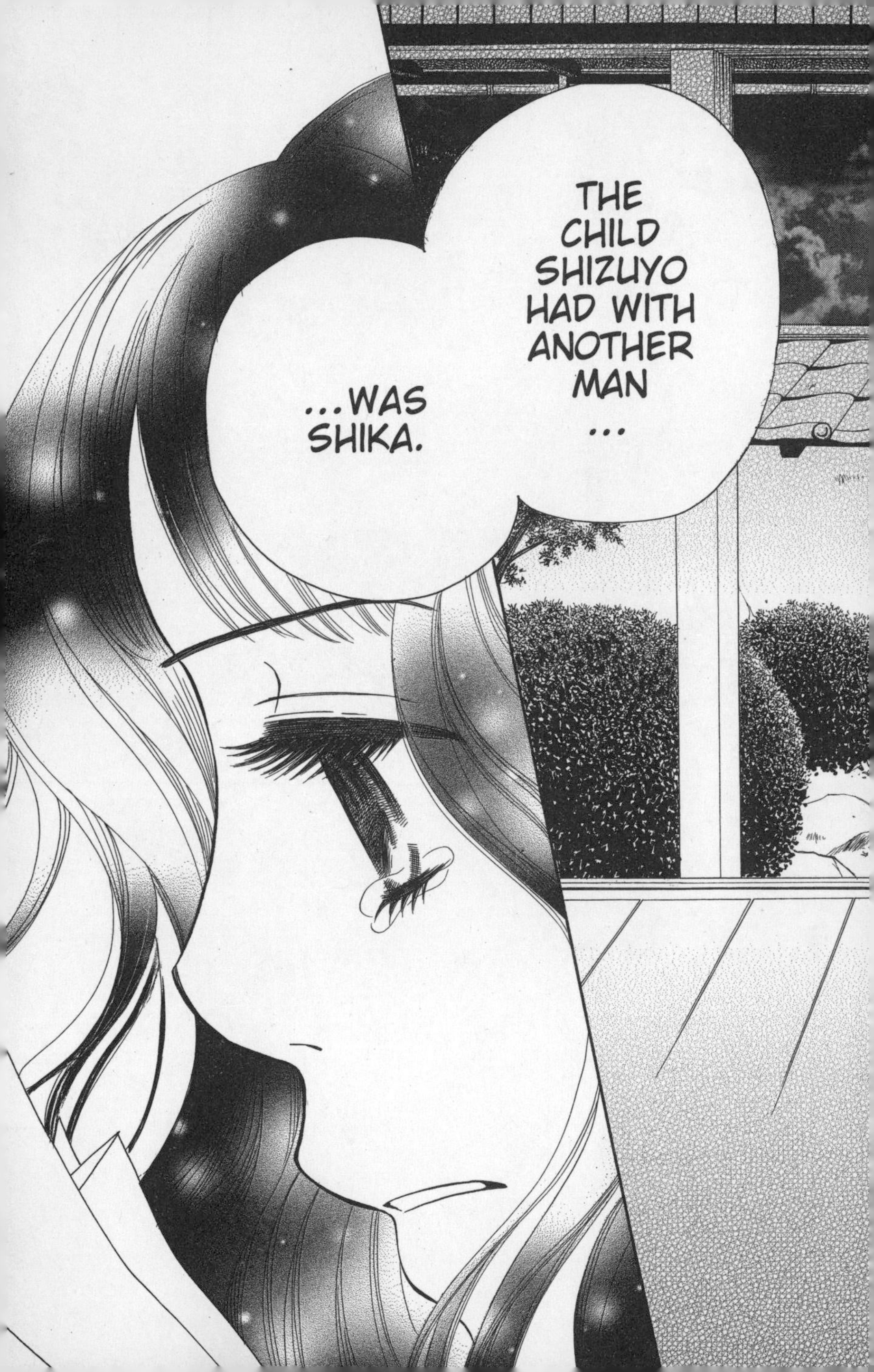
THE CHILD SHIZUYO HAD WITH ANOTHER MAN ...
...WAS SHIKA.

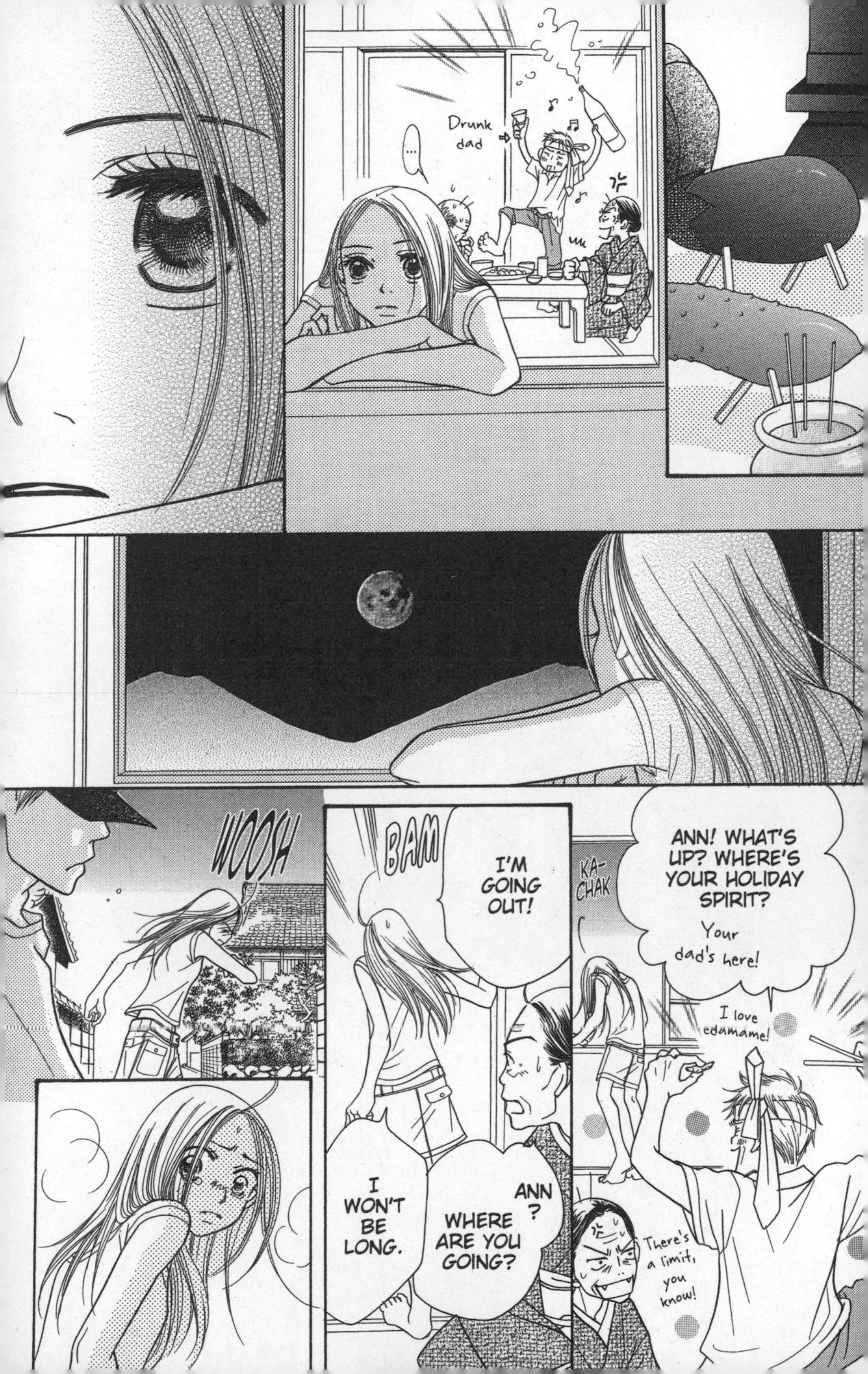
Drunk dad
...
ANN! WHAT'S UP? WHERE'S YOUR HOLIDAY SPIRIT?
Your dad's here!
KA-CHAK
I love edamame!
There's a limit, you know!
BAM
I'M GOING OUT!
ANN? WHERE ARE YOU GOING?
I WON'T BE LONG.
WOOSH

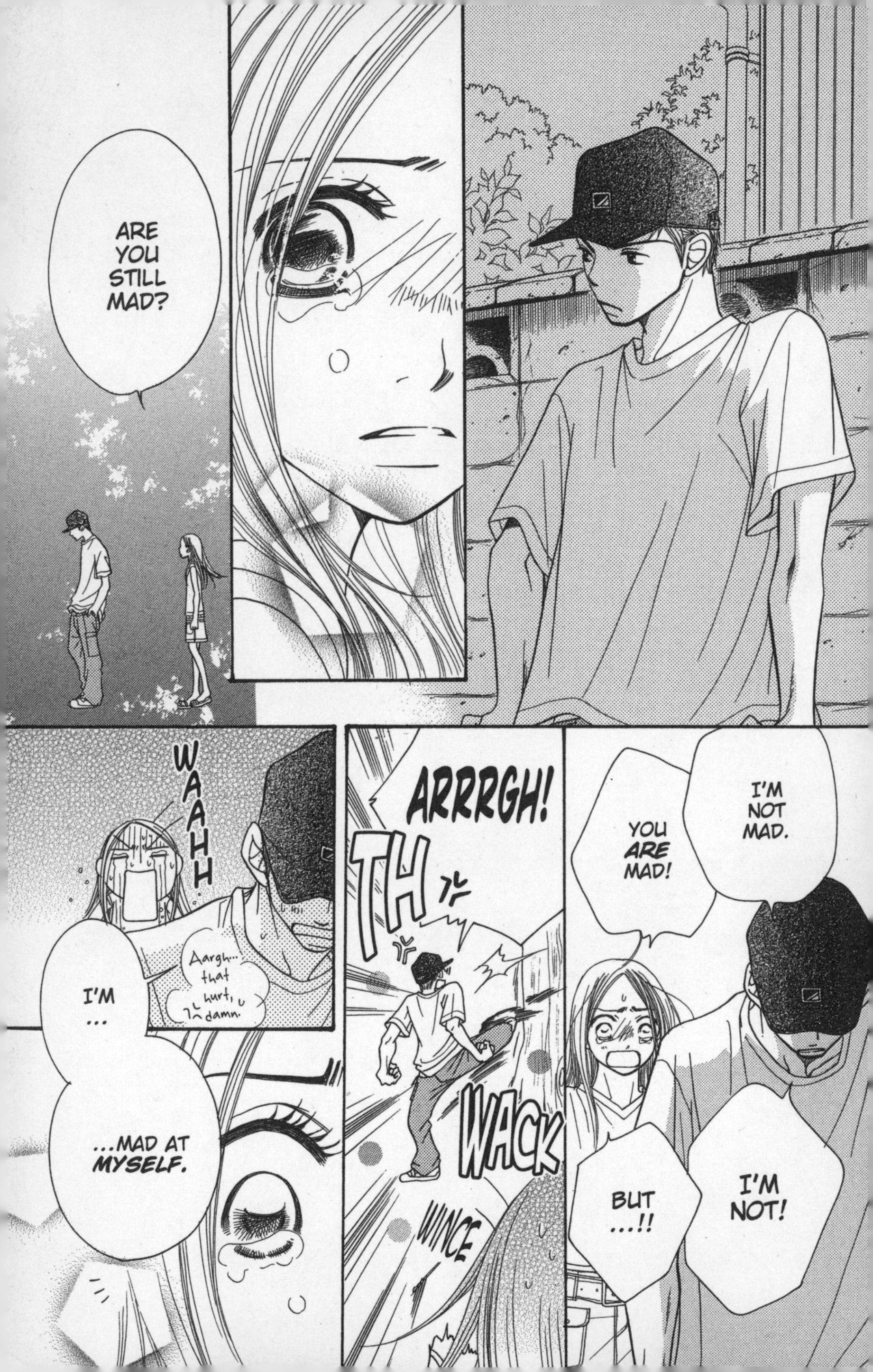
ARE YOU STILL MAD?
I'M NOT MAD.
YOU ARE MAD!
I'M NOT!
BUT ...!!
ARRRGH!
TH
WACK
WINCE
WAAHH
Aargh... that hurt, damn.
I'M ...
...MAD AT MYSELF.

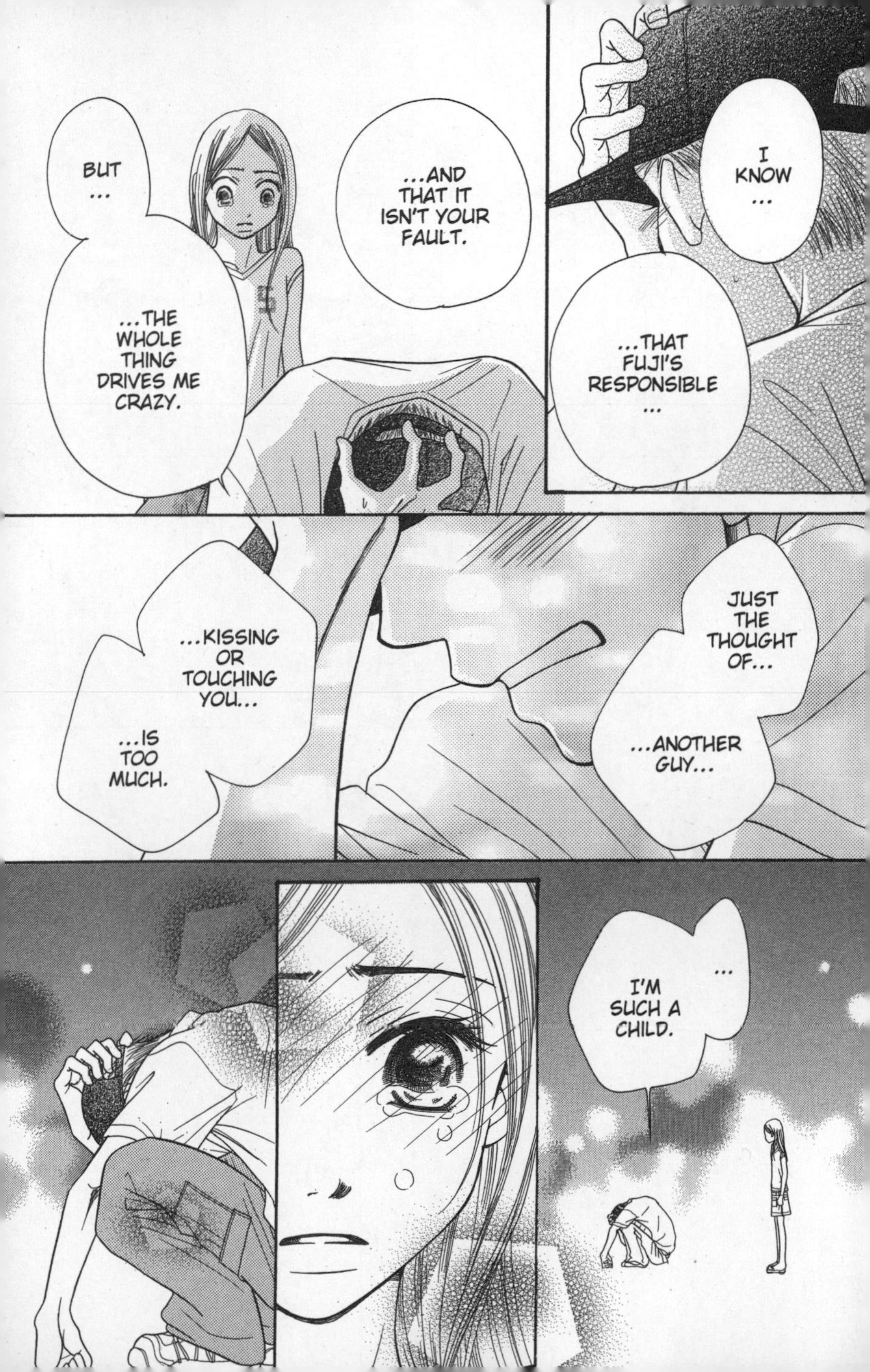
I KNOW...
...THAT FUJI'S RESPONSIBLE...
...AND THAT IT ISN'T YOUR FAULT.
BUT...
...THE WHOLE THING DRIVES ME CRAZY.
JUST THE THOUGHT OF...
...ANOTHER GUY...
...KISSING OR TOUCHING YOU...
...IS TOO MUCH.
... I'M SUCH A CHILD.

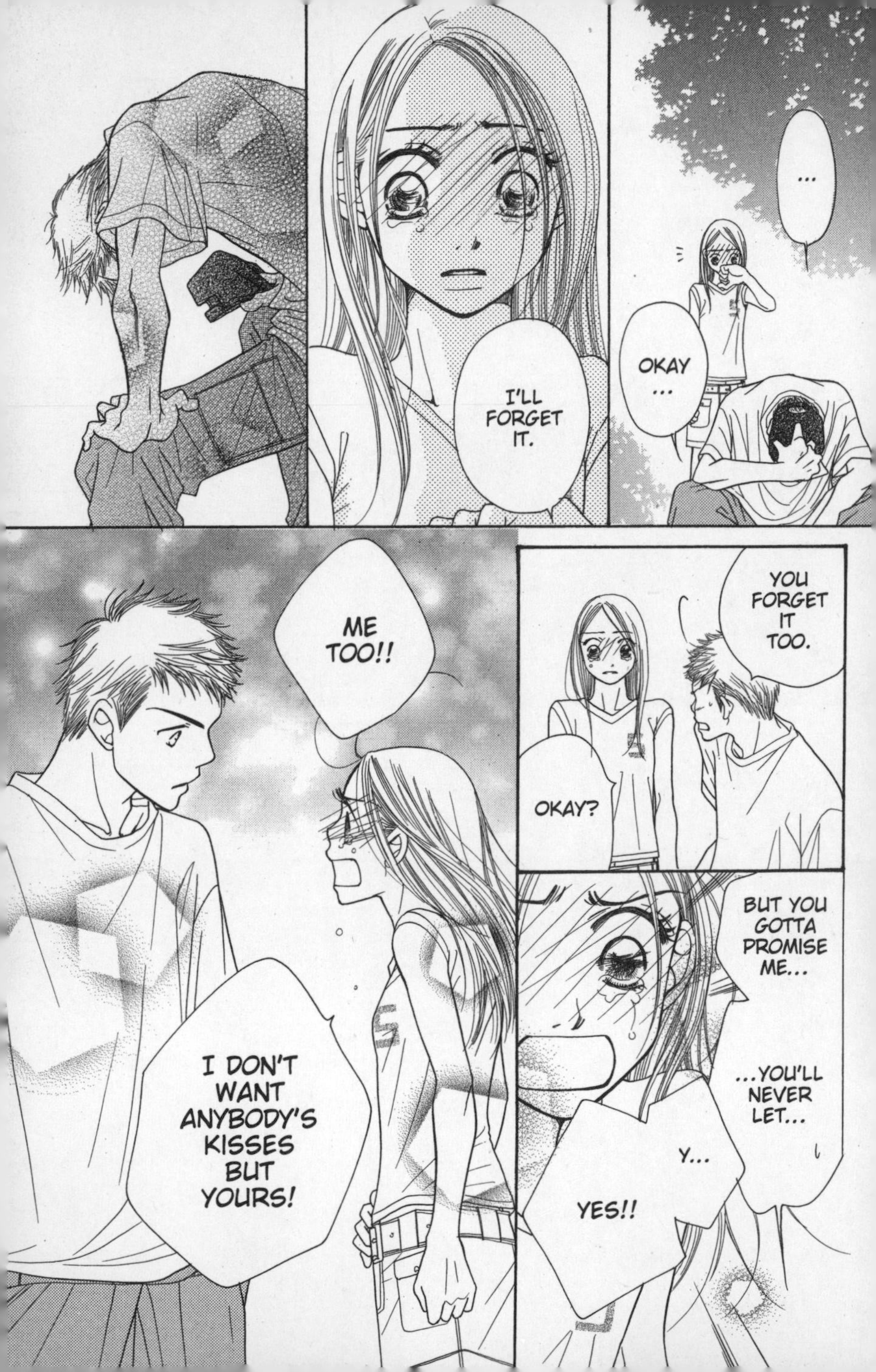
...
OKAY ...
I'LL FORGET IT.
YOU FORGET IT TOO.
OKAY?
BUT YOU GOTTA PROMISE ME...
...YOU'LL NEVER LET...
Y...
YES!!
ME TOO!!
I DON'T WANT ANYBODY'S KISSES BUT YOURS!

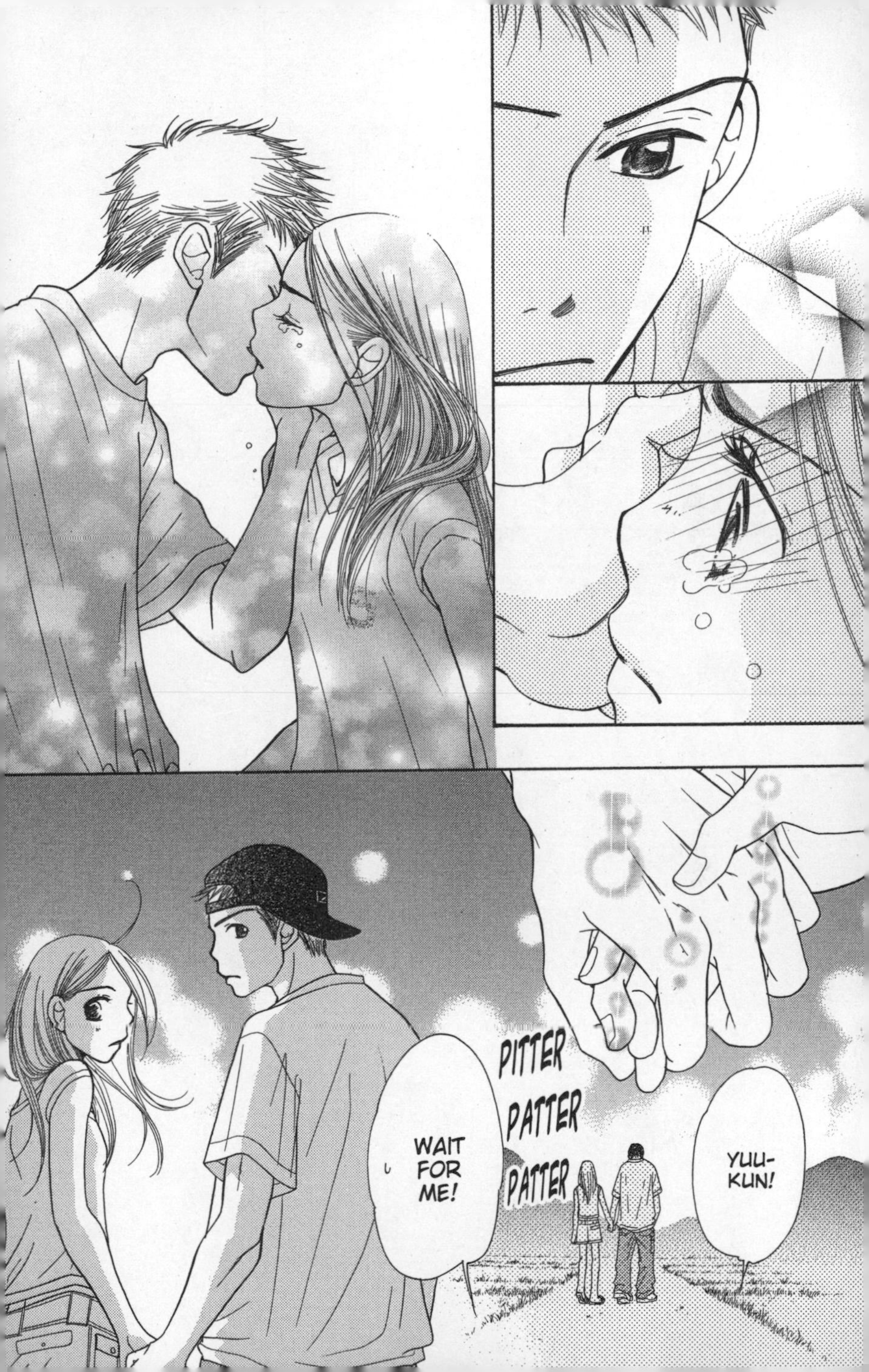
YUU-KUN!
PITTER PATTER PATTER
WAIT FOR ME!

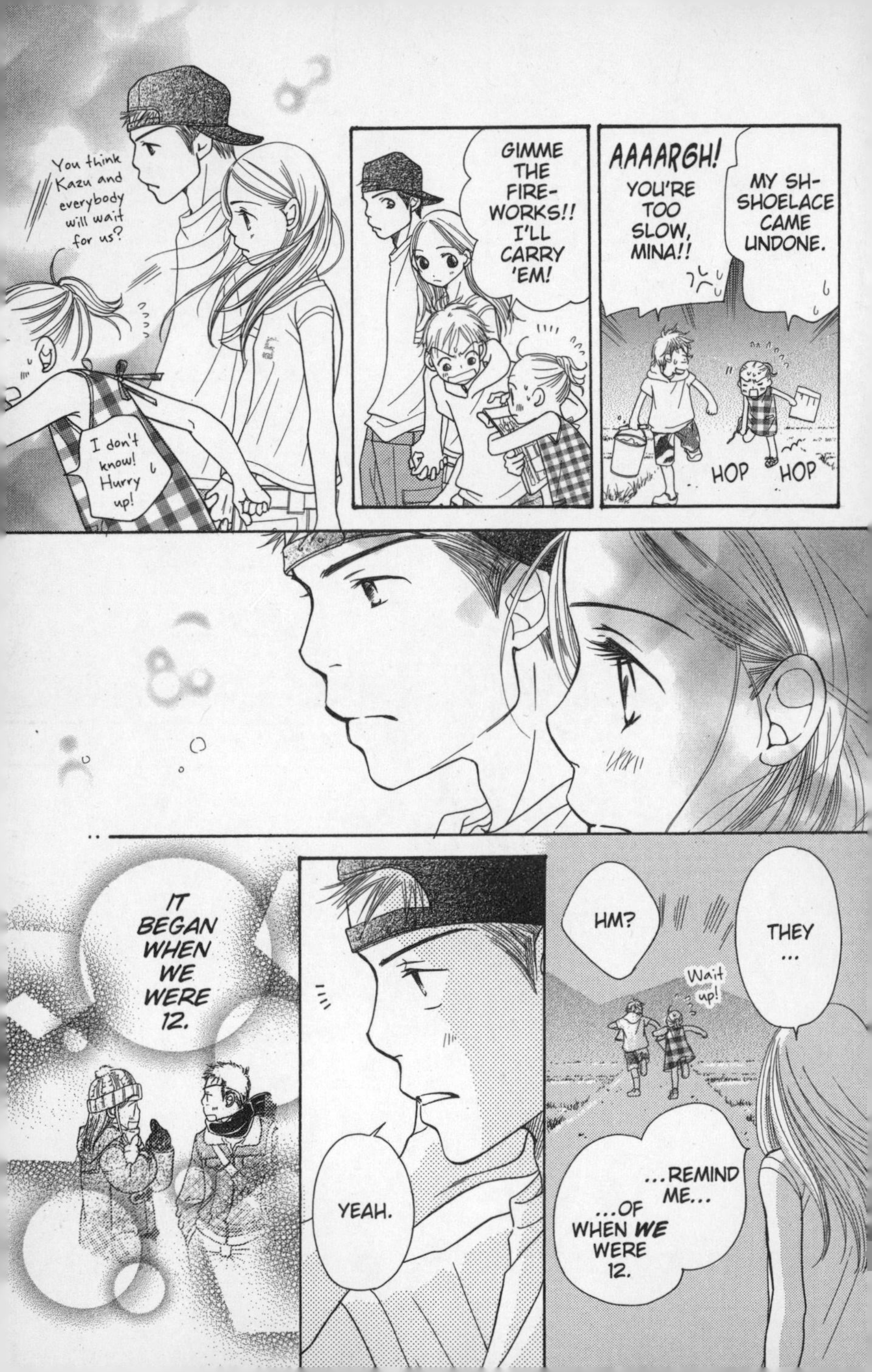
MY SH-SHOELACE CAME UNDONE.
AAAARGH! YOU'RE TOO SLOW, MINA!!
HOP HOP
GIMME THE FIRE-WORKS!! I'LL CARRY 'EM!
You think Kazu and everybody will wait for us?
I don't know! Hurry up!
THEY ...
HM?
Wait up!
...REMIND ME...
...OF WHEN WE WERE 12.
YEAH.
IT BEGAN WHEN WE WERE 12.

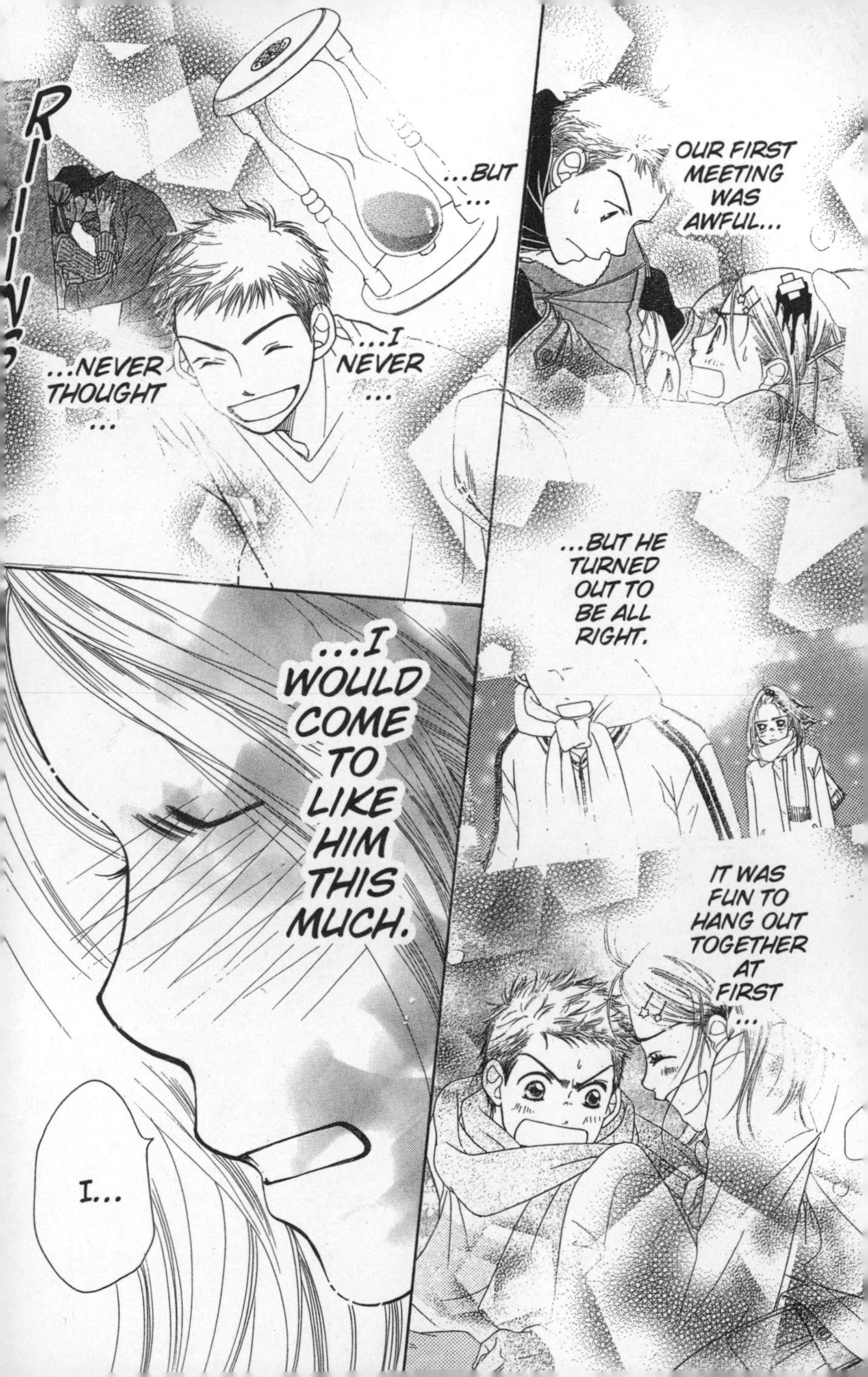
OUR FIRST MEETING WAS AWFUL...
...BUT HE TURNED OUT TO BE ALL RIGHT.
IT WAS FUN TO HANG OUT TOGETHER AT FIRST ...
...BUT ...
RIIING
...I NEVER ...
...NEVER THOUGHT ...
...I WOULD COME TO LIKE HIM THIS MUCH.
I...

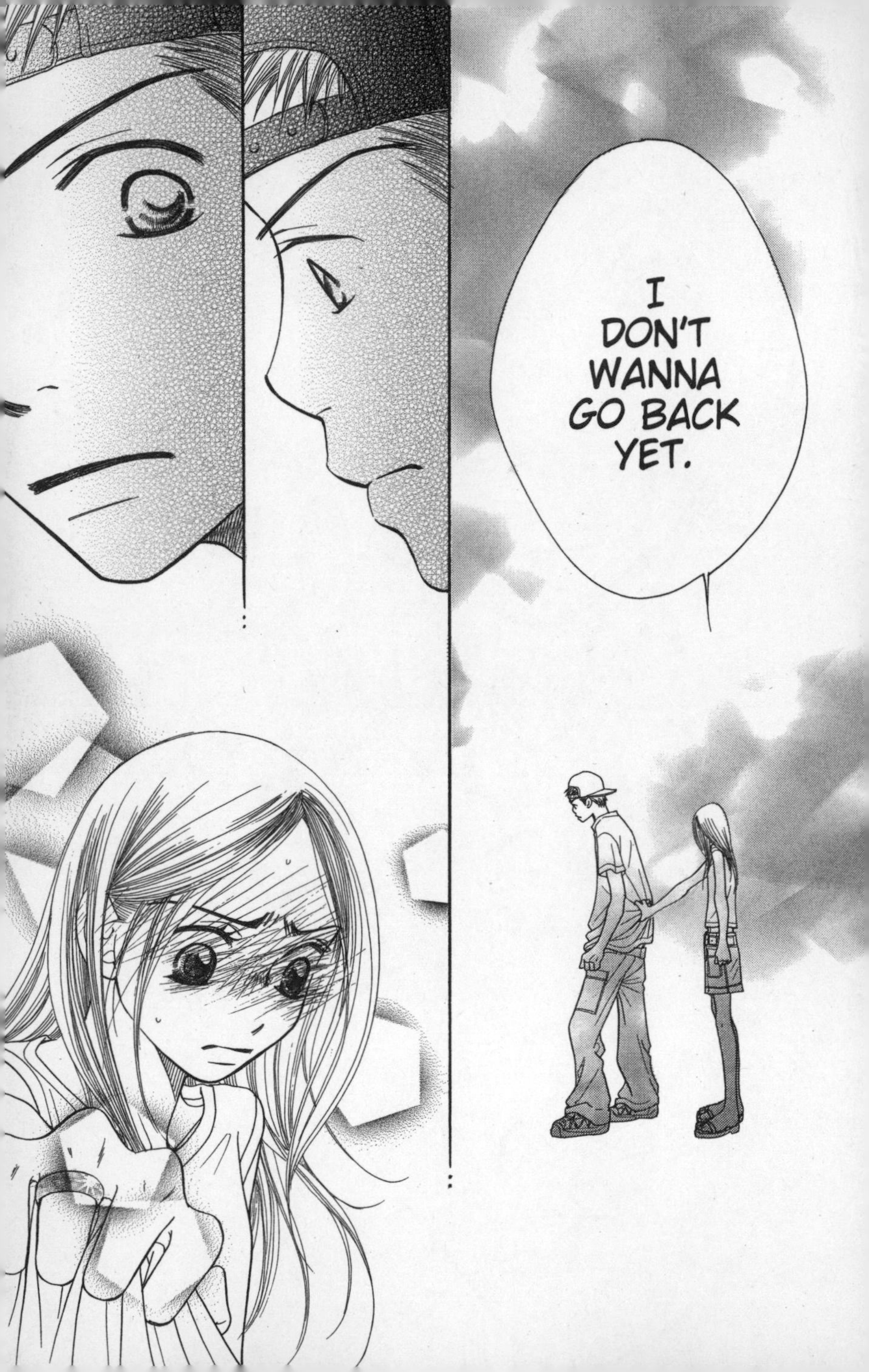
I DON'T WANNA GO BACK YET.

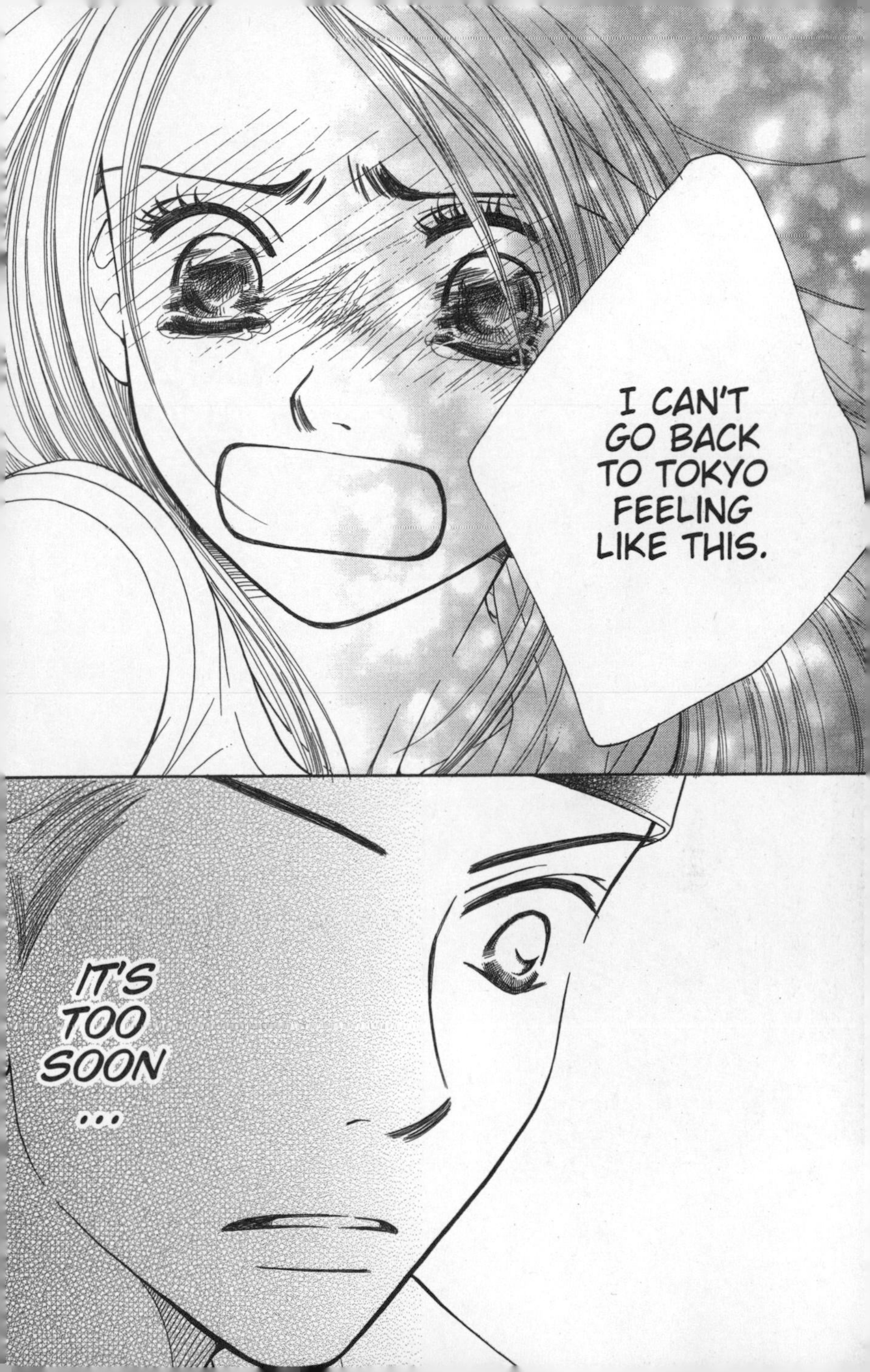
I CAN'T GO BACK TO TOKYO FEELING LIKE THIS.
IT'S TOO SOON ...

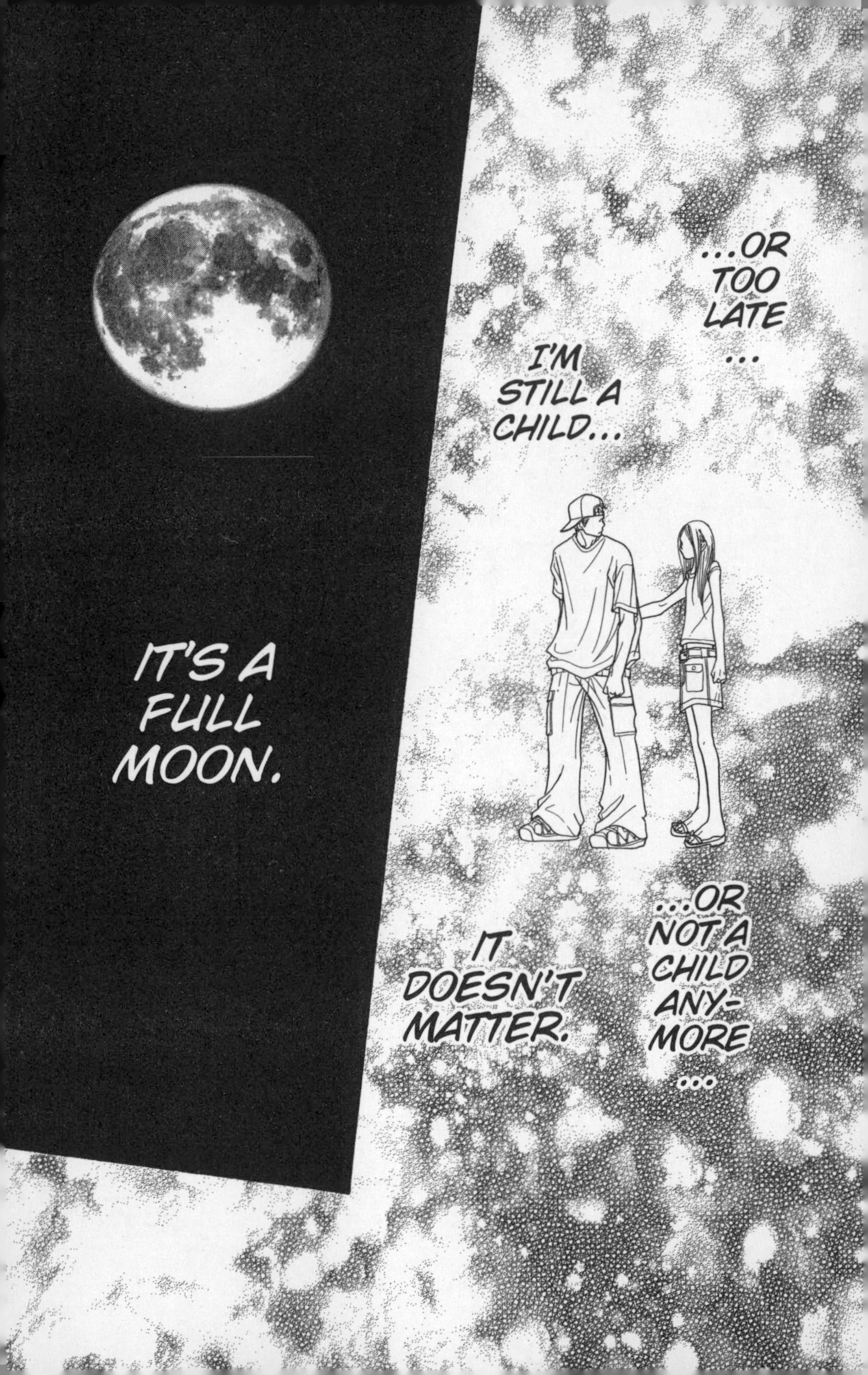
...OR TOO LATE...
I'M STILL A CHILD...
...OR NOT A CHILD ANYMORE...
IT DOESN'T MATTER.
IT'S A FULL MOON.

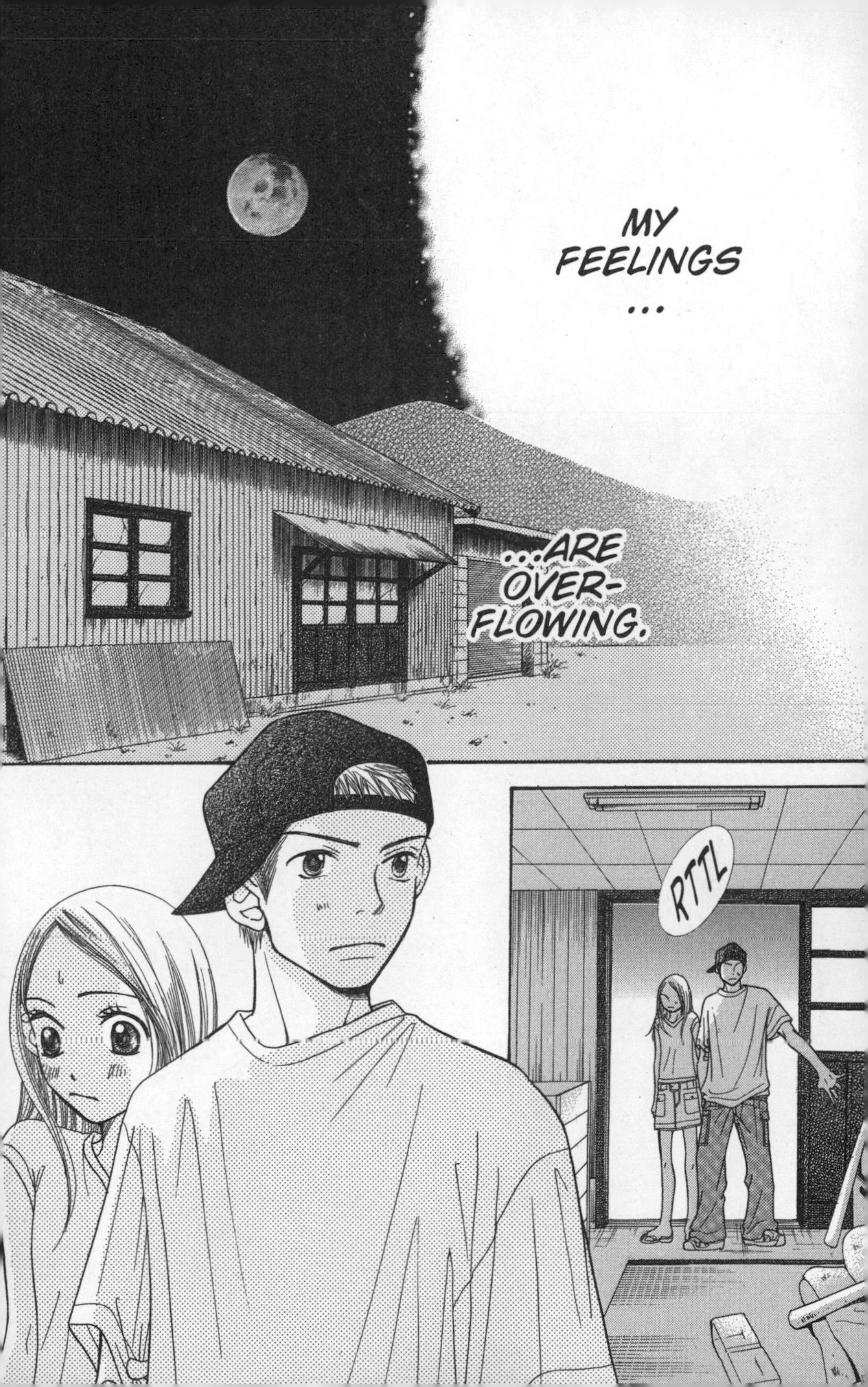
MY FEELINGS ...
...ARE OVER-FLOWING.
RTTL

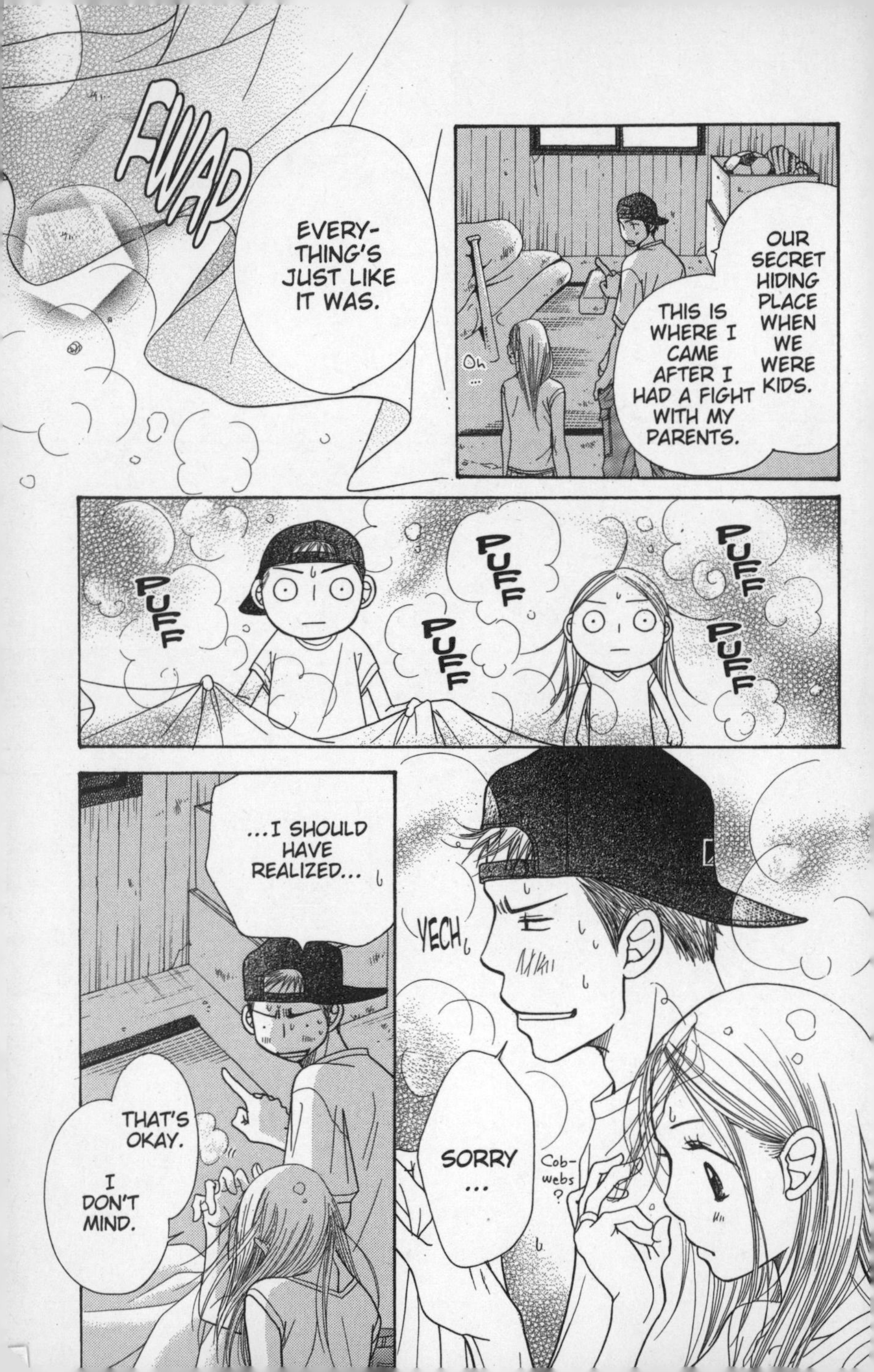
OUR SECRET HIDING PLACE WHEN WE WERE KIDS.
THIS IS WHERE I CAME AFTER I HAD A FIGHT WITH MY PARENTS.
Oh ...
FWAP
EVERY-THING'S JUST LIKE IT WAS.
PUFF
PUFF
PUFF
PUFF
PUFF
YECH
Cob-webs?
SORRY ...
...I SHOULD HAVE REALIZED...
THAT'S OKAY.
I DON'T MIND.

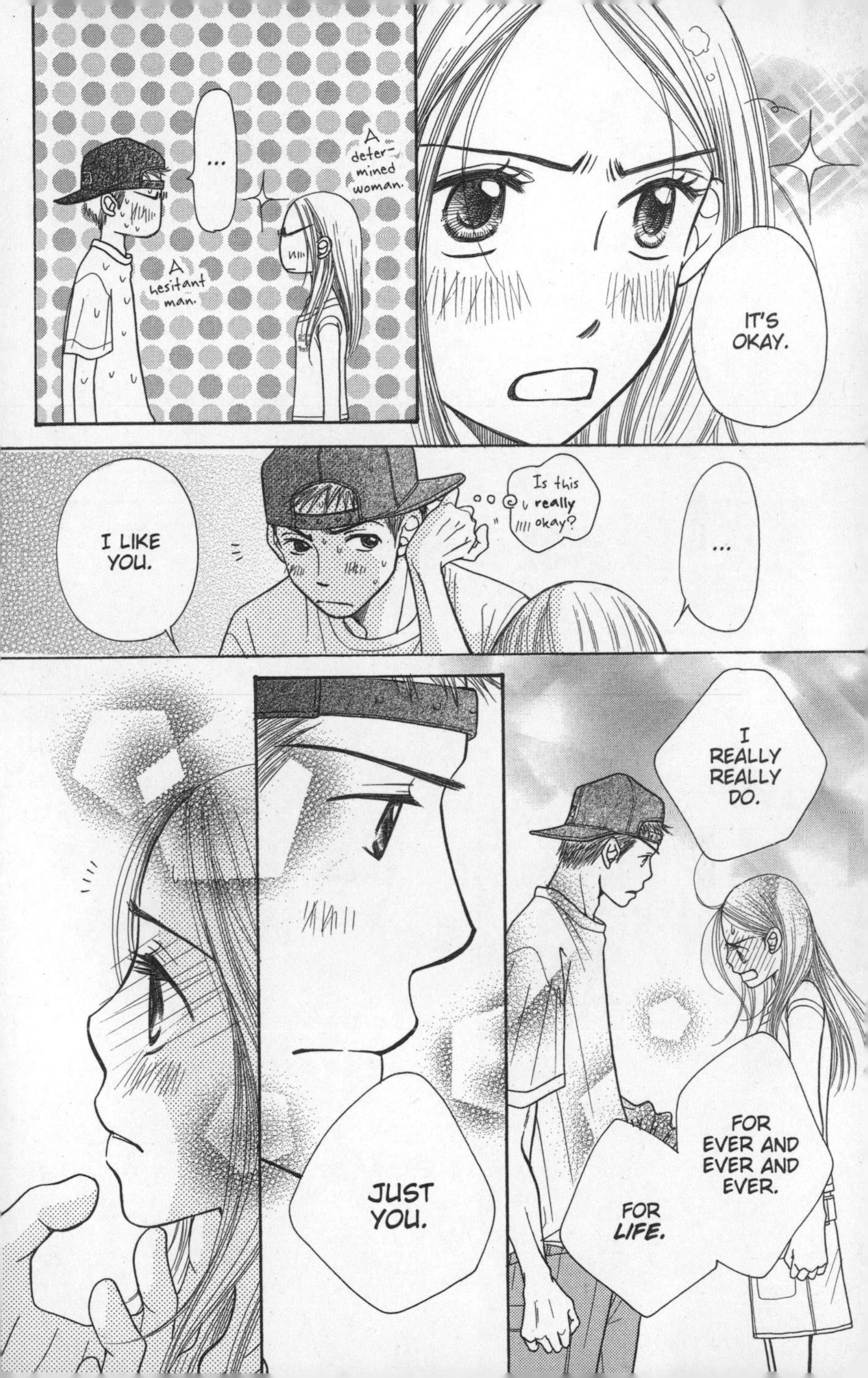
IT'S OKAY.
A deter-mined woman.
...
A hesitant man.
...
Is this really okay?
I LIKE YOU.
I REALLY REALLY DO.
FOR EVER AND EVER AND EVER.
FOR LIFE.
JUST YOU.

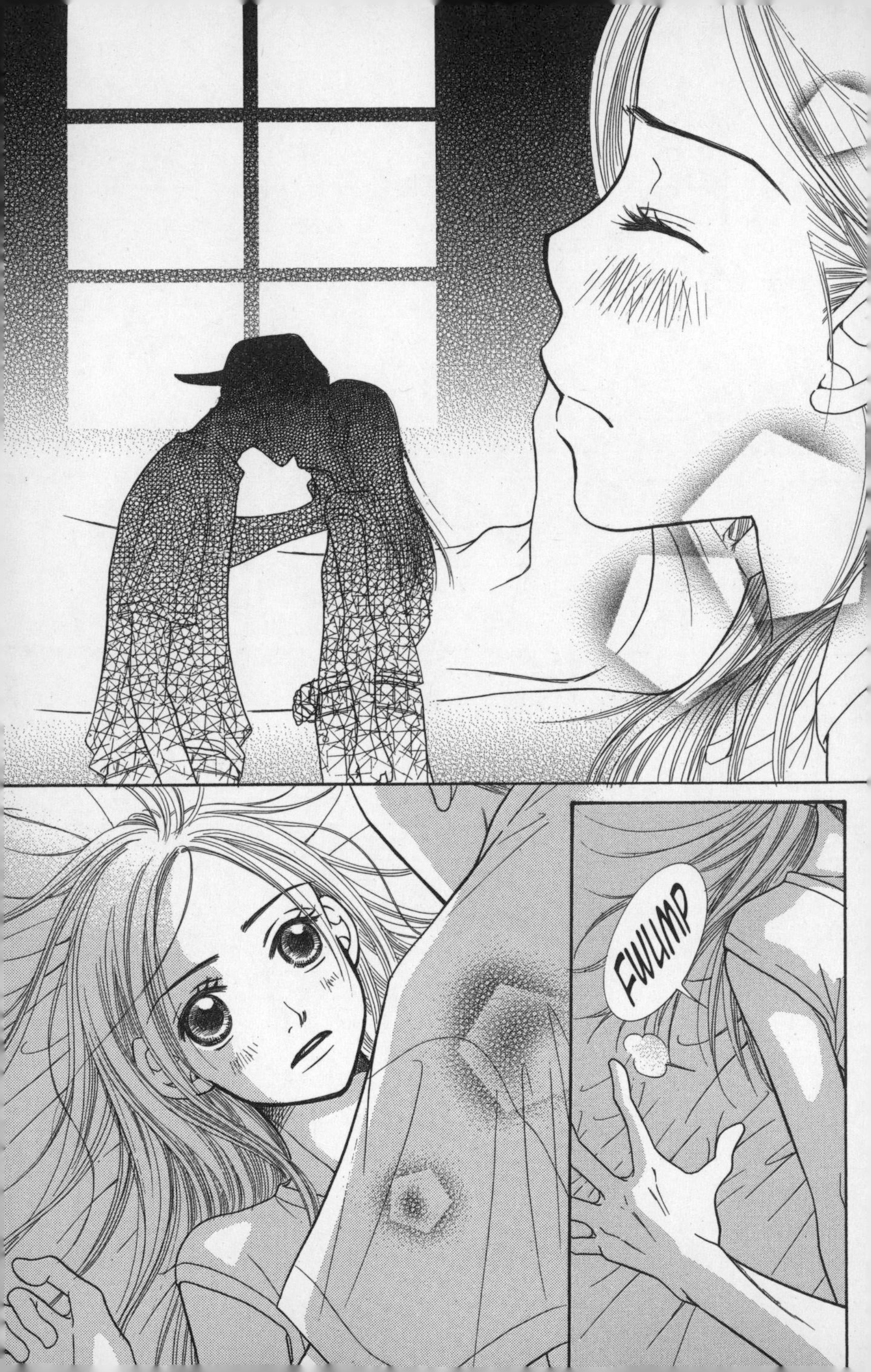
FWUMP

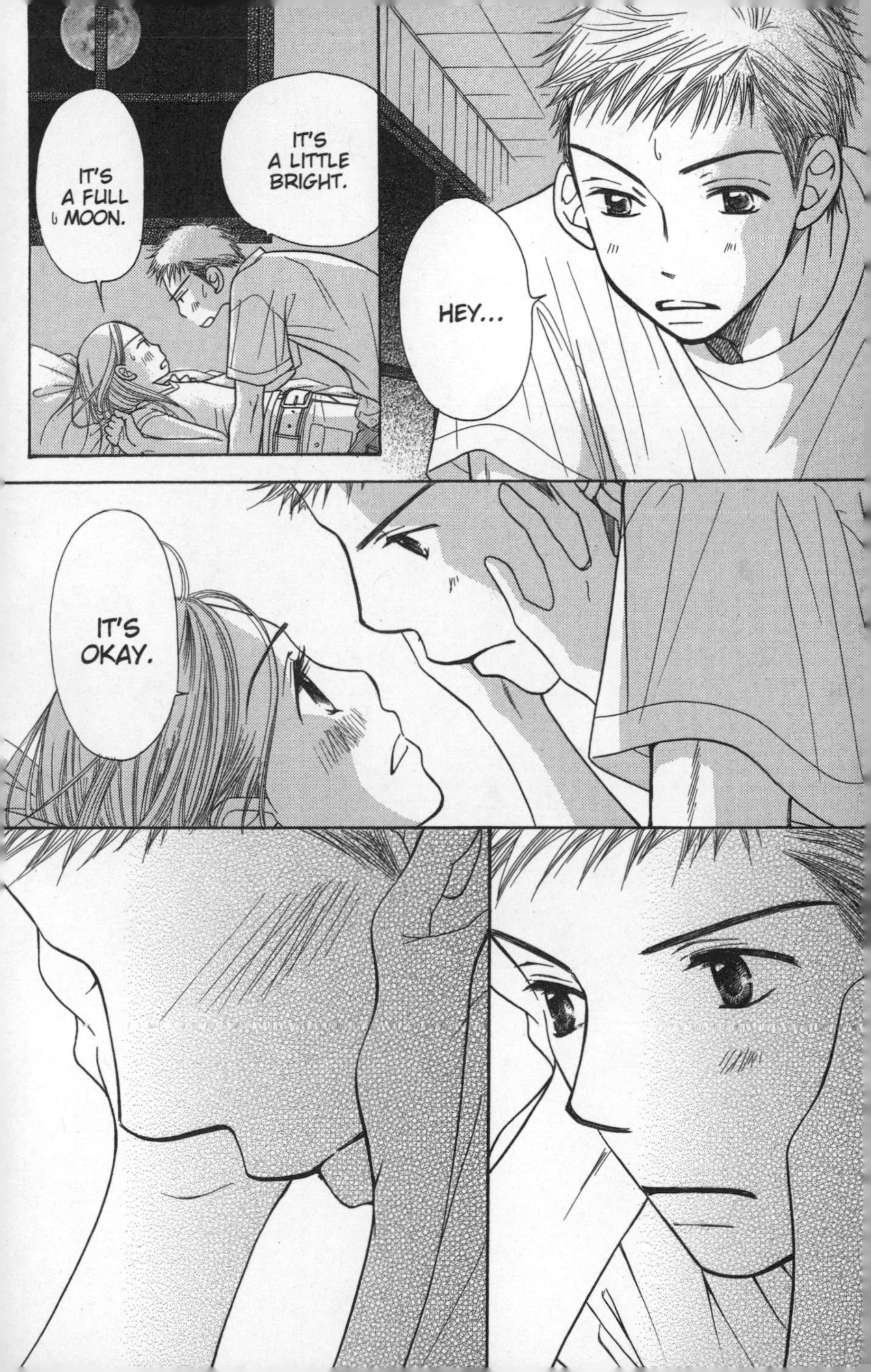
HEY...
IT'S A LITTLE BRIGHT.
IT'S A FULL MOON.
IT'S OKAY.

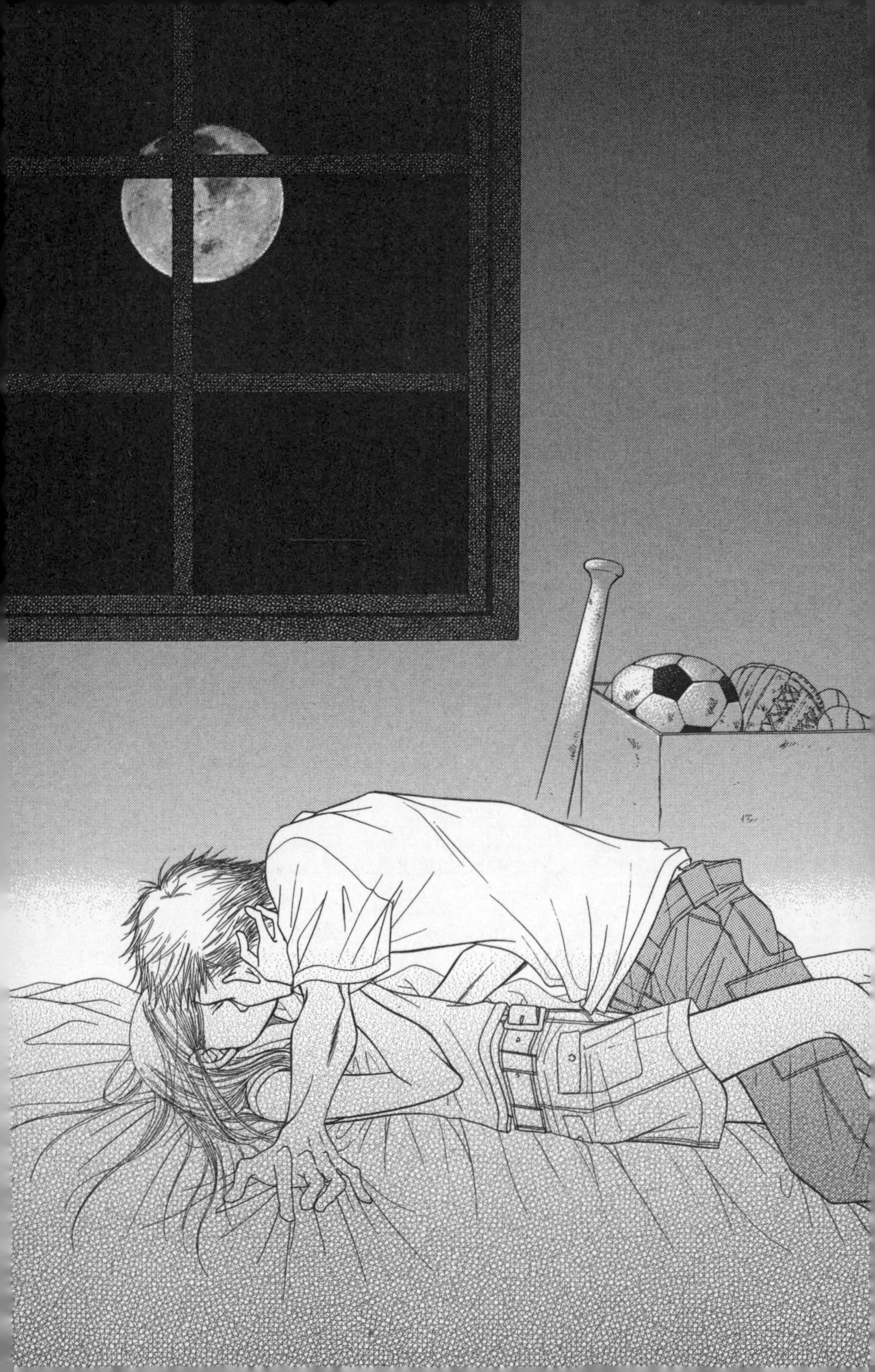

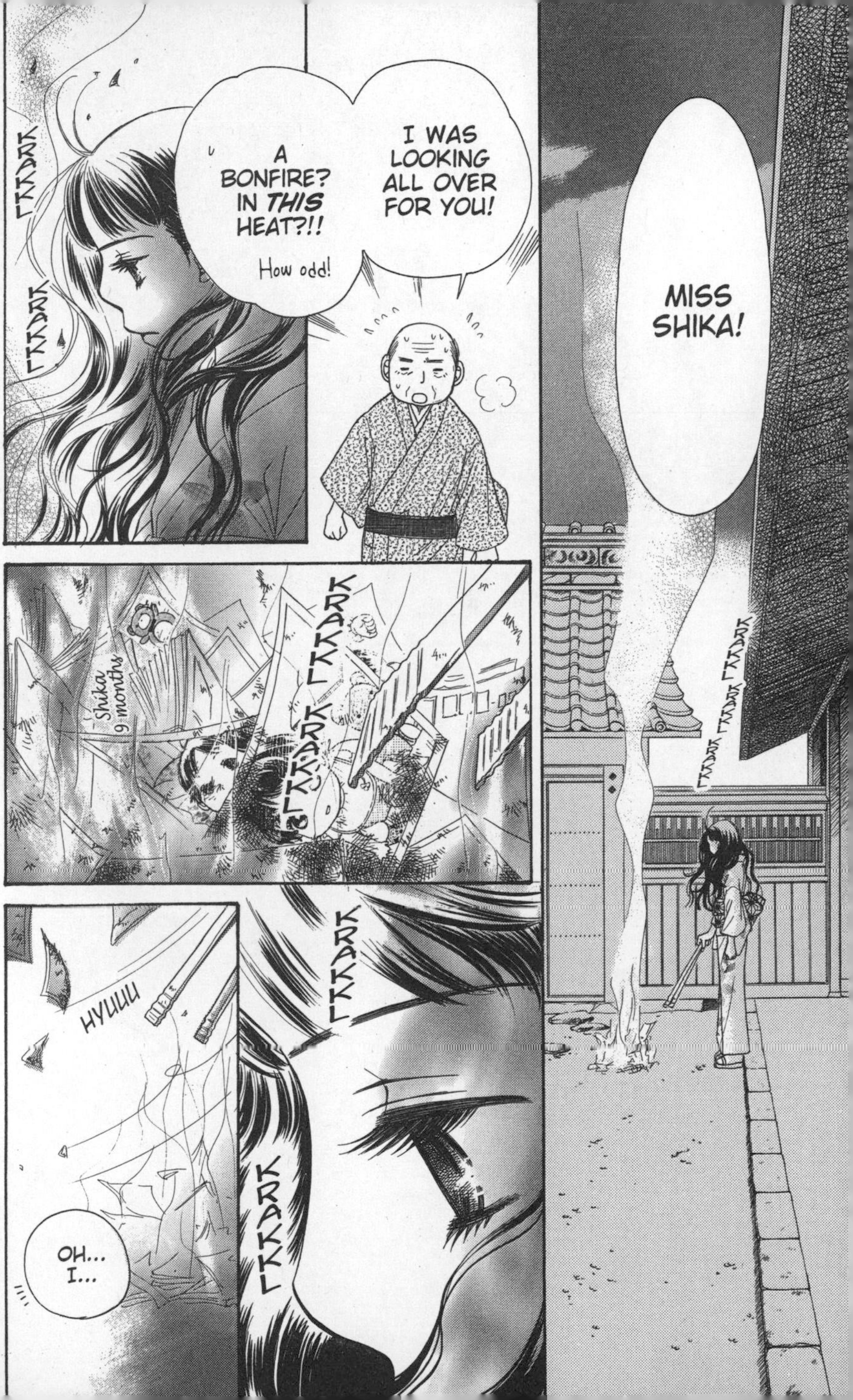
MISS SHIKA!
KRAKKL KRAKKL KRAKKL
KRAKKL
I WAS LOOKING ALL OVER FOR YOU!
A BONFIRE? IN *THIS* HEAT?!!
How odd!
KRAKKL
KRAKKL
KRAKKL KRAKKL KRAKKL
Shika 9 months
KRAKKL
KRAKKL
HYUUU
OH... I...

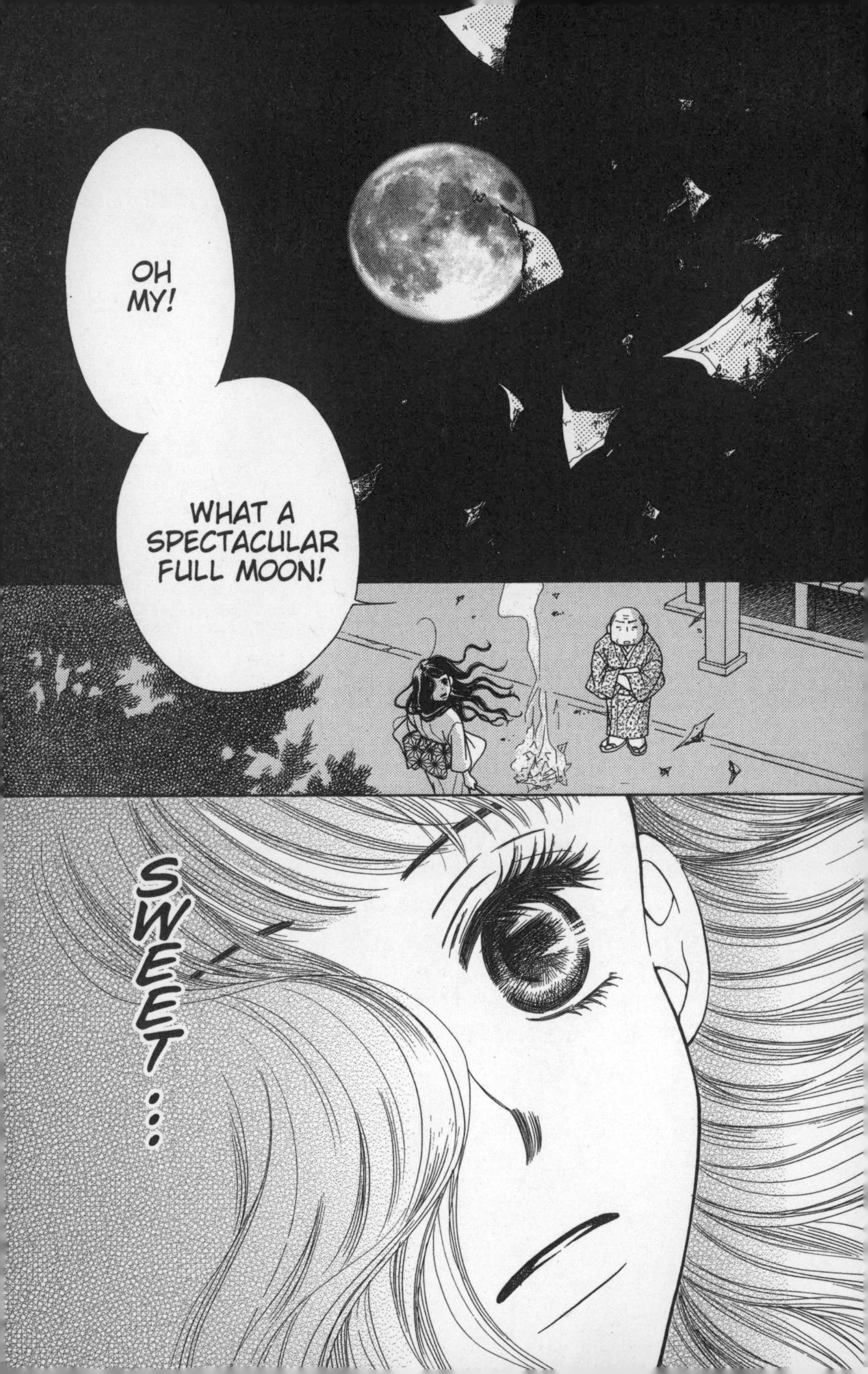
OH MY!
WHAT A SPECTACULAR FULL MOON!
SWEET...

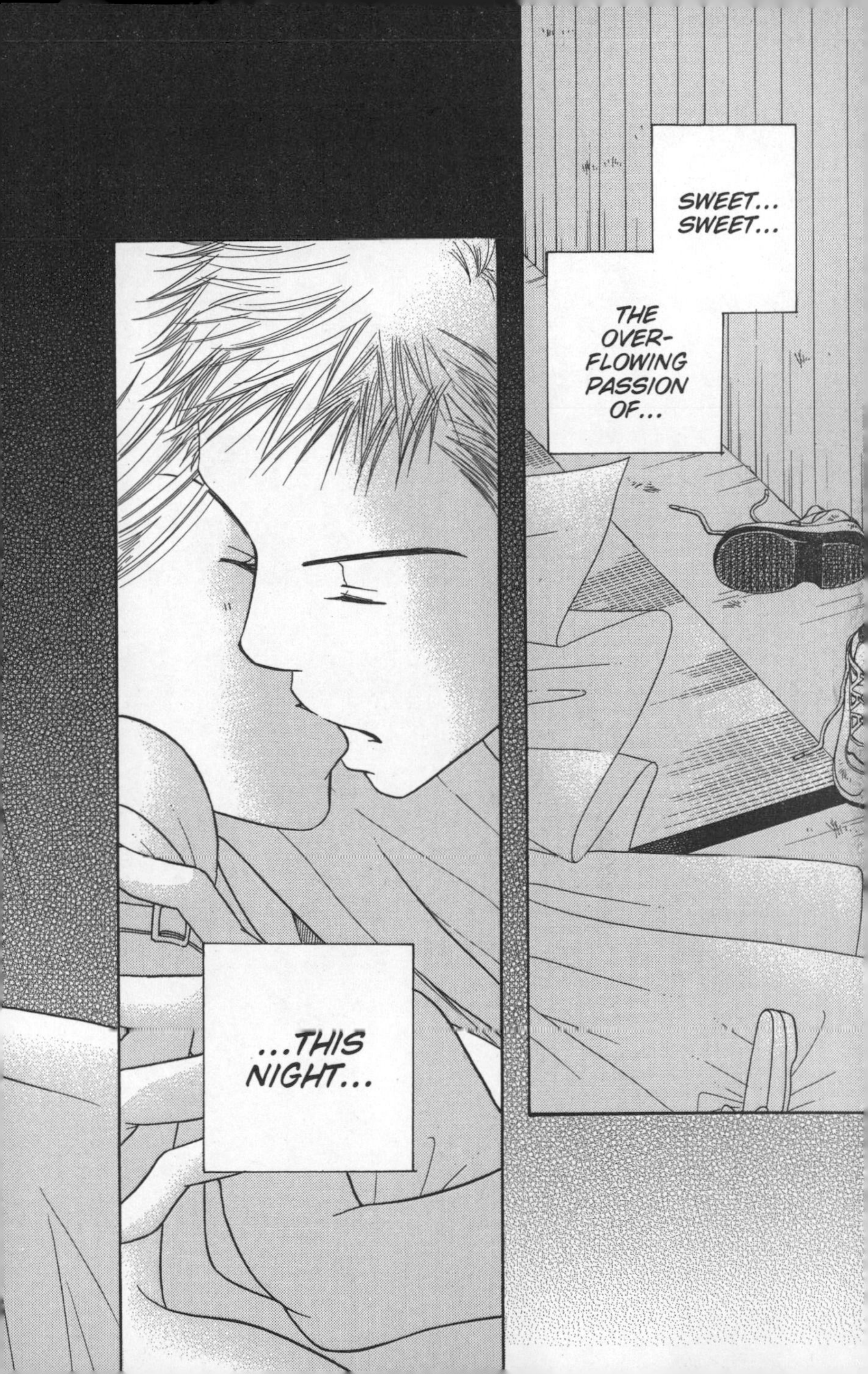
SWEET... SWEET...
THE OVER-FLOWING PASSION OF...
...THIS NIGHT...

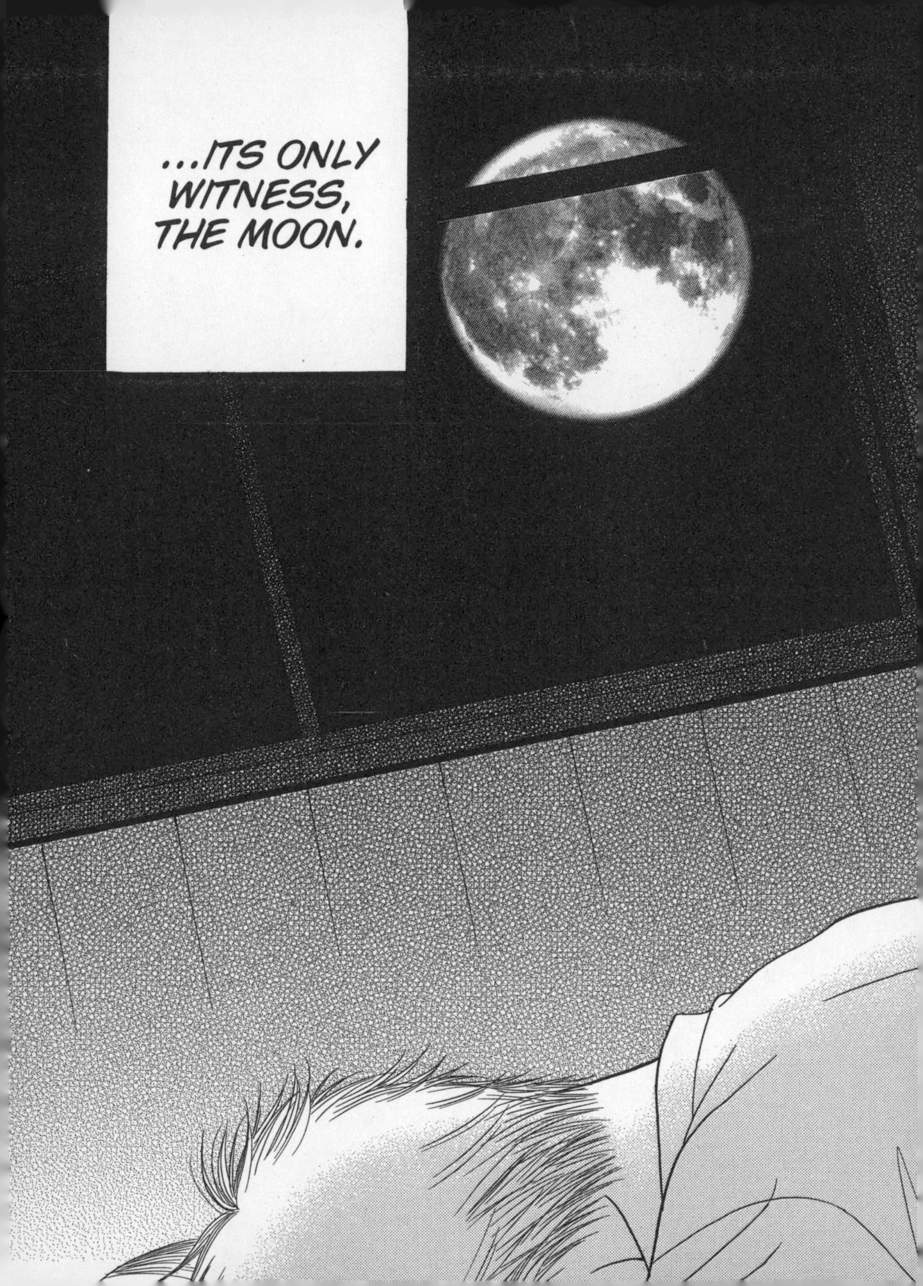
...ITS ONLY WITNESS, THE MOON.

## Sand Chronicles

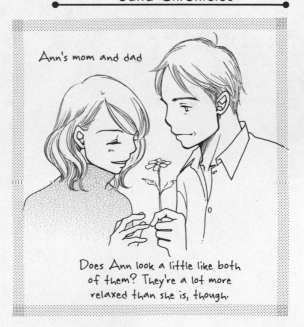

Ann's mom and dad

Does Ann look a little like both of them? They're a lot more relaxed than she is, though.

# AUTUMN, AGE 16: CICADA SHELLS

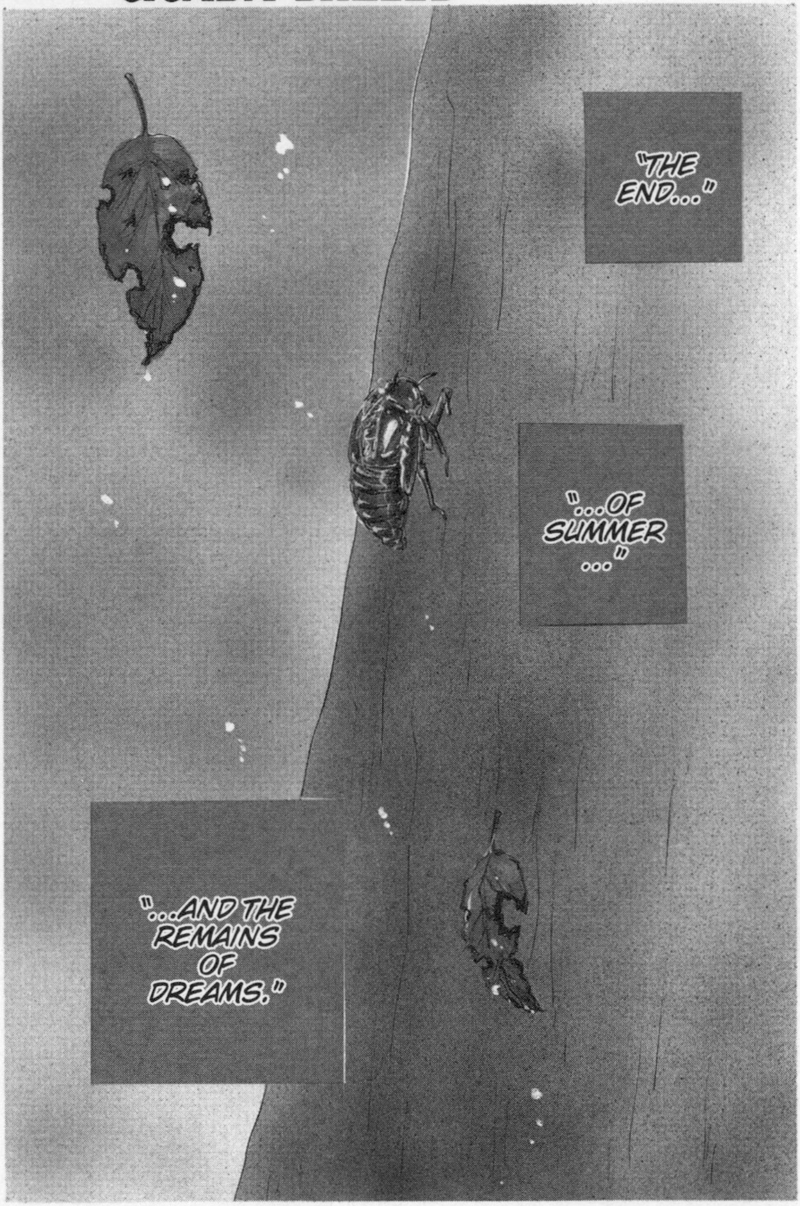
"THE END..."
"...OF SUMMER..."
"...AND THE REMAINS OF DREAMS."

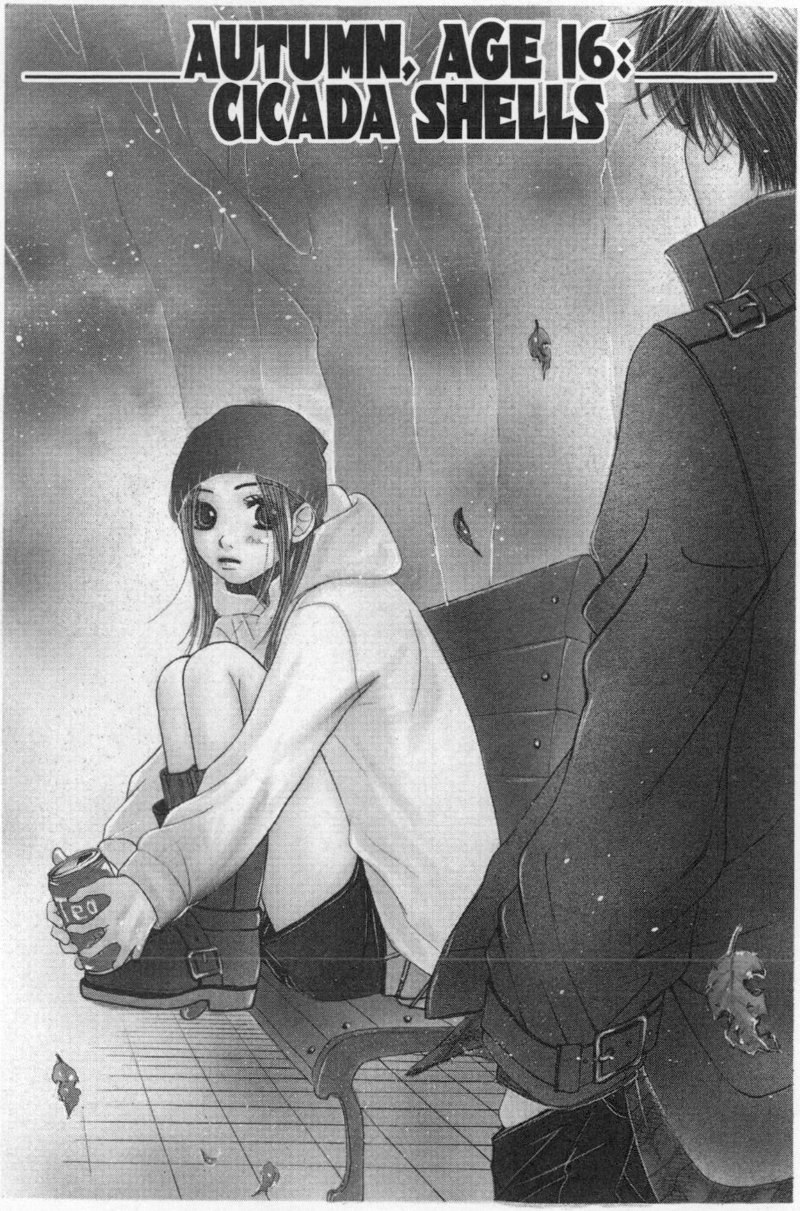
AUTUMN, AGE 16:
CICADA SHELLS

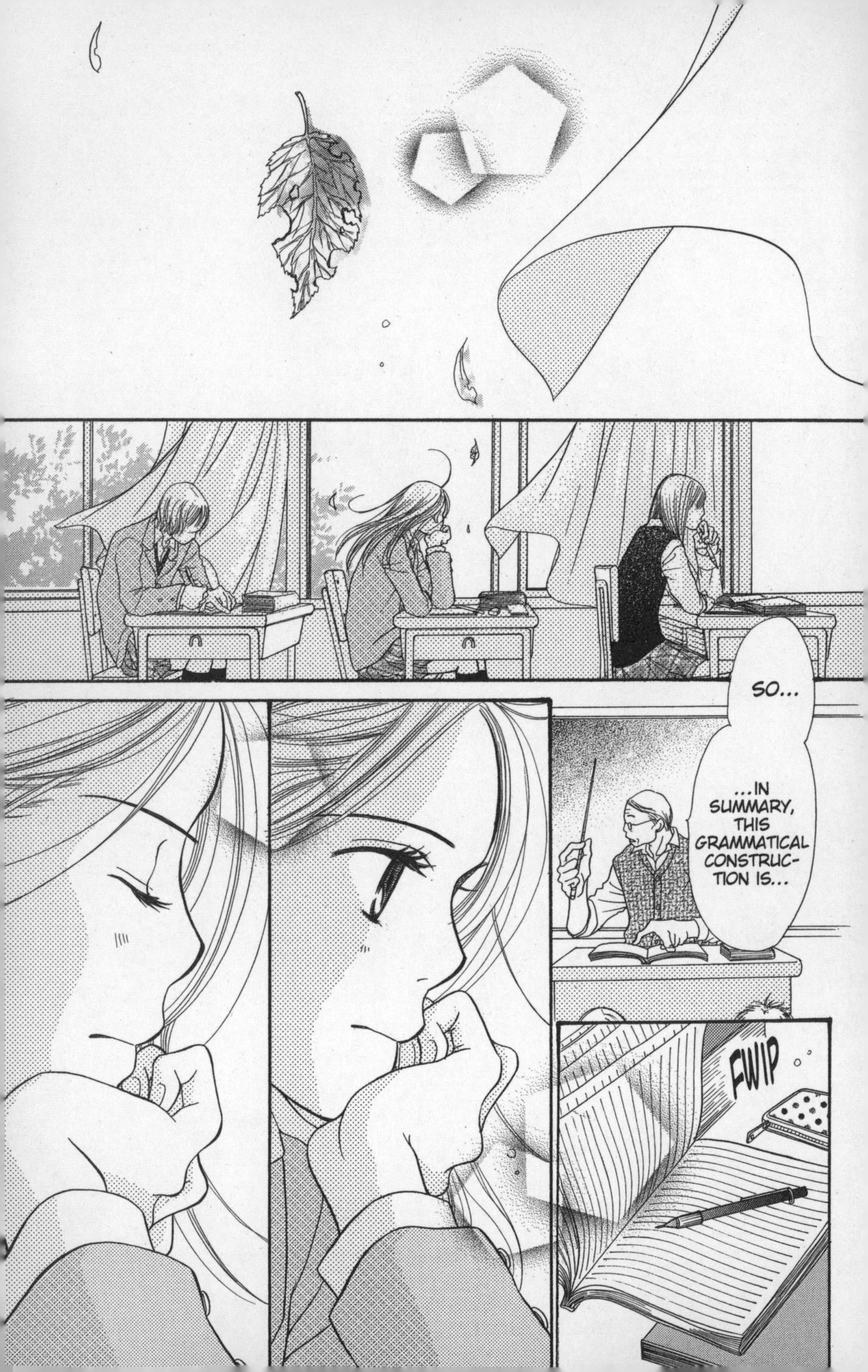
SO...
...IN SUMMARY, THIS GRAMMATICAL CONSTRUC- TION IS...
FWIP

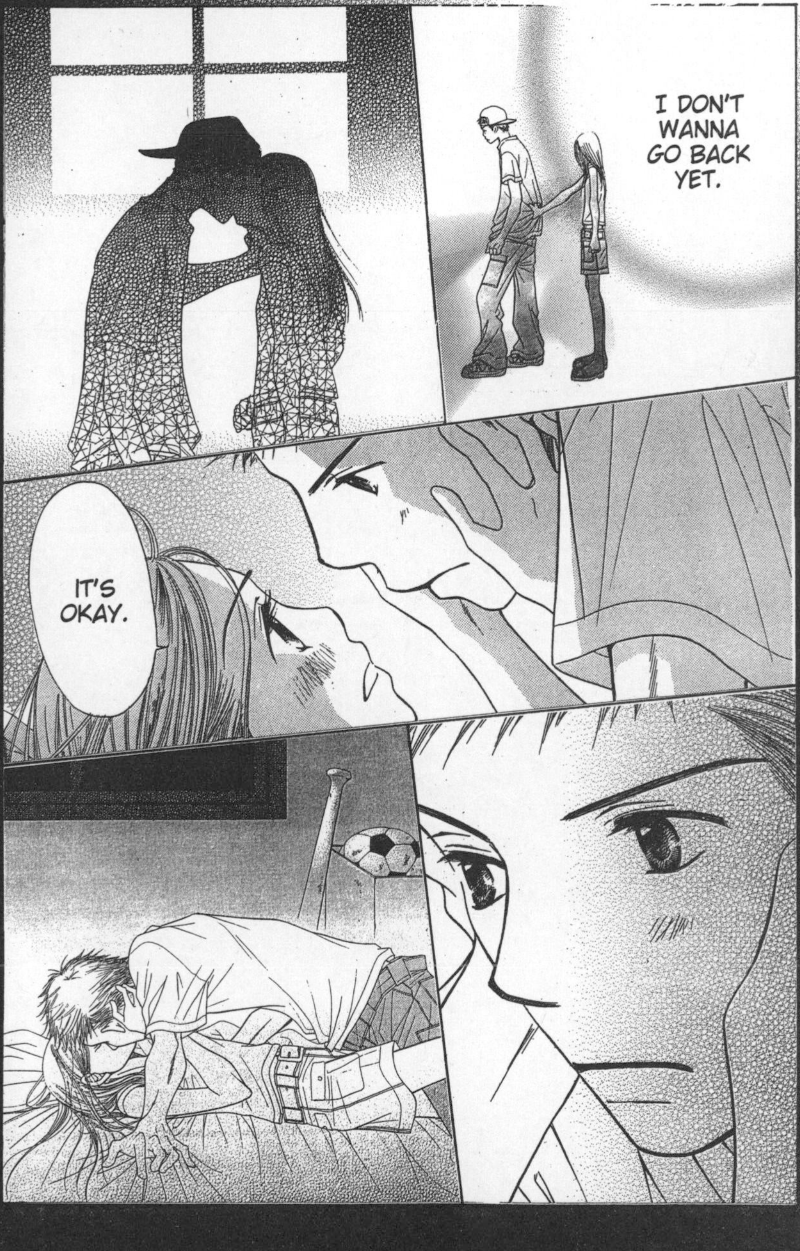
I DON'T WANNA GO BACK YET.
IT'S OKAY.

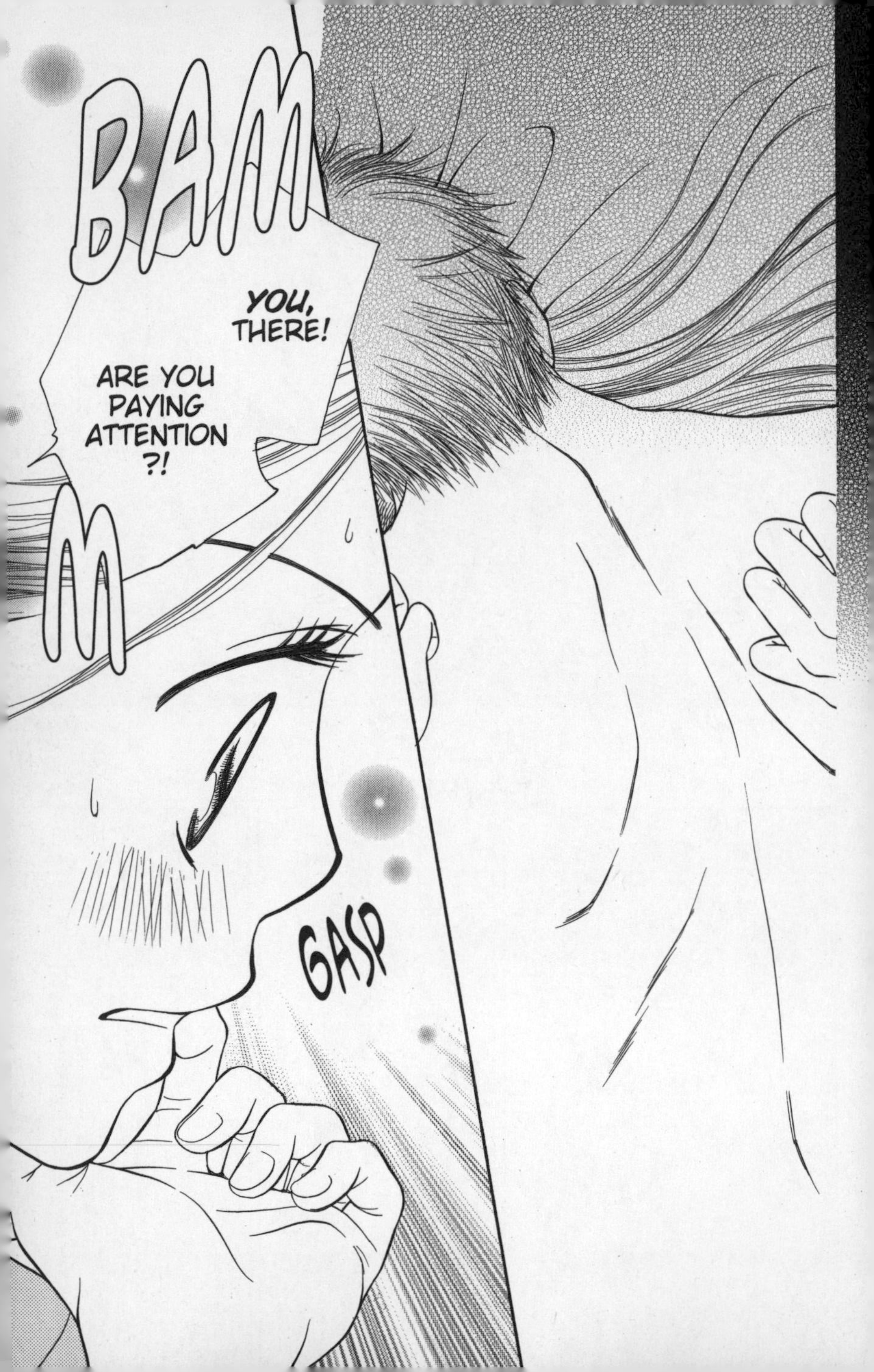
BAMM
YOU, THERE!
ARE YOU PAYING ATTENTION ?!
GASP

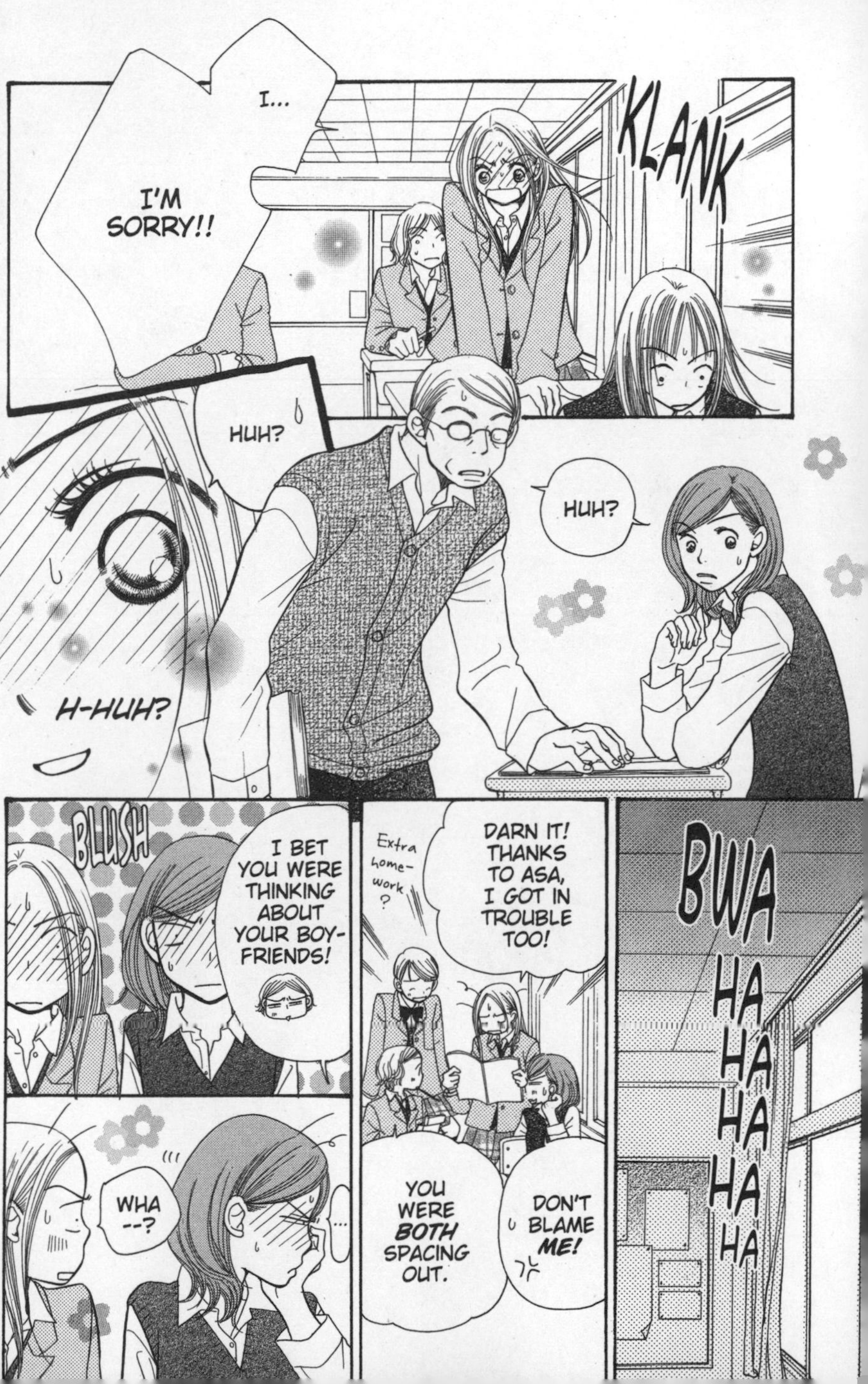
KLANK
I...
I'M SORRY!!
HUH?
HUH?
H-HUH?
BWA HA HA HA HA HA HA
DARN IT! THANKS TO ASA, I GOT IN TROUBLE TOO!
Extra home-work?
DON'T BLAME ME!
YOU WERE BOTH SPACING OUT.
BLUSH
I BET YOU WERE THINKING ABOUT YOUR BOY-FRIENDS!
...
WHA --?

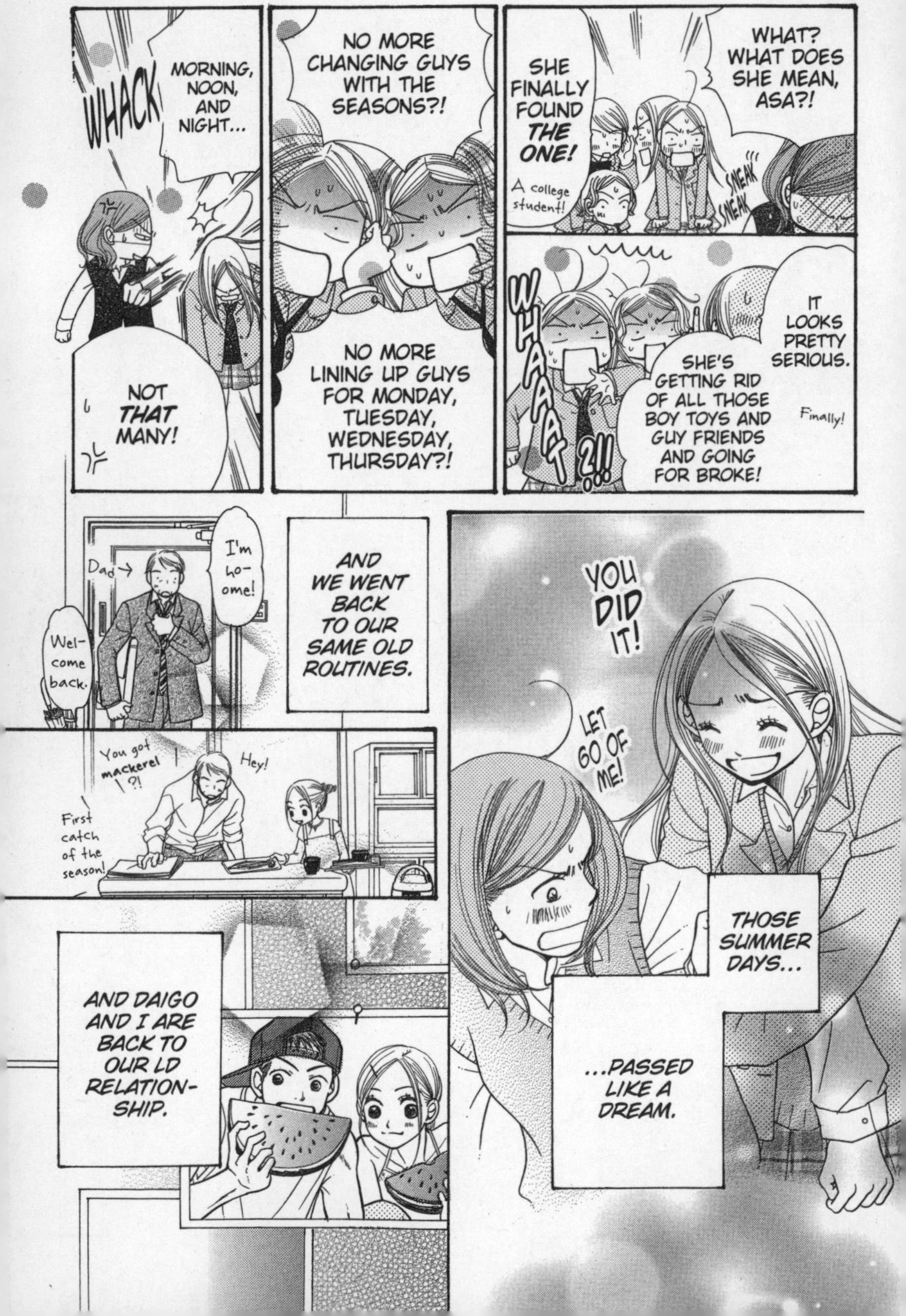
WHAT? WHAT DOES SHE MEAN, ASA?!
SHE FINALLY FOUND THE ONE!
A college student!
SNEAK SNEAK
IT LOOKS PRETTY SERIOUS.
WHAAAT?!!
SHE'S GETTING RID OF ALL THOSE BOY TOYS AND GUY FRIENDS AND GOING FOR BROKE!
Finally!
NO MORE CHANGING GUYS WITH THE SEASONS?!
NO MORE LINING UP GUYS FOR MONDAY, TUESDAY, WEDNESDAY, THURSDAY?!
MORNING, NOON, AND NIGHT...
WHACK
NOT THAT MANY!
YOU DID IT!
LET GO OF ME!
THOSE SUMMER DAYS...
...PASSED LIKE A DREAM.
AND WE WENT BACK TO OUR SAME OLD ROUTINES.
I'm ho-ome!
Dad
Wel-come back.
Hey!
You got mackerel?!
First catch of the season!
AND DAIGO AND I ARE BACK TO OUR LD RELATION-SHIP.

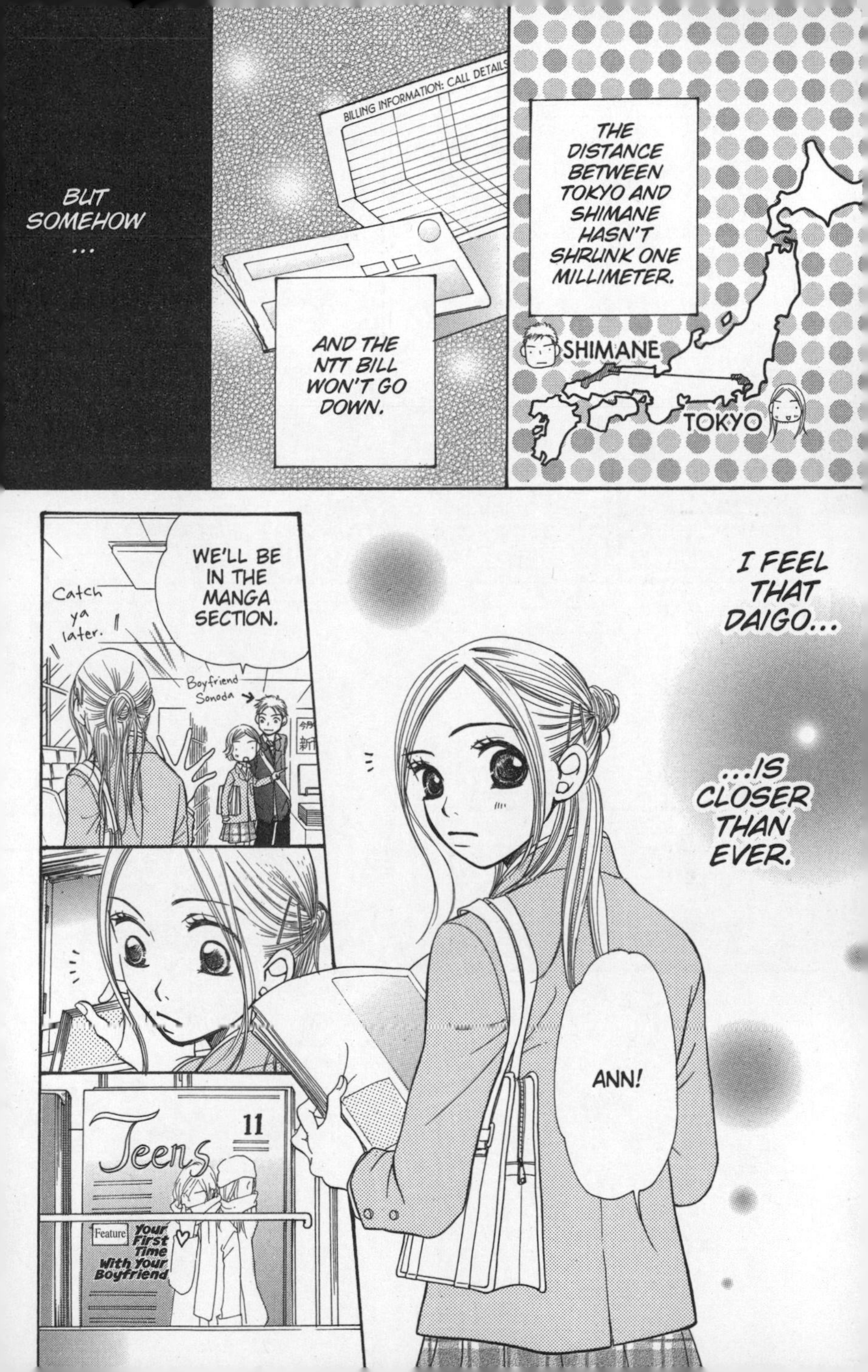
THE DISTANCE BETWEEN TOKYO AND SHIMANE HASN'T SHRUNK ONE MILLIMETER.
SHIMANE
TOKYO
BILLING INFORMATION: CALL DETAILS
AND THE NTT BILL WON'T GO DOWN.
BUT SOMEHOW ...
I FEEL THAT DAIGO...
...IS CLOSER THAN EVER.
ANN!
WE'LL BE IN THE MANGA SECTION.
Catch ya later.
Boyfriend Sonoda
Teens
11
Feature
Your First Time With Your Boyfriend

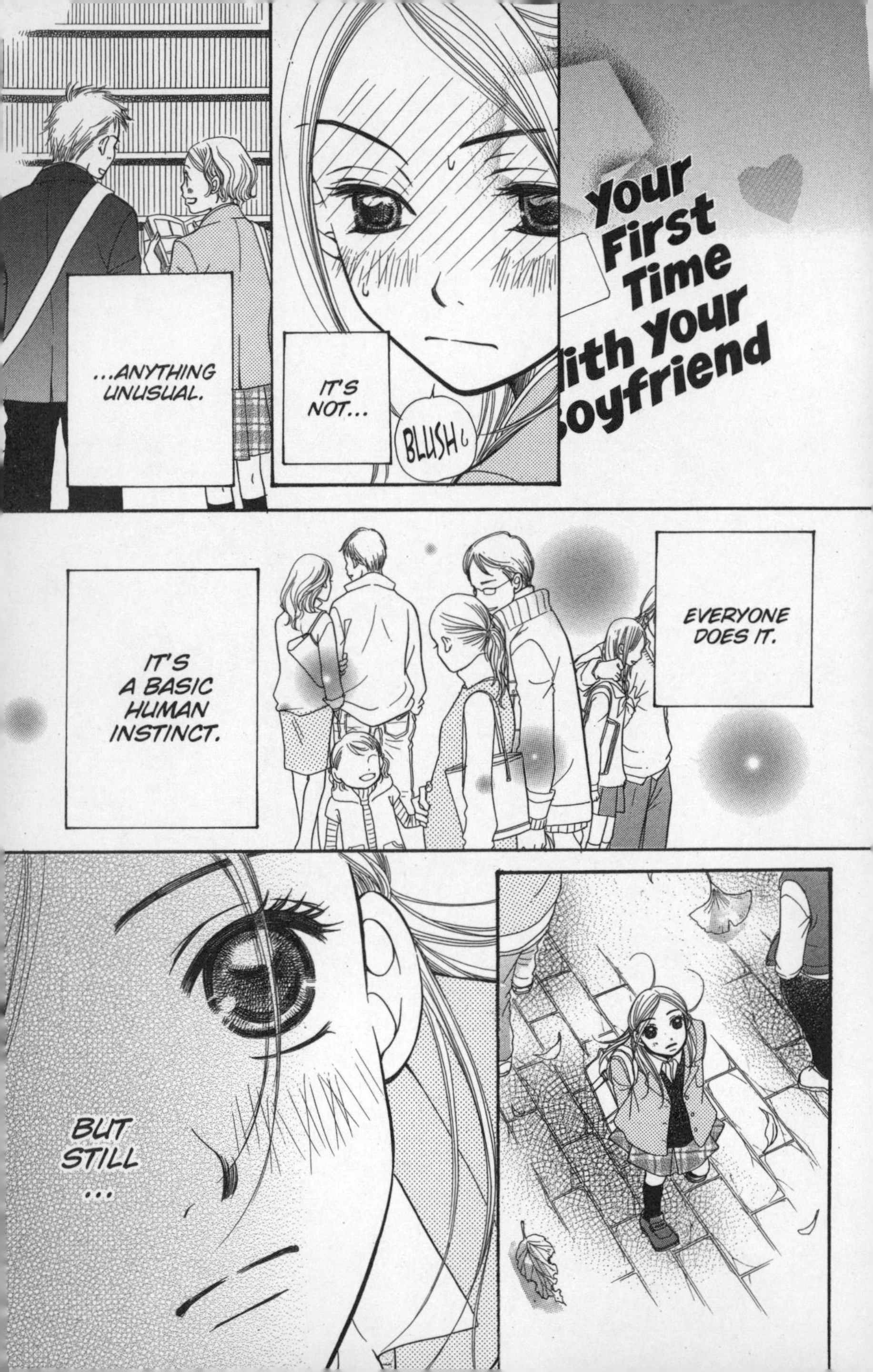
Your First Time
ith Your
oyfriend
IT'S NOT...
BLUSH
...ANYTHING UNUSUAL.
EVERYONE DOES IT.
IT'S A BASIC HUMAN INSTINCT.
BUT STILL ...

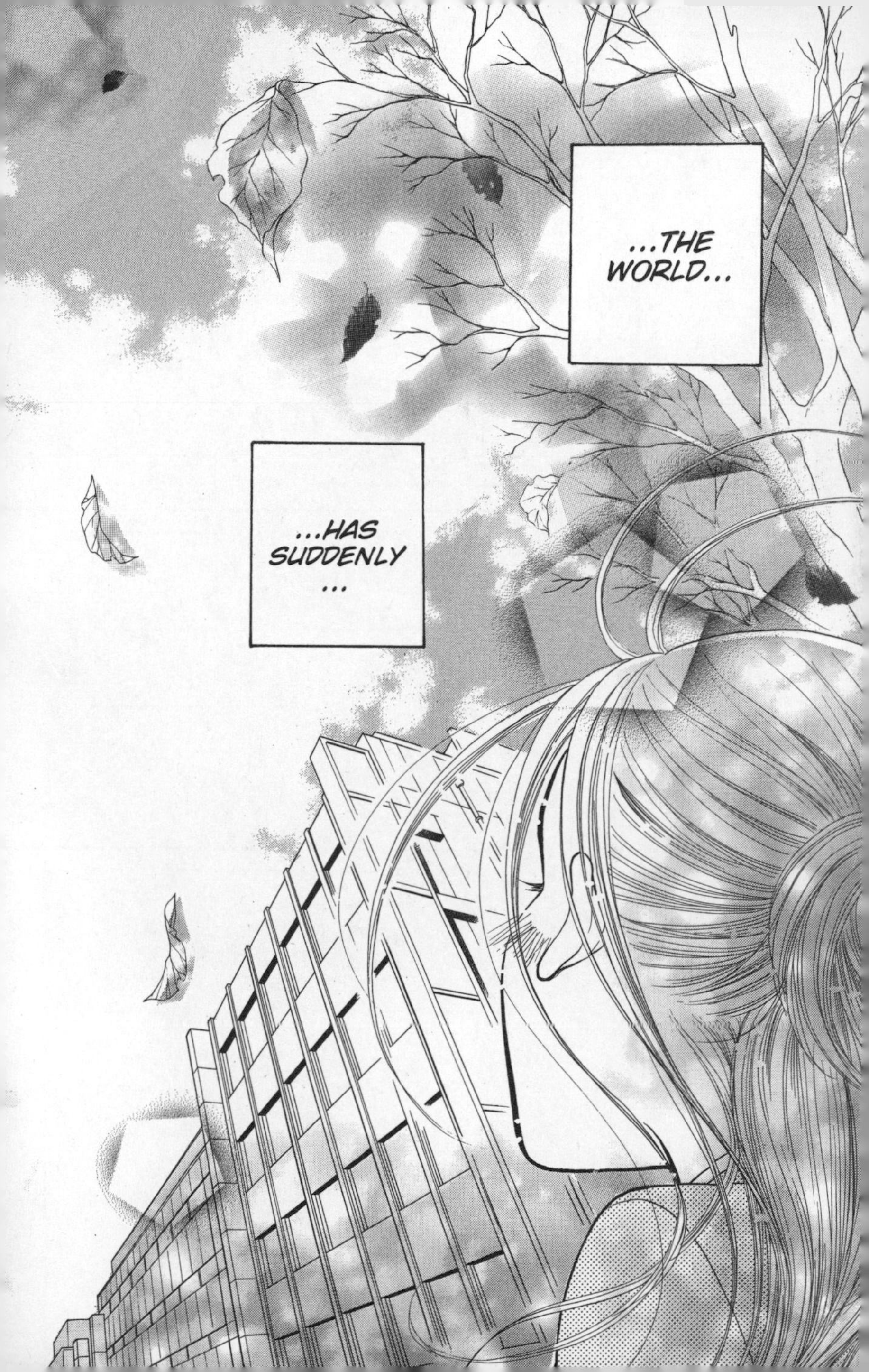
...THE WORLD...
...HAS SUDDENLY ...

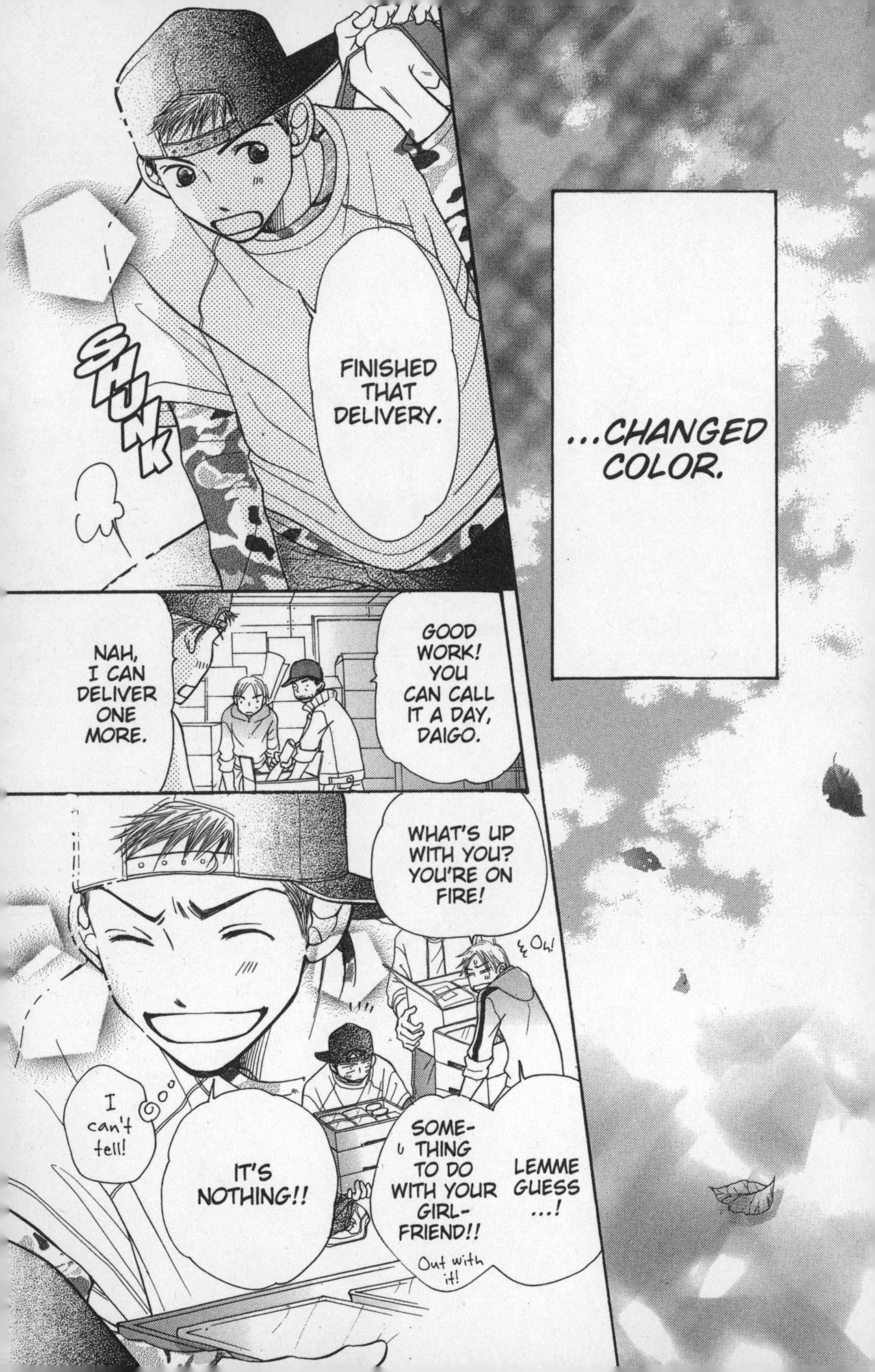
...CHANGED COLOR.
SHUNK
FINISHED THAT DELIVERY.
GOOD WORK! YOU CAN CALL IT A DAY, DAIGO.
NAH, I CAN DELIVER ONE MORE.
WHAT'S UP WITH YOU? YOU'RE ON FIRE!
Oh!
LEMME GUESS...!
SOME-THING TO DO WITH YOUR GIRL-FRIEND!!
Out with it!
IT'S NOTHING!!
I can't tell!

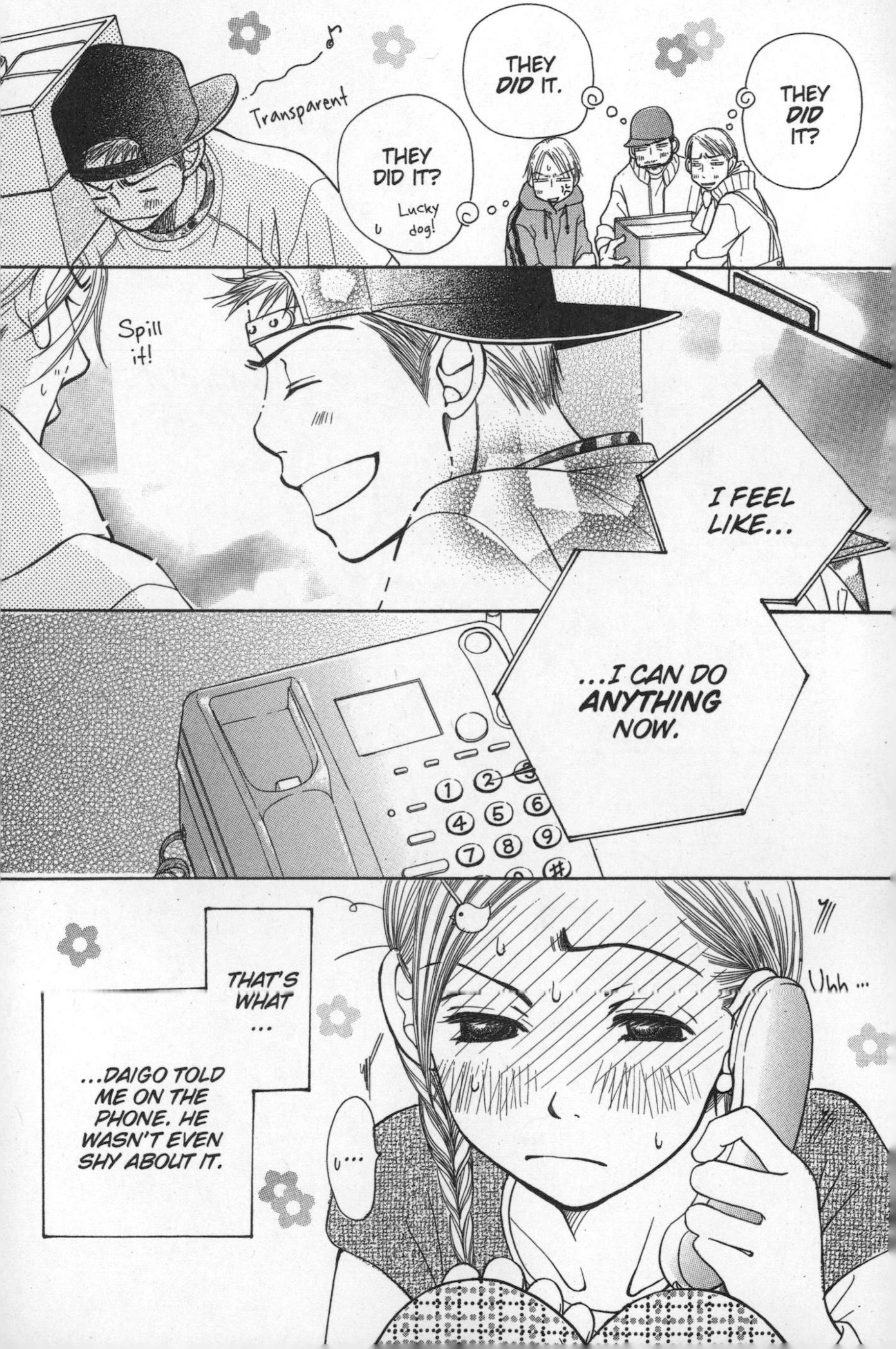
THEY DID IT?
THEY DID IT.
THEY DID IT?
Lucky dog!
Transparent
I FEEL LIKE...
Spill it!
...I CAN DO ANYTHING NOW.
Uhh ...
THAT'S WHAT ...
...DAIGO TOLD ME ON THE PHONE. HE WASN'T EVEN SHY ABOUT IT.

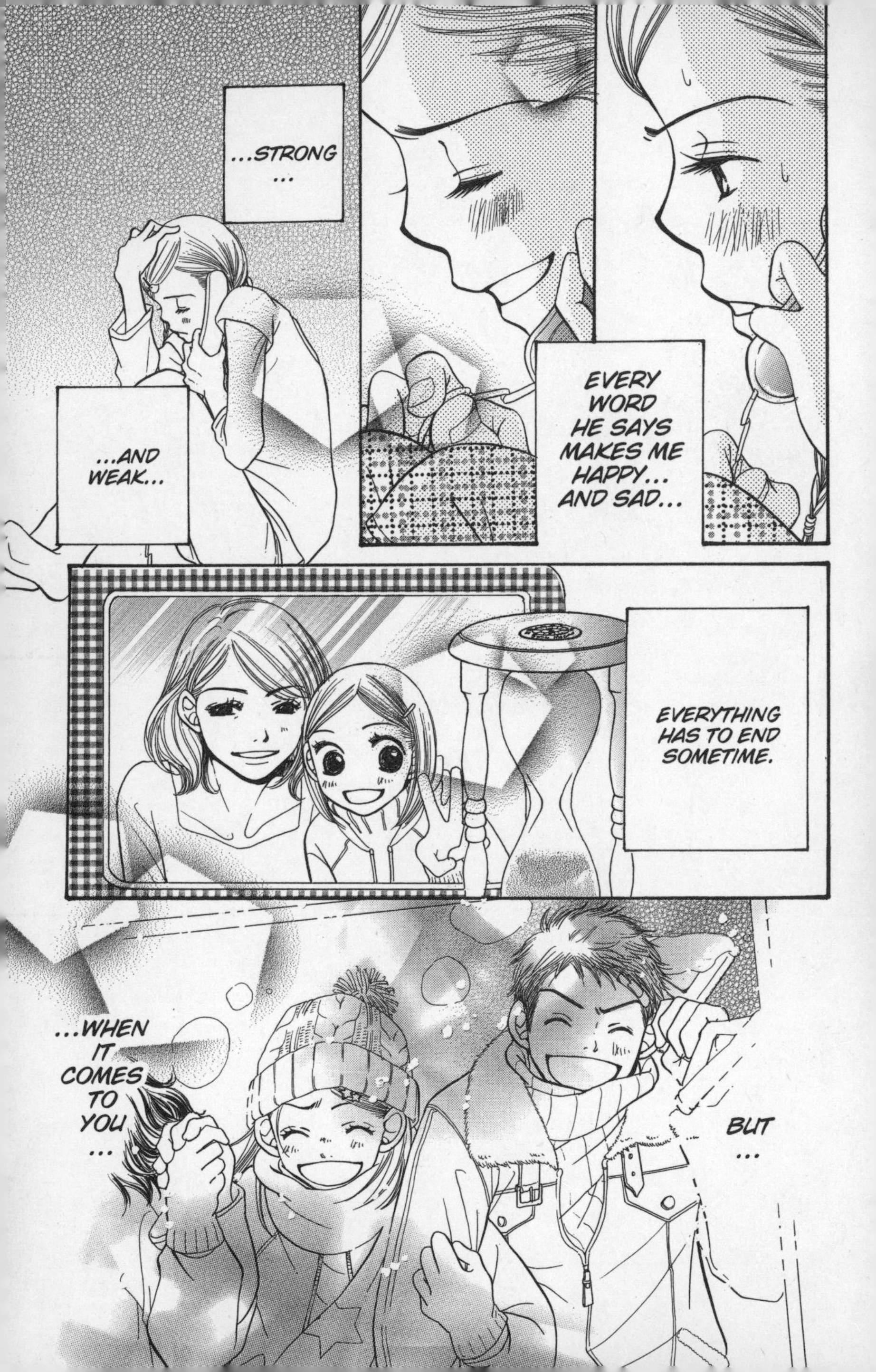
EVERY WORD HE SAYS MAKES ME HAPPY... AND SAD...
...STRONG...
...AND WEAK...
EVERYTHING HAS TO END SOMETIME.
BUT...
...WHEN IT COMES TO YOU...

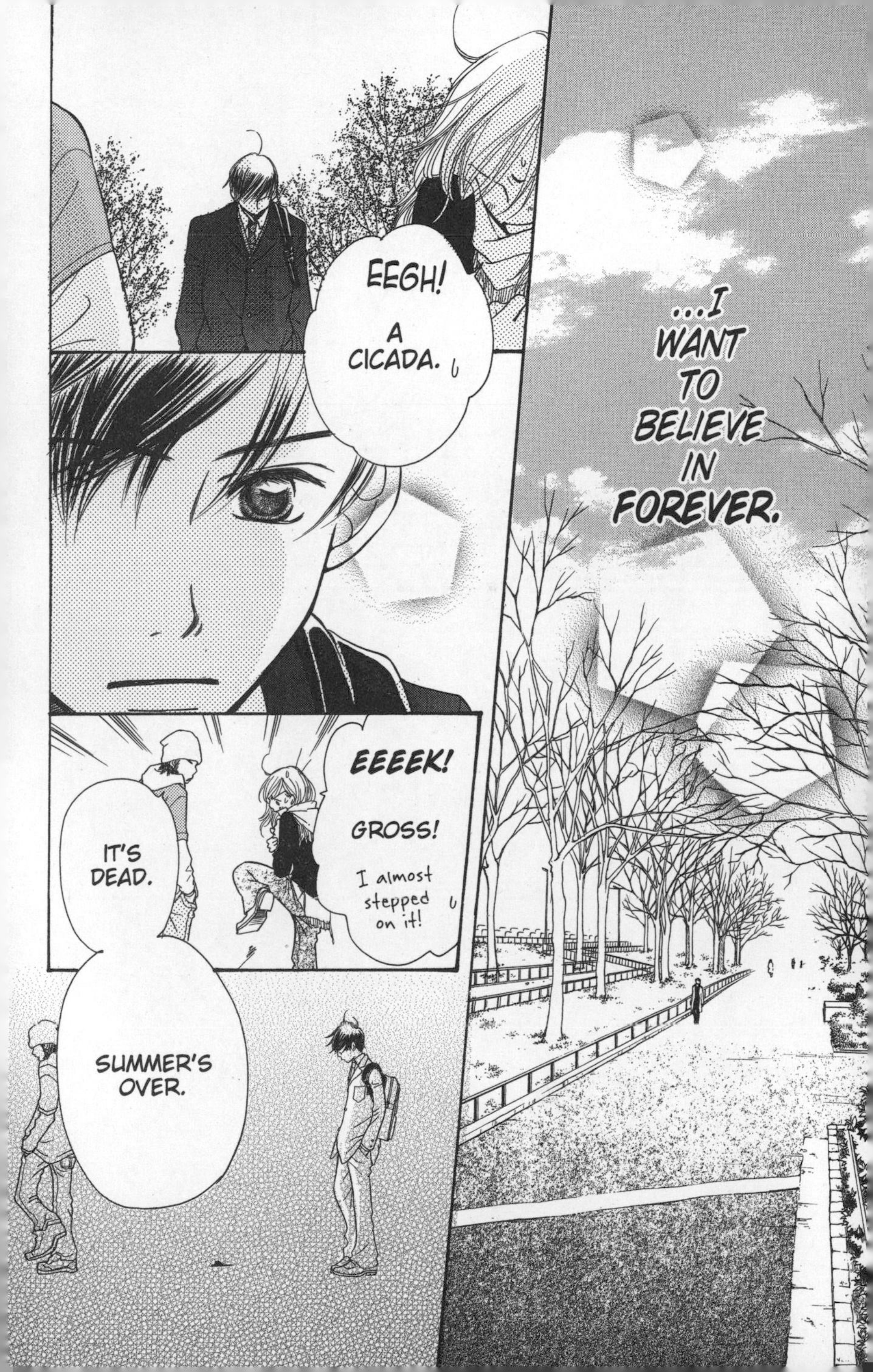
...I WANT TO BELIEVE IN FOREVER.
EEGH!
A CICADA.
EEEEK!
GROSS!
I almost stepped on it!
IT'S DEAD.
SUMMER'S OVER.

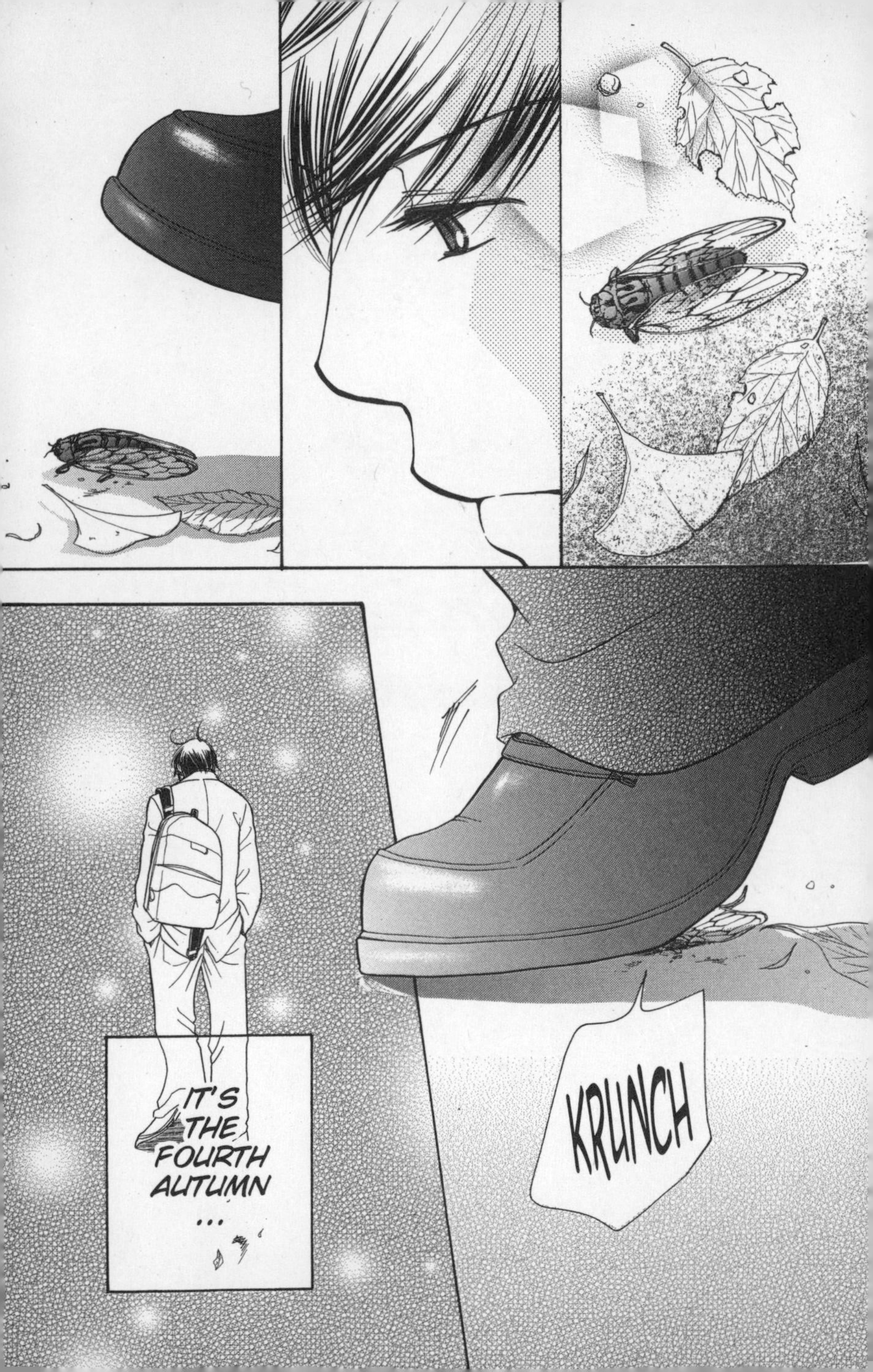
KRUNCH
IT'S THE FOURTH AUTUMN ...

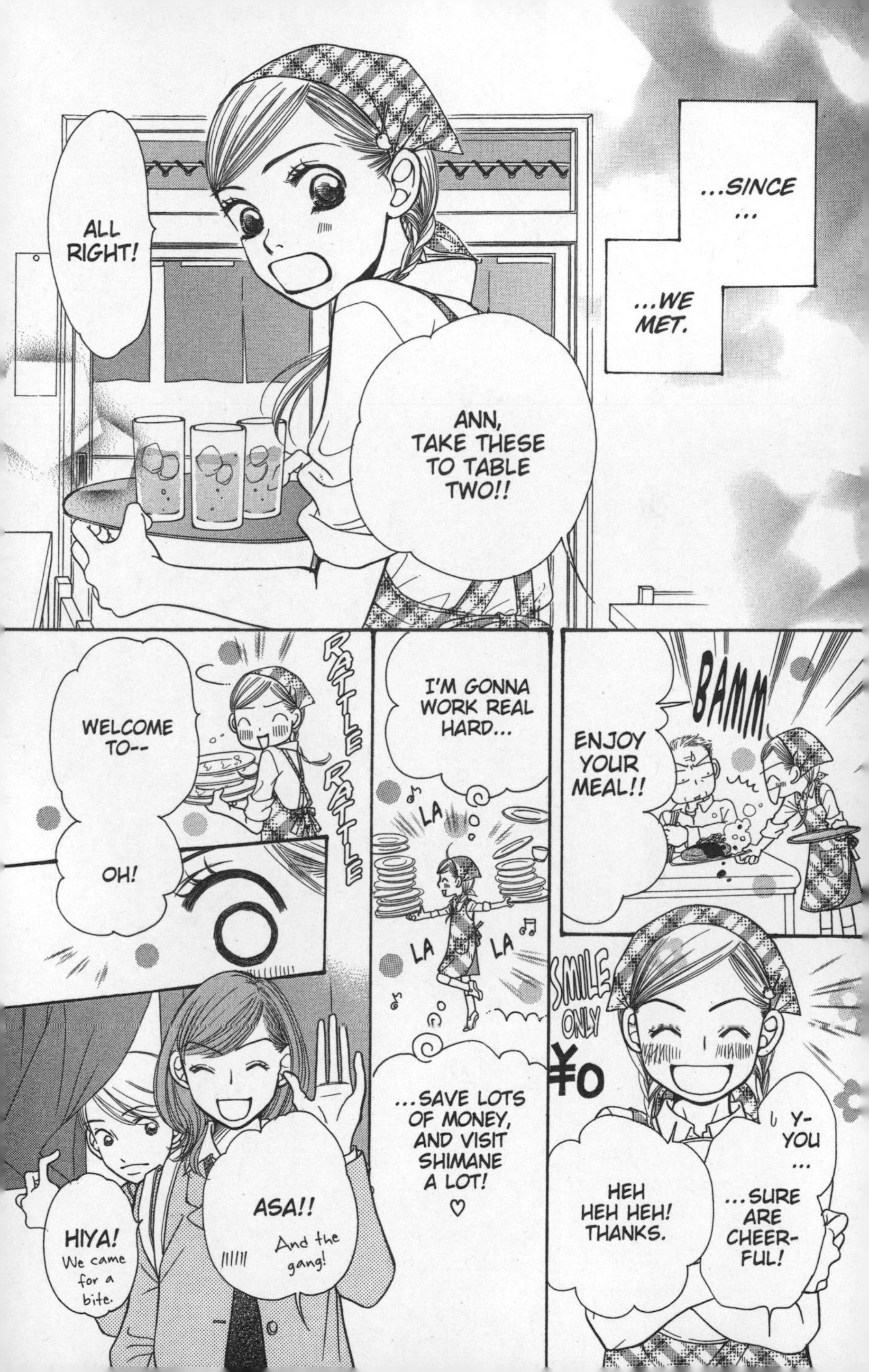
...SINCE
...
...WE MET.
ANN, TAKE THESE TO TABLE TWO!!
ALL RIGHT!
BAMM
ENJOY YOUR MEAL!!
SMILE ONLY ¥0
Y-YOU ...
...SURE ARE CHEERFUL!
HEH HEH HEH! THANKS.
I'M GONNA WORK REAL HARD...
LA
LA
LA
...SAVE LOTS OF MONEY, AND VISIT SHIMANE A LOT! ♡
WELCOME TO--
RATTLE RATTLE
OH!
ASA!!
And the gang!
HIYA! We came for a bite.

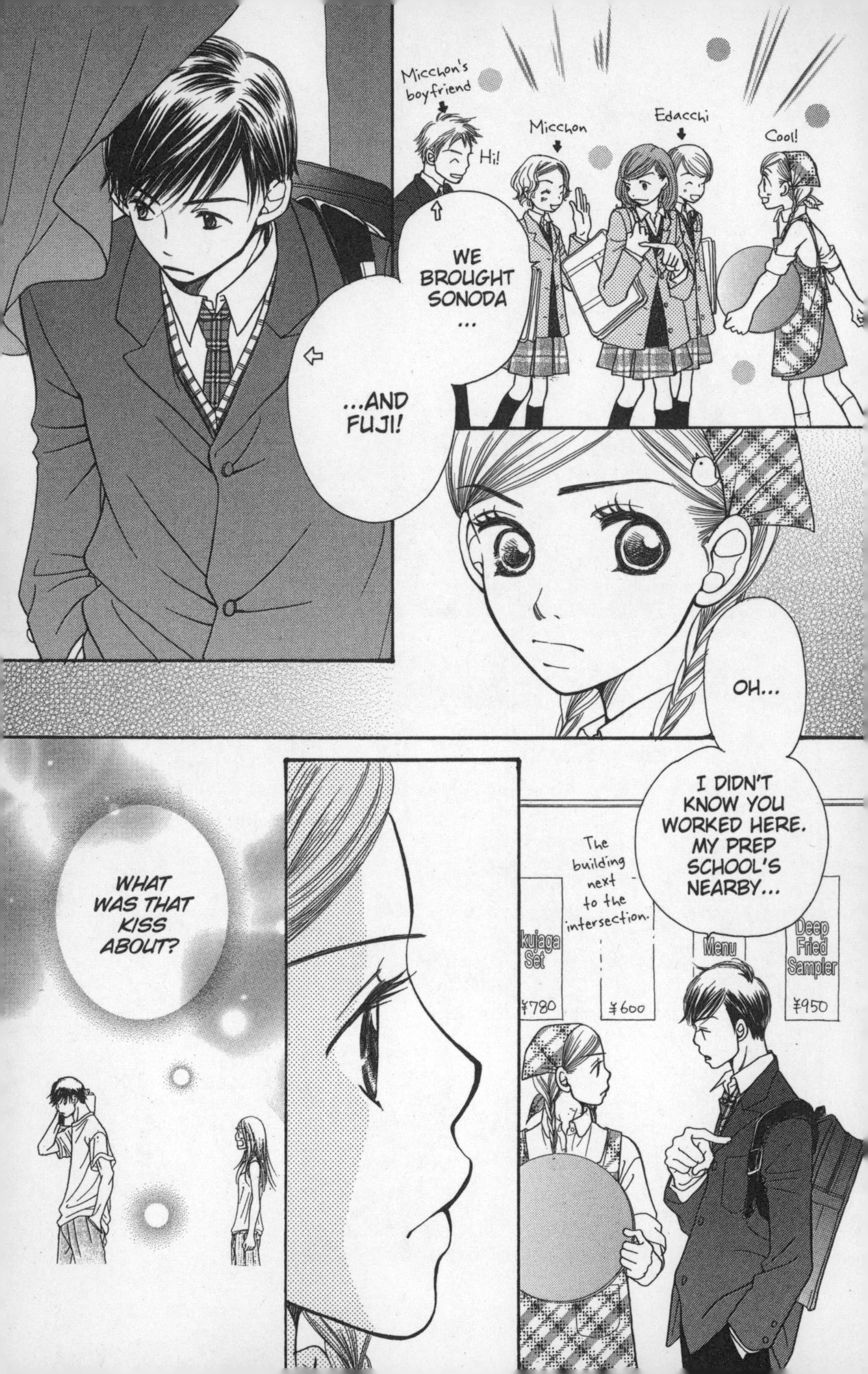

Cool!
Edacchi
Micchon
Hi!
Micchon's boyfriend
WE BROUGHT SONODA...
...AND FUJI!
OH...
I DIDN'T KNOW YOU WORKED HERE. MY PREP SCHOOL'S NEARBY...
Deep Fried Sampler ¥950
Menu
¥600
The building next to the intersection.
kujaga Set ¥780
WHAT WAS THAT KISS ABOUT?

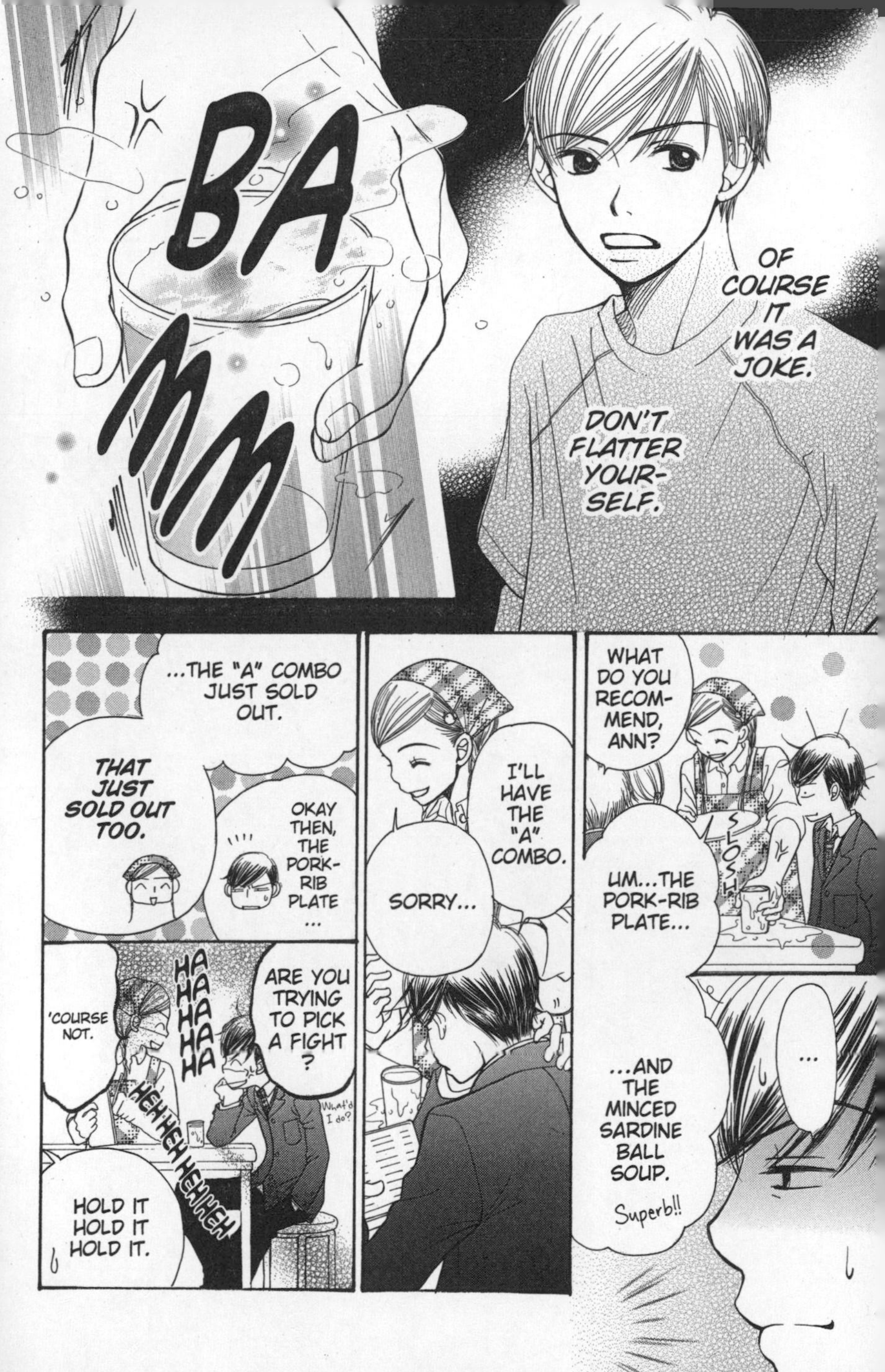
OF COURSE IT WAS A JOKE.
DON'T FLATTER YOURSELF.
BAMM
WHAT DO YOU RECOMMEND, ANN?
SLOSH
UM...THE PORK-RIB PLATE...
I'LL HAVE THE "A" COMBO.
SORRY...
...THE "A" COMBO JUST SOLD OUT.
OKAY THEN, THE PORK-RIB PLATE ...
THAT JUST SOLD OUT TOO.
...
...AND THE MINCED SARDINE BALL SOUP.
Superb!!
What'd I do?
ARE YOU TRYING TO PICK A FIGHT?
HAHAHAHAHAHA
'COURSE NOT.
HEH HEH HEH HEH HEH
HOLD IT HOLD IT HOLD IT.

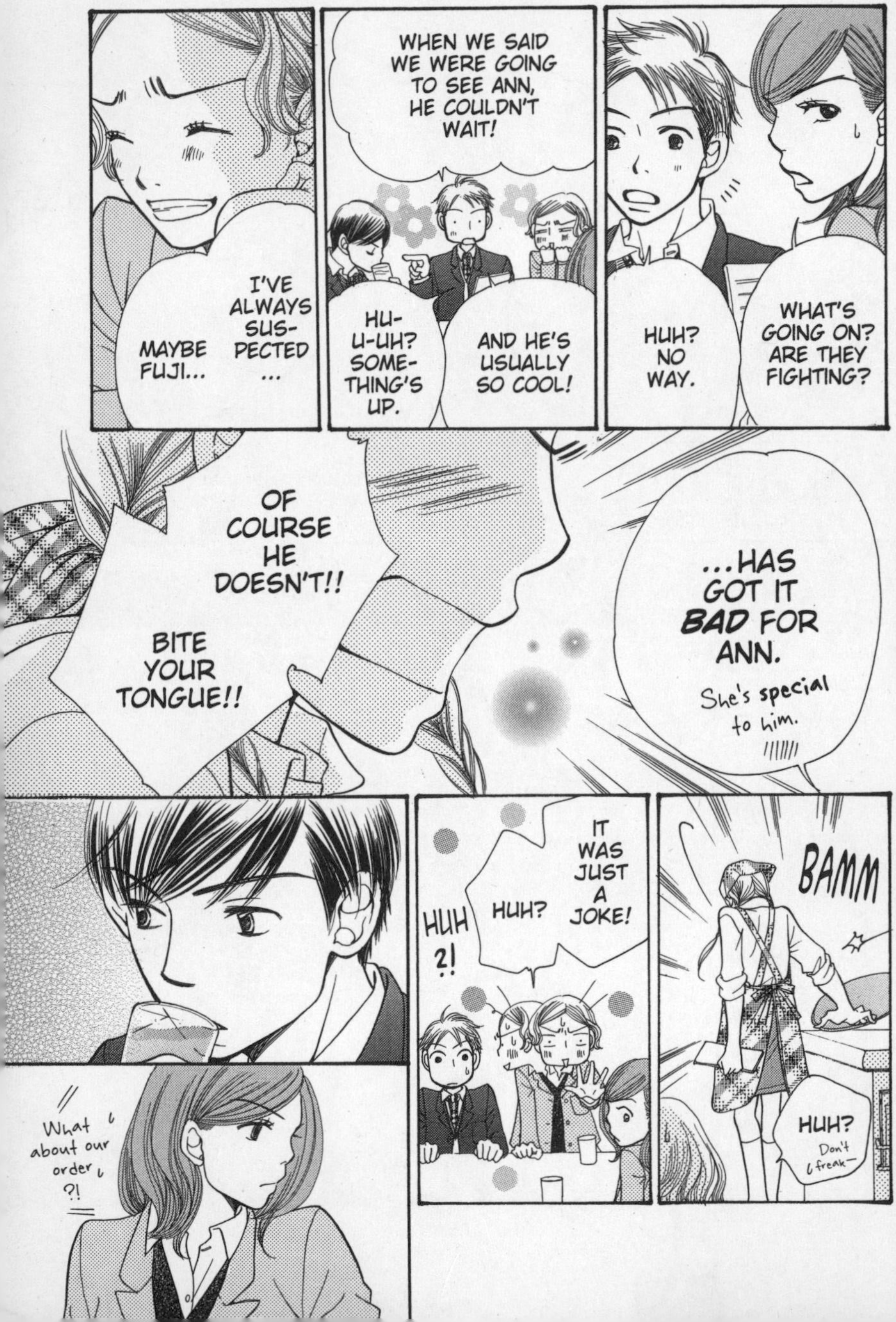
WHAT'S GOING ON? ARE THEY FIGHTING?
HUH? NO WAY.
WHEN WE SAID WE WERE GOING TO SEE ANN, HE COULDN'T WAIT!
AND HE'S USUALLY SO COOL!
HU-U-UH? SOME-THING'S UP.
I'VE ALWAYS SUS-PECTED ...
MAYBE FUJI...
...HAS GOT IT BAD FOR ANN.
She's special to him.
OF COURSE HE DOESN'T!!
BITE YOUR TONGUE!!
BAMM
HUH?
Don't freak—
IT WAS JUST A JOKE!
HUH?
HUH ?!
What about our order ?!

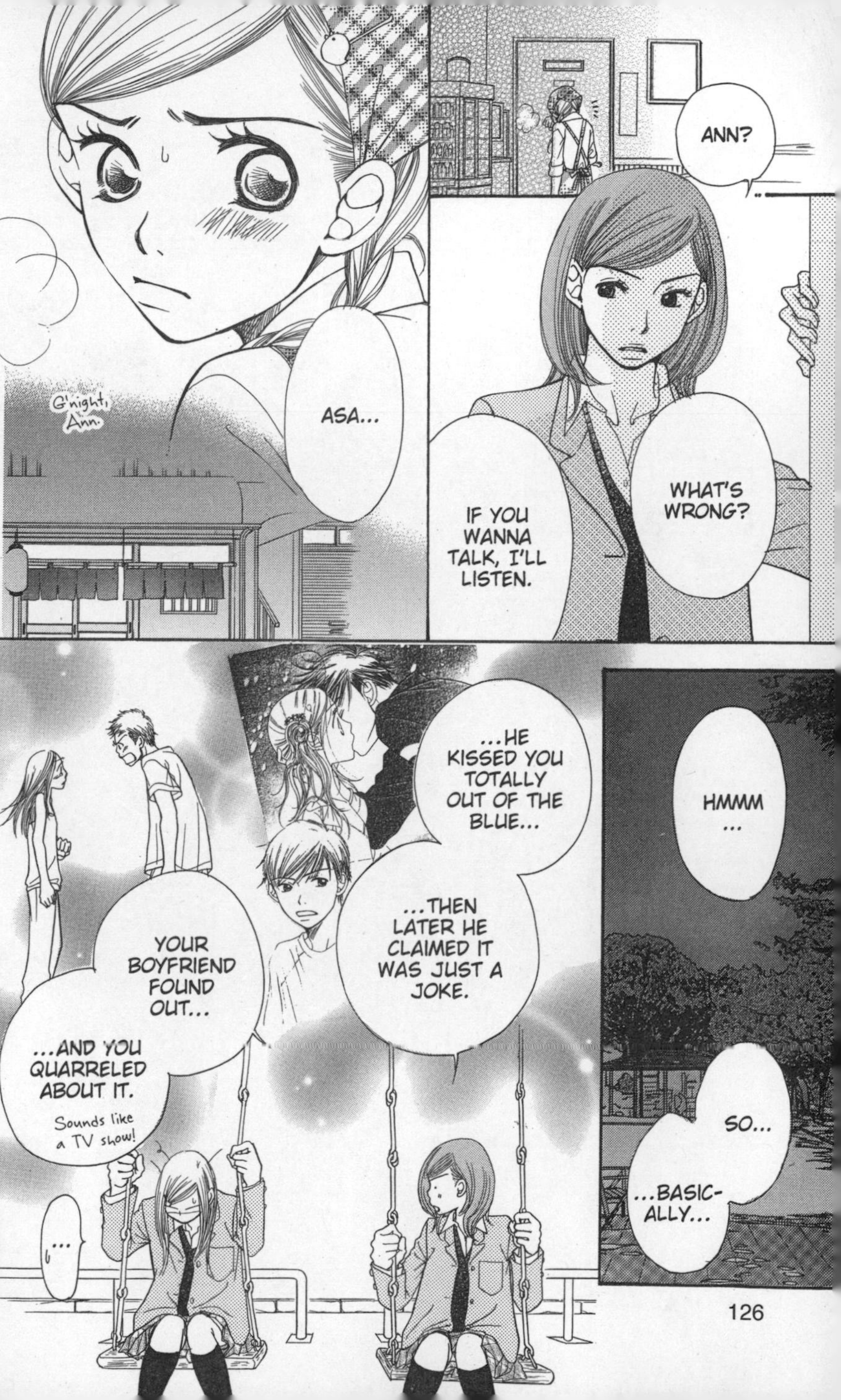
ANN?
WHAT'S WRONG?
IF YOU WANNA TALK, I'LL LISTEN.
ASA...
G'night, Ann.
HMMM ...
SO...
...BASIC-ALLY...
...HE KISSED YOU TOTALLY OUT OF THE BLUE...
...THEN LATER HE CLAIMED IT WAS JUST A JOKE.
YOUR BOYFRIEND FOUND OUT...
...AND YOU QUARRELED ABOUT IT.
Sounds like a TV show!
...

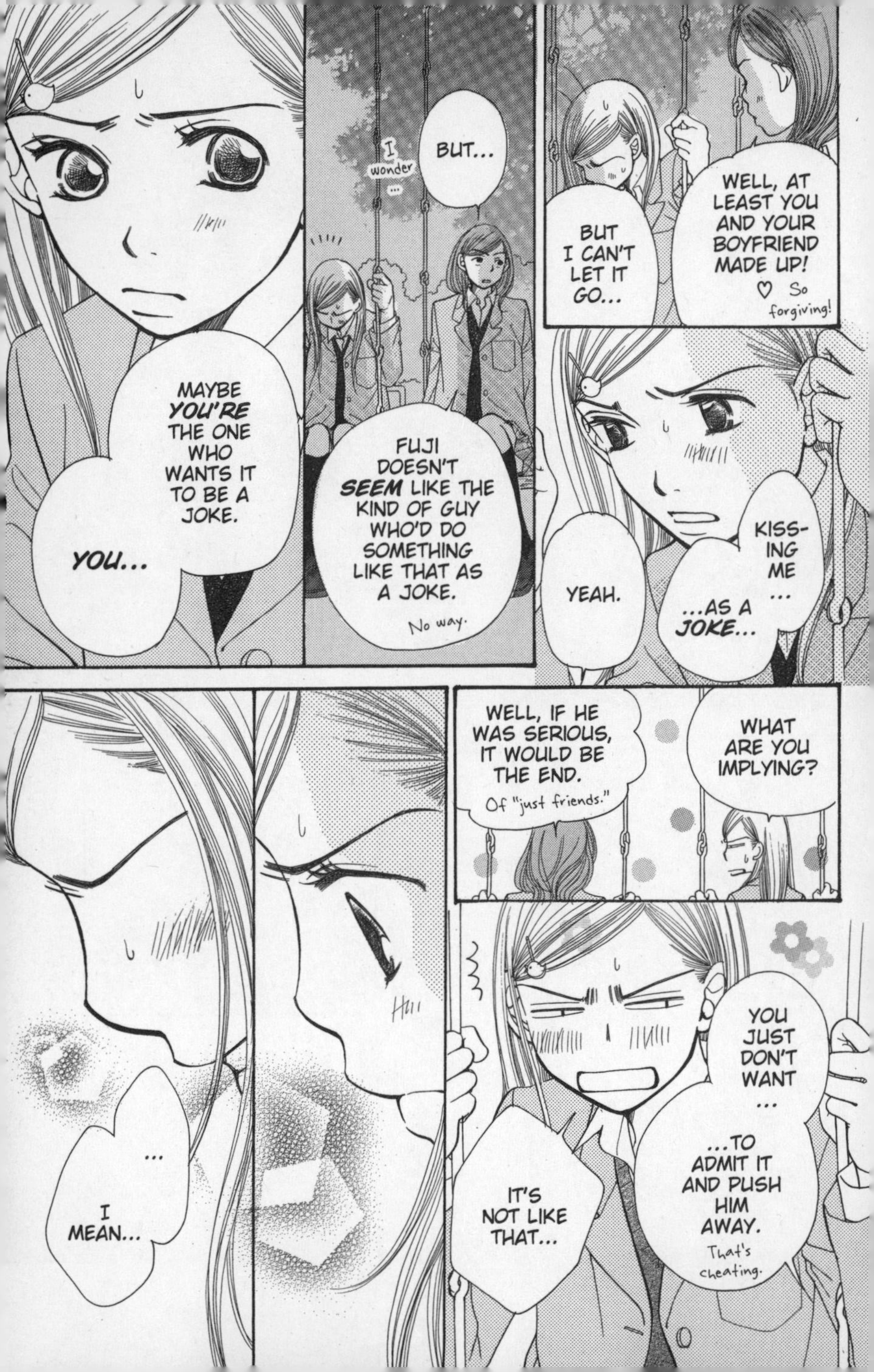
WELL, AT LEAST YOU AND YOUR BOYFRIEND MADE UP! ♡
So forgiving!
BUT I CAN'T LET IT GO...
KISSING ME...
...AS A JOKE...
YEAH.
BUT...
I wonder...
FUJI DOESN'T SEEM LIKE THE KIND OF GUY WHO'D DO SOMETHING LIKE THAT AS A JOKE.
No way.
MAYBE YOU'RE THE ONE WHO WANTS IT TO BE A JOKE.
YOU...
WHAT ARE YOU IMPLYING?
WELL, IF HE WAS SERIOUS, IT WOULD BE THE END.
Of "just friends."
YOU JUST DON'T WANT...
...TO ADMIT IT AND PUSH HIM AWAY.
That's cheating.
IT'S NOT LIKE THAT...
... I MEAN...

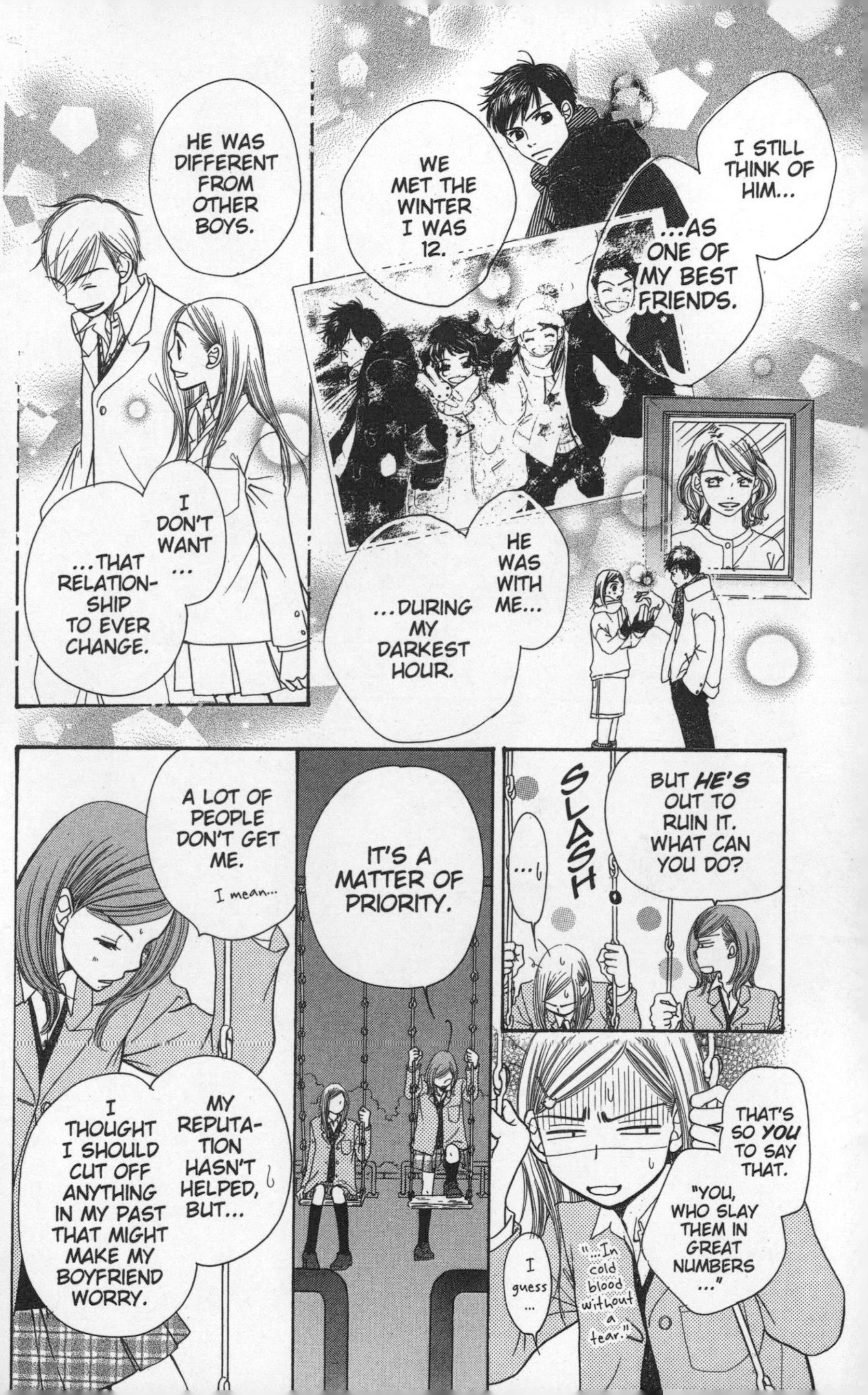
I STILL THINK OF HIM...
...AS ONE OF MY BEST FRIENDS.
WE MET THE WINTER I WAS 12.
HE WAS WITH ME...
...DURING MY DARKEST HOUR.
HE WAS DIFFERENT FROM OTHER BOYS.
I DON'T WANT...
...THAT RELATIONSHIP TO EVER CHANGE.
BUT ***HE'S*** OUT TO RUIN IT. WHAT CAN YOU DO?
SLASH
...!
THAT'S SO ***YOU*** TO SAY THAT.
"YOU, WHO SLAY THEM IN GREAT NUMBERS..."
"...In cold blood without a tear."
I guess...
IT'S A MATTER OF PRIORITY.
A LOT OF PEOPLE DON'T GET ME.
I mean...
MY REPUTATION HASN'T HELPED, BUT...
I THOUGHT I SHOULD CUT OFF ANYTHING IN MY PAST THAT MIGHT MAKE MY BOYFRIEND WORRY.

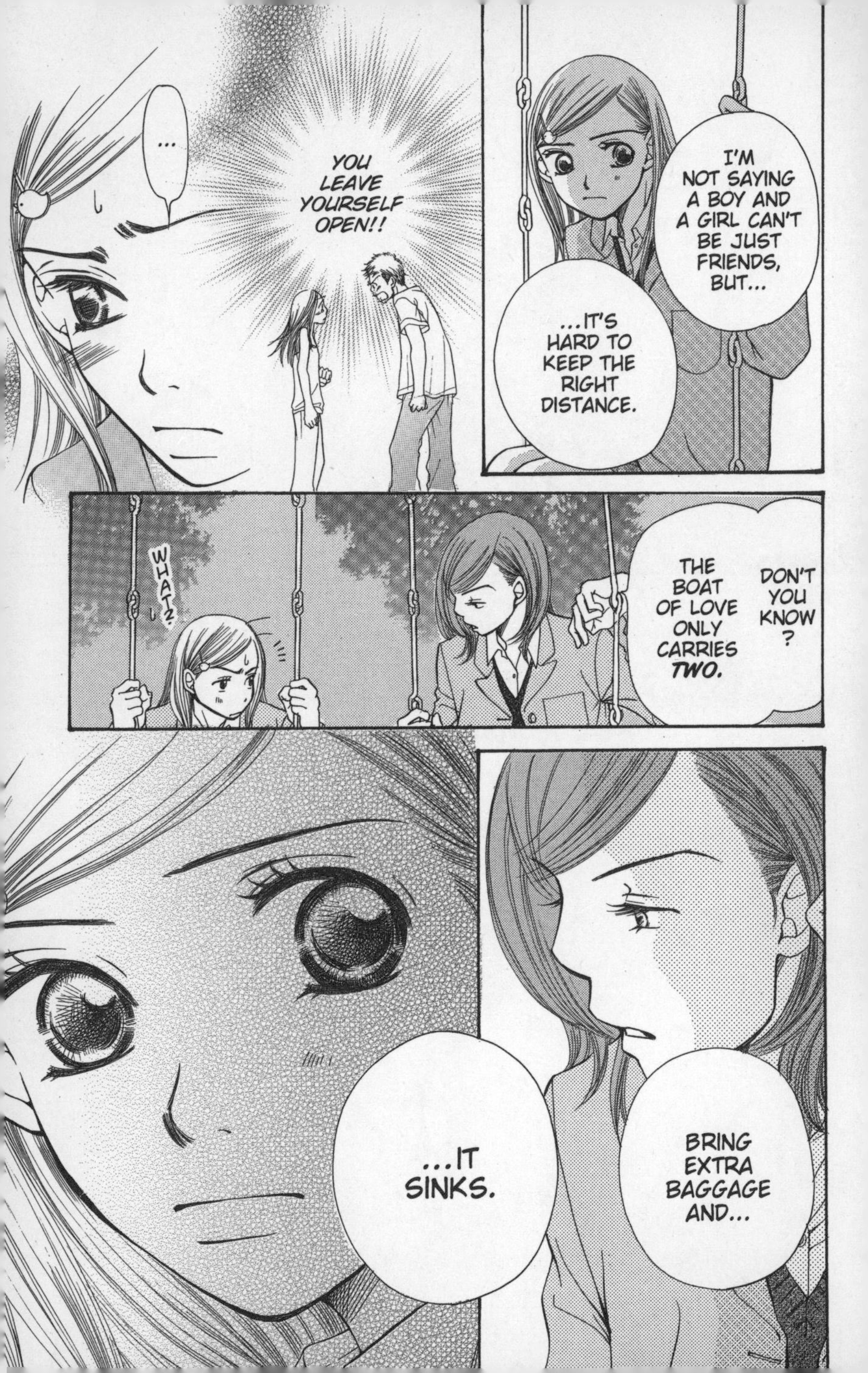
I'M NOT SAYING A BOY AND A GIRL CAN'T BE JUST FRIENDS, BUT...
...IT'S HARD TO KEEP THE RIGHT DISTANCE.
YOU LEAVE YOURSELF OPEN!!
...
DON'T YOU KNOW?
THE BOAT OF LOVE ONLY CARRIES TWO.
WHAT?
BRING EXTRA BAGGAGE AND...
...IT SINKS.

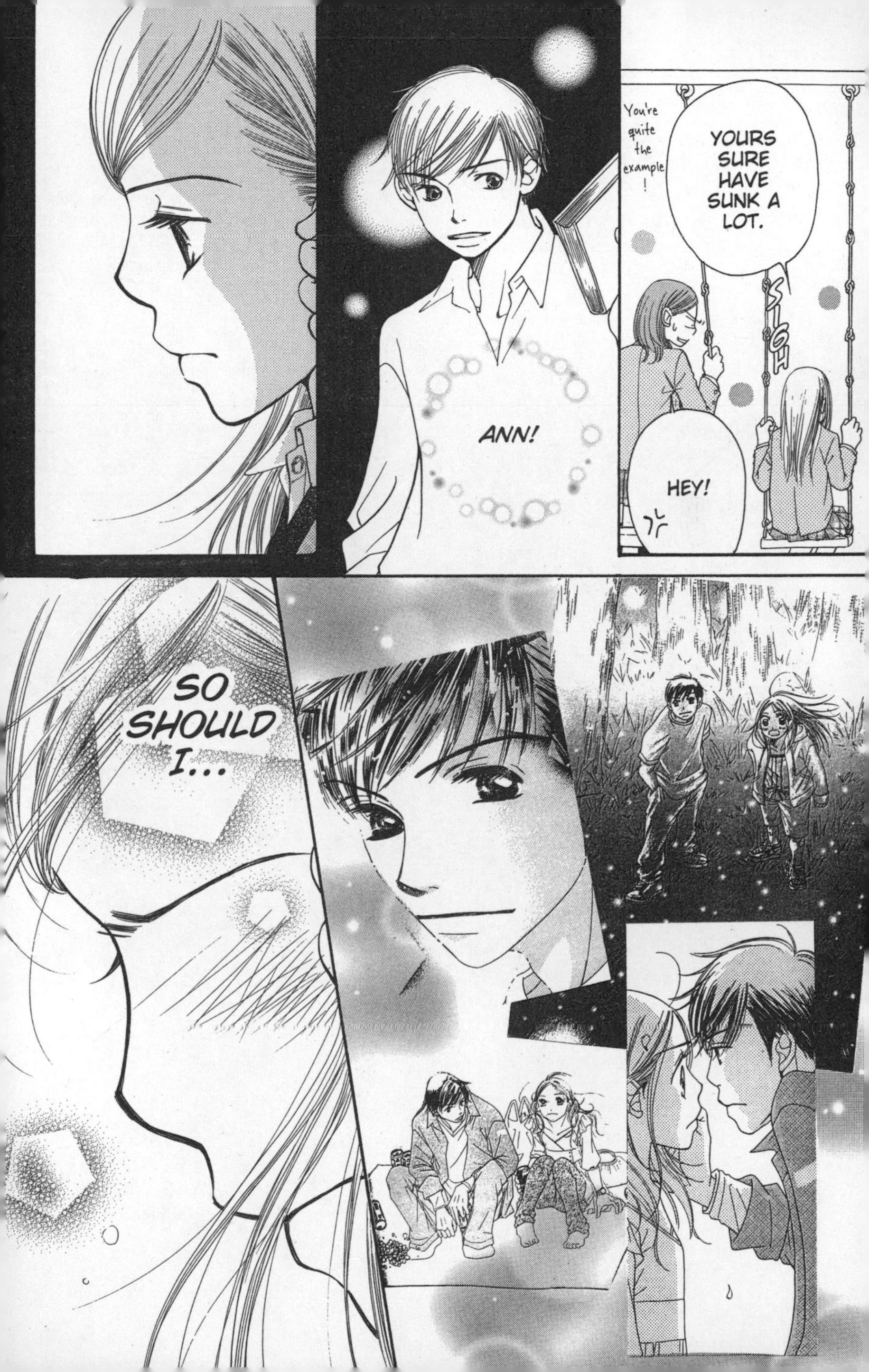
YOURS SURE HAVE SUNK A LOT.
You're quite the example!
SIGH
HEY!
ANN!
SO SHOULD I...

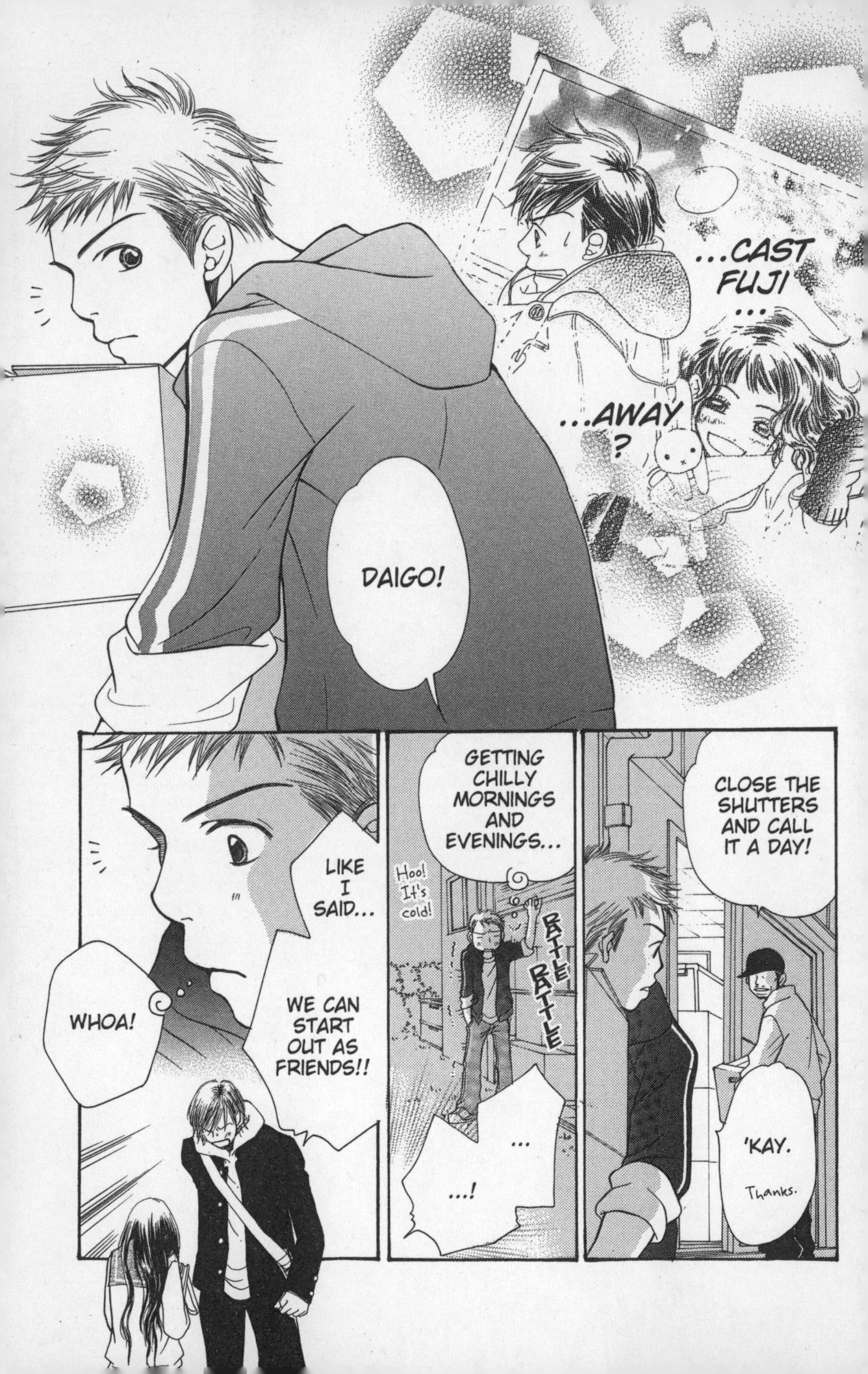
...CAST FUJI ...
...AWAY ?
DAIGO!
CLOSE THE SHUTTERS AND CALL IT A DAY!
'KAY.
Thanks.
GETTING CHILLY MORNINGS AND EVENINGS...
Hoo! It's cold!
RATTLE RATTLE
...
...!
LIKE I SAID...
WE CAN START OUT AS FRIENDS!!
WHOA!

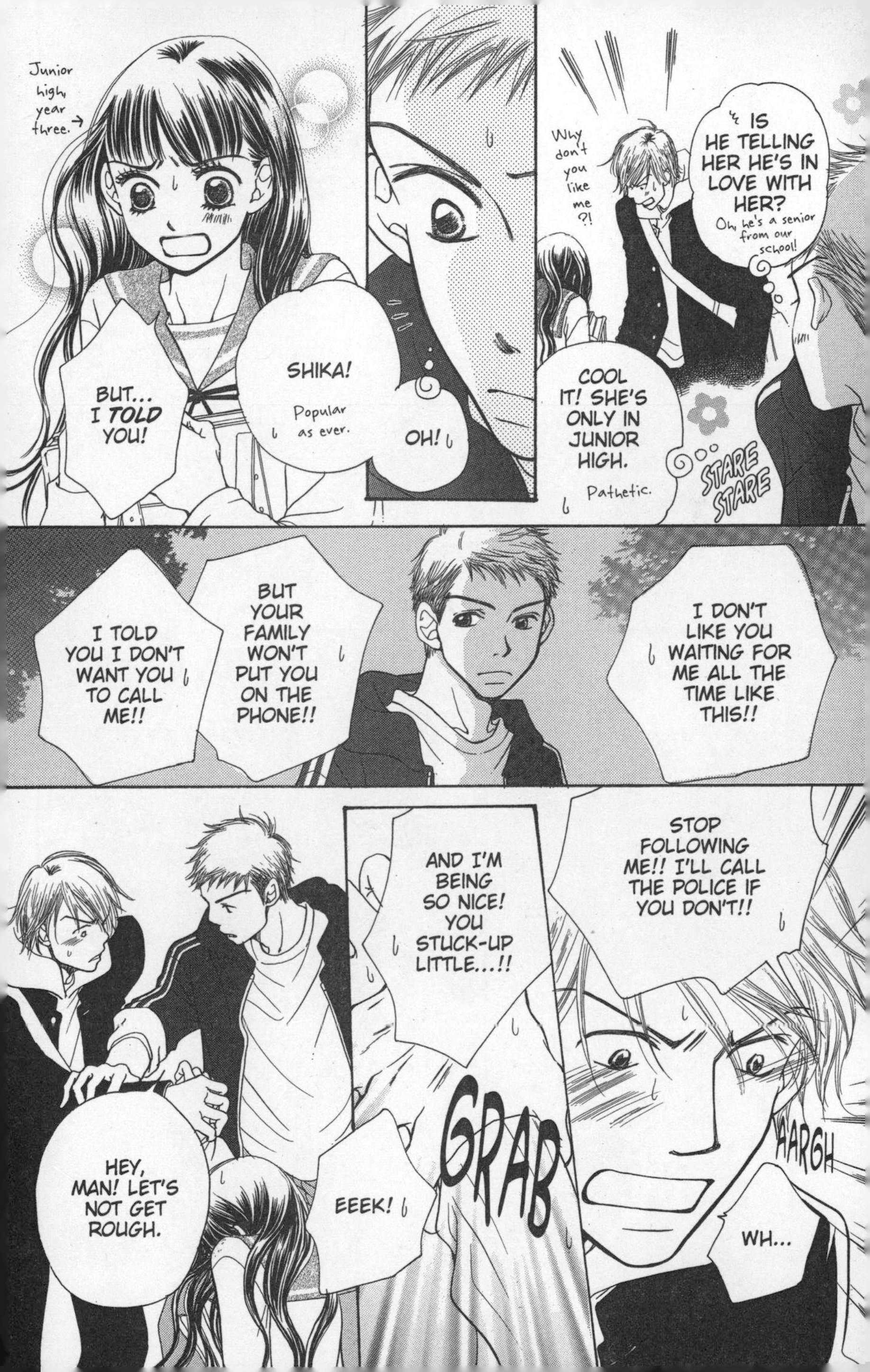
IS HE TELLING HER HE'S IN LOVE WITH HER?
Oh, he's a senior from our school!
Why don't you like me ?!
STARE STARE
COOL IT! SHE'S ONLY IN JUNIOR HIGH.
Pathetic.
OH!
SHIKA!
Popular as ever.
Junior high, year three.
BUT... I *TOLD* YOU!
I DON'T LIKE YOU WAITING FOR ME ALL THE TIME LIKE THIS!!
BUT YOUR FAMILY WON'T PUT YOU ON THE PHONE!!
I TOLD YOU I DON'T WANT YOU TO CALL ME!!
STOP FOLLOWING ME!! I'LL CALL THE POLICE IF YOU DON'T!!
HARGH
WH...
AND I'M BEING SO NICE! YOU STUCK-UP LITTLE...!!
GRAB
EEEK!
HEY, MAN! LET'S NOT GET ROUGH.

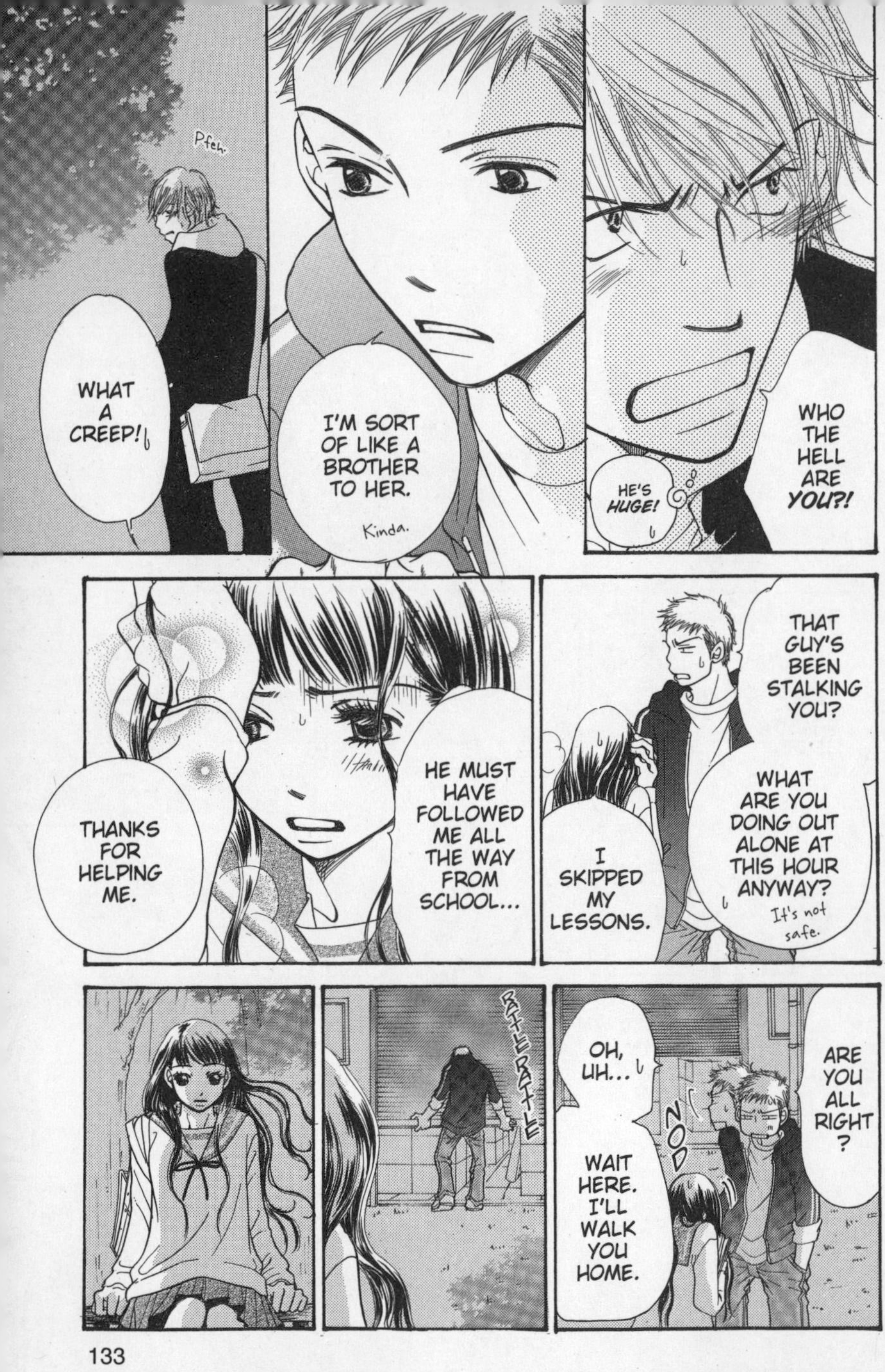
WHO THE HELL ARE YOU?!
HE'S HUGE!
I'M SORT OF LIKE A BROTHER TO HER.
Kinda.
Pfeh.
WHAT A CREEP!
THAT GUY'S BEEN STALKING YOU?
WHAT ARE YOU DOING OUT ALONE AT THIS HOUR ANYWAY?
It's not safe.
I SKIPPED MY LESSONS.
HE MUST HAVE FOLLOWED ME ALL THE WAY FROM SCHOOL...
THANKS FOR HELPING ME.
ARE YOU ALL RIGHT?
OH, UH...
NOD
WAIT HERE. I'LL WALK YOU HOME.
RATTLE RATTLE

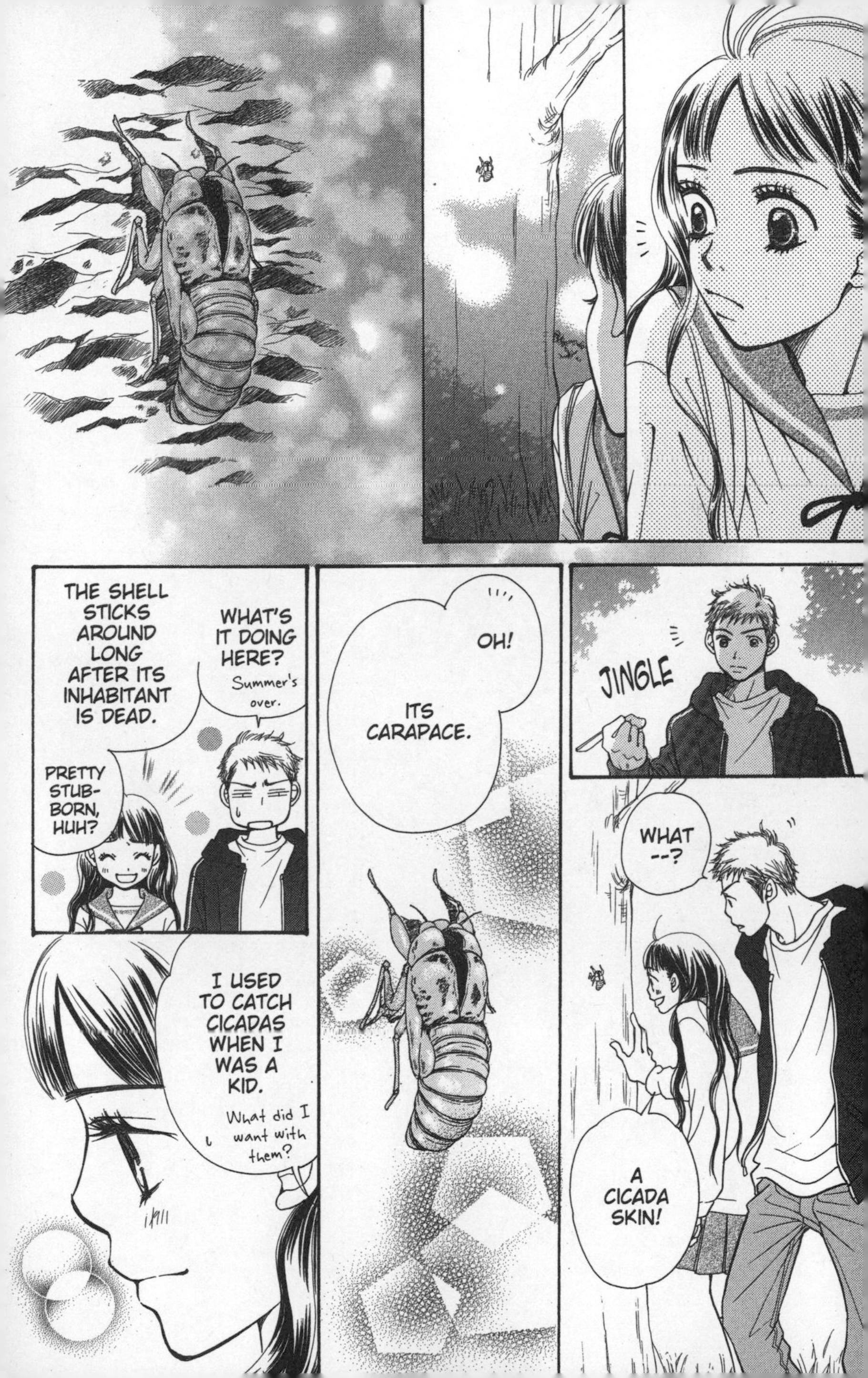
JINGLE
WHAT --?
A CICADA SKIN!
OH!
ITS CARAPACE.
WHAT'S IT DOING HERE?
Summer's over.
THE SHELL STICKS AROUND LONG AFTER ITS INHABITANT IS DEAD.
PRETTY STUB-BORN, HUH?
I USED TO CATCH CICADAS WHEN I WAS A KID.
What did I want with them?

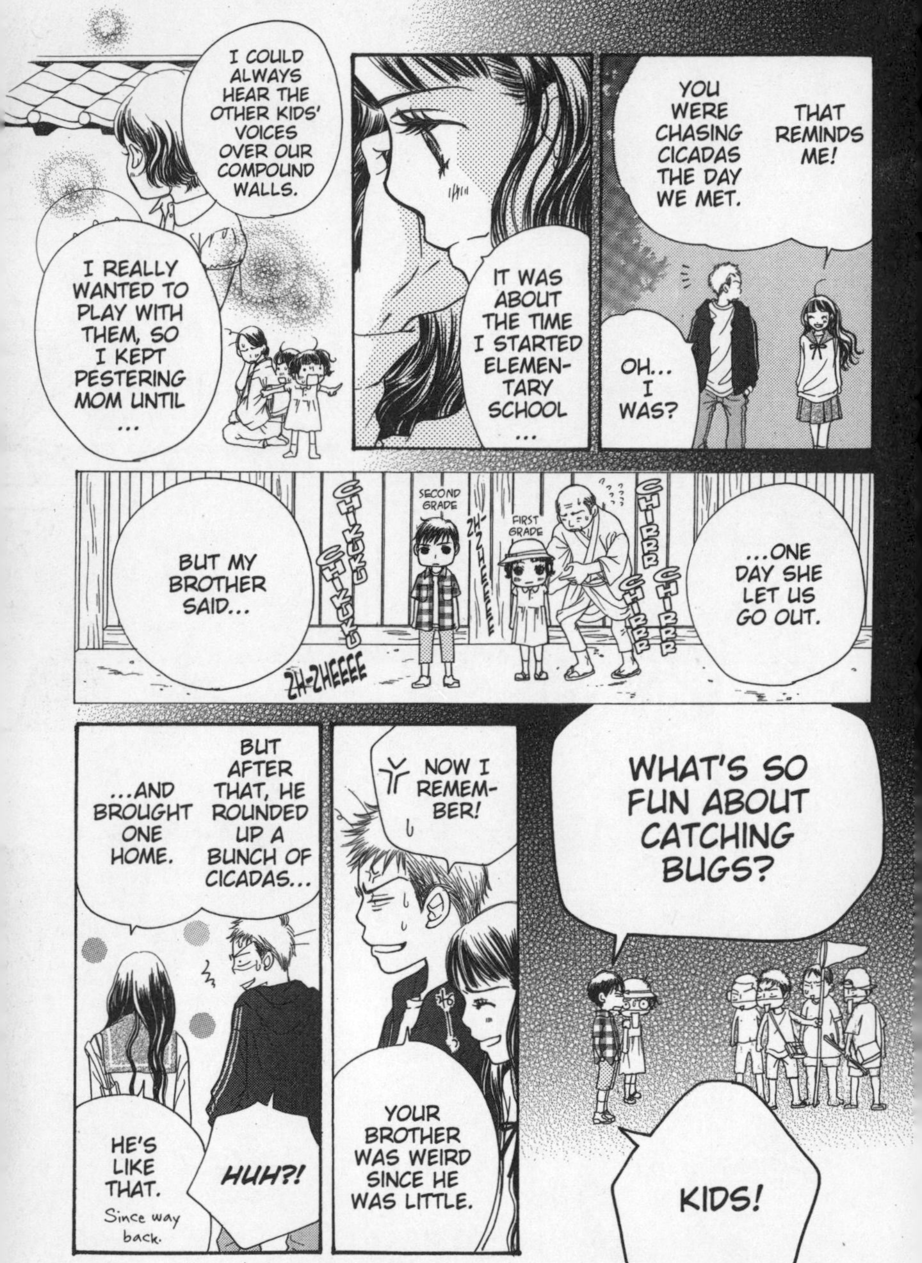
THAT REMINDS ME!
YOU WERE CHASING CICADAS THE DAY WE MET.
OH... I WAS?
IT WAS ABOUT THE TIME I STARTED ELEMENTARY SCHOOL...
I COULD ALWAYS HEAR THE OTHER KIDS' VOICES OVER OUR COMPOUND WALLS.
I REALLY WANTED TO PLAY WITH THEM, SO I KEPT PESTERING MOM UNTIL...
...ONE DAY SHE LET US GO OUT.
CHIRRR
FIRST GRADE
SECOND GRADE
BUT MY BROTHER SAID...
WHAT'S SO FUN ABOUT CATCHING BUGS?
KIDS!
NOW I REMEMBER!
YOUR BROTHER WAS WEIRD SINCE HE WAS LITTLE.
BUT AFTER THAT, HE ROUNDED UP A BUNCH OF CICADAS...
...AND BROUGHT ONE HOME.
HUH?!
HE'S LIKE THAT.
Since way back.

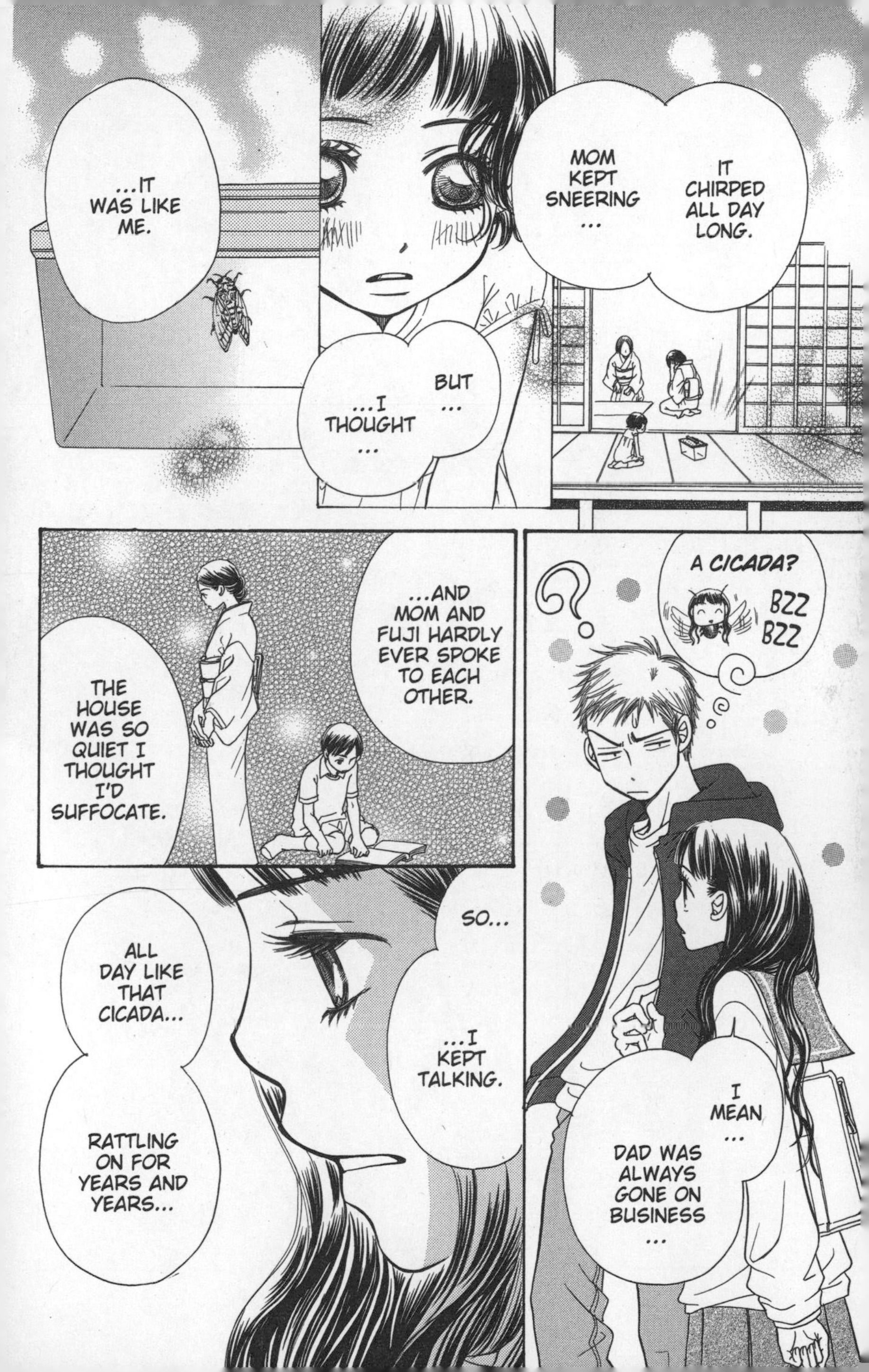
IT CHIRPED ALL DAY LONG.
MOM KEPT SNEERING ...
BUT ...
...I THOUGHT ...
...IT WAS LIKE ME.
A CICADA?
BZZ BZZ
I MEAN ...
DAD WAS ALWAYS GONE ON BUSINESS ...
...AND MOM AND FUJI HARDLY EVER SPOKE TO EACH OTHER.
THE HOUSE WAS SO QUIET I THOUGHT I'D SUFFOCATE.
SO...
...I KEPT TALKING.
ALL DAY LIKE THAT CICADA...
RATTLING ON FOR YEARS AND YEARS...

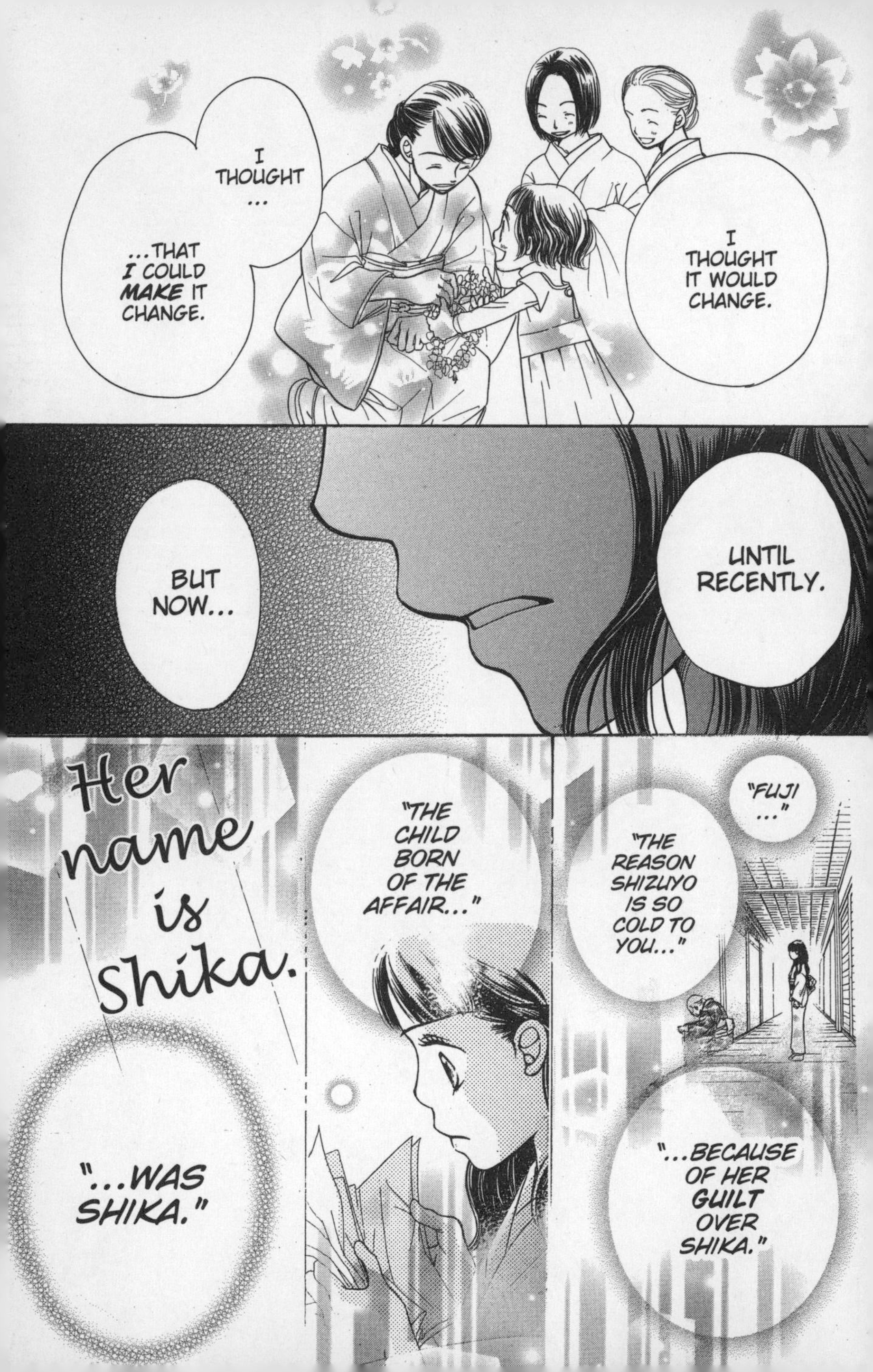
I THOUGHT IT WOULD CHANGE.
I THOUGHT ... ...THAT I COULD MAKE IT CHANGE.
UNTIL RECENTLY.
BUT NOW...
"FUJI ..."
"THE REASON SHIZUYO IS SO COLD TO YOU..."
"...BECAUSE OF HER GUILT OVER SHIKA."
"THE CHILD BORN OF THE AFFAIR..."
Her name is Shika.
"...WAS SHIKA."

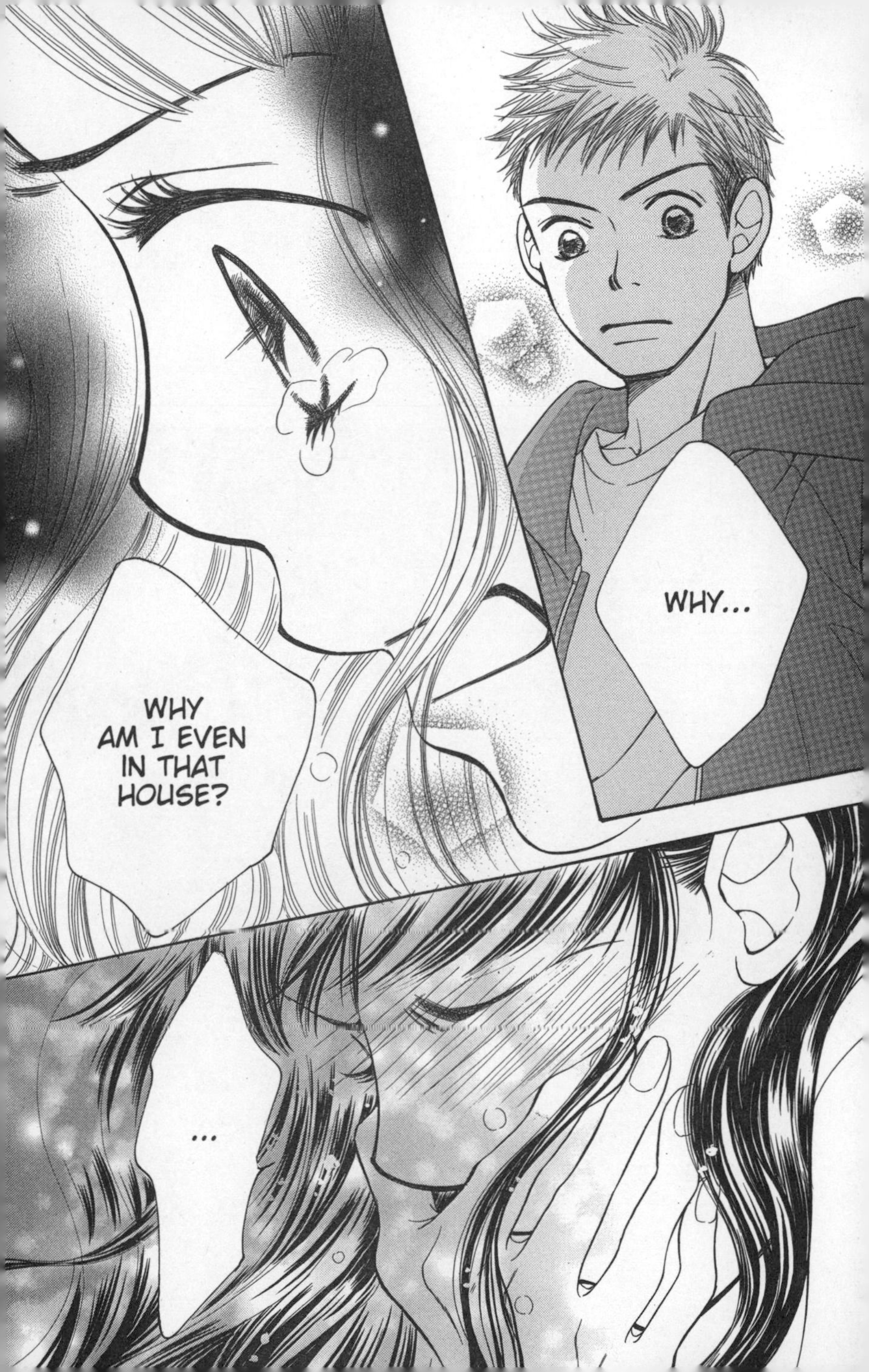
WHY...
WHY AM I EVEN IN THAT HOUSE?
...

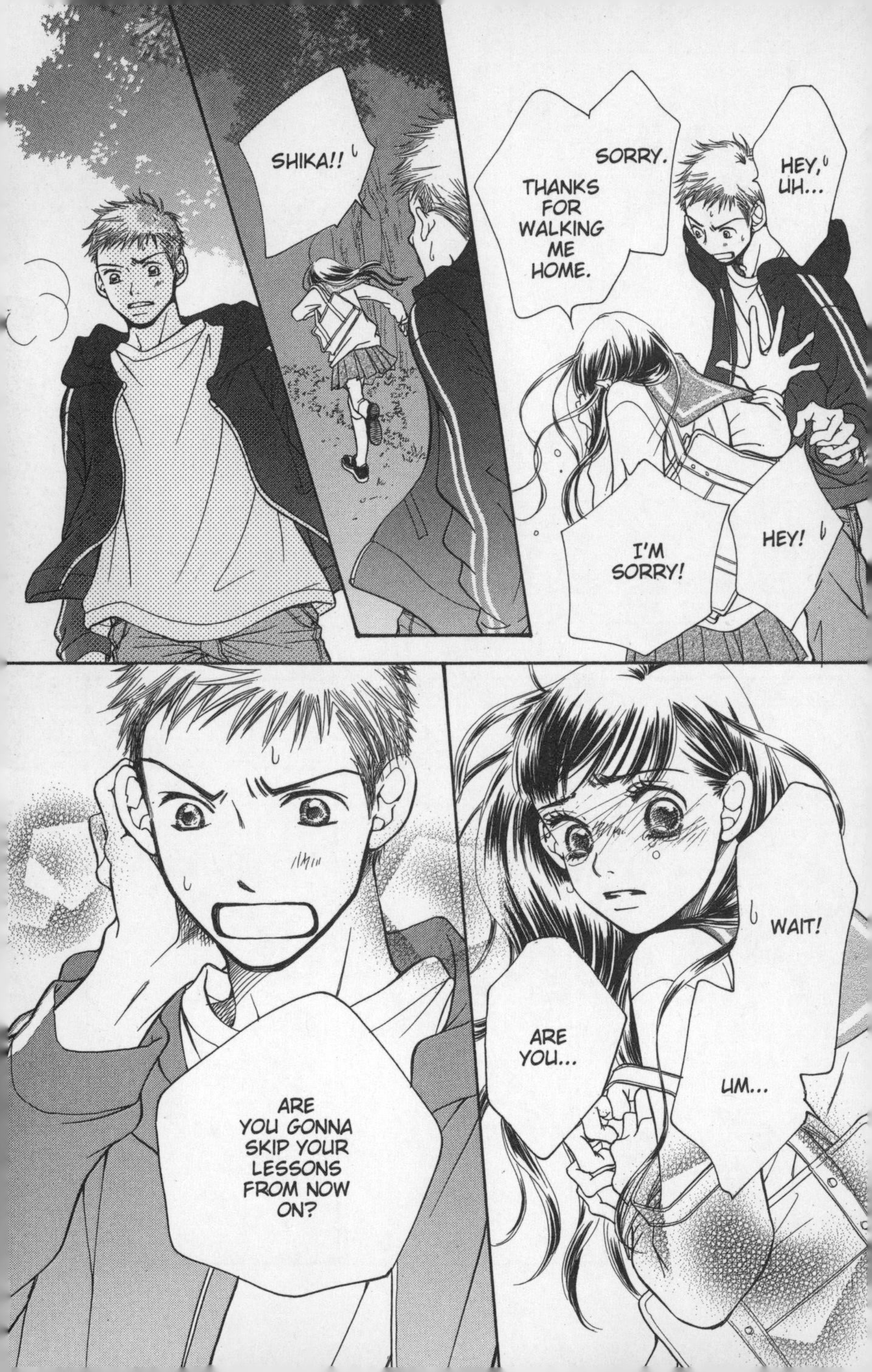
HEY, UH...
SORRY. THANKS FOR WALKING ME HOME.
HEY!
I'M SORRY!
SHIKA!!
WAIT!
UM...
ARE YOU...
ARE YOU GONNA SKIP YOUR LESSONS FROM NOW ON?

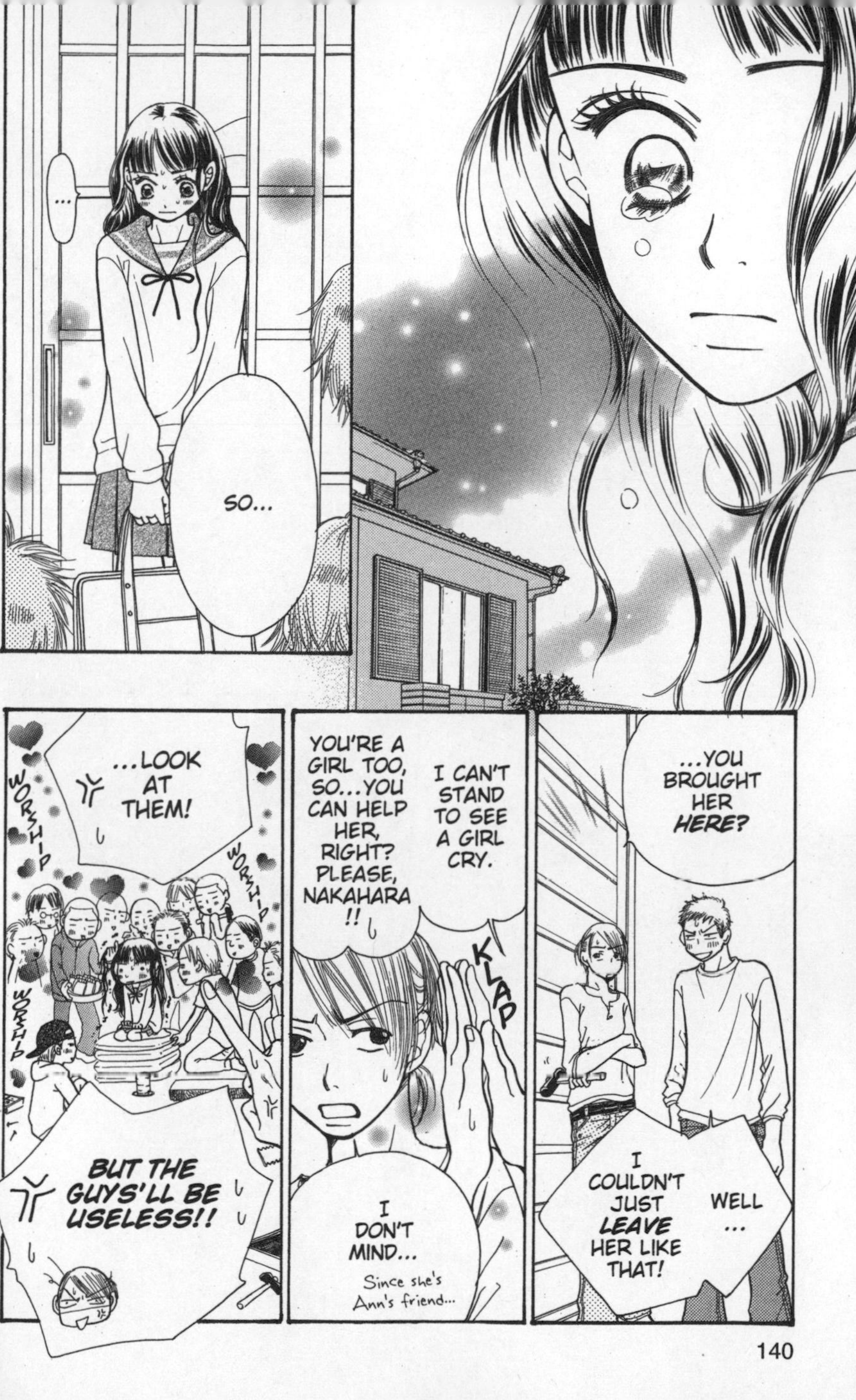
...
SO...
...YOU BROUGHT HER HERE?
WELL...
I COULDN'T JUST LEAVE HER LIKE THAT!
I CAN'T STAND TO SEE A GIRL CRY.
YOU'RE A GIRL TOO, SO...YOU CAN HELP HER, RIGHT? PLEASE, NAKAHARA!!
KLAP
I DON'T MIND...
Since she's Ann's friend...
...LOOK AT THEM!
WORSHIP
WORSHIP
WORSHIP
BUT THE GUYS'LL BE USELESS!!

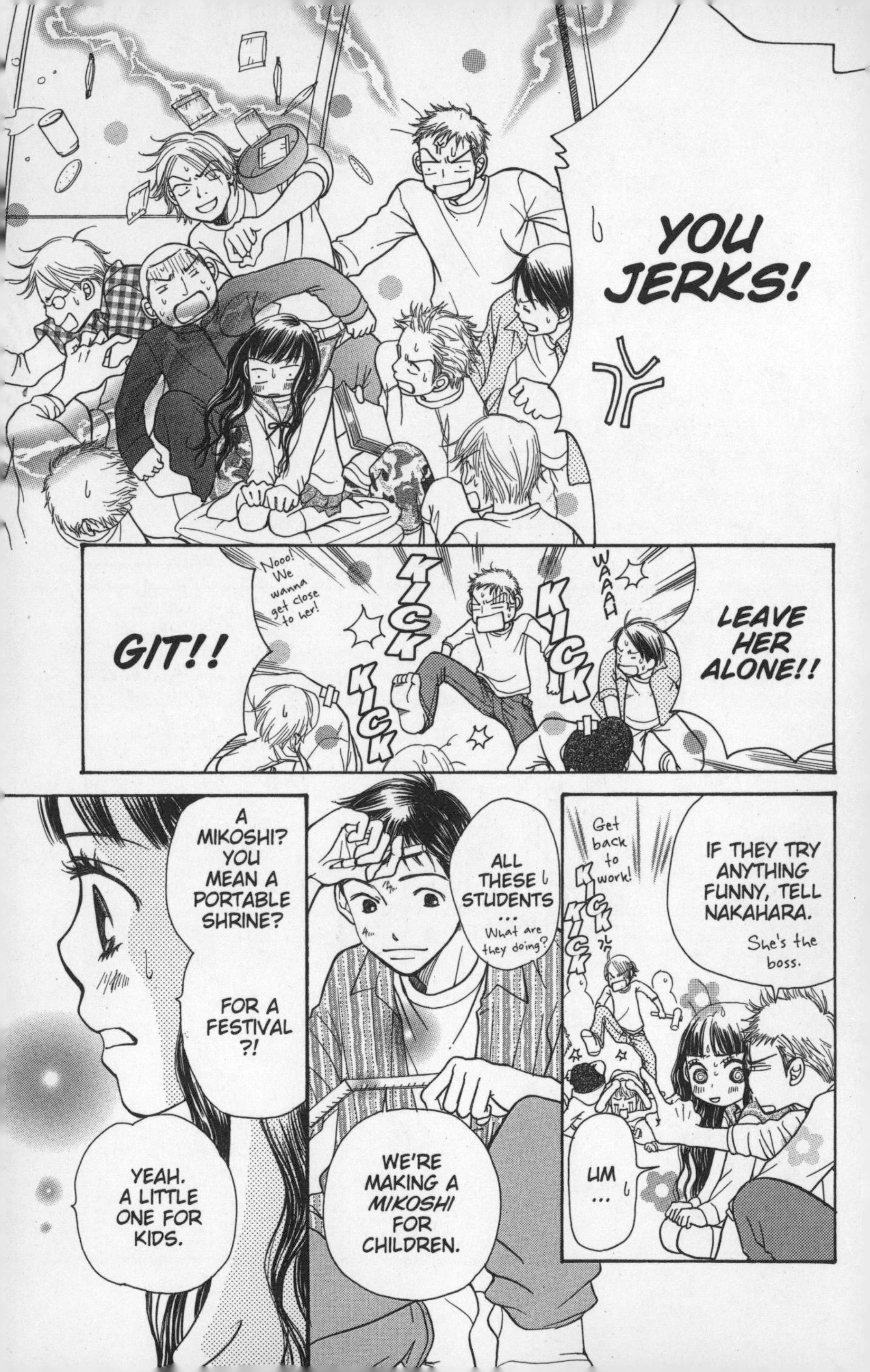
YOU JERKS!
LEAVE HER ALONE!!
WAAAH
KICK
KICK
Nooo! We wanna get close to her!
KICK
GIT!!
IF THEY TRY ANYTHING FUNNY, TELL NAKAHARA.
She's the boss.
Get back to work!
KICK
KICK
UM ...
ALL THESE STUDENTS ...
What are they doing?
WE'RE MAKING A MIKOSHI FOR CHILDREN.
A MIKOSHI? YOU MEAN A PORTABLE SHRINE?
FOR A FESTIVAL ?!
YEAH. A LITTLE ONE FOR KIDS.

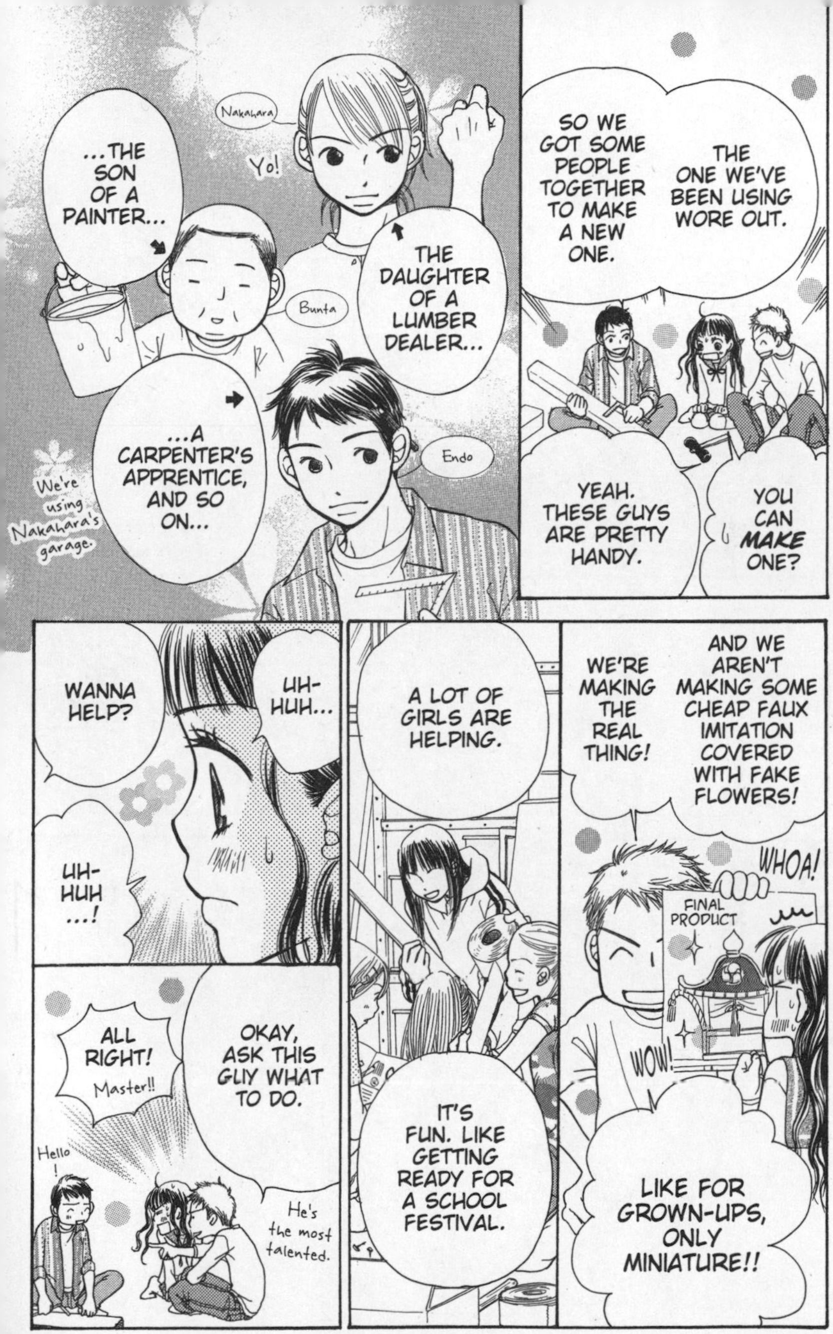
THE ONE WE'VE BEEN USING WORE OUT.
SO WE GOT SOME PEOPLE TOGETHER TO MAKE A NEW ONE.
YOU CAN *MAKE* ONE?
YEAH. THESE GUYS ARE PRETTY HANDY.
Nakahara
Yo!
THE DAUGHTER OF A LUMBER DEALER...
...THE SON OF A PAINTER...
Bunta
...A CARPENTER'S APPRENTICE, AND SO ON...
Endo
We're using Nakahara's garage.
AND WE AREN'T MAKING SOME CHEAP FAUX IMITATION COVERED WITH FAKE FLOWERS!
WE'RE MAKING THE REAL THING!
WHOA!
FINAL PRODUCT
WOW!
LIKE FOR GROWN-UPS, ONLY MINIATURE!!
A LOT OF GIRLS ARE HELPING.
IT'S FUN. LIKE GETTING READY FOR A SCHOOL FESTIVAL.
UH-HUH...
WANNA HELP?
UH-HUH ...!
OKAY, ASK THIS GUY WHAT TO DO.
ALL RIGHT!
Master!!
He's the most talented.
Hello!

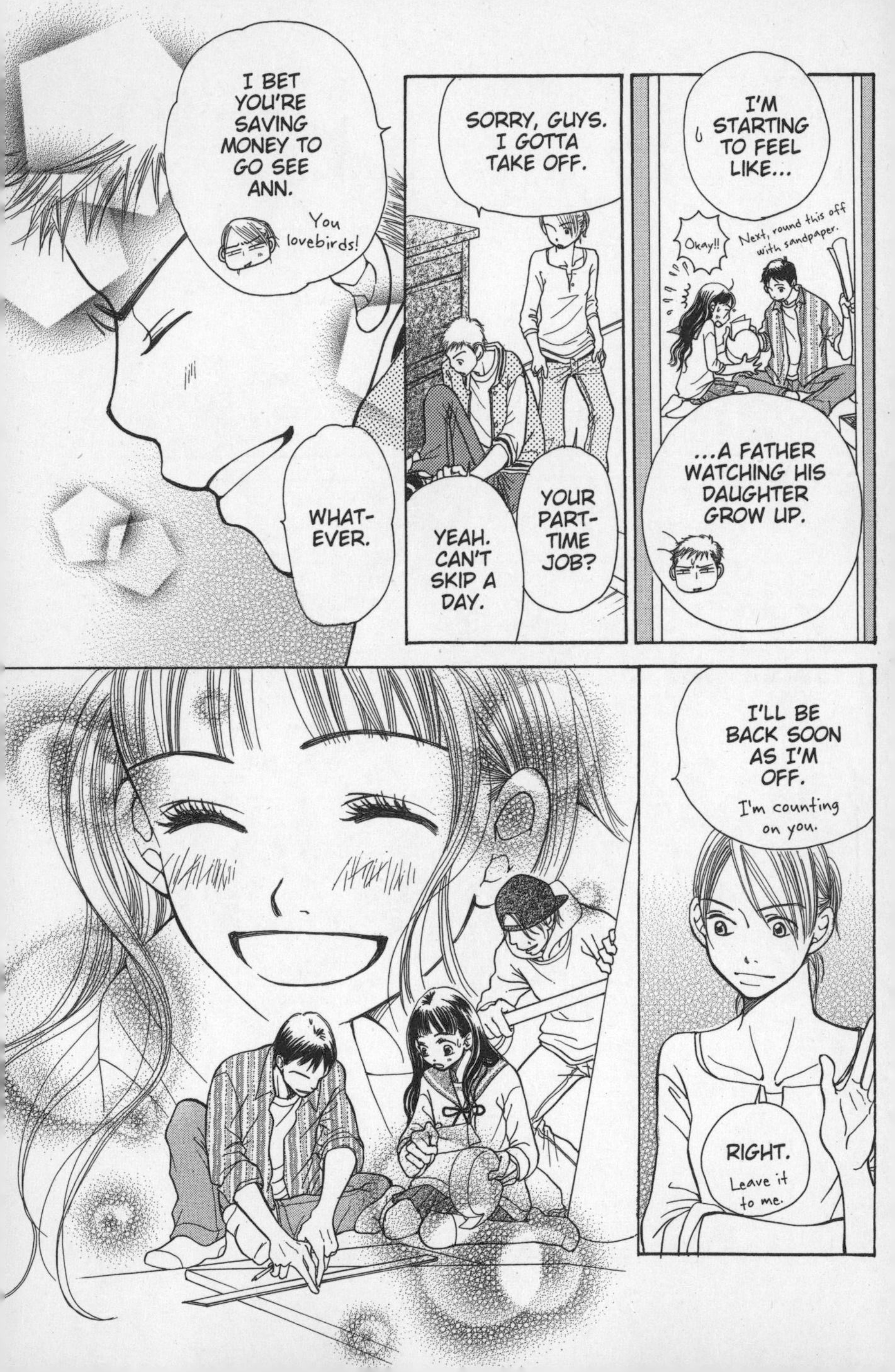
I'M STARTING TO FEEL LIKE...
Next, round this off with sandpaper.
Okay!!
...A FATHER WATCHING HIS DAUGHTER GROW UP.
SORRY, GUYS. I GOTTA TAKE OFF.
YOUR PART-TIME JOB?
YEAH. CAN'T SKIP A DAY.
I BET YOU'RE SAVING MONEY TO GO SEE ANN.
You lovebirds!
WHATEVER.
I'LL BE BACK SOON AS I'M OFF.
I'm counting on you.
RIGHT.
Leave it to me.

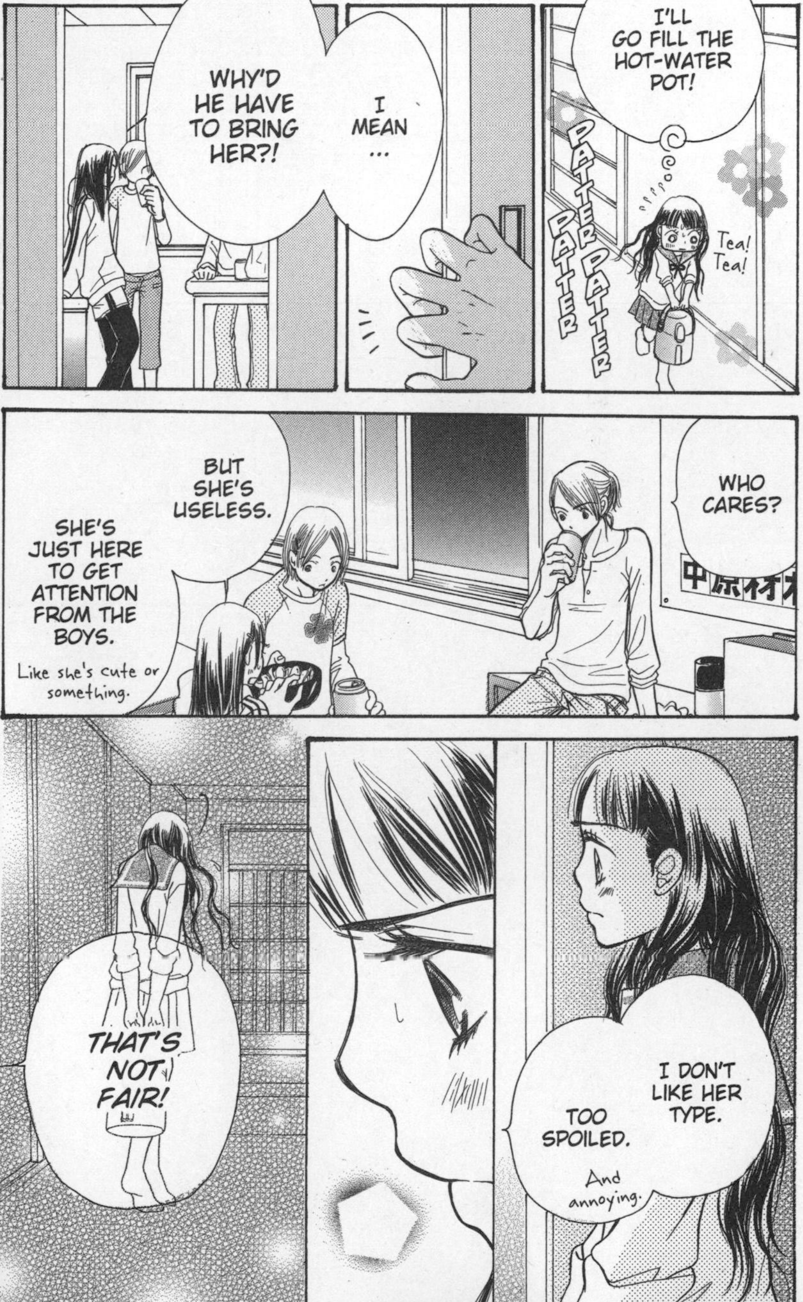
I'LL GO FILL THE HOT-WATER POT!
PATTER PATTER
PATTER PATTER
Tea! Tea!
I MEAN ...
WHY'D HE HAVE TO BRING HER?!
WHO CARES?
BUT SHE'S USELESS.
SHE'S JUST HERE TO GET ATTENTION FROM THE BOYS.
Like she's cute or something.
I DON'T LIKE HER TYPE.
TOO SPOILED.
And annoying.
THAT'S NOT FAIR!

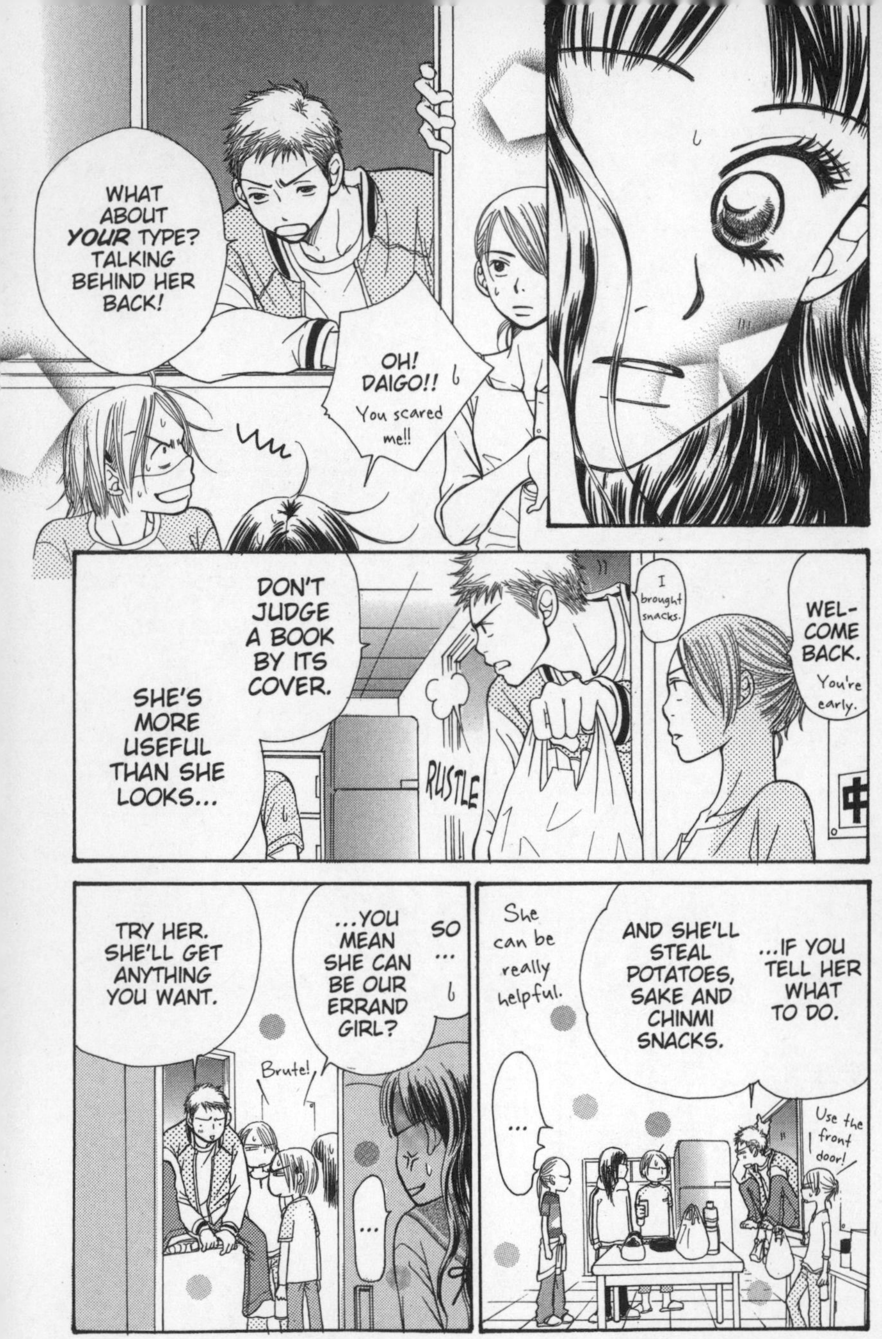
WHAT ABOUT YOUR TYPE? TALKING BEHIND HER BACK!
OH! DAIGO!! You scared me!!
WEL-COME BACK. You're early.
I brought snacks.
DON'T JUDGE A BOOK BY ITS COVER.
SHE'S MORE USEFUL THAN SHE LOOKS...
RUSTLE
...IF YOU TELL HER WHAT TO DO.
AND SHE'LL STEAL POTATOES, SAKE AND CHINMI SNACKS.
She can be really helpful.
Use the front door!
...
SO...
...YOU MEAN SHE CAN BE OUR ERRAND GIRL?
TRY HER. SHE'LL GET ANYTHING YOU WANT.
Brute!
...

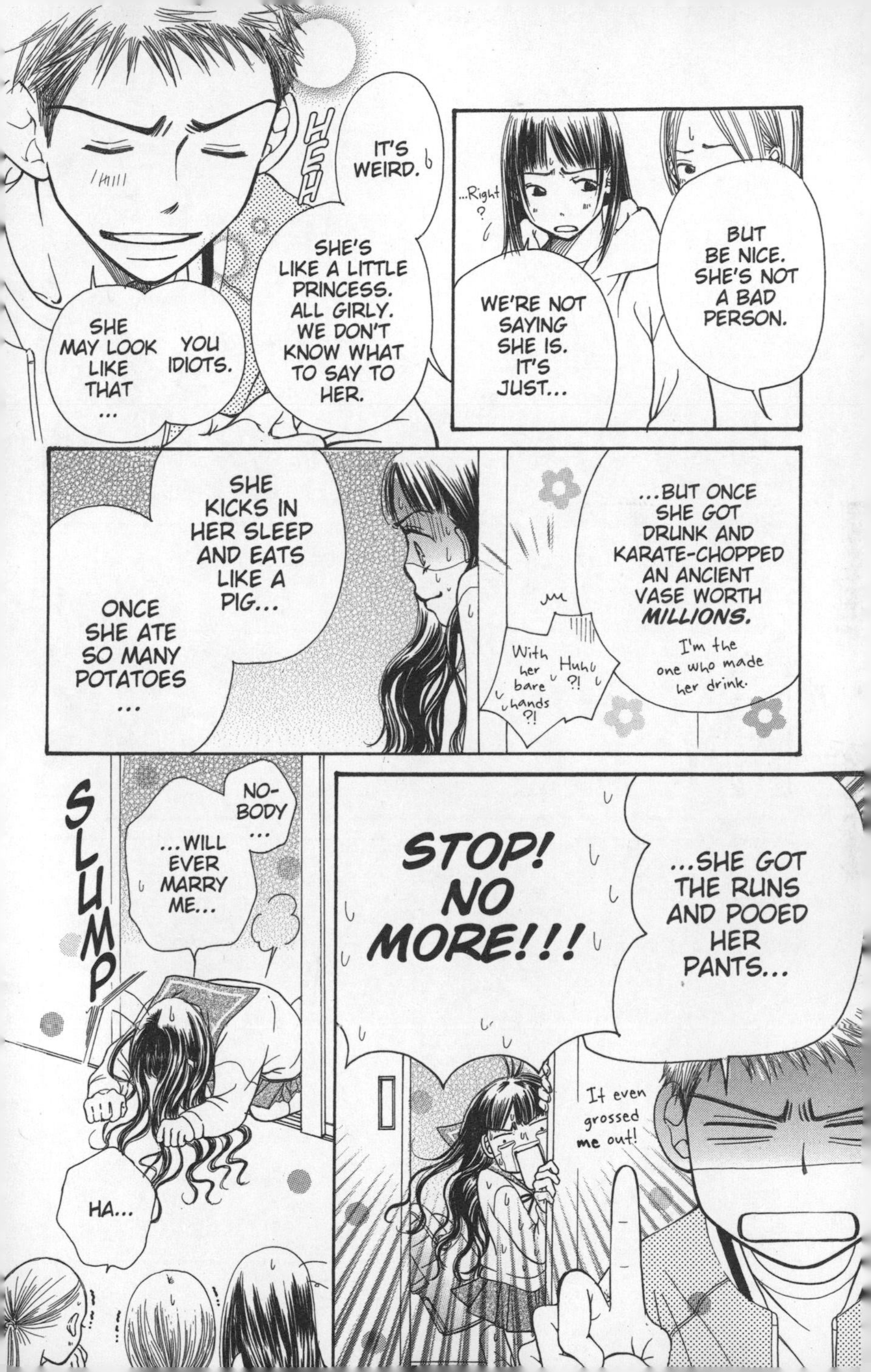
BUT BE NICE. SHE'S NOT A BAD PERSON.
...Right ?
WE'RE NOT SAYING SHE IS. IT'S JUST...
IT'S WEIRD.
SHE'S LIKE A LITTLE PRINCESS. ALL GIRLY. WE DON'T KNOW WHAT TO SAY TO HER.
HEH
YOU IDIOTS.
SHE MAY LOOK LIKE THAT...
...BUT ONCE SHE GOT DRUNK AND KARATE-CHOPPED AN ANCIENT VASE WORTH MILLIONS.
I'm the one who made her drink.
Huh?!
With her bare hands?!
SHE KICKS IN HER SLEEP AND EATS LIKE A PIG...
ONCE SHE ATE SO MANY POTATOES...
...SHE GOT THE RUNS AND POOED HER PANTS...
STOP! NO MORE!!!
It even grossed me out!
NO-BODY...
...WILL EVER MARRY ME...
SLUMP
HA...

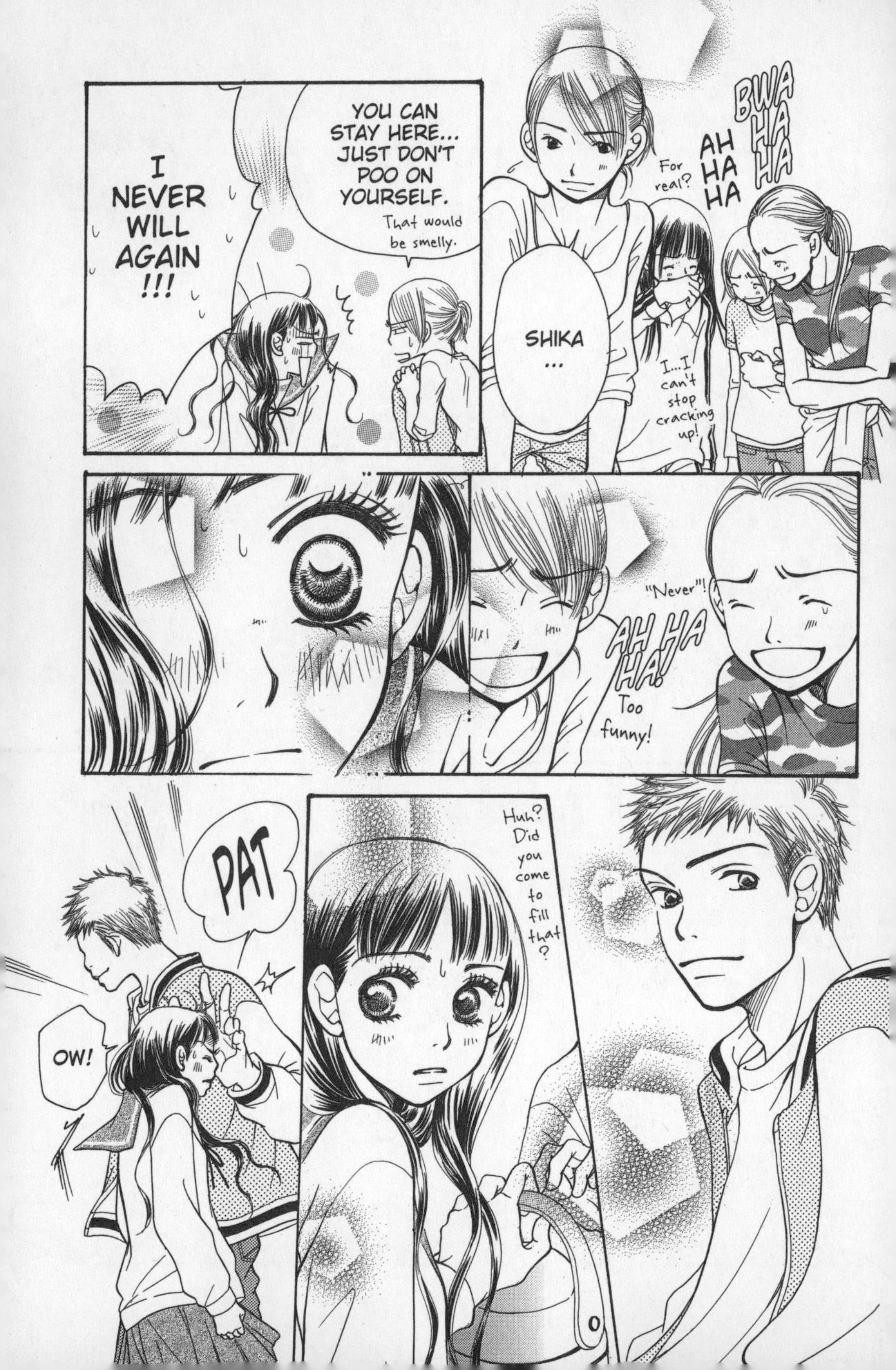
YOU CAN STAY HERE... JUST DON'T POO ON YOURSELF.
That would be smelly.
I NEVER WILL AGAIN !!!
SHIKA ...
For real?
AH HA HA
BWA HA HA HA
I...I can't stop cracking up!
"Never"!
AH HA HA!
Too funny!
PAT
OW!
Huh? Did you come to fill that?

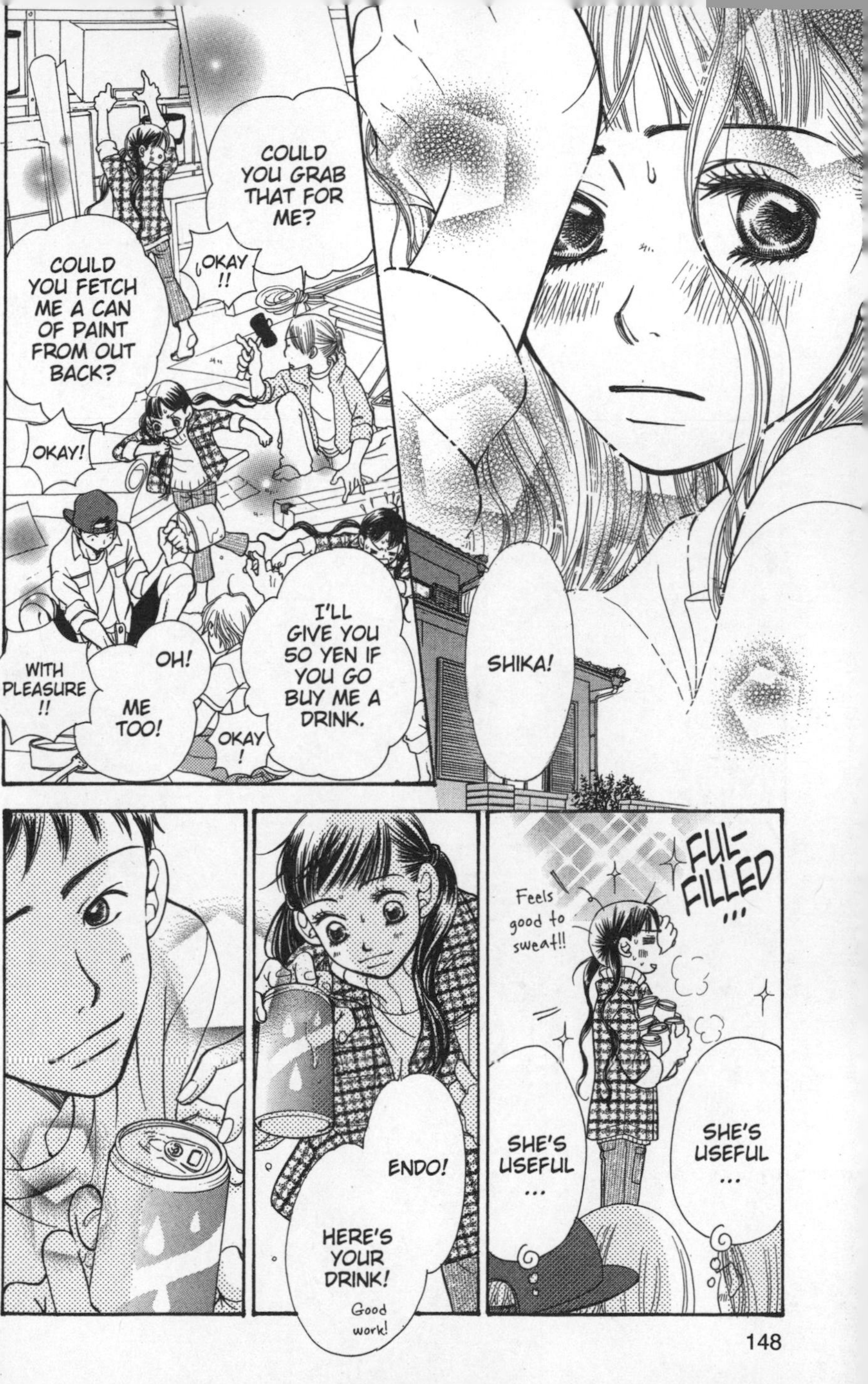
SHIKA!
COULD YOU GRAB THAT FOR ME?
OKAY !!
COULD YOU FETCH ME A CAN OF PAINT FROM OUT BACK?
OKAY!
I'LL GIVE YOU 50 YEN IF YOU GO BUY ME A DRINK.
OKAY !
OH!
ME TOO!
WITH PLEASURE !!
FUL-FILLED ...
Feels good to sweat!!
SHE'S USEFUL ...
SHE'S USEFUL ...
ENDO!
HERE'S YOUR DRINK!
Good work!

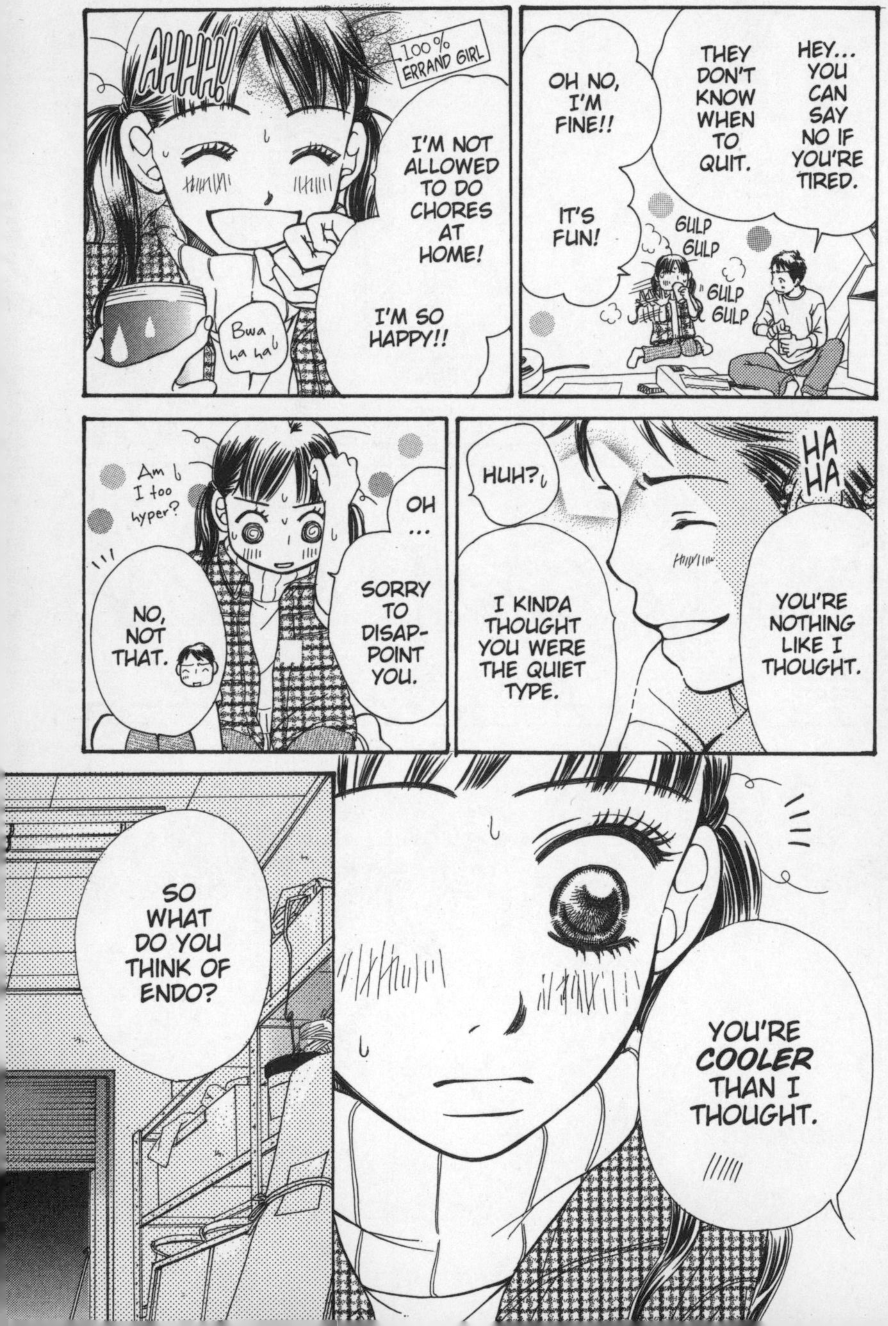
HEY... YOU CAN SAY NO IF YOU'RE TIRED.
THEY DON'T KNOW WHEN TO QUIT.
OH NO, I'M FINE!!
IT'S FUN!
GULP GULP
GULP GULP
AHHH!
100% ERRAND GIRL
I'M NOT ALLOWED TO DO CHORES AT HOME!
I'M SO HAPPY!!
Bwa ha ha
HA HA
YOU'RE NOTHING LIKE I THOUGHT.
HUH?
I KINDA THOUGHT YOU WERE THE QUIET TYPE.
OH ...
SORRY TO DISAPPOINT YOU.
Am I too hyper?
NO, NOT THAT.
YOU'RE COOLER THAN I THOUGHT.
SO WHAT DO YOU THINK OF ENDO?

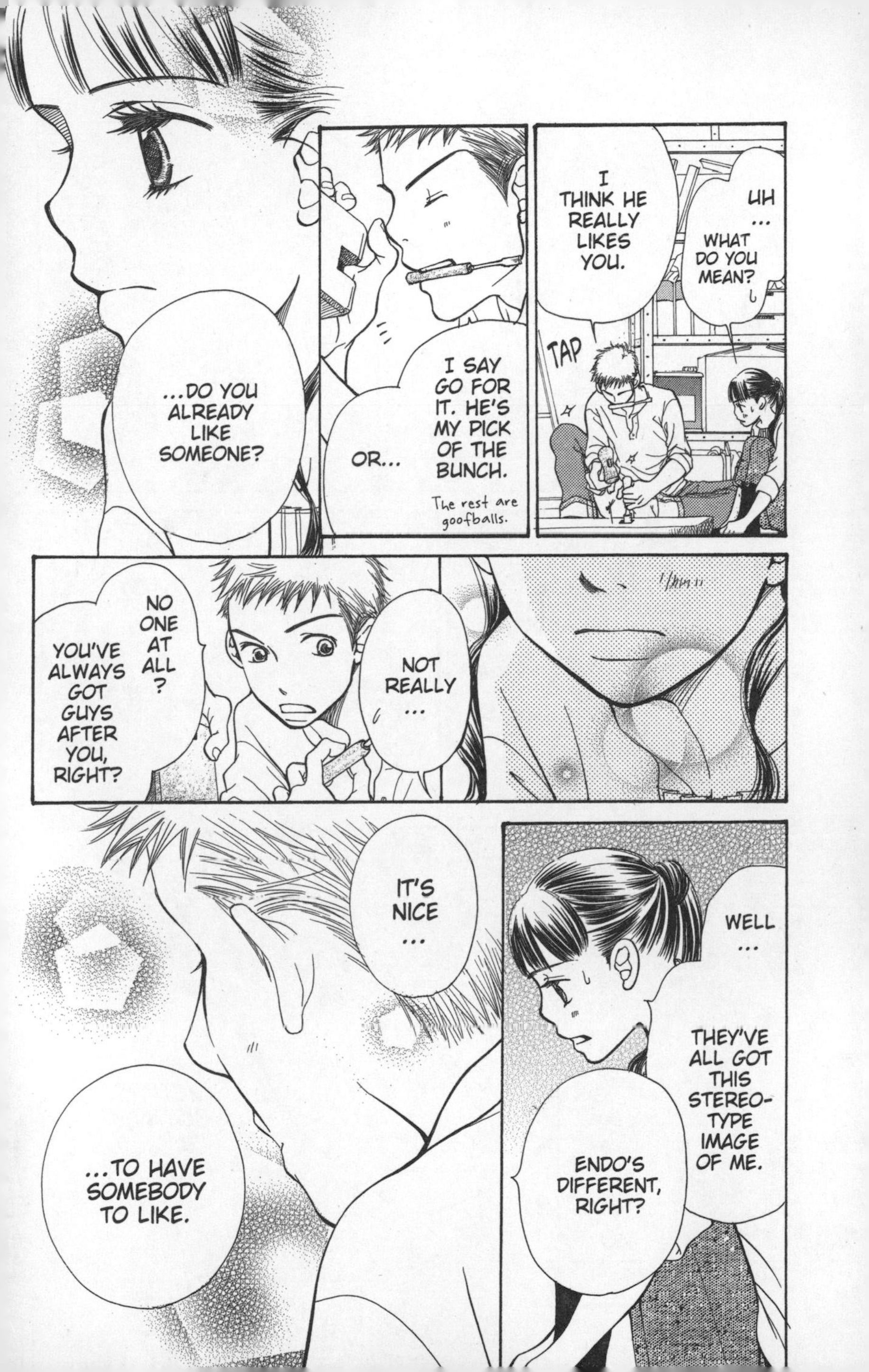
I THINK HE REALLY LIKES YOU.
UH ... WHAT DO YOU MEAN?
TAP
I SAY GO FOR IT. HE'S MY PICK OF THE BUNCH.
The rest are goofballs.
OR...
...DO YOU ALREADY LIKE SOMEONE?
NOT REALLY ...
NO ONE AT ALL?
YOU'VE ALWAYS GOT GUYS AFTER YOU, RIGHT?
WELL ...
THEY'VE ALL GOT THIS STEREO-TYPE IMAGE OF ME.
ENDO'S DIFFERENT, RIGHT?
IT'S NICE ...
...TO HAVE SOMEBODY TO LIKE.

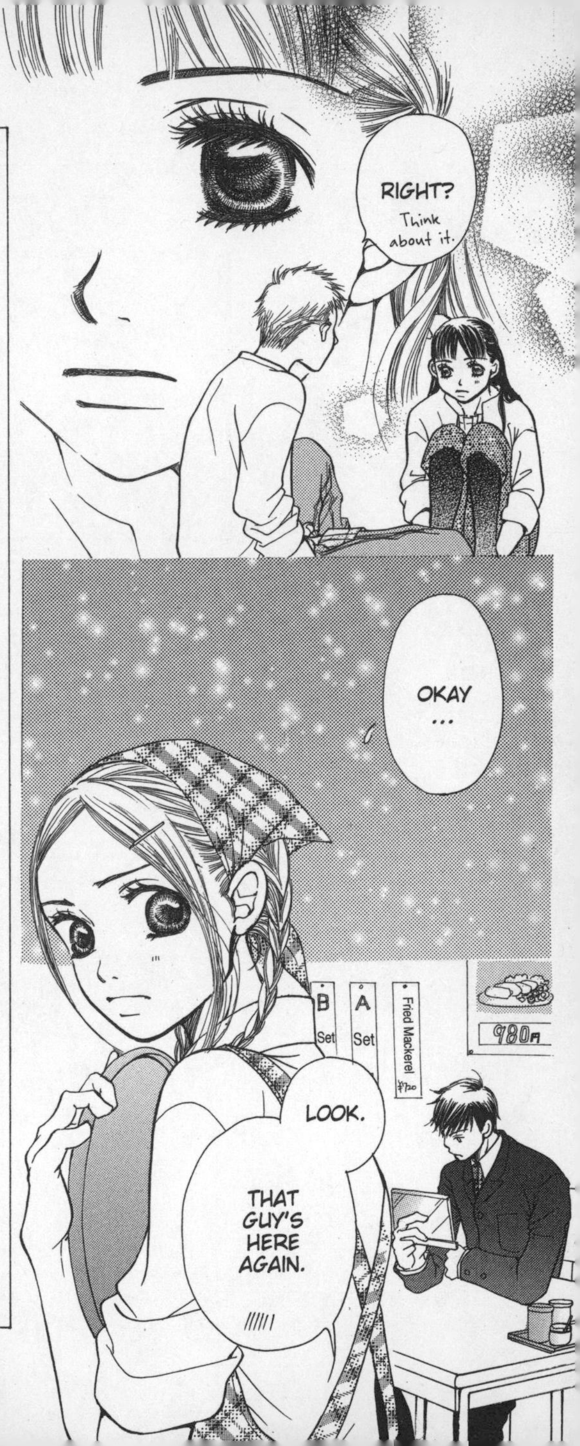
RIGHT? Think about it.
OKAY ...
Fried Mackerel ¥720
A Set
B Set
980円
LOOK.
THAT GUY'S HERE AGAIN.

## AGE 16, FALL: CICADA CARAPACES

To tell the truth, I've hated cicadas ever since one slammed into my forehead one day when I was in junior high and going to cram school on my bike. But without their singing, it doesn't really feel like summer.

Anyway, this chapter is set in the autumn...

I bought a book on insects as a reference, and it had all these pictures of cicadas and cockroaches and flies and grubs all wriggling, wriggling, wriggling...and I can't drive those images out of my head! Ick!

I've been asked how often I can put out one volume of manga. At my recent pace, about one every four months (...maybe). I hope that helps.

Well, I'll see you again in volume 4. Please keep reading while Ann and the others grow up little by little!

02.10.07 Hinako Ashihara

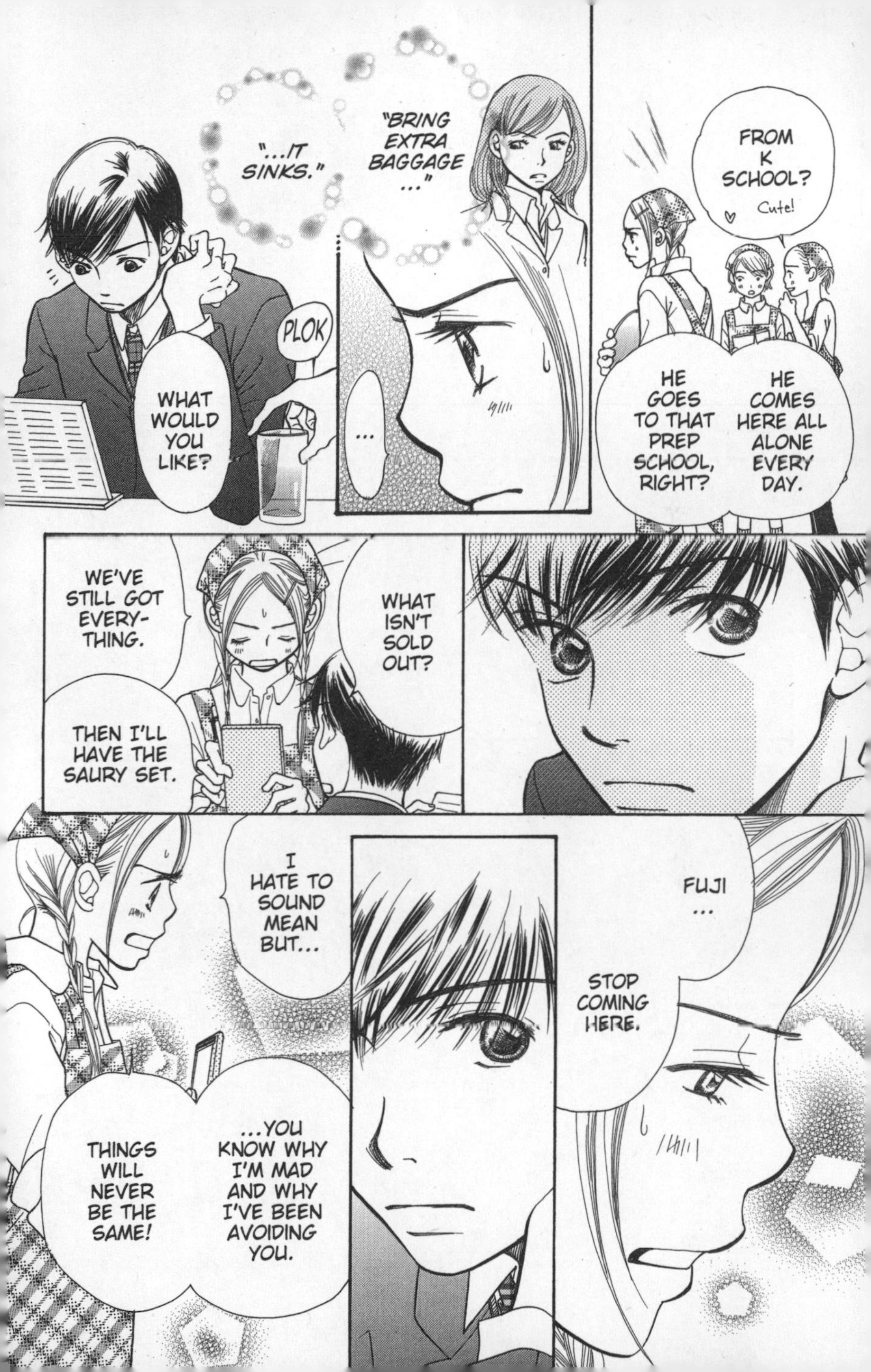
FROM K SCHOOL?
Cute!
HE COMES HERE ALL ALONE EVERY DAY.
HE GOES TO THAT PREP SCHOOL, RIGHT?
"BRING EXTRA BAGGAGE ..."
"...IT SINKS."
...
PLOK
WHAT WOULD YOU LIKE?
WHAT ISN'T SOLD OUT?
WE'VE STILL GOT EVERYTHING.
THEN I'LL HAVE THE SAURY SET.
FUJI ...
STOP COMING HERE.
I HATE TO SOUND MEAN BUT...
...YOU KNOW WHY I'M MAD AND WHY I'VE BEEN AVOIDING YOU.
THINGS WILL NEVER BE THE SAME!

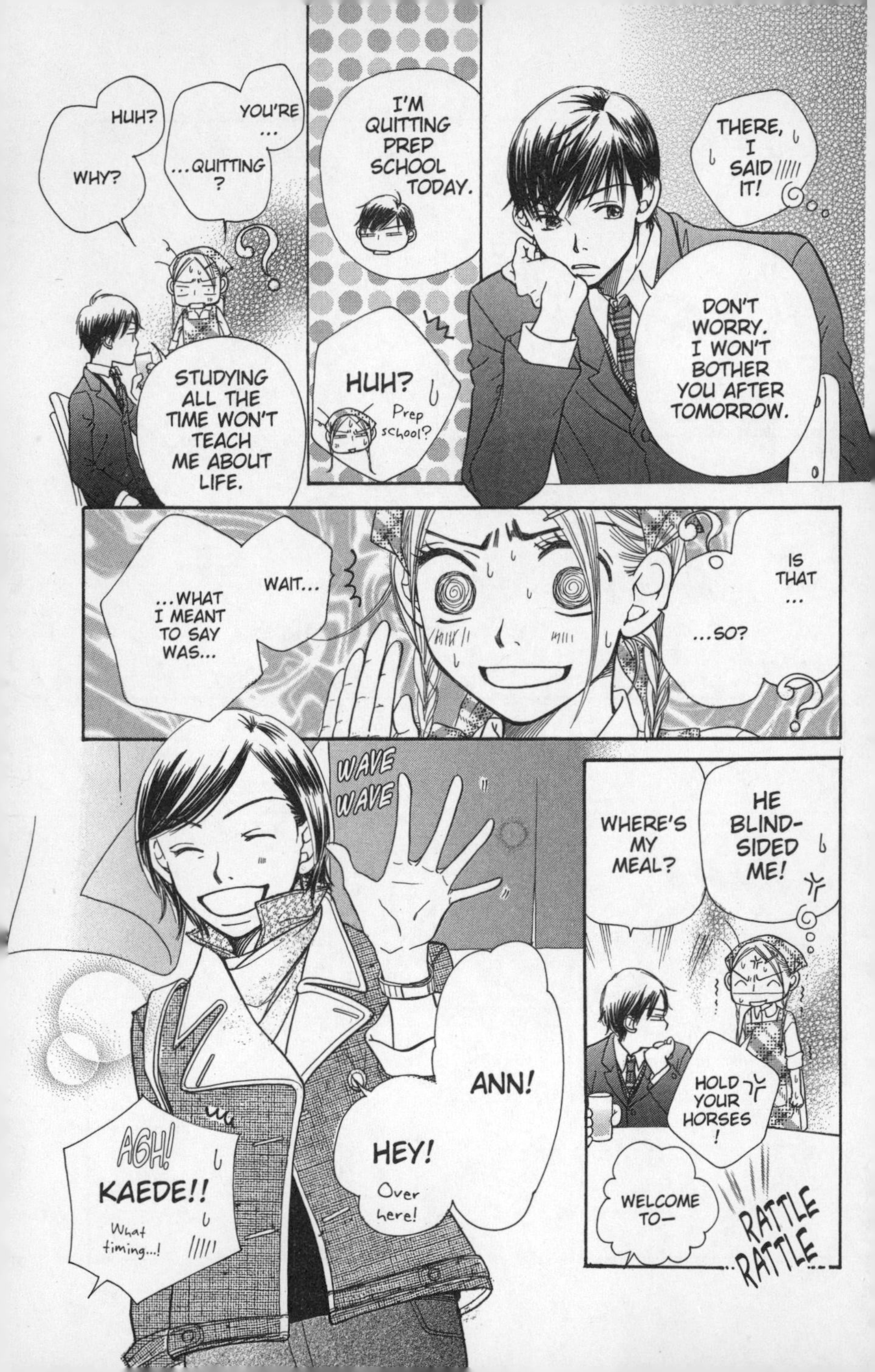
THERE, I SAID IT!
DON'T WORRY. I WON'T BOTHER YOU AFTER TOMORROW.
I'M QUITTING PREP SCHOOL TODAY.
HUH?
Prep school?
YOU'RE ... ...QUITTING?
HUH? WHY?
STUDYING ALL THE TIME WON'T TEACH ME ABOUT LIFE.
IS THAT ... ...SO?
WAIT...
...WHAT I MEANT TO SAY WAS...
HE BLIND-SIDED ME!
WHERE'S MY MEAL?
HOLD YOUR HORSES!
WELCOME TO—
RATTLE RATTLE
WAVE WAVE
ANN!
HEY!
Over here!
AGH!
KAEDE!!
What timing...!

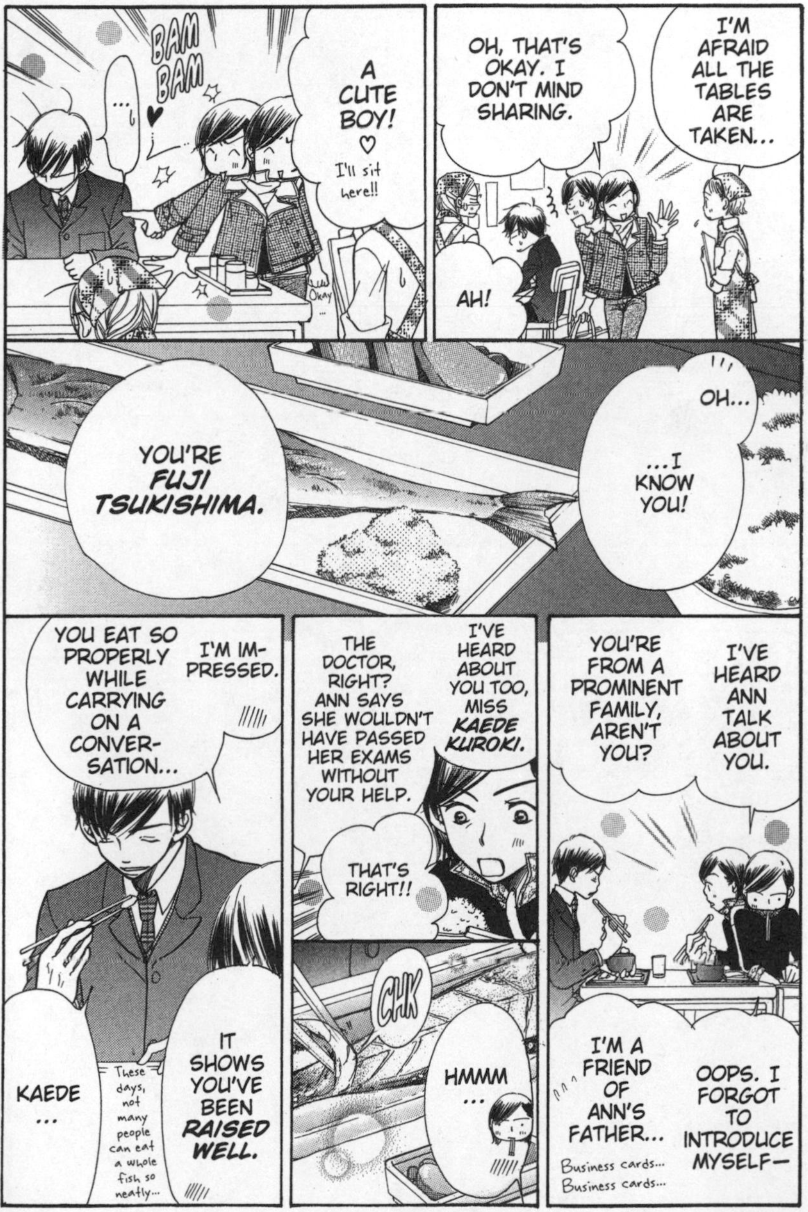
I'M AFRAID ALL THE TABLES ARE TAKEN...
OH, THAT'S OKAY. I DON'T MIND SHARING.
AH!
A CUTE BOY! ♡
I'll sit here!!
BAM BAM
...
Okay ...
OH...
...I KNOW YOU!
YOU'RE FUJI TSUKISHIMA.
I'VE HEARD ANN TALK ABOUT YOU.
YOU'RE FROM A PROMINENT FAMILY, AREN'T YOU?
OOPS. I FORGOT TO INTRODUCE MYSELF—
I'M A FRIEND OF ANN'S FATHER...
Business cards... Business cards...
I'VE HEARD ABOUT YOU TOO, MISS KAEDE KUROKI.
THE DOCTOR, RIGHT? ANN SAYS SHE WOULDN'T HAVE PASSED HER EXAMS WITHOUT YOUR HELP.
THAT'S RIGHT!!
CHK
HMMM ...
I'M IM-PRESSED.
YOU EAT SO PROPERLY WHILE CARRYING ON A CONVER-SATION...
IT SHOWS YOU'VE BEEN RAISED WELL.
These days, not many people can eat a whole fish so neatly...
KAEDE ...

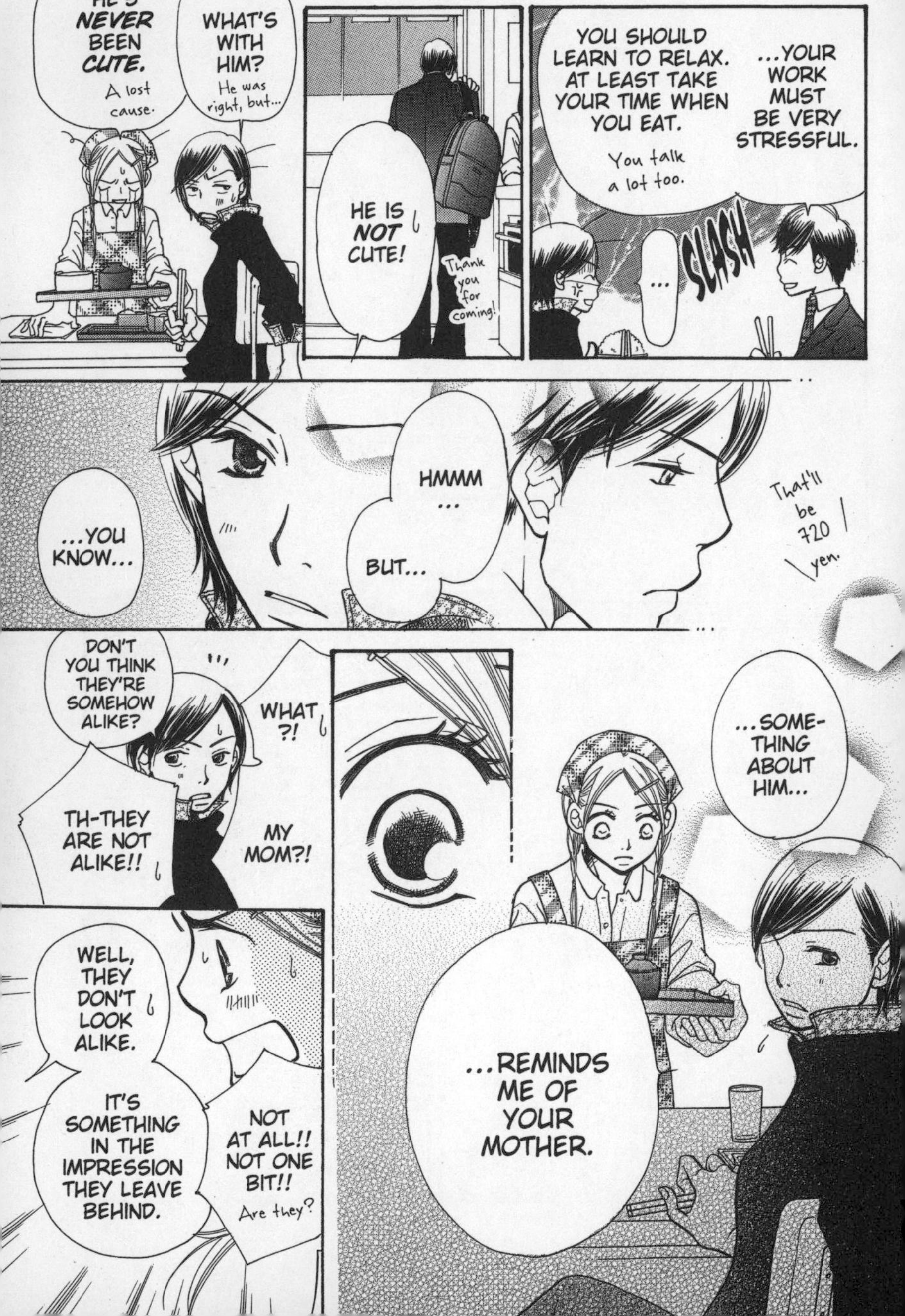
...YOUR WORK MUST BE VERY STRESSFUL.
YOU SHOULD LEARN TO RELAX. AT LEAST TAKE YOUR TIME WHEN YOU EAT.
You talk a lot too.
...
SLASH
HE IS NOT CUTE!
Thank you for coming!
WHAT'S WITH HIM?
He was right, but...
HE'S NEVER BEEN CUTE.
A lost cause.
That'll be 720 yen.
HMMM...
BUT...
...YOU KNOW...
...SOME-THING ABOUT HIM...
...REMINDS ME OF YOUR MOTHER.
WHAT?!
MY MOM?!
DON'T YOU THINK THEY'RE SOMEHOW ALIKE?
TH-THEY ARE NOT ALIKE!!
NOT AT ALL!! NOT ONE BIT!!
Are they?
WELL, THEY DON'T LOOK ALIKE.
IT'S SOMETHING IN THE IMPRESSION THEY LEAVE BEHIND.

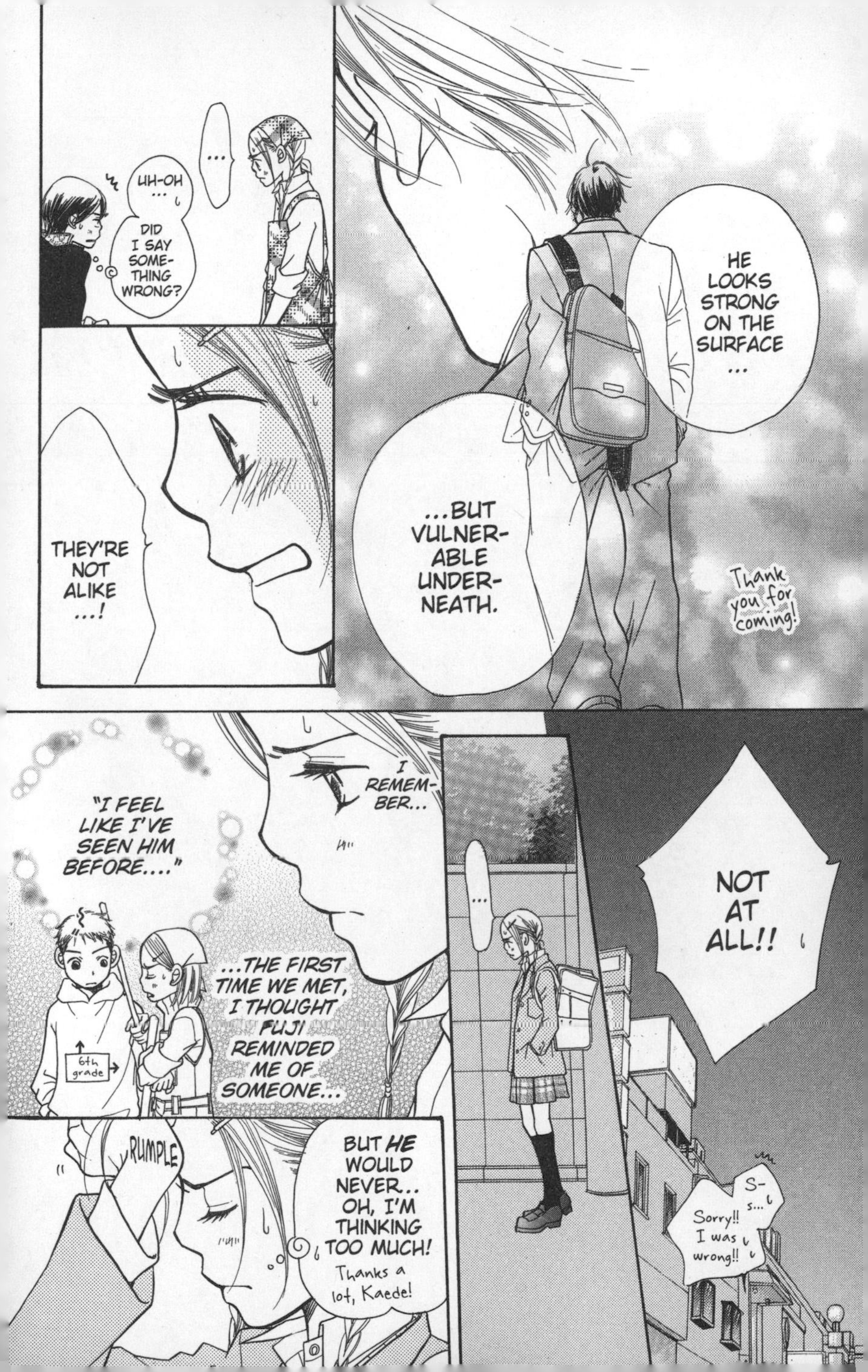
HE LOOKS STRONG ON THE SURFACE...
...BUT VULNERABLE UNDERNEATH.
Thank you for coming!
...
UH-OH...
DID I SAY SOMETHING WRONG?
THEY'RE NOT ALIKE...!
NOT AT ALL!!
...
S- s...
Sorry!! I was wrong!!
I REMEMBER...
"I FEEL LIKE I'VE SEEN HIM BEFORE...."
...THE FIRST TIME WE MET, I THOUGHT FUJI REMINDED ME OF SOMEONE...
6th grade
RUMPLE
BUT HE WOULD NEVER... OH, I'M THINKING TOO MUCH!
Thanks a lot, Kaede!

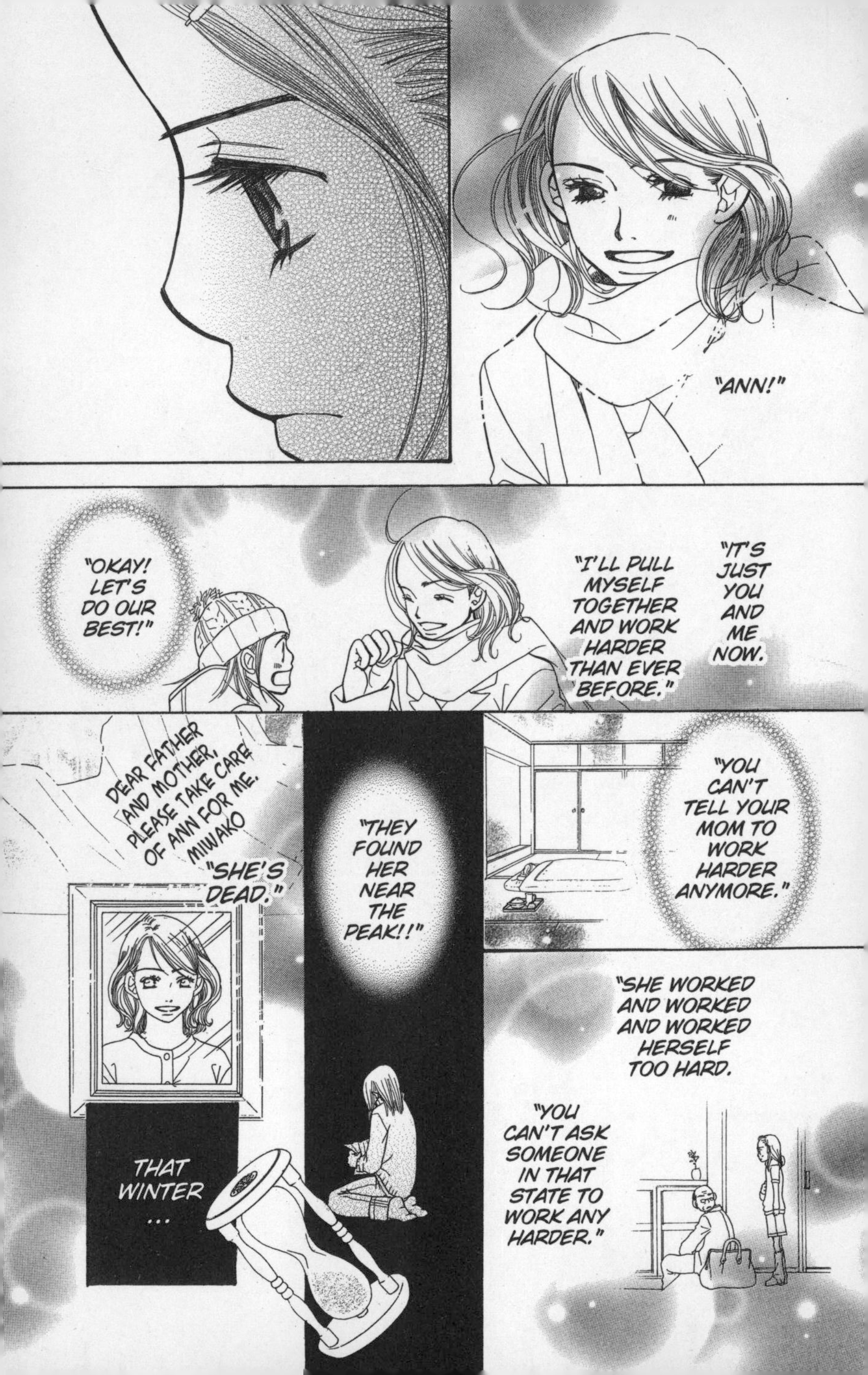
"ANN!"
"IT'S JUST YOU AND ME NOW.
"I'LL PULL MYSELF TOGETHER AND WORK HARDER THAN EVER BEFORE."
"OKAY! LET'S DO OUR BEST!"
"YOU CAN'T TELL YOUR MOM TO WORK HARDER ANYMORE."
"SHE WORKED AND WORKED AND WORKED HERSELF TOO HARD.
"YOU CAN'T ASK SOMEONE IN THAT STATE TO WORK ANY HARDER."
"THEY FOUND HER NEAR THE PEAK!!"
DEAR FATHER AND MOTHER, PLEASE TAKE CARE OF ANN FOR ME. MIWAKO
"SHE'S DEAD."
THAT WINTER ...

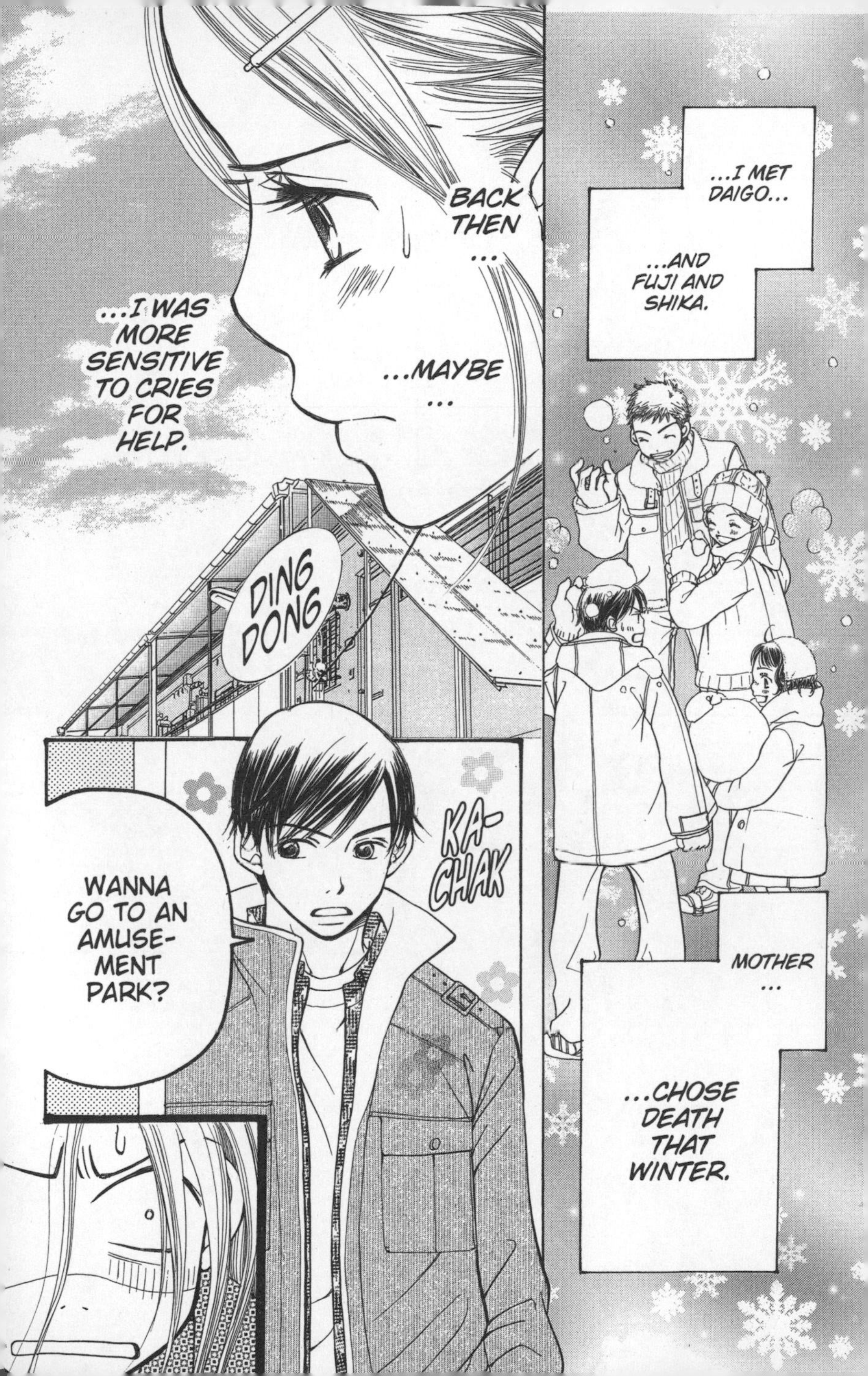
...I MET DAIGO...
...AND FUJI AND SHIKA.
MOTHER...
...CHOSE DEATH THAT WINTER.
BACK THEN...
...MAYBE...
...I WAS MORE SENSITIVE TO CRIES FOR HELP.
DING DONG
KA-CHAK
WANNA GO TO AN AMUSEMENT PARK?

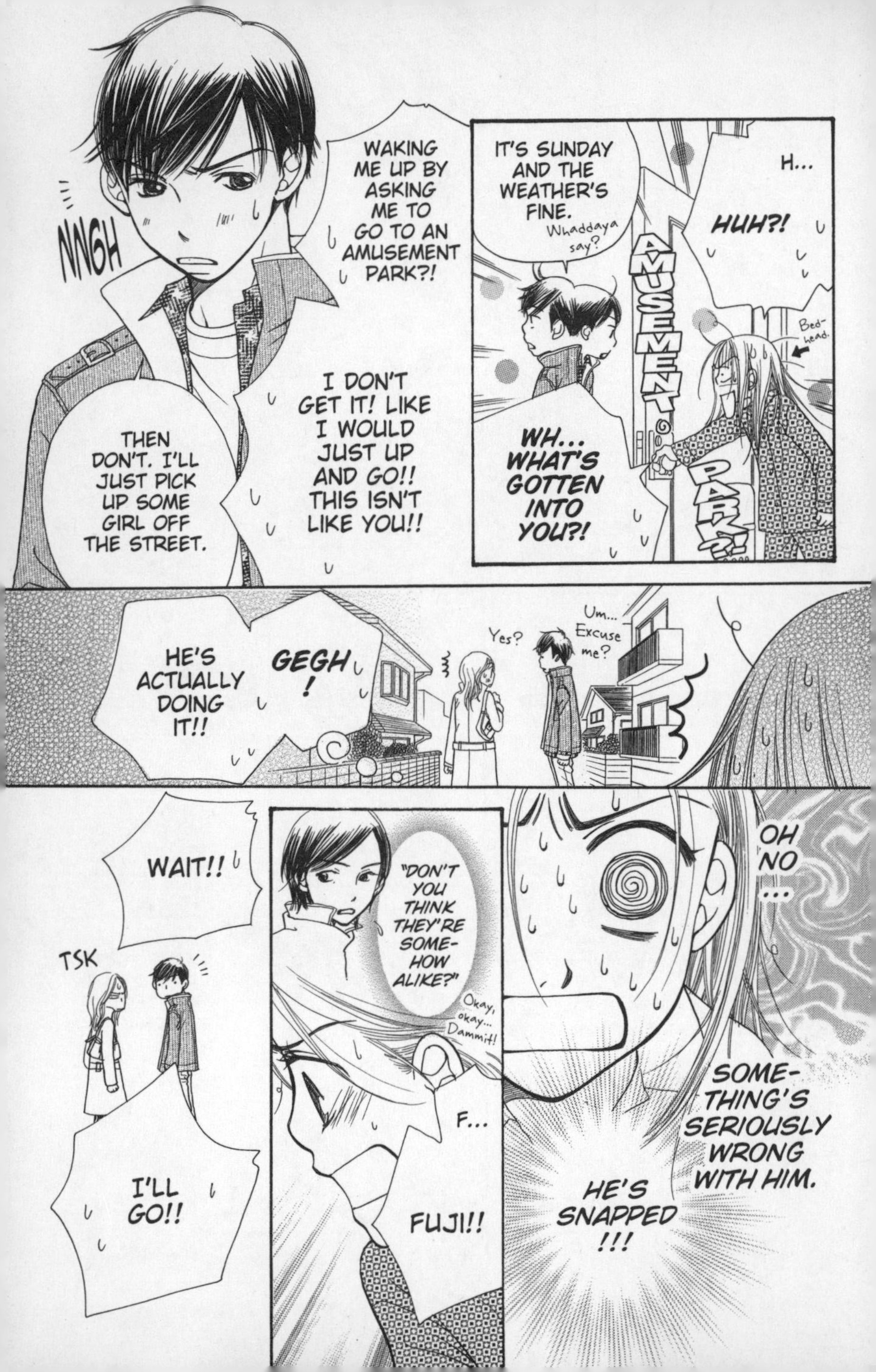
H...
HUH?!
Bed-head.
IT'S SUNDAY AND THE WEATHER'S FINE.
Whaddaya say?
AMUSEMENT PARK
WH... WHAT'S GOTTEN INTO YOU?!
WAKING ME UP BY ASKING ME TO GO TO AN AMUSEMENT PARK?!
NNGH
I DON'T GET IT! LIKE I WOULD JUST UP AND GO!! THIS ISN'T LIKE YOU!!
THEN DON'T. I'LL JUST PICK UP SOME GIRL OFF THE STREET.
Um... Excuse me?
Yes?
GEGH!
HE'S ACTUALLY DOING IT!!
OH NO...
SOME-THING'S SERIOUSLY WRONG WITH HIM.
HE'S SNAPPED!!!
"DON'T YOU THINK THEY'RE SOME-HOW ALIKE?"
Okay, okay... Dammit!
F...
FUJI!!
WAIT!!
TSK
I'LL GO!!

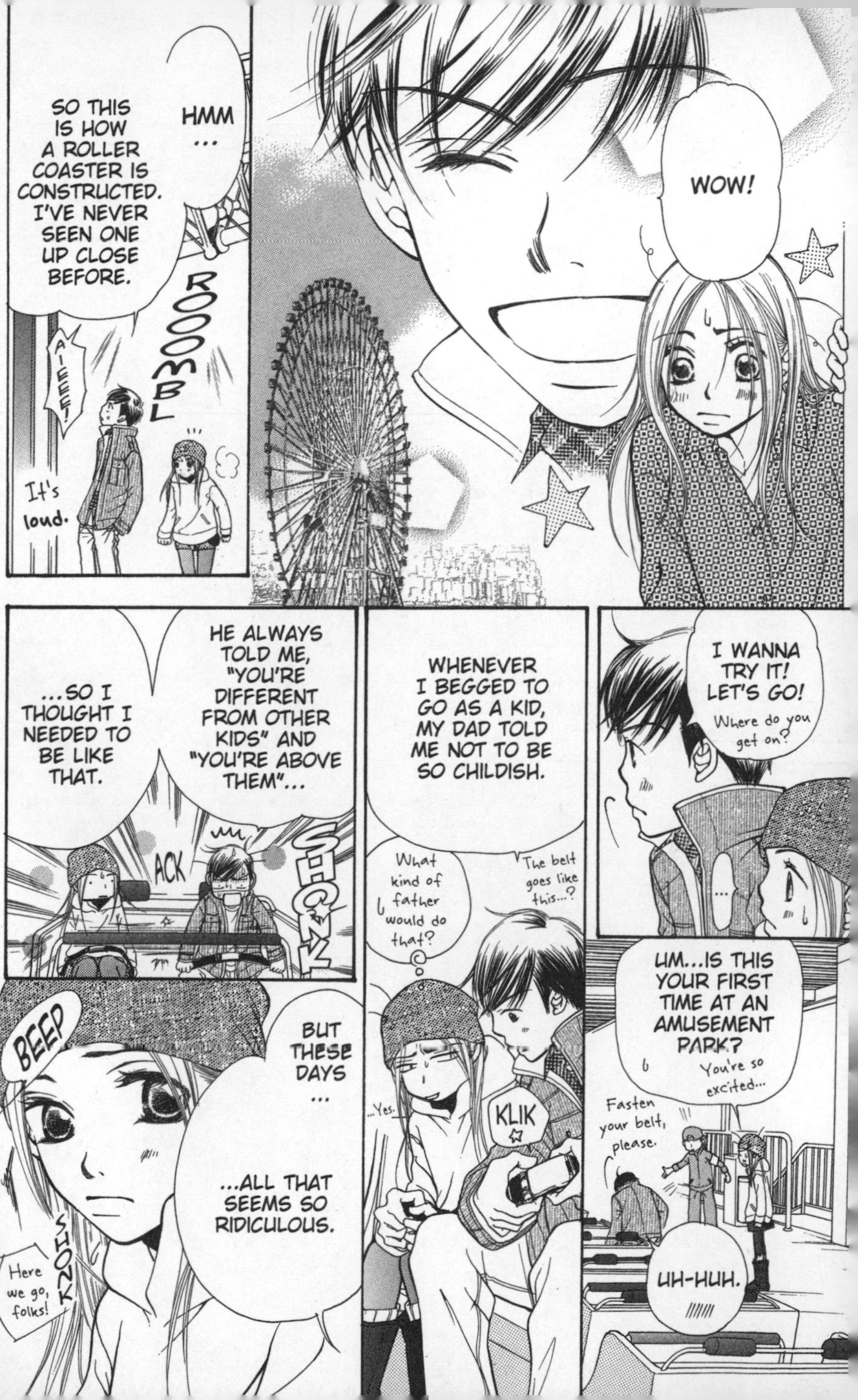
WOW!
HMM...
SO THIS IS HOW A ROLLER COASTER IS CONSTRUCTED. I'VE NEVER SEEN ONE UP CLOSE BEFORE.
ROOOMBL
AIEEE!
It's loud.
I WANNA TRY IT! LET'S GO!
Where do you get on?
...
UM...IS THIS YOUR FIRST TIME AT AN AMUSEMENT PARK?
You're so excited...
Fasten your belt, please.
UH-HUH.
WHENEVER I BEGGED TO GO AS A KID, MY DAD TOLD ME NOT TO BE SO CHILDISH.
The belt goes like this...?
What kind of father would do that?
KLIK
...Yes.
HE ALWAYS TOLD ME, "YOU'RE DIFFERENT FROM OTHER KIDS" AND "YOU'RE ABOVE THEM"...
...SO I THOUGHT I NEEDED TO BE LIKE THAT.
SHONK
ACK
BUT THESE DAYS...
...ALL THAT SEEMS SO RIDICULOUS.
BEEP
SHONK
Here we go, folks!

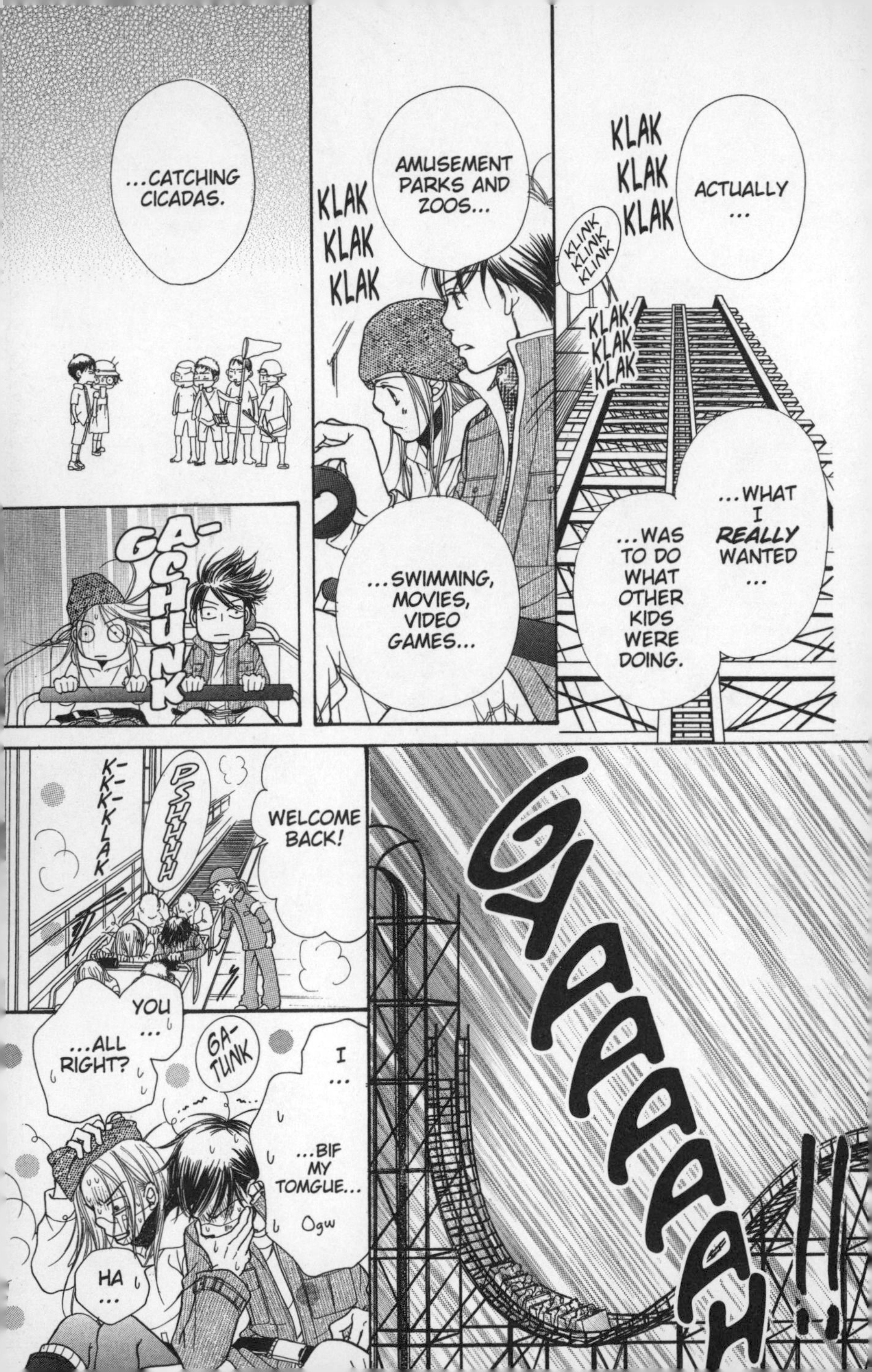
KLAK KLAK KLAK
ACTUALLY ...
KLINK KLINK KLINK
KLAK KLAK KLAK
...WHAT I *REALLY* WANTED ...
...WAS TO DO WHAT OTHER KIDS WERE DOING.
AMUSEMENT PARKS AND ZOOS...
KLAK KLAK KLAK
...SWIMMING, MOVIES, VIDEO GAMES...
...CATCHING CICADAS.
GA-CHUNK
GYAAAAAH!!
WELCOME BACK!
PSHHHH
K-K-K-KLAK
YOU ...
...ALL RIGHT?
GA-TUNK
I ...
...BIF MY TOMGUE...
Ogw
HA ...

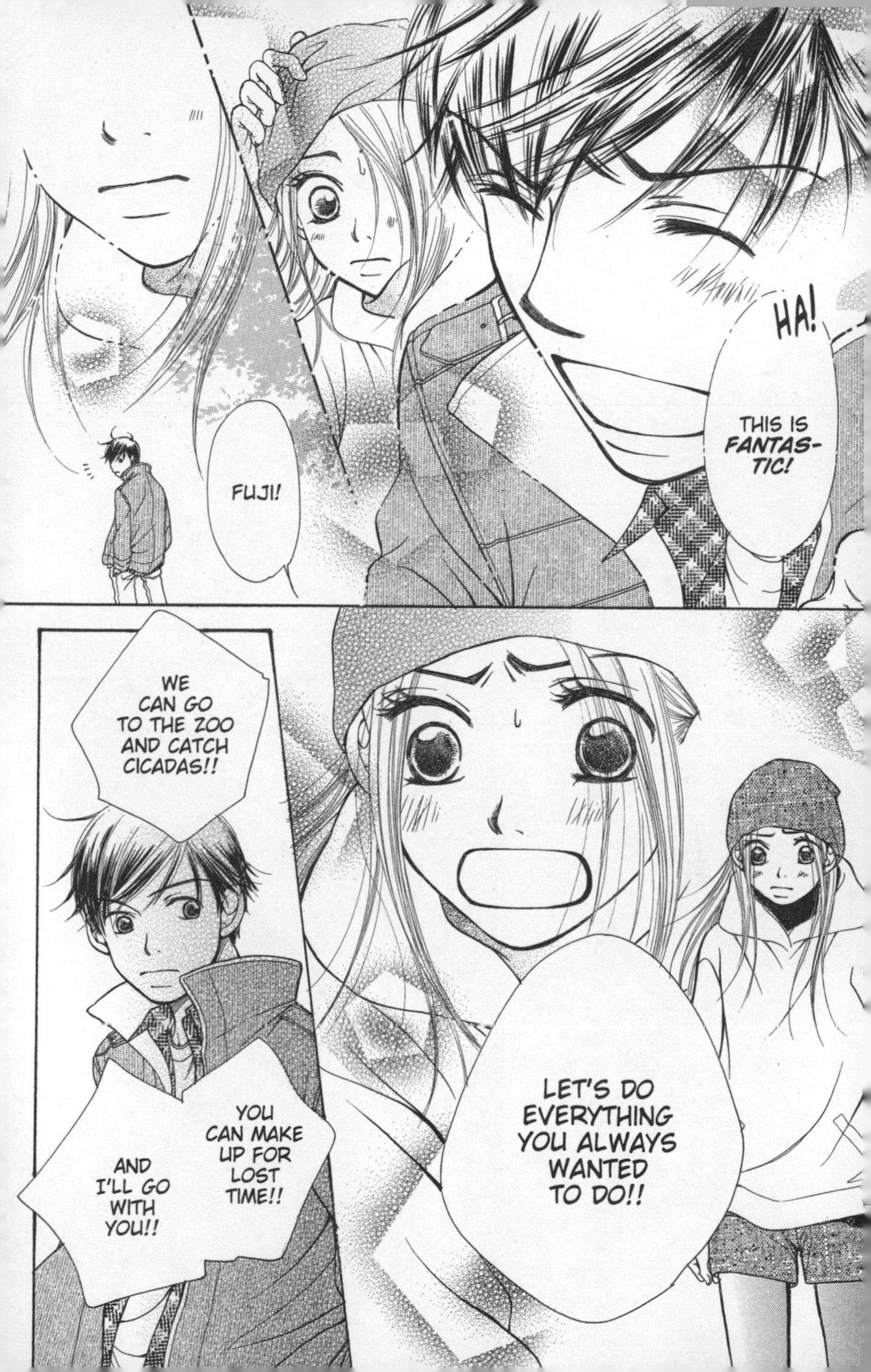
HA!
THIS IS FANTASTIC!
FUJI!
LET'S DO EVERYTHING YOU ALWAYS WANTED TO DO!!
WE CAN GO TO THE ZOO AND CATCH CICADAS!!
YOU CAN MAKE UP FOR LOST TIME!!
AND I'LL GO WITH YOU!!

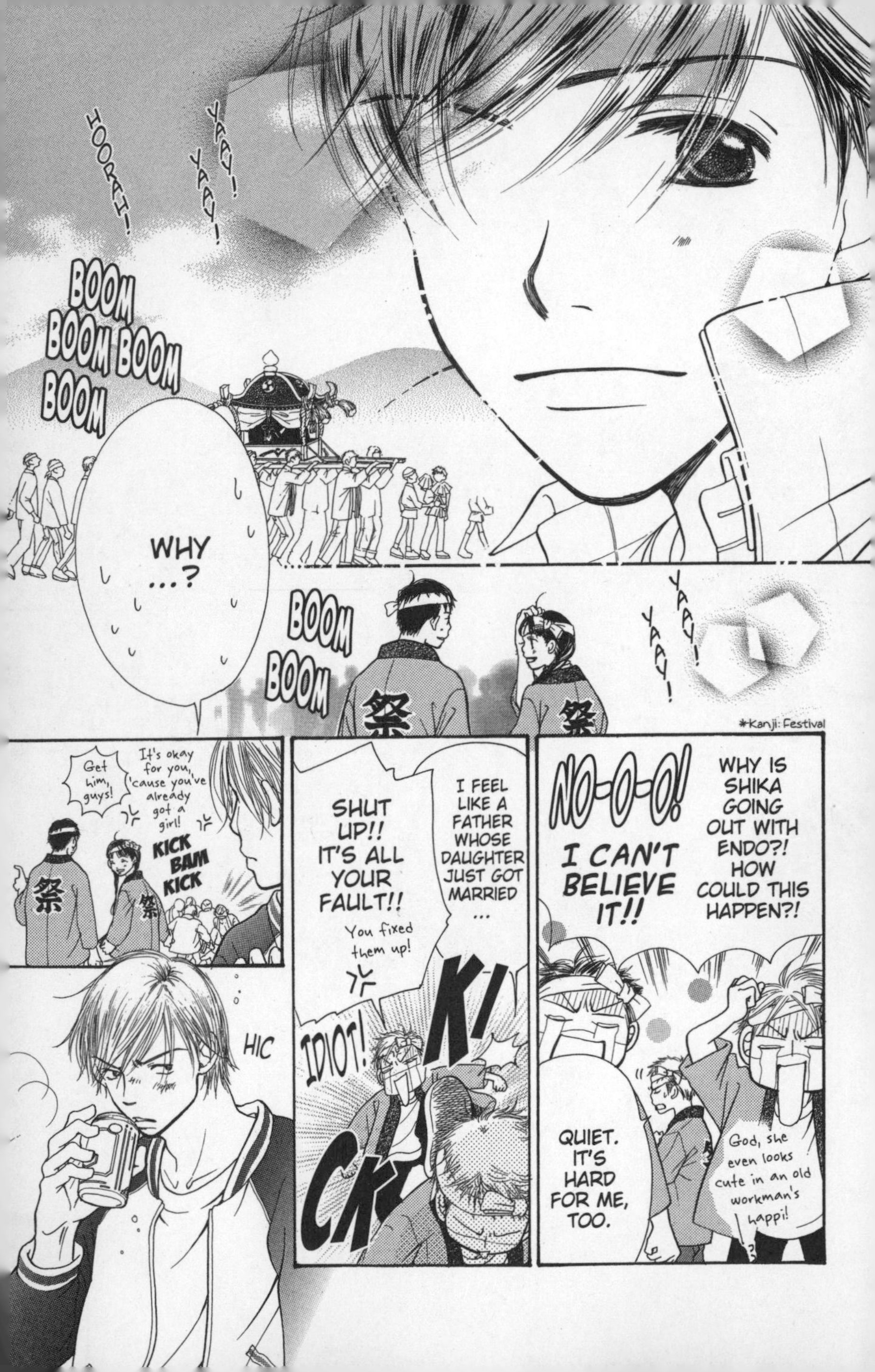
YAAY! YAAY!
HOORAH!
BOOM BOOM BOOM BOOM
WHY ...?
YAAY! YAAY!
BOOM BOOM
*Kanji: Festival
NO-O-O-O!
WHY IS SHIKA GOING OUT WITH ENDO?! HOW COULD THIS HAPPEN?!
I CAN'T BELIEVE IT!!
God, she even looks cute in an old workman's happi!
QUIET. IT'S HARD FOR ME, TOO.
I FEEL LIKE A FATHER WHOSE DAUGHTER JUST GOT MARRIED ...
SHUT UP!! IT'S ALL YOUR FAULT!!
You fixed them up!
KICK
IDIOT!
It's okay for you, 'cause you've already got a girl!
Get him, guys!
KICK BAM KICK
HIC

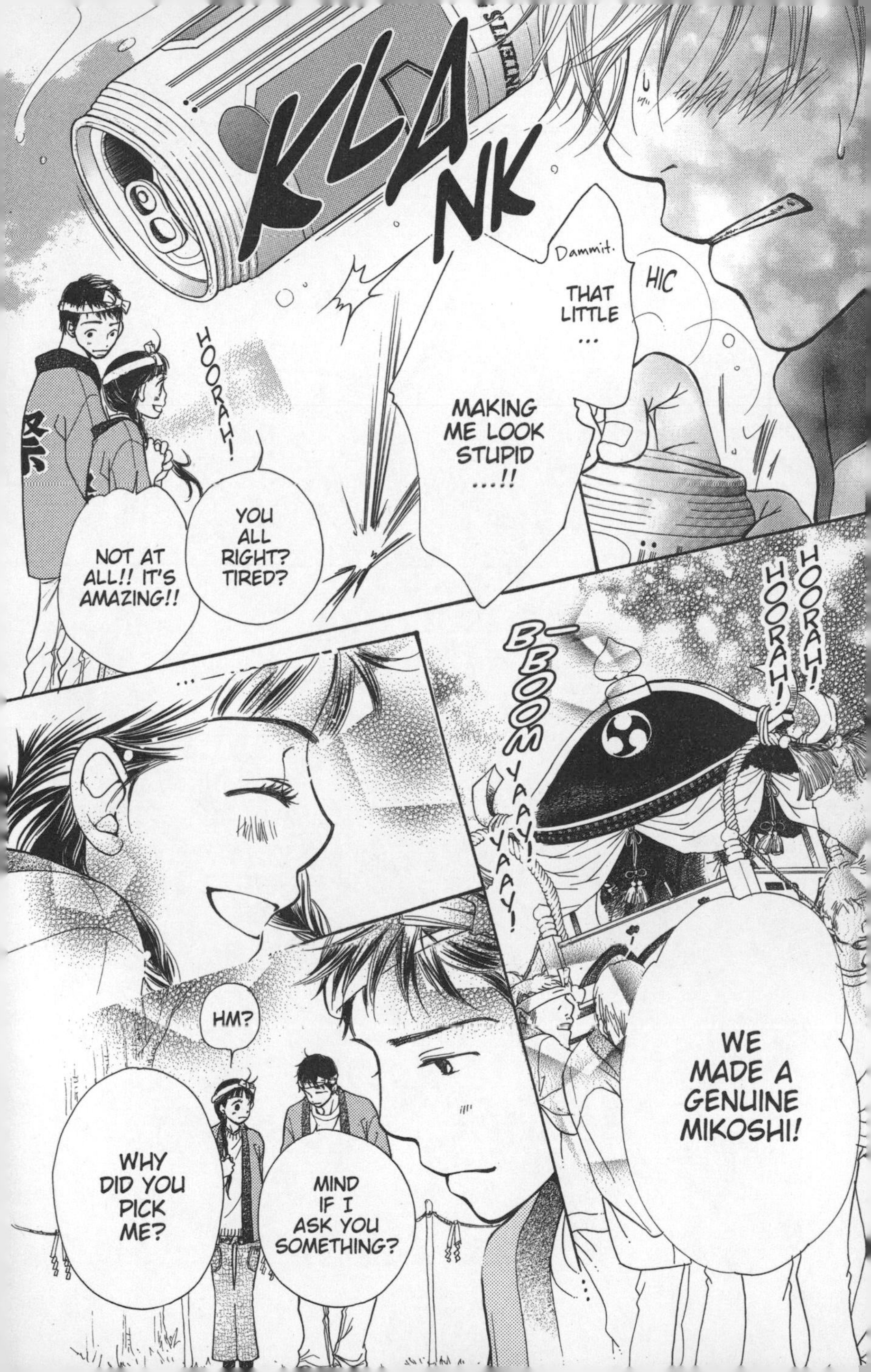
KLANK
Dammit.
HIC
THAT LITTLE ...
MAKING ME LOOK STUPID ...!!
HOORAH!
YOU ALL RIGHT? TIRED?
NOT AT ALL!! IT'S AMAZING!!
HOORAH! HOORAH!
B-BOOM
YAAY! YAAY!
WE MADE A GENUINE MIKOSHI!
...
MIND IF I ASK YOU SOMETHING?
HM?
WHY DID YOU PICK ME?

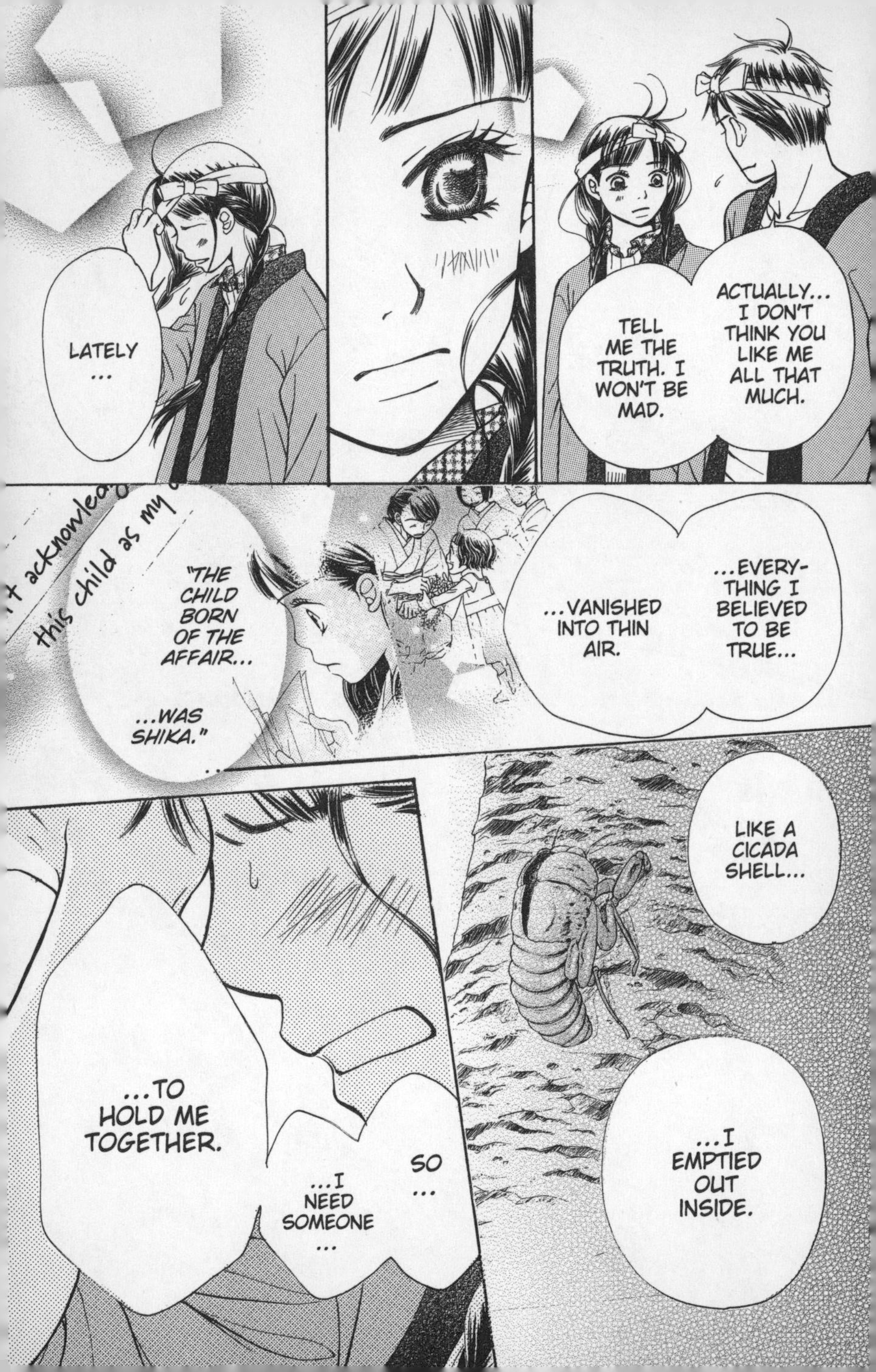
ACTUALLY... I DON'T THINK YOU LIKE ME ALL THAT MUCH.
TELL ME THE TRUTH. I WON'T BE MAD.
LATELY ...
...EVERY-THING I BELIEVED TO BE TRUE...
...VANISHED INTO THIN AIR.
"THE CHILD BORN OF THE AFFAIR...
...WAS SHIKA."
this child as my
LIKE A CICADA SHELL...
...I EMPTIED OUT INSIDE.
SO ...
...I NEED SOMEONE ...
...TO HOLD ME TOGETHER.

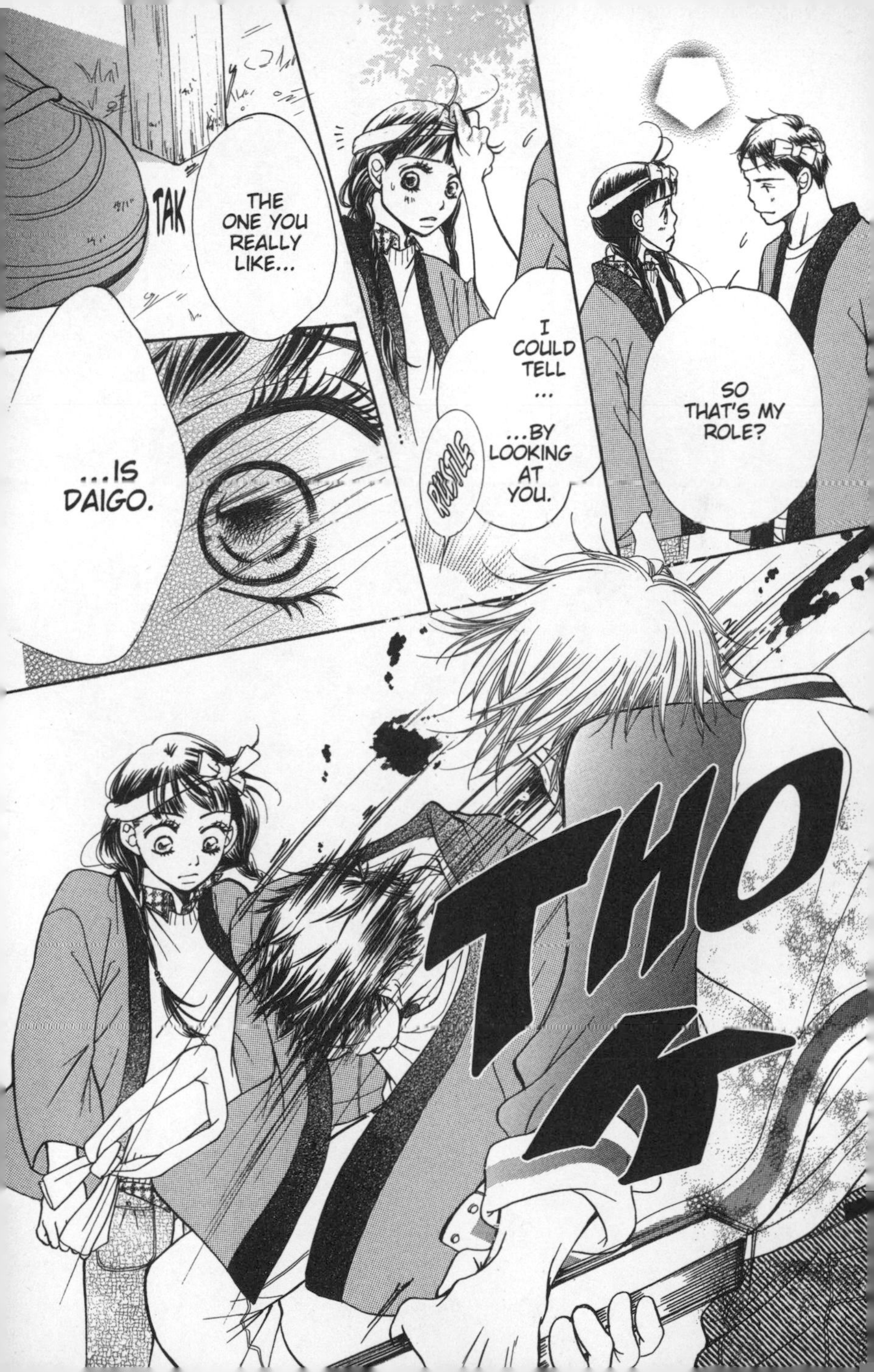
SO THAT'S MY ROLE?
I COULD TELL ...
...BY LOOKING AT YOU.
RUSTLE
TAK
THE ONE YOU REALLY LIKE...
...IS DAIGO.
THOK

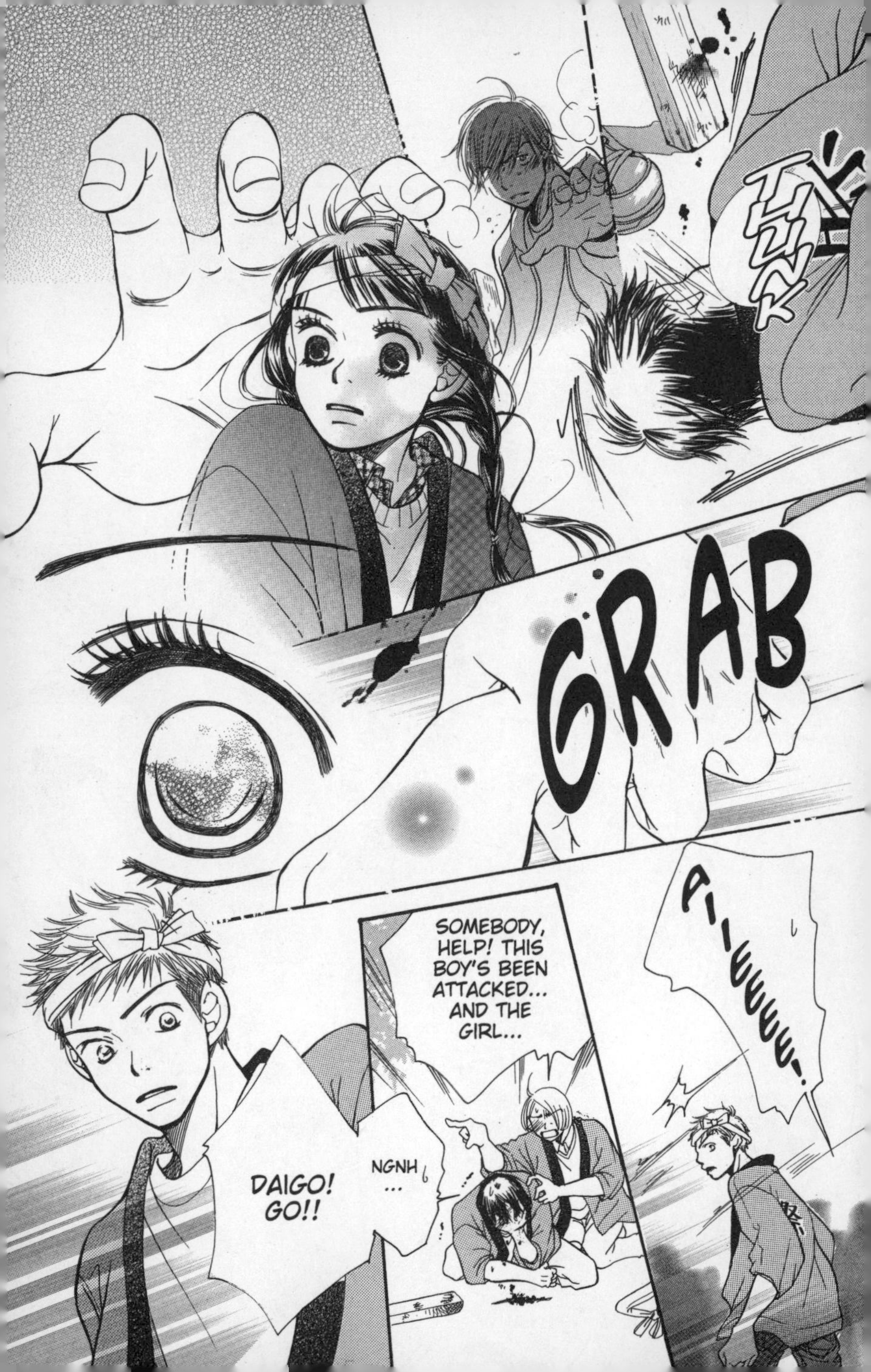
THUNK
GRAB
AIEEEEE!
SOMEBODY, HELP! THIS BOY'S BEEN ATTACKED... AND THE GIRL...
NGNH...
DAIGO! GO!!

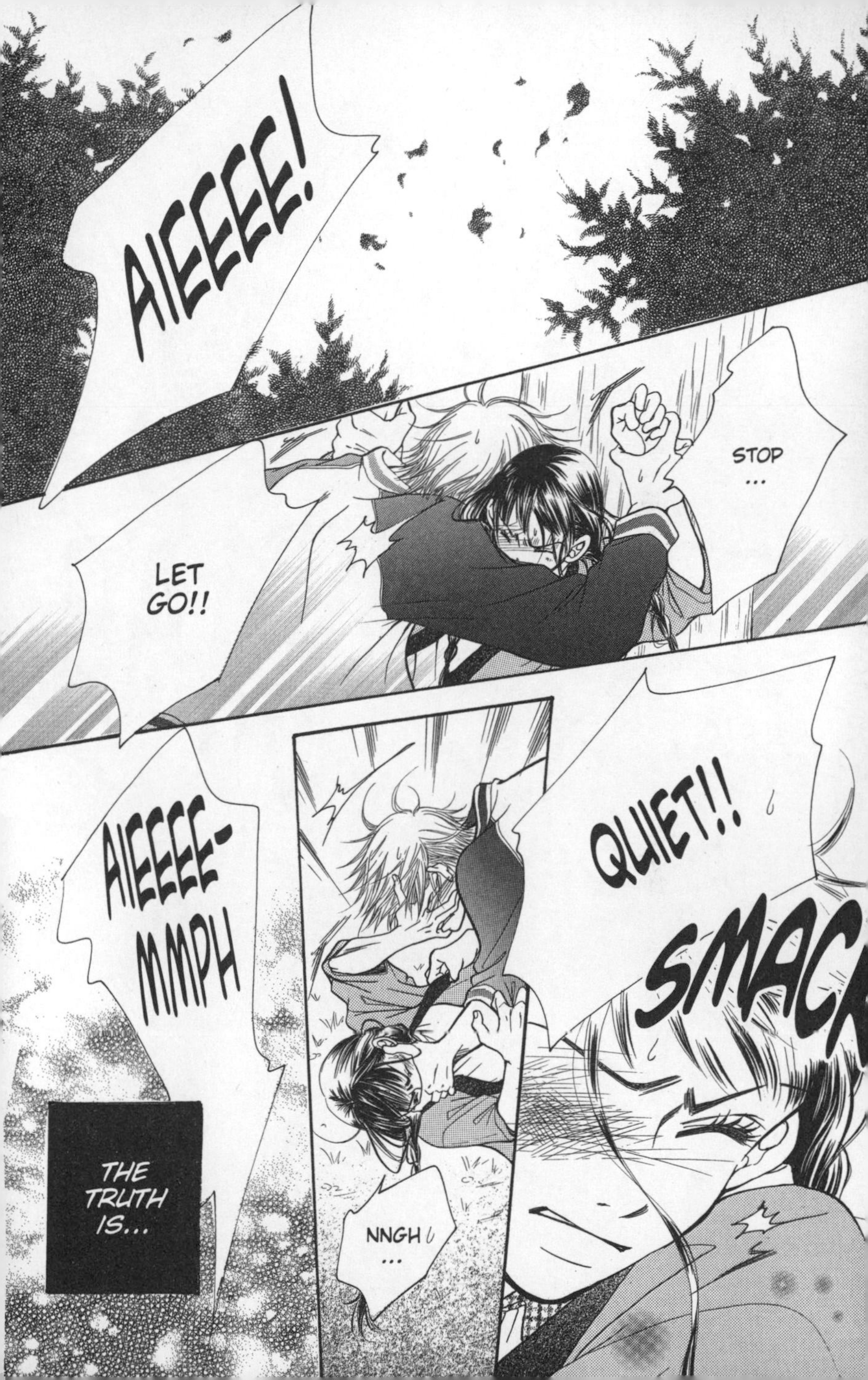
AIEEEE!
STOP ...
LET GO!!
QUIET!!
SMACK
NNGH ...
AIEEEE-MMPH
THE TRUTH IS...

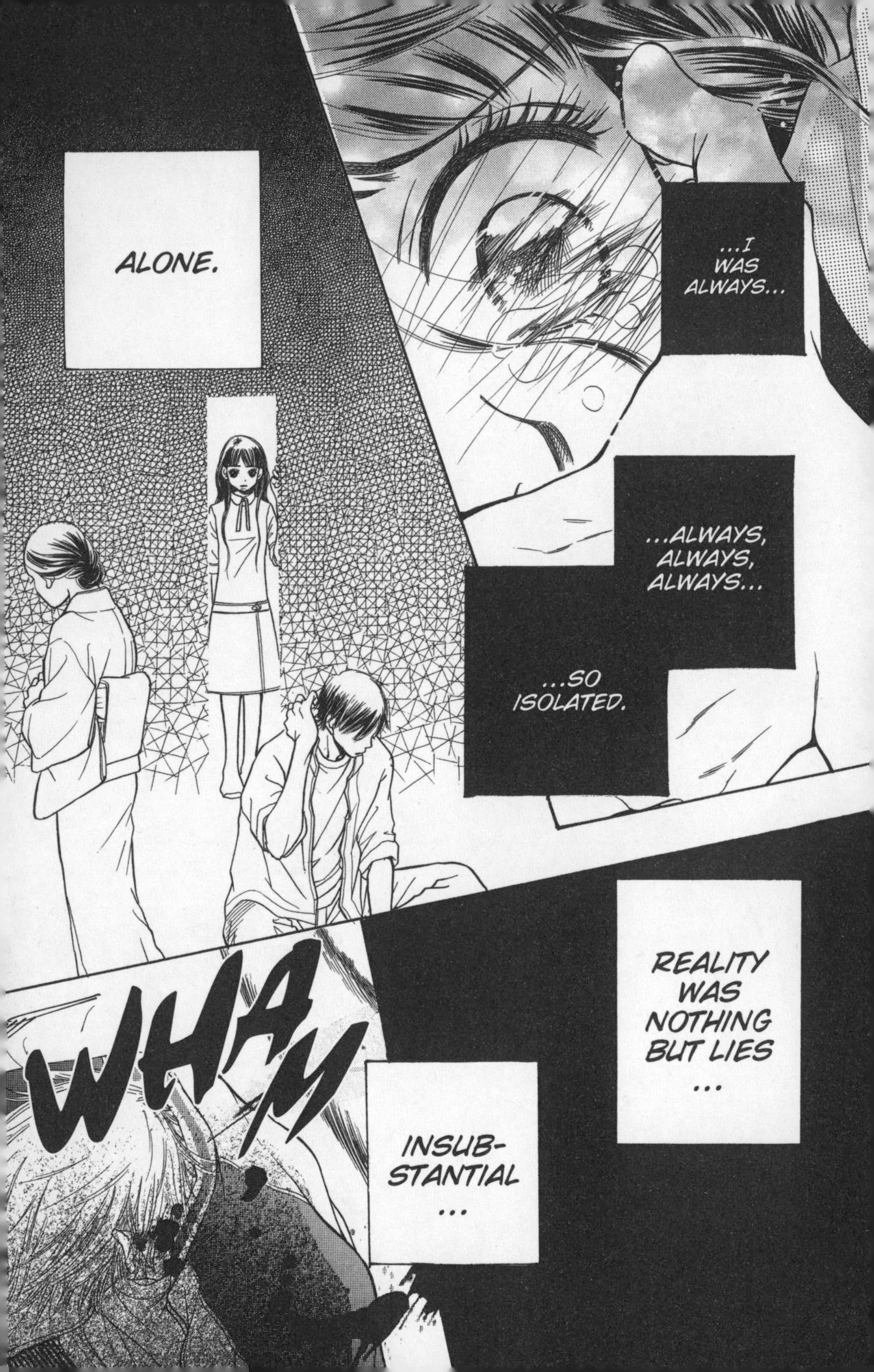
...I WAS ALWAYS...
...ALWAYS, ALWAYS, ALWAYS...
...SO ISOLATED.
ALONE.
REALITY WAS NOTHING BUT LIES ...
INSUB-STANTIAL ...
WHAM

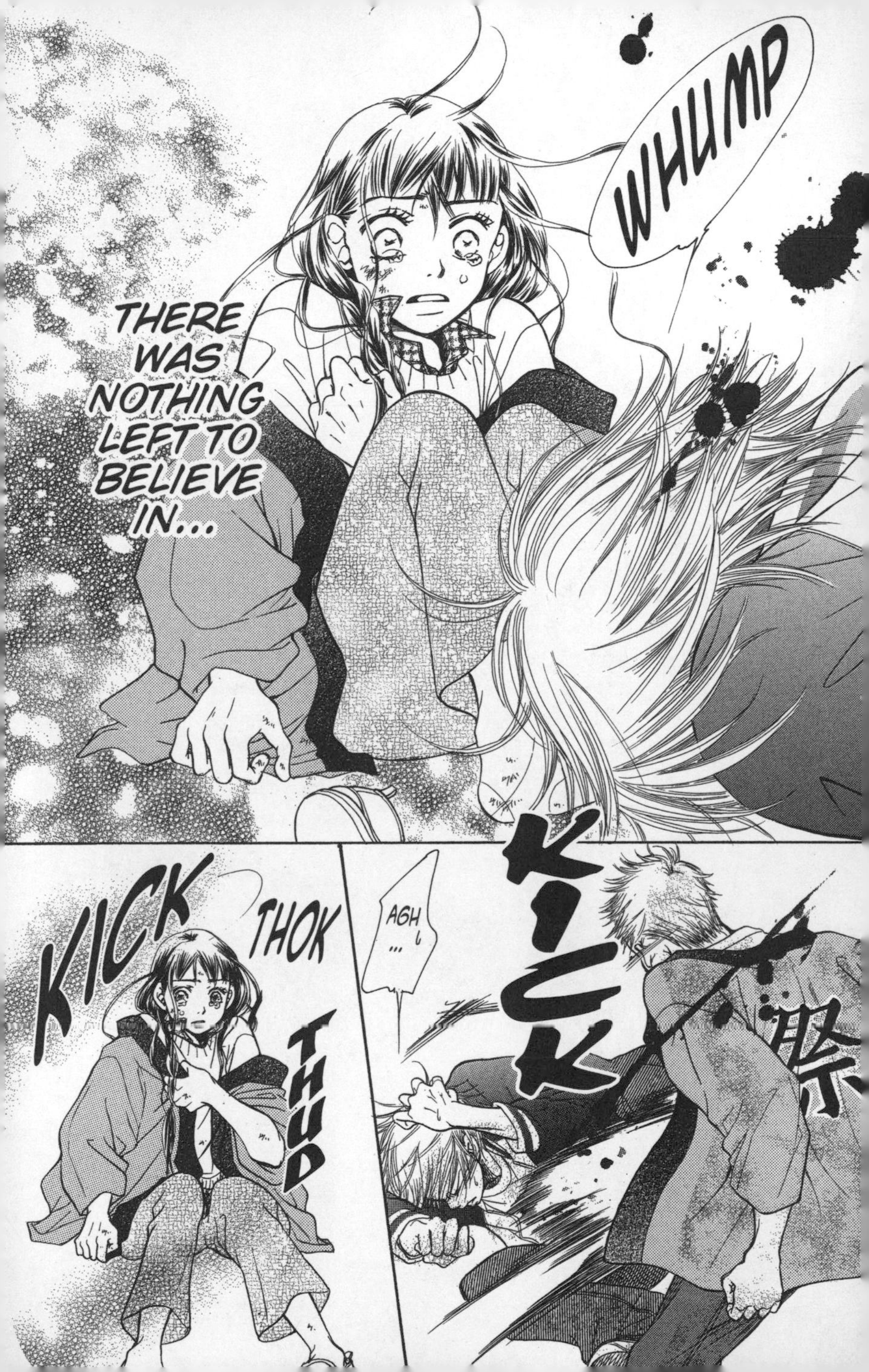
WHUMP
THERE WAS NOTHING LEFT TO BELIEVE IN...
KICK
AGH ...
KICK
THOK
THUD

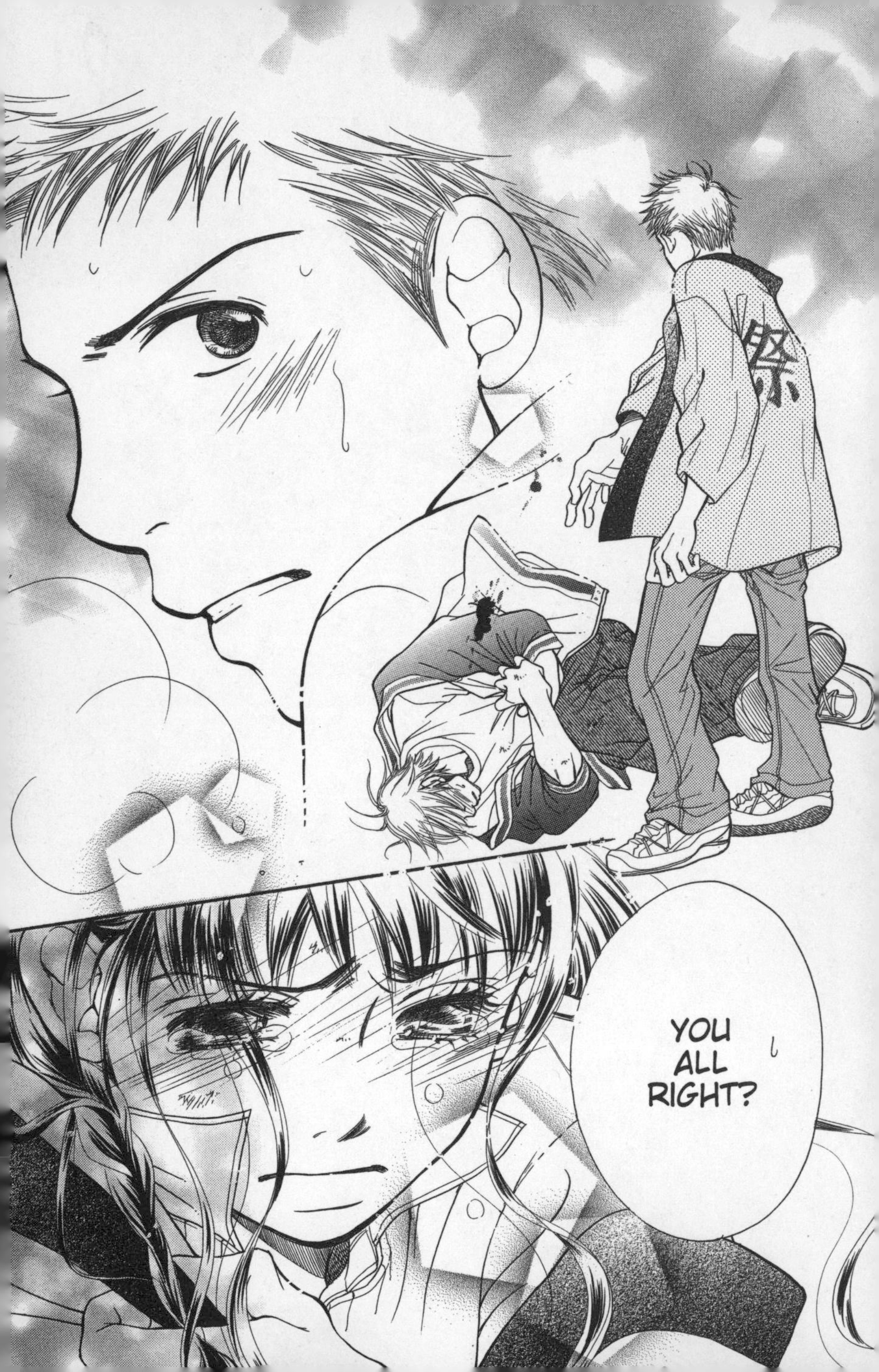
祭
YOU ALL RIGHT?

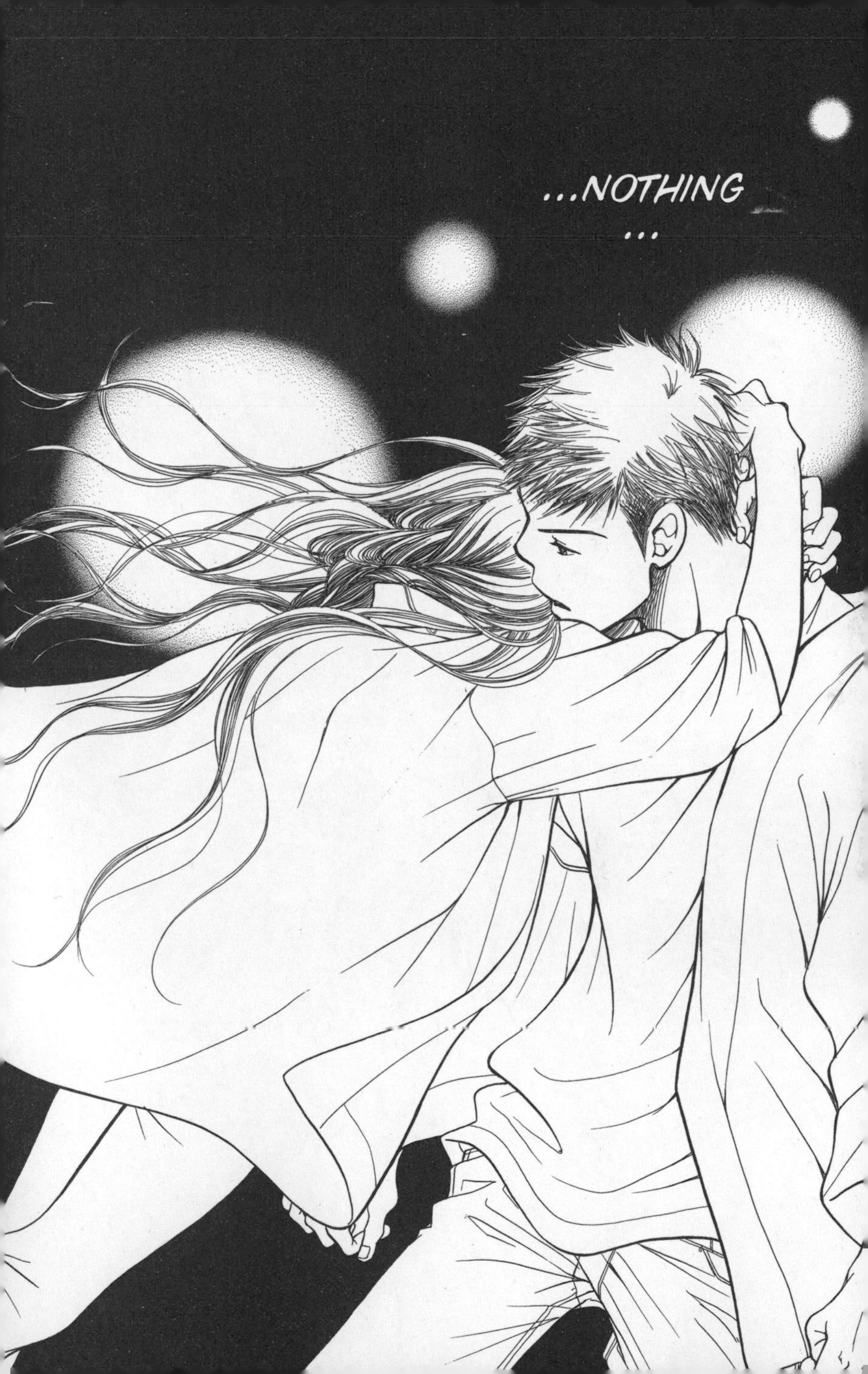
...NOTHING
...

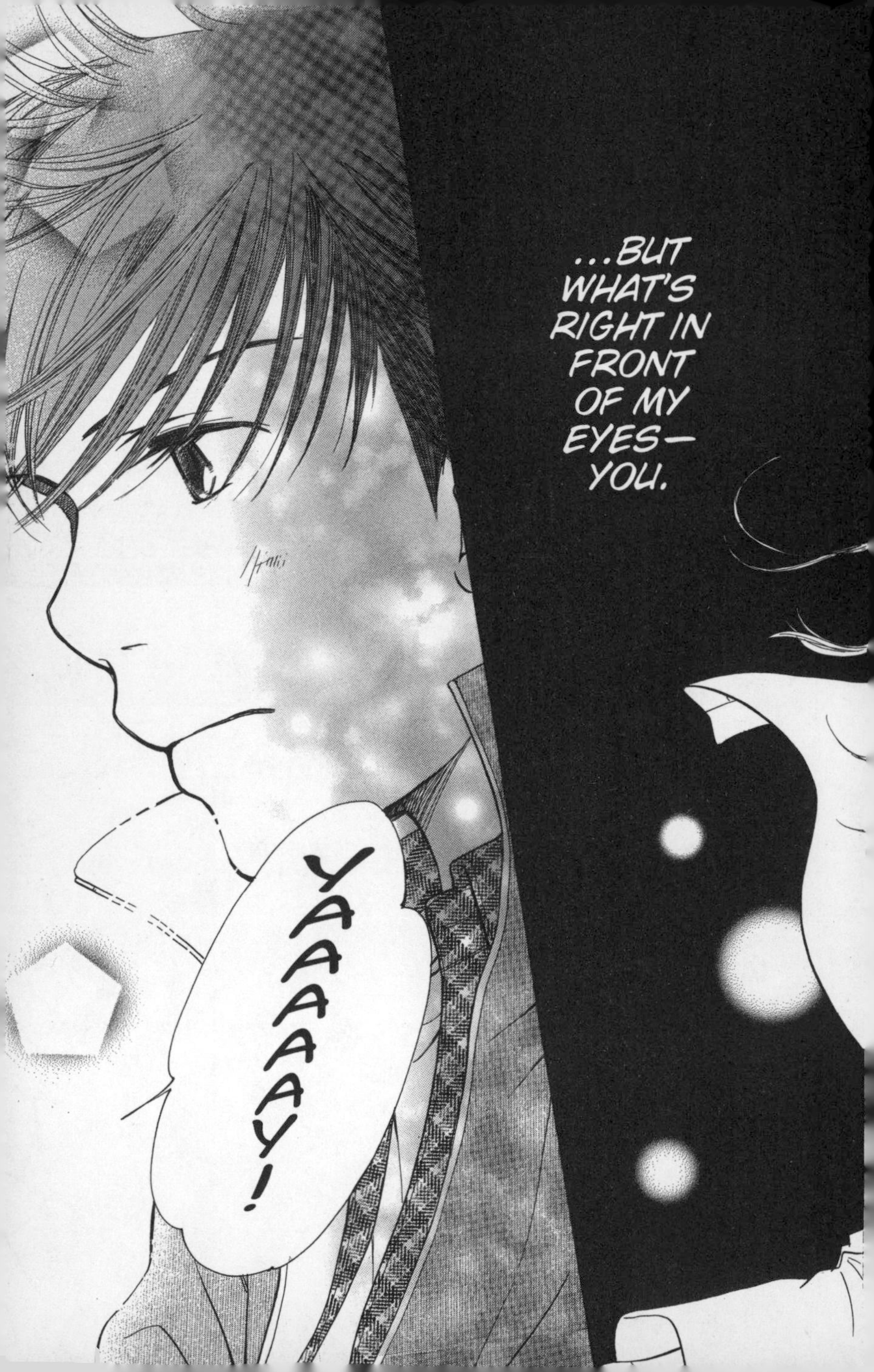
...BUT WHAT'S RIGHT IN FRONT OF MY EYES— YOU.
YAAAAAAY!

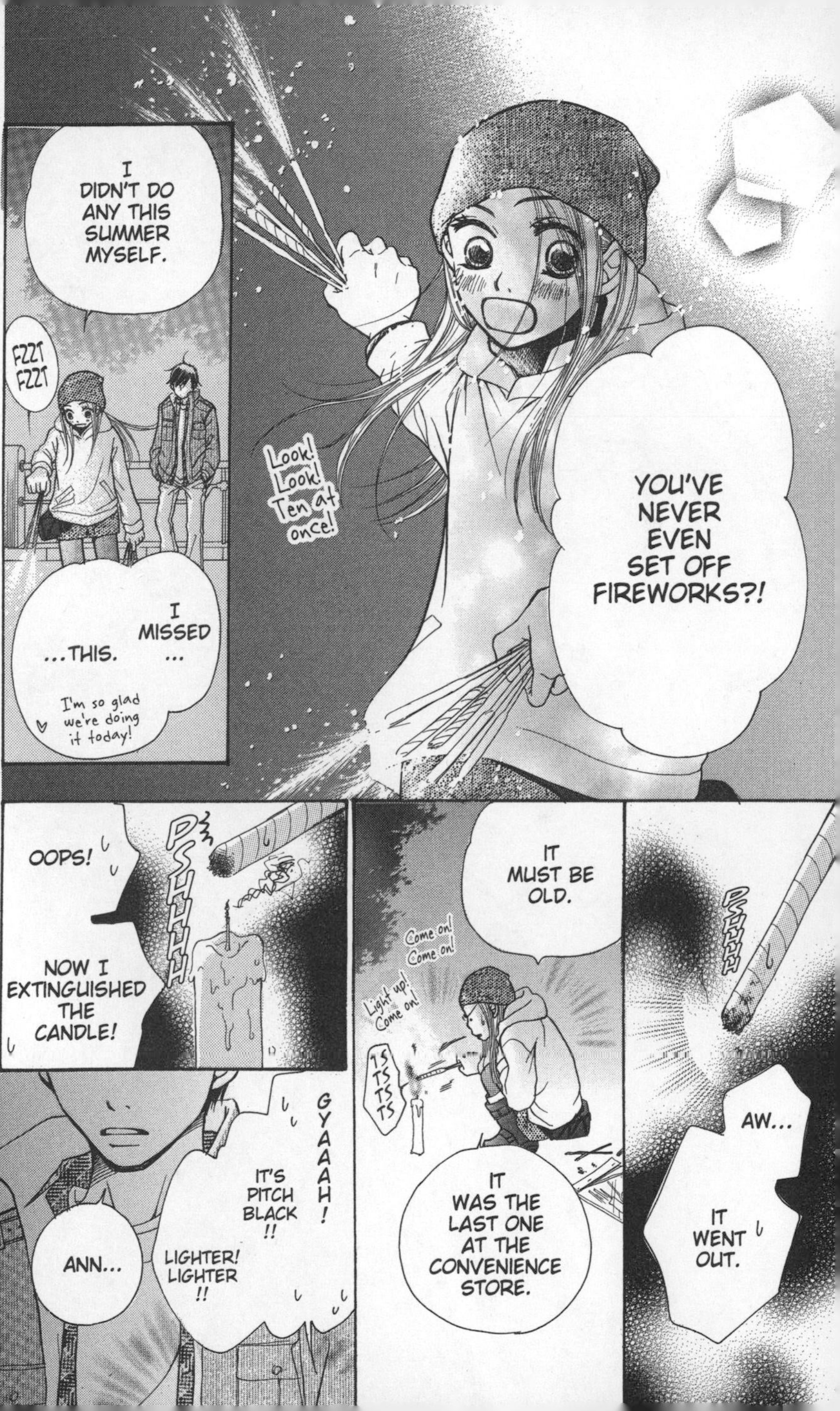
YOU'VE NEVER EVEN SET OFF FIREWORKS?!
Look! Look! Ten at once!
I DIDN'T DO ANY THIS SUMMER MYSELF.
FZZT FZZT
I MISSED ...
...THIS.
I'm so glad we're doing it today!
PSHHHH
AW...
IT WENT OUT.
IT MUST BE OLD.
Come on! Come on!
Light up! Come on!
TS TS TS TS
IT WAS THE LAST ONE AT THE CONVENIENCE STORE.
OOPS!
PSHHHH
NOW I EXTINGUISHED THE CANDLE!
GYAAAAH!
IT'S PITCH BLACK!!
LIGHTER! LIGHTER!!
ANN...

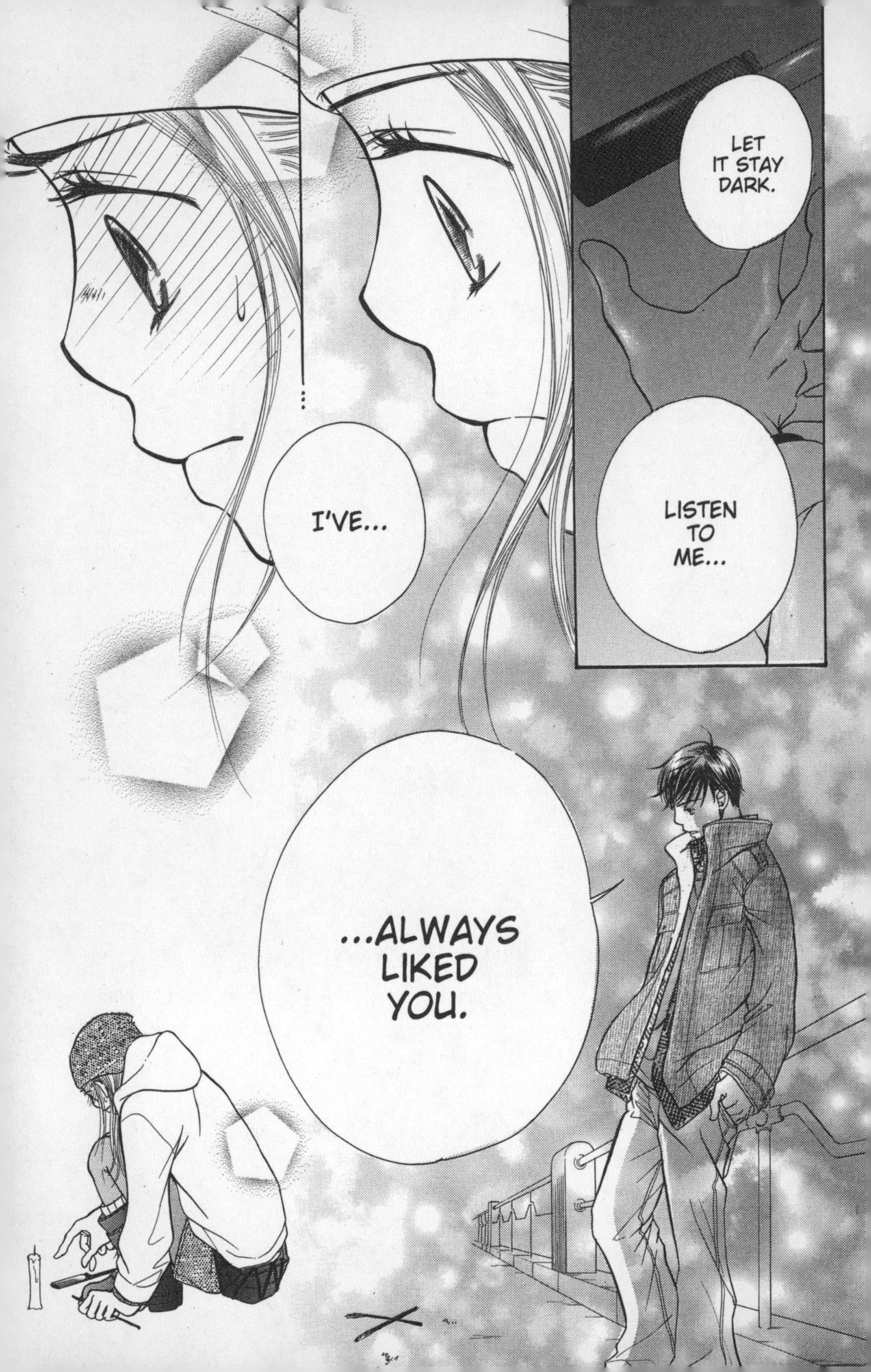
LET IT STAY DARK.
LISTEN TO ME...
I'VE...
...ALWAYS LIKED YOU.

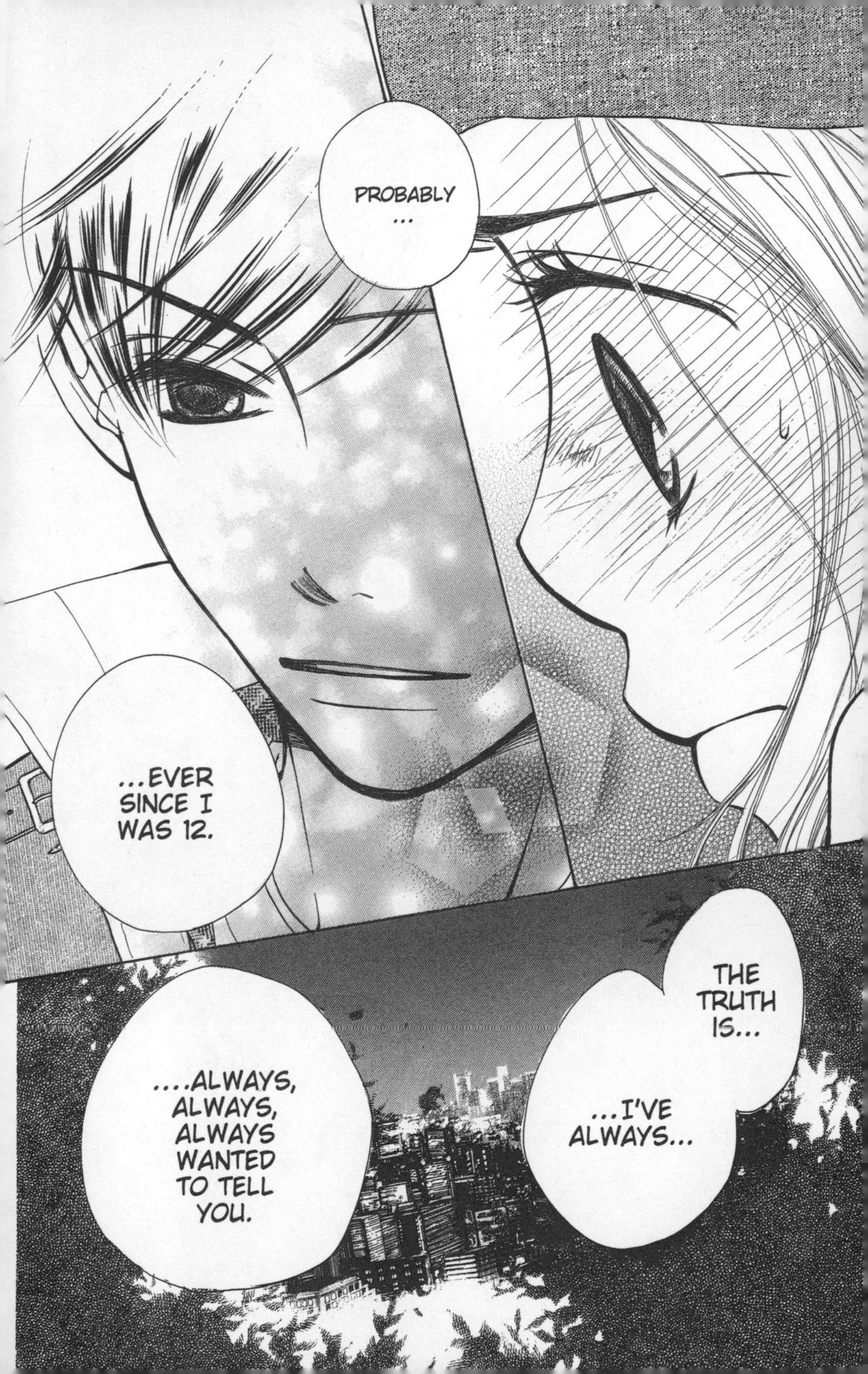
PROBABLY ...
...EVER SINCE I WAS 12.
THE TRUTH IS...
...I'VE ALWAYS...
....ALWAYS, ALWAYS, ALWAYS WANTED TO TELL YOU.

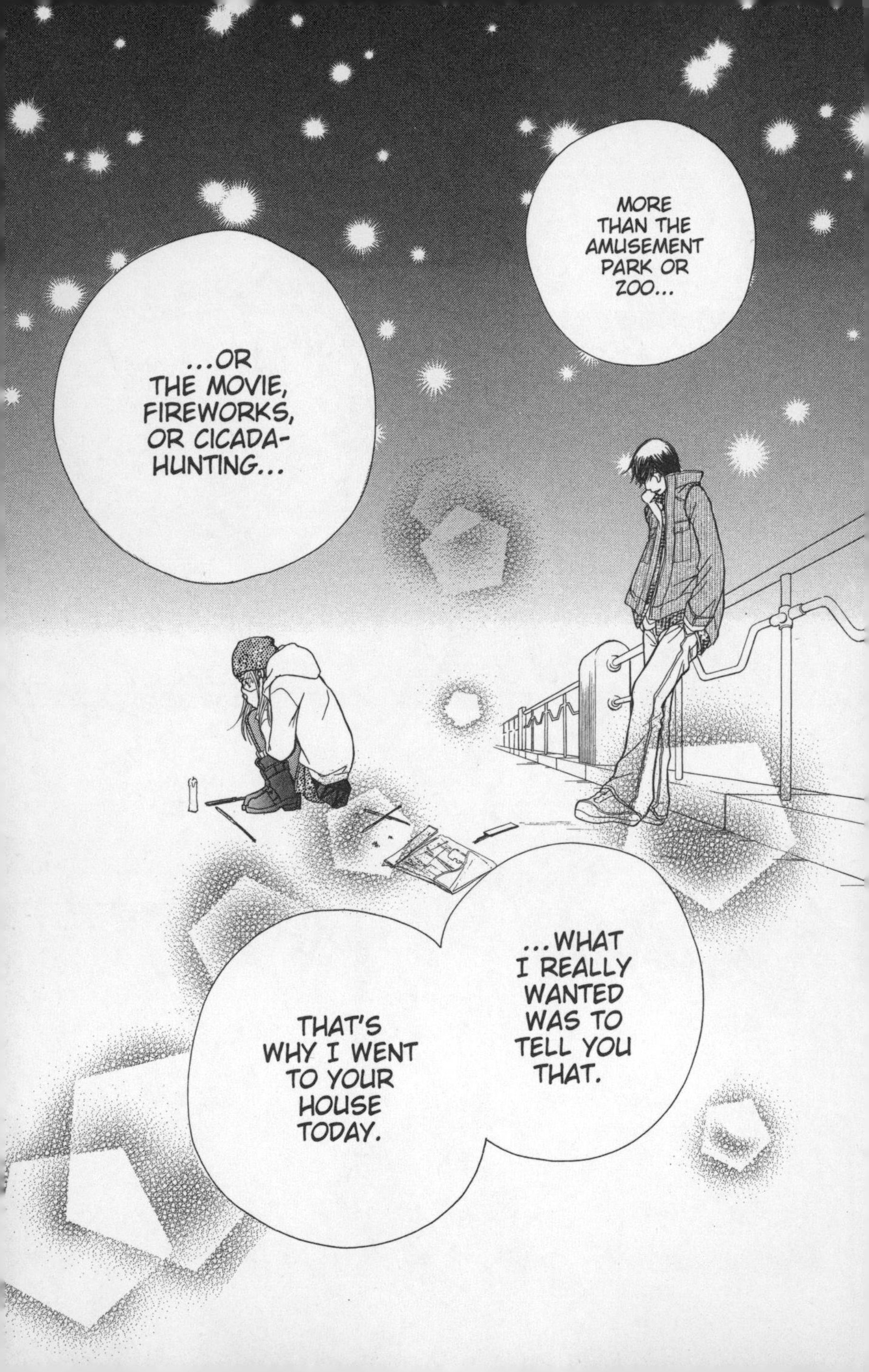
MORE THAN THE AMUSEMENT PARK OR ZOO...
...OR THE MOVIE, FIREWORKS, OR CICADA-HUNTING...
...WHAT I REALLY WANTED WAS TO TELL YOU THAT.
THAT'S WHY I WENT TO YOUR HOUSE TODAY.

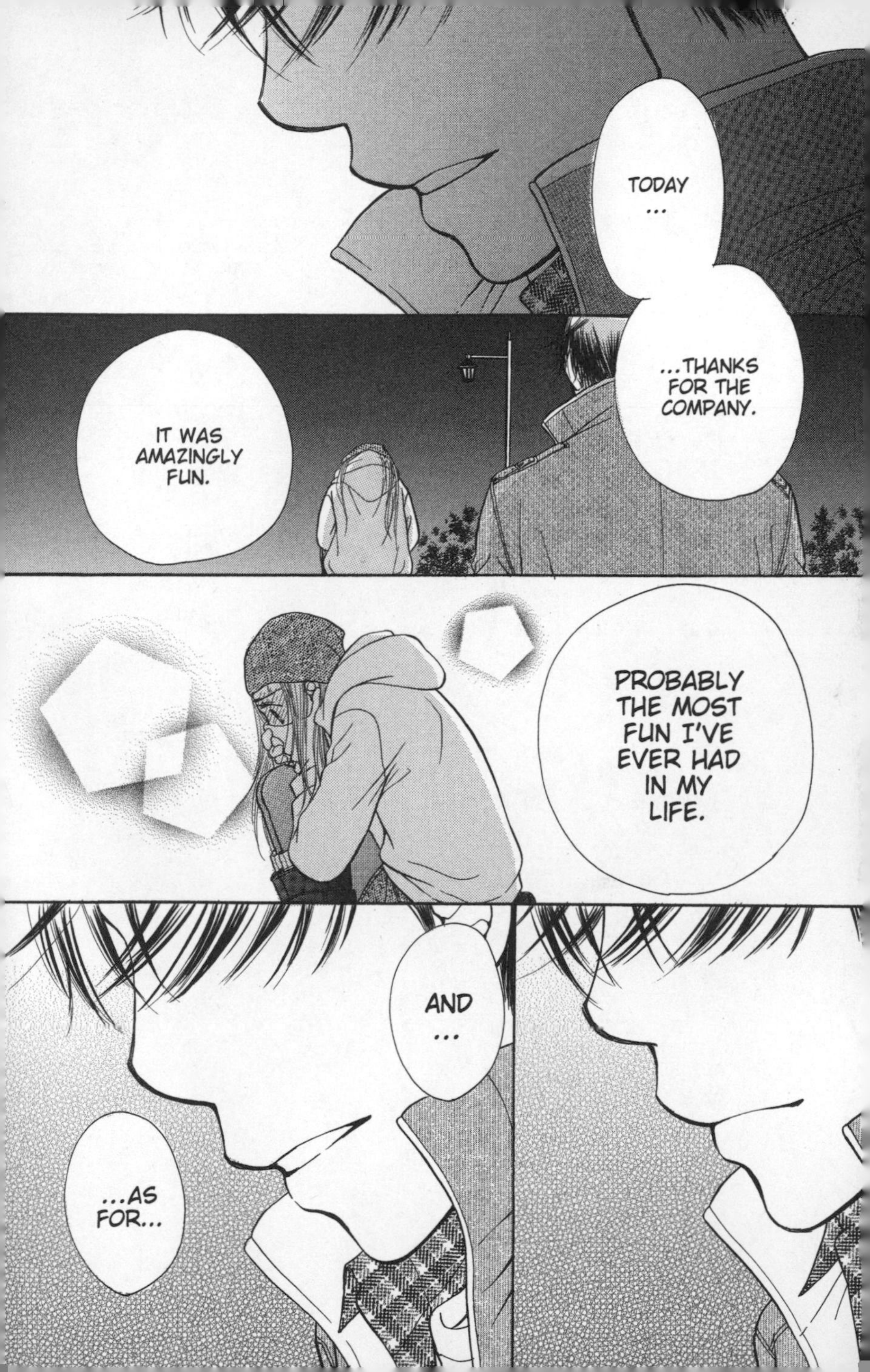
TODAY ...
...THANKS FOR THE COMPANY.
IT WAS AMAZINGLY FUN.
PROBABLY THE MOST FUN I'VE EVER HAD IN MY LIFE.
AND ...
...AS FOR...

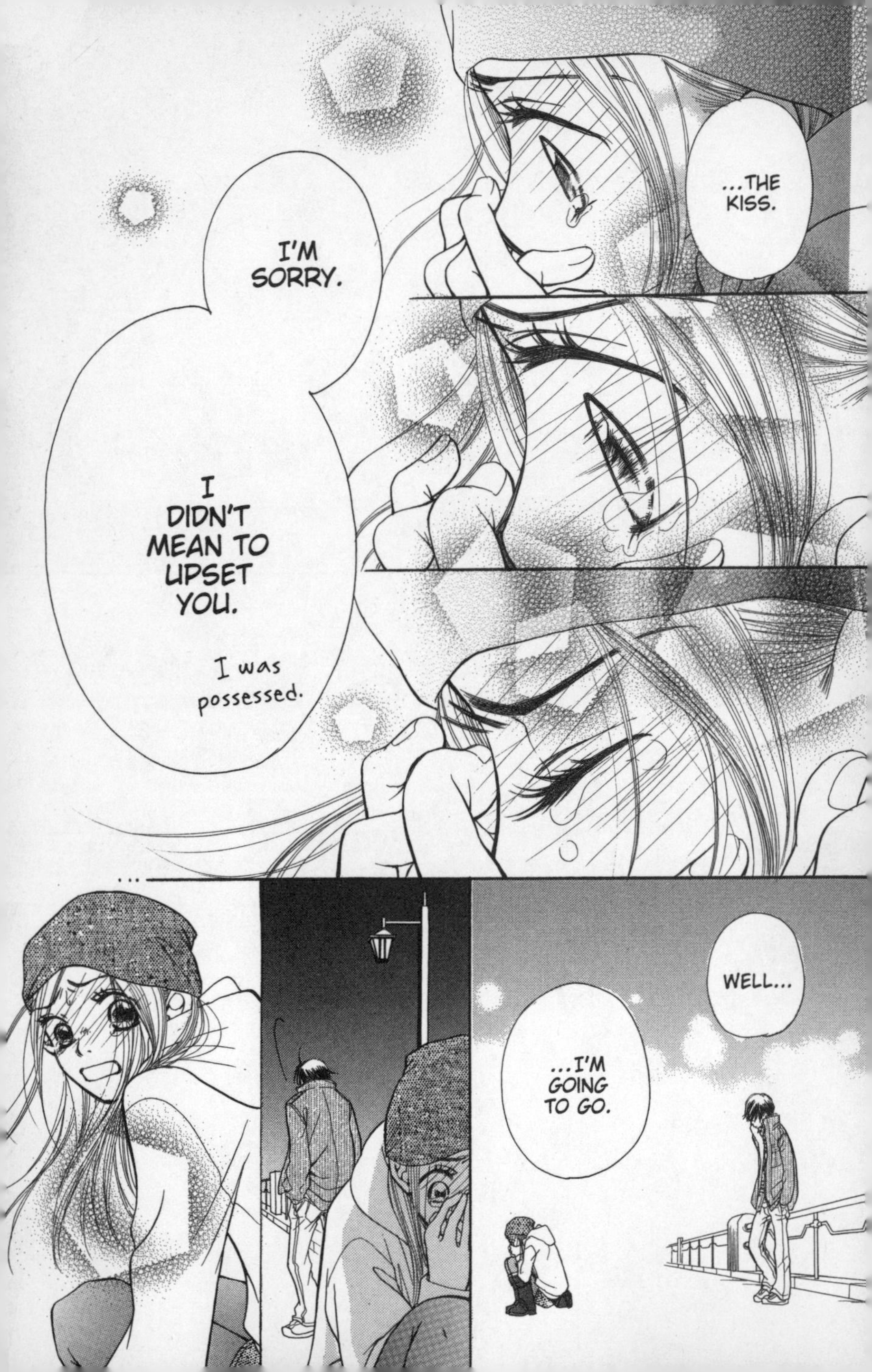
...THE KISS.
I'M SORRY.
I DIDN'T MEAN TO UPSET YOU.
I was possessed.
WELL...
...I'M GOING TO GO.
...

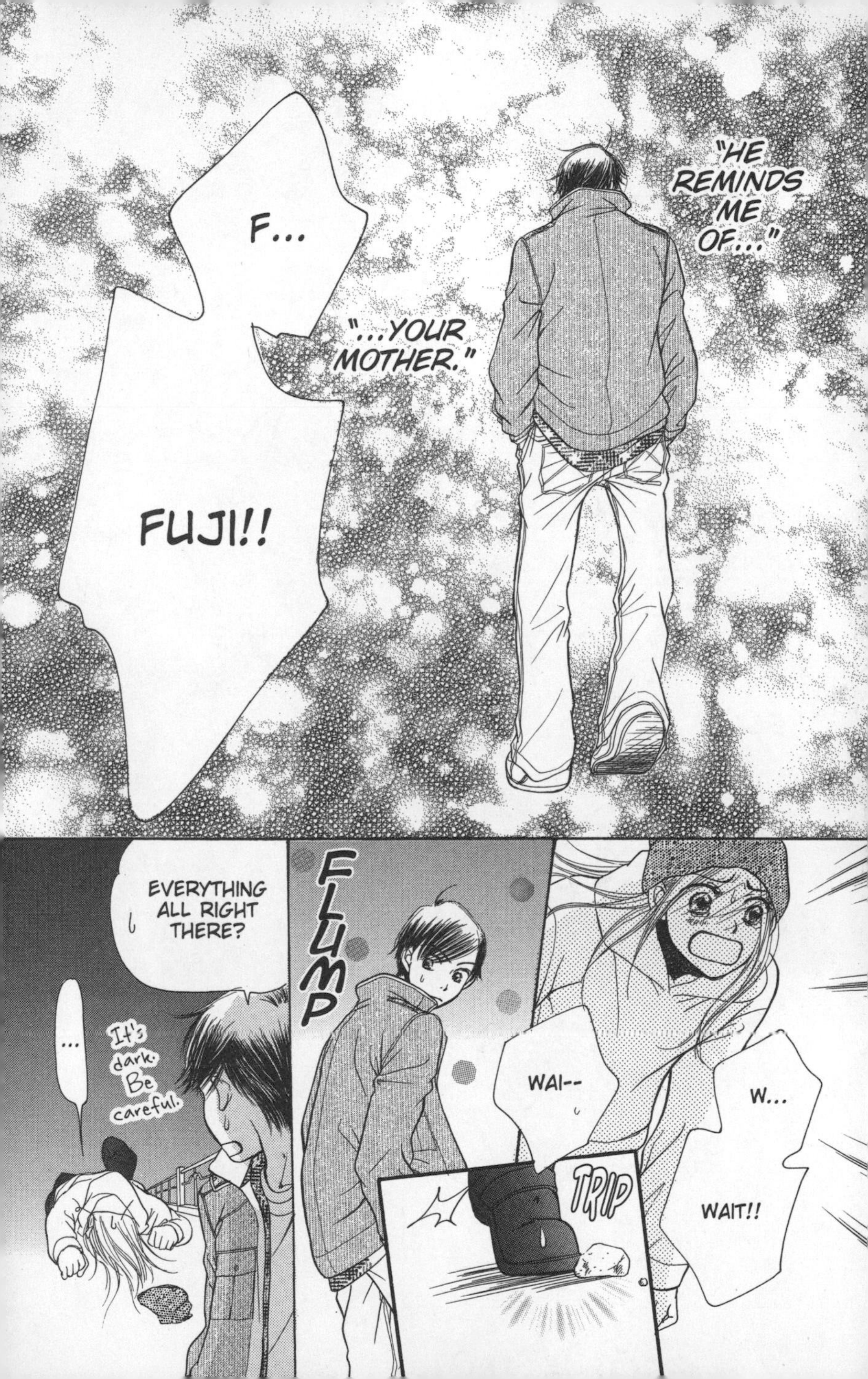
"HE REMINDS ME OF..."
"...YOUR MOTHER."
F...
FUJI!!
W...
WAIT!!
WAI--
TRIP
FLUMP
EVERYTHING ALL RIGHT THERE?
...
It's dark. Be careful.

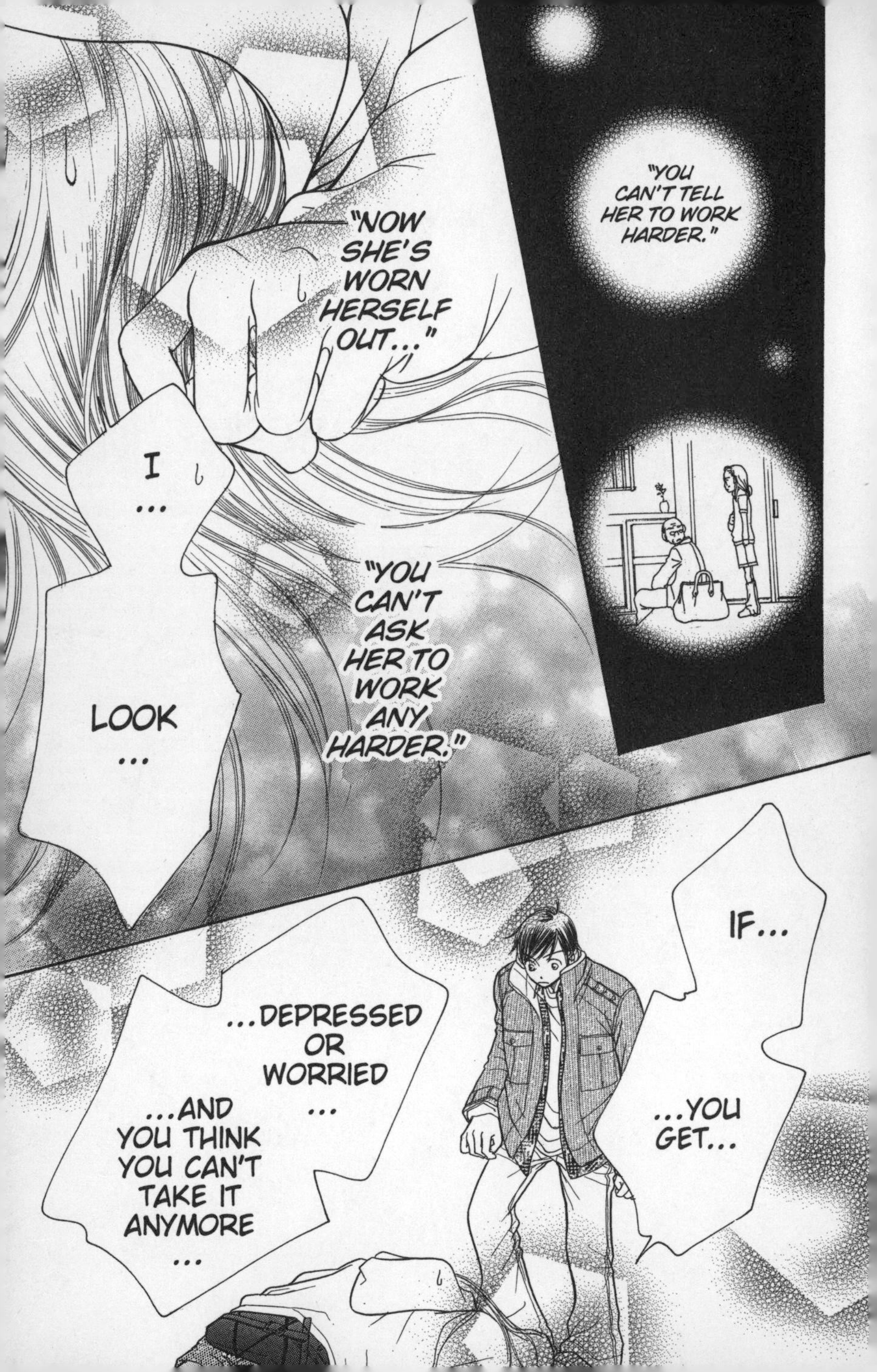
"YOU CAN'T TELL HER TO WORK HARDER."
"NOW SHE'S WORN HERSELF OUT..."
I...
"YOU CAN'T ASK HER TO WORK ANY HARDER."
LOOK...
IF...
...YOU GET...
...DEPRESSED OR WORRIED...
...AND YOU THINK YOU CAN'T TAKE IT ANYMORE...

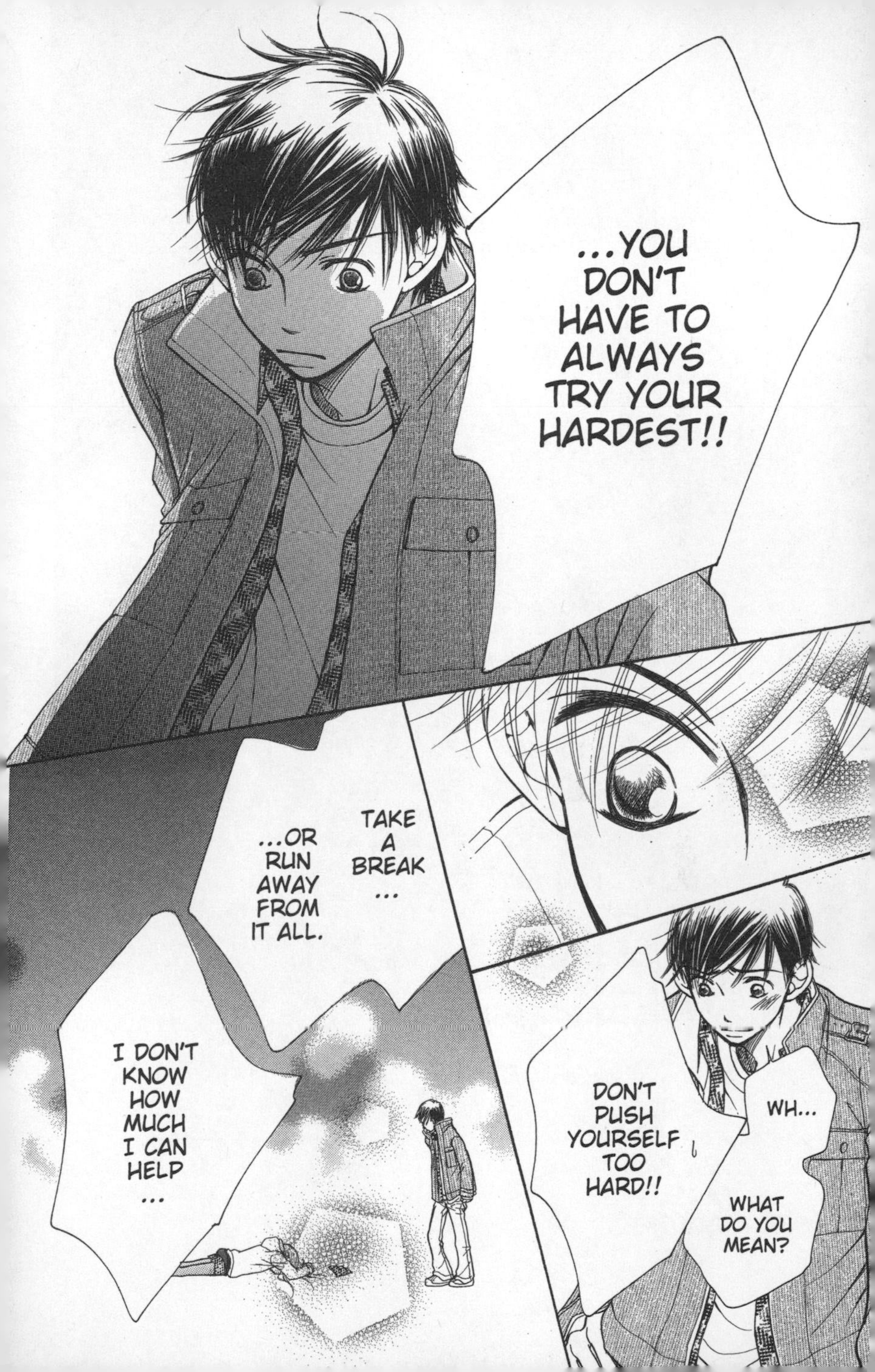
...YOU DON'T HAVE TO ALWAYS TRY YOUR HARDEST!!
DON'T PUSH YOURSELF TOO HARD!!
WH...
WHAT DO YOU MEAN?
TAKE A BREAK...
...OR RUN AWAY FROM IT ALL.
I DON'T KNOW HOW MUCH I CAN HELP...

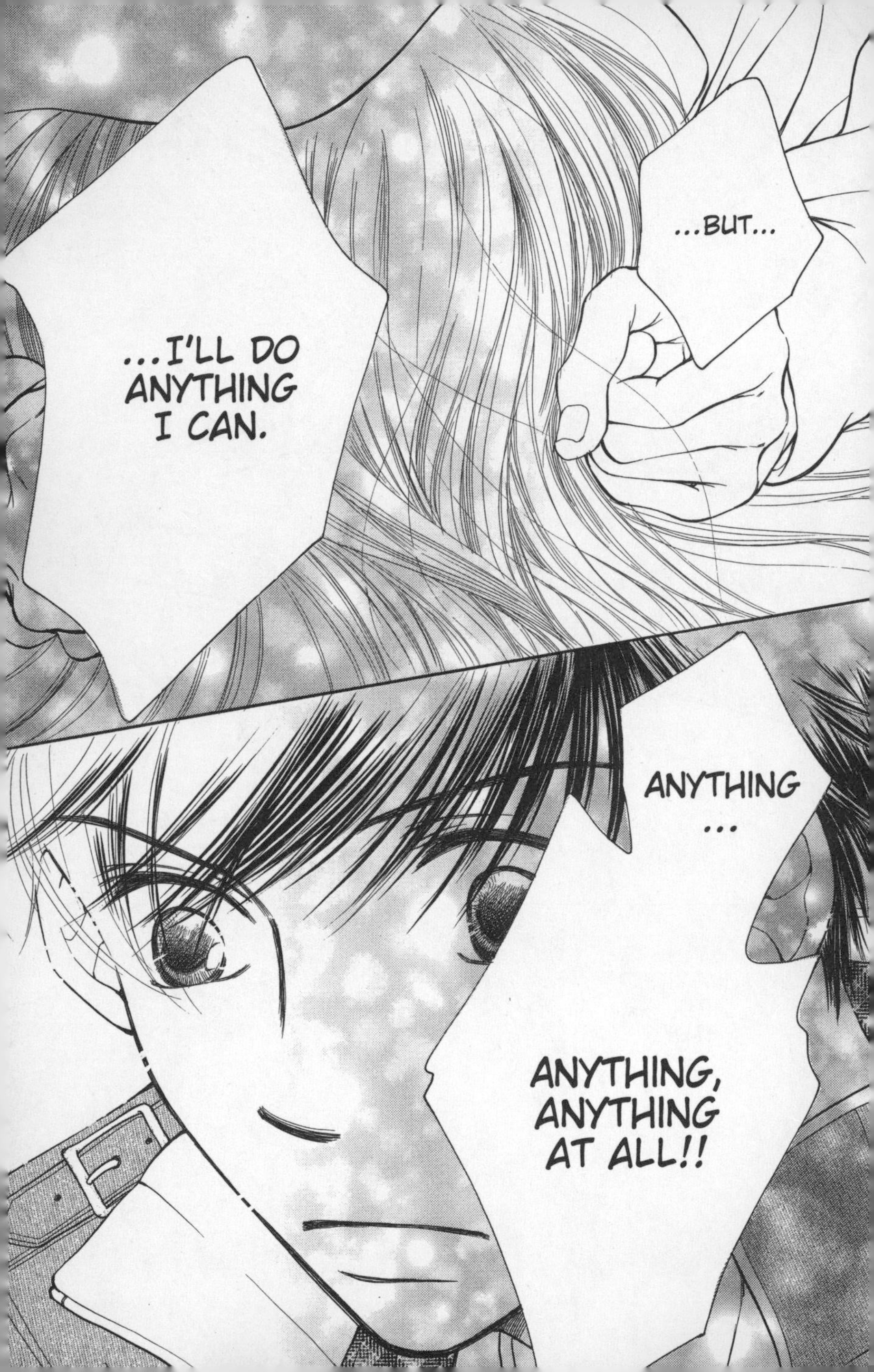
...BUT...
...I'LL DO ANYTHING I CAN.
ANYTHING ...
ANYTHING, ANYTHING AT ALL!!

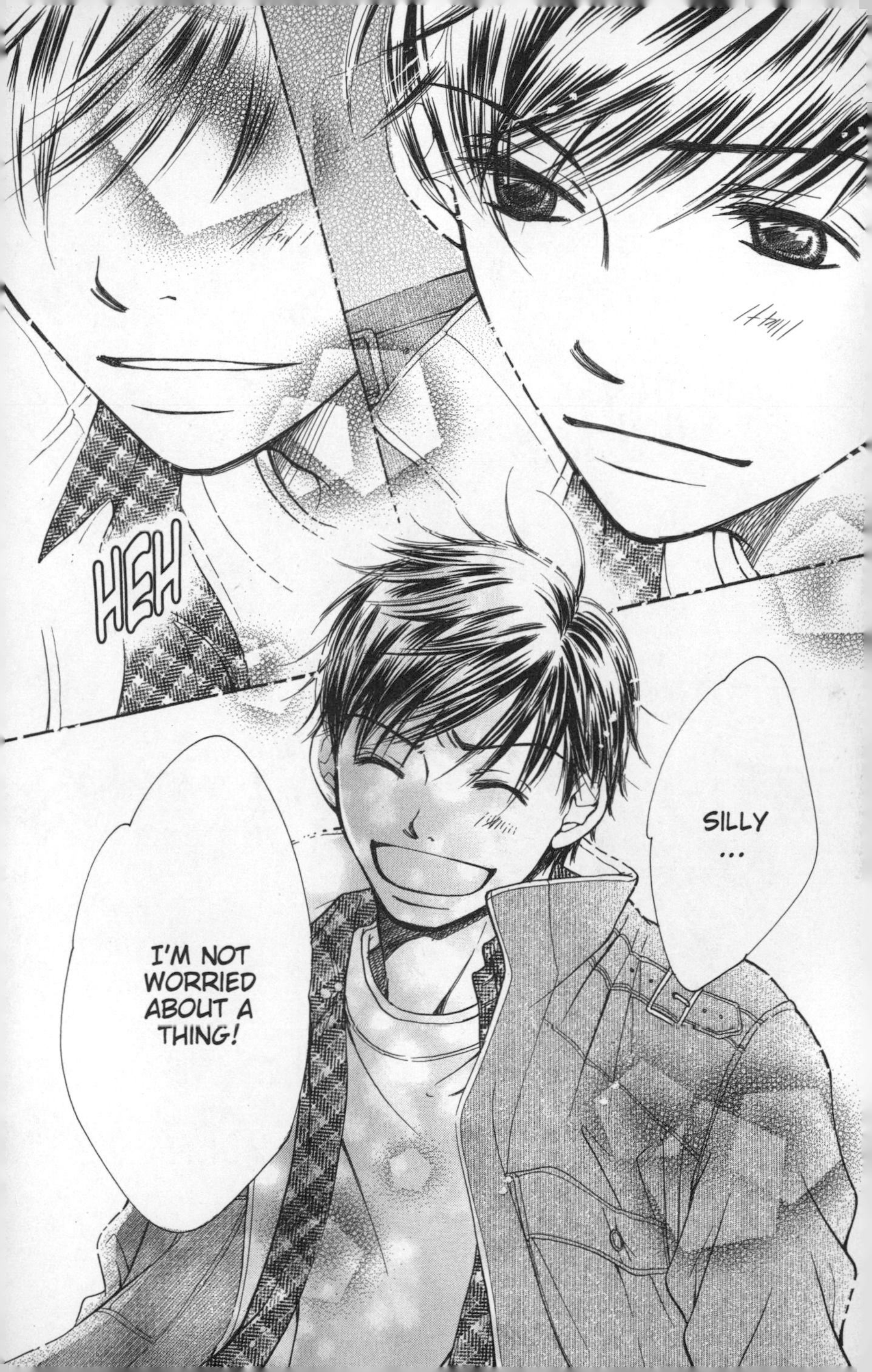
HEH
SILLY ...
I'M NOT WORRIED ABOUT A THING!

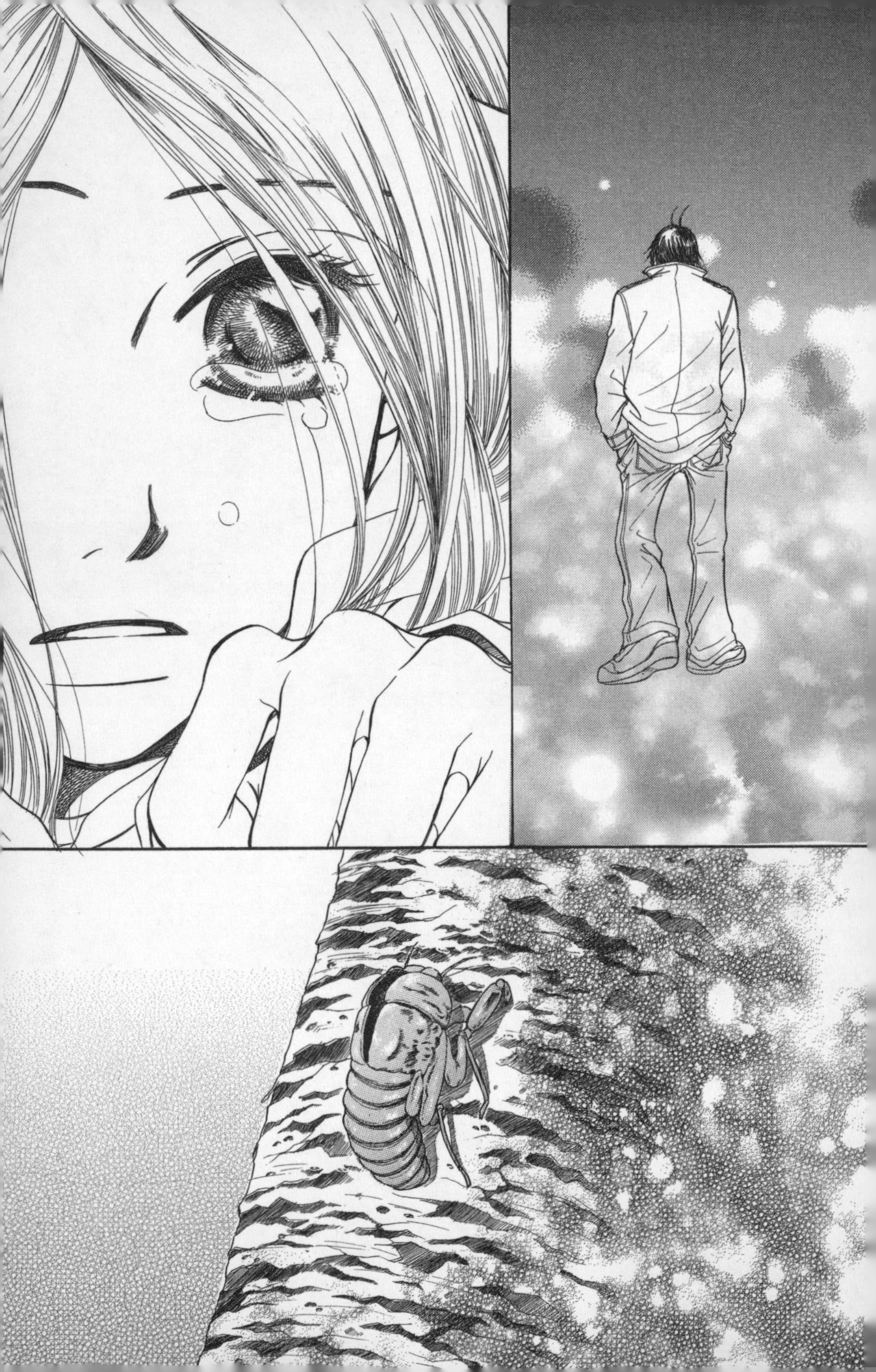

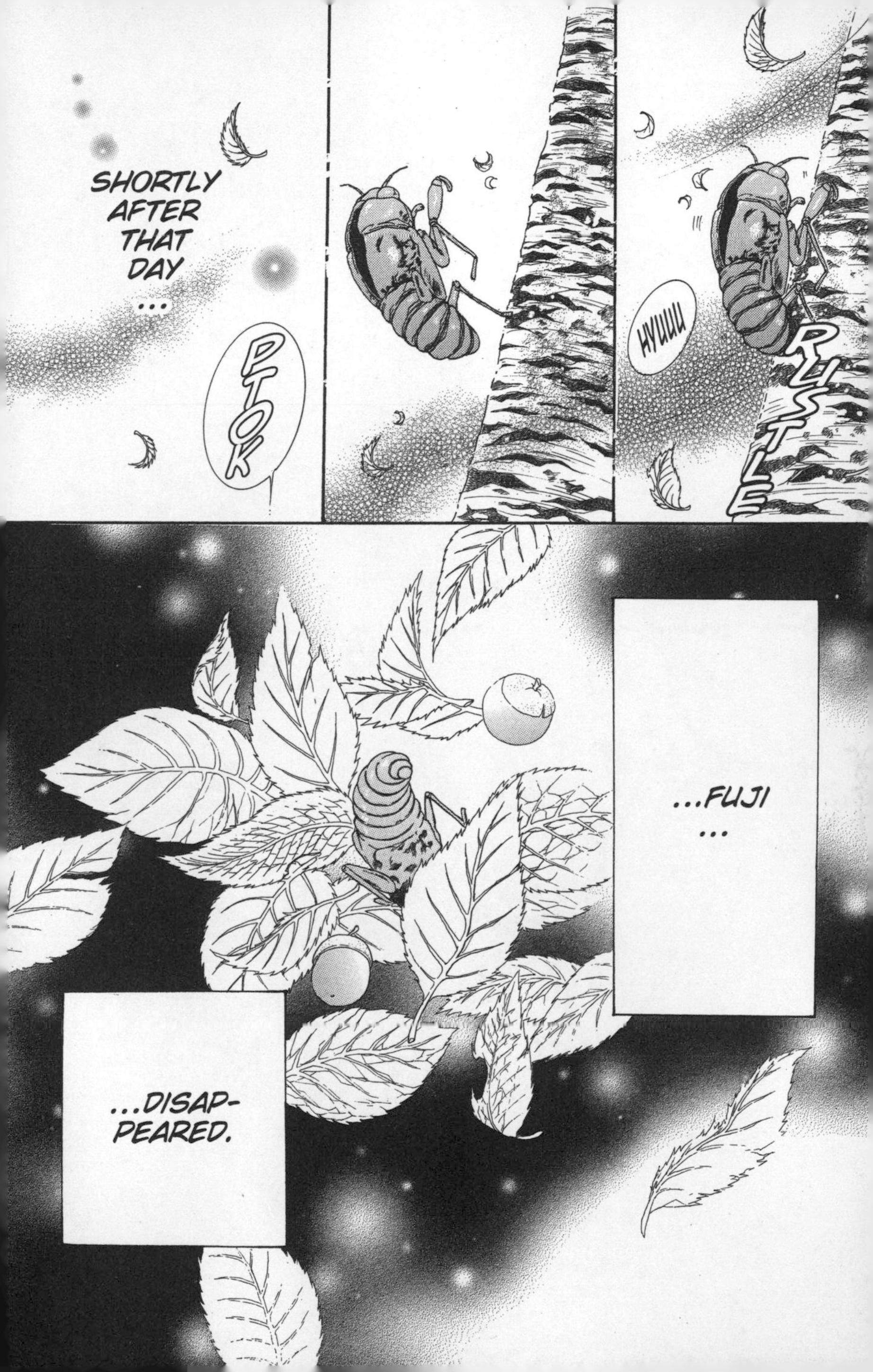
HYUUU
RUSTLE
SHORTLY AFTER THAT DAY ...
PTOK
...FUJI ...
...DISAP-PEARED.

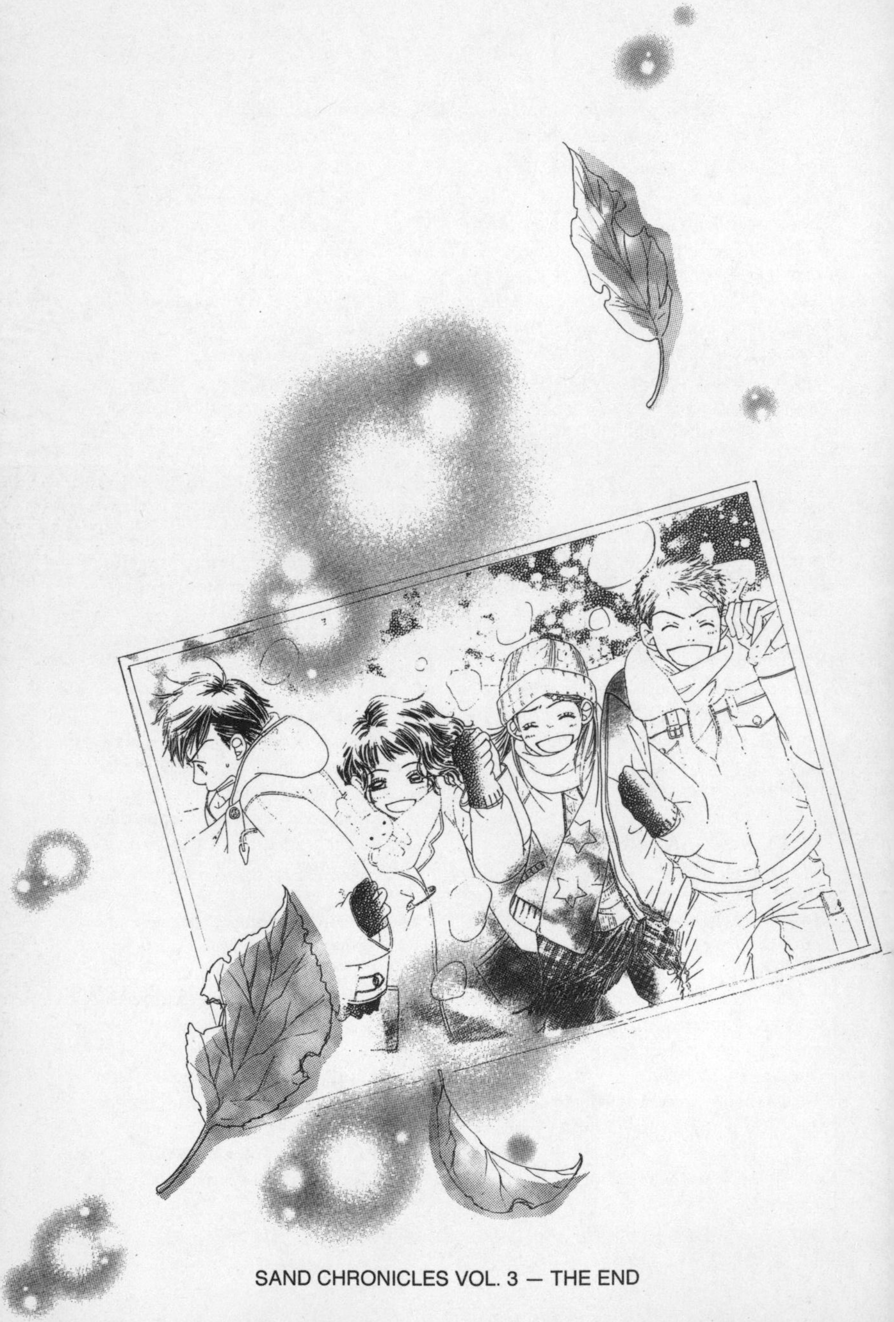

SAND CHRONICLES VOL. 3 — THE END

# Glossary

If only adolescence came with an instruction manual. We can't give you that, but this glossary of terms might prove useful for this volume.

**Page 4: Utsusemi**
The cast-off shells of the cicada are known as *utsusemi*. In Buddhist thought, because of the insects' short lifespan, they have connotations of the impermanence of the physical world. Thus, this chapter title, "Cicada Shells," might refer to the lives of people in this transient world. Cicadas appear frequently in this volume as symbols. Most noticeably, Shika and Fuji are both compared to cicadas.

**Page 8, panel 4: School breaks**
Even during vacations, a couple days are usually designated for showing up at school. Exactly what days and for what purpose differs from school to school.

**Page 10, panel 1: Obon**
Obon is a holiday held in mid-August when it is customary for people to return to their hometown and tend to the family grave. Many people get time off from work during this period.

**Page 15, panel 1: Kaminari okoshi, Tokyo banana, Funawa, sweet-potato yokan**
Kaminari okoshi is a traditional sweet from Tokyo made from rice, malt syrup, sugar, and peanuts. They look like crisped rice. *Kaminari* means "thunder," but this sweet is actually associated with the Kaminari Gate in Asakusa.

Tokyo bananas are a brand of small sponge cakes filled with banana custard.

Funawa is a brand name for a type of

yokan made from sweet potatoes. Most yokan is a gelatin-like beancake made from azuki beans.

**Page 15, panel 4: Common phrase when entering a house**
When Japanese people enter a house, they often say "excuse me," much the way we might say, "I don't mean to trouble you" or "I hope it's no bother." But that seems too formal for Ann to say to Daigo, so we adapted the translation to capture the appropriate tone in English.

**Page 45, panel 8: Classical dance, epic song, tea ceremony, flower arranging, cooking, comportment**
These are all very traditional and expensive lessons in Japanese culture.

**Page 56, panel 6: Hiyashiame**
Hiyashiame (*hiyashi* = cold + *ame* = sweet) is a cold drink consisting of malt sugar dissolved in water and squeezed ginger. It is a popular drink in western Japan that many people from other regions may not be familiar with.

**Page 71, panel 3: Common phrase when sitting down or embarking on a task**
Great-grandma says "yokkoisho" in the original. This is something said when starting to do something that requires some encouragement. It is usually said when standing up, sitting down, or starting on a new task. It's old-fashioned, though.

**Page 107, panel 1: Poem by Basho**
Ann ends her words with a line of poetry:

"…the end of summer and the remains of dreams." This phrase is from a famous poem by Basho.

**Page 122, panel 2: Common phrase a waitress says when bringing a meal**

"Sorry to have kept you waiting!!!" is what Ann actually said. But she hasn't kept Daigo waiting any more than would be usual in a restaurant. It's just something that is said when serving a customer food in Japan.

**Page 140, panel 4: Praying gesture**

Daigo claps his hands together before him the way one would when praying at a shrine.

**Page 114, panel 2: NTT bill**

NTT stands for "Nippon Telegraph and Telephone"

**Page 114, panel 7: Slang for sex**

The magazine title literally reads: First H with ♥ Your Boyfriend. The letter H is sometimes used to symbolize sex in Japanese because saying the letter H in Japanese (eicchi/eitchi) sounds like the Japanese word for sex (ecchi/etchi). It's not a very elegant expression, but it's not terribly crude either.

**Page 131, panel 2: Common phrase said at the end of a workday**

Daigo's aside actually reads, "Good work today." This is a set phrase used after any kind of work, practice, etc. However, in English, it would sound odd for an employee to say these words to his employer, so we adapted it.

**Page 140, panel 4: Praying gesture**

Once again, note that Daigo claps his hands together the way one would when praying at a shrine. This seems to be an ongoing joke with him.

**Page 141, panel 4~5: Mikoshi**

A mikoshi is a portable shrine carried through the streets in a parade. Endo uses the word *kodomo-mikoshi*. Shika is not sure she has heard properly. She asks, "Mikoshi? You mean an o-mikoshi?" The reason she confirms the honorific is because "mikoshi" is usually used that way. Endo didn't use the honorific because *mikoshi* was tacked onto *kodomo* (child). We did some rewriting here to make this literal content work in English.

**Page 145, panel 4: Chinmi**

Chinmi are snack foods with unusual flavors, mostly seafood such as octopus, squid, dried fish and so on, that are often eaten while drinking sake, an alcoholic beverage made from fermented rice.

**Page 163, panel 1: Japanese cheers**

In Japanese, the kids yell, "Yoooiyasaaa." This is something called out in situations such as this one—carrying a cumbersome o-mikoshi—in order to cheer oneself and one's companions along. It has no literal meaning.

**Page 163, panel 3: Happi**

The happi that Shika is wearing in the parade is a jacket-like garment that used to be a traditional workman's coat, but is now usually worn by festival participants.

**Page 164, panel 2: Japanese cheers (cont.)**

The boys yell, "Wasshoi." It is a kind of cheer.

# Profile of Hinako Ashihara

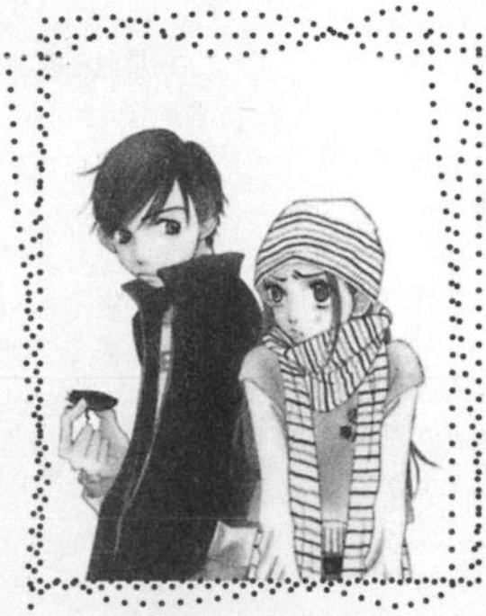

Lately, more and more people around me have succeeded in losing weight. D-Don't leave me behind! I think I need sweets to facilitate my work. Or is that just a lame excuse? Okay…it is.
—Hinako Ashihara

**Hinako Ashihara** won the 50th Shogakukan Manga Award for *Sunadokei*. She debuted with *Sono Hanashi Okotowari Shimasu* in Bessatsu Shojo Comics in 1994. Her other works include *SOS*, *Forbidden Dance*, and *Tennen Bitter Chocolate*.

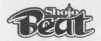

# SAND CHRONICLES
## Vol. 3
### The Shojo Beat Manga Edition

This manga volume contains material that was originally
published in English in *Shojo Beat* magazine, April 2008~July 2008 issues.
Artwork in the magazine may have been
slightly altered from that presented here.

## STORY AND ART BY HINAKO ASHIHARA

English Adaptation/John Werry
Translation/Kinami Watabe
Touch-up Art & Lettering/Rina Mapa
Additional Touch-up/Rachel Lightfoot
Cover design/Yukiko Whitley
Interior design/Izumi Evers
Editor/Annette Roman

Editor in Chief, Books/Alvin Lu
Editor in Chief, Magazines/Marc Weidenbaum
VP, Publishing Licensing/Rika Inouye
VP, Sales and Product Marketing/Gonzalo Ferreyra
VP, Creative/Linda Espinosa
Publisher/Hyoe Narita

Printed in Canada

Published by VIZ Media, LLC
P.O. Box 77010
San Francisco, CA 94107

Shojo Beat Manga Edition
10 9 8 7 6 5 4 3 2 1
First printing, September 2008

store.viz.com

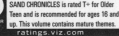
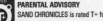

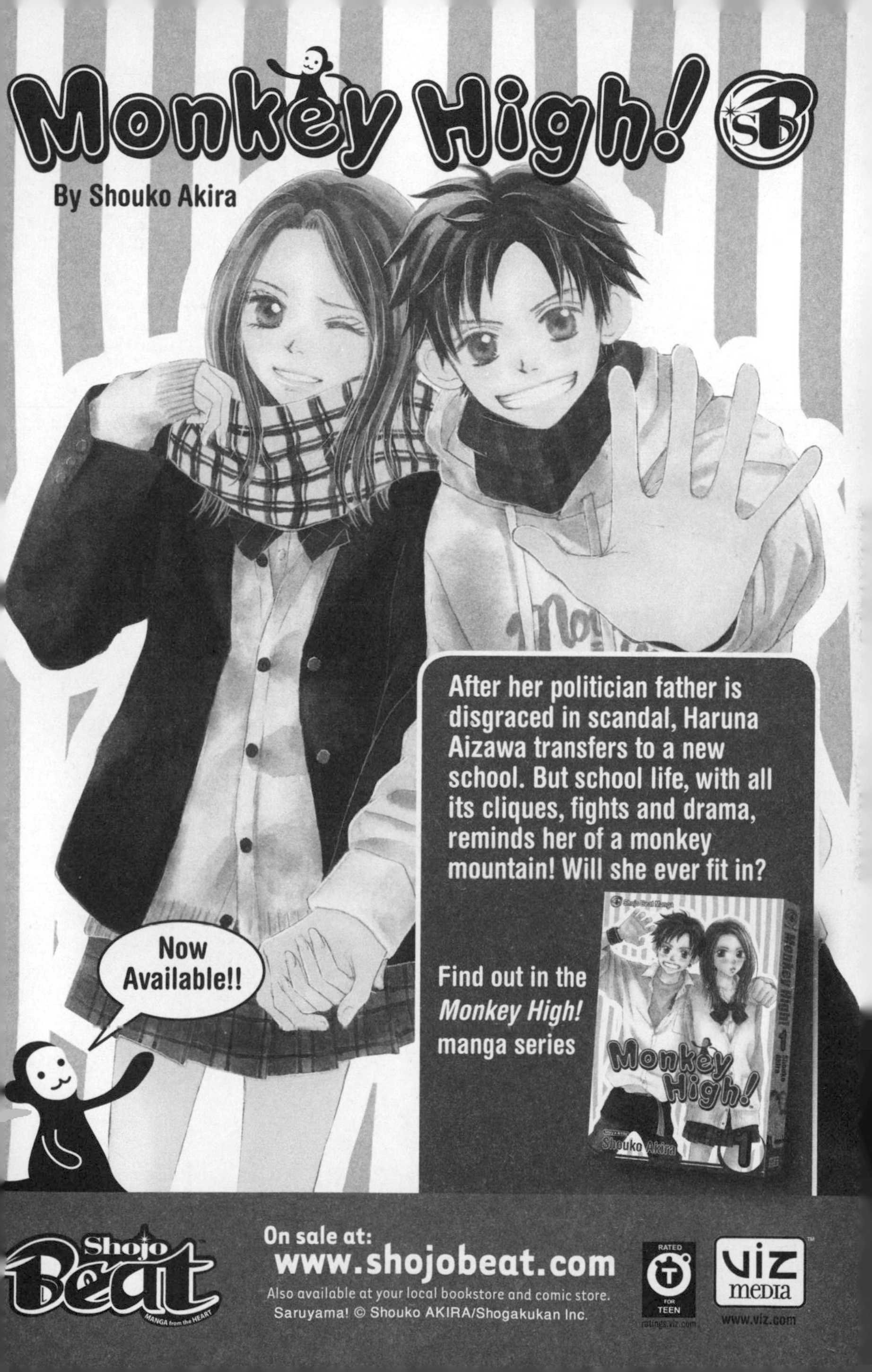
Monkey High!
SB
By Shouko Akira
After her politician father is disgraced in scandal, Haruna Aizawa transfers to a new school. But school life, with all its cliques, fights and drama, reminds her of a monkey mountain! Will she ever fit in?
Now Available!!
Find out in the *Monkey High!* manga series
Monkey High!
Shouko Akira
1
Shojo Beat
MANGA from the HEART
On sale at:
www.shojobeat.com
Also available at your local bookstore and comic store.
Saruyama! © Shouko AKIRA/Shogakukan Inc.
RATED
T
FOR TEEN
ratings.viz.com
VIZ media
www.viz.com

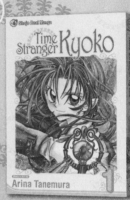
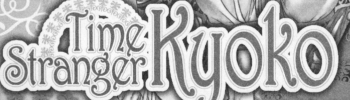
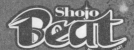

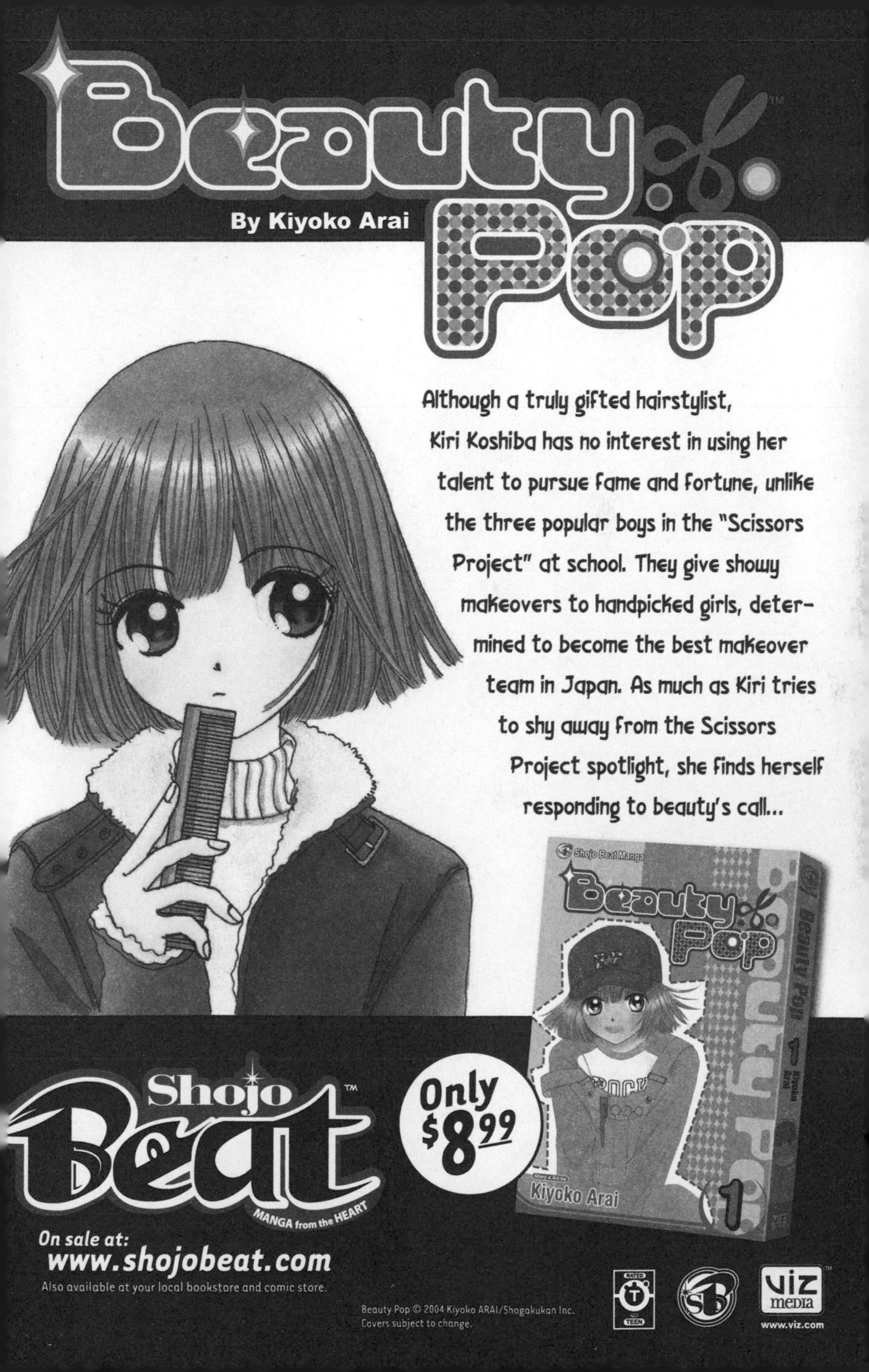

Beauty Pop™
By Kiyoko Arai
Although a truly gifted hairstylist, Kiri Koshiba has no interest in using her talent to pursue fame and fortune, unlike the three popular boys in the "Scissors Project" at school. They give showy makeovers to handpicked girls, determined to become the best makeover team in Japan. As much as Kiri tries to shy away from the Scissors Project spotlight, she finds herself responding to beauty's call...
Shojo Beat Manga
Beauty Pop
Kiyoko Arai
1
Shojo Beat™
MANGA from the HEART
Only $8.99
On sale at:
www.shojobeat.com
Also available at your local bookstore and comic store.
Beauty Pop © 2004 Kiyoko ARAI/Shogakukan Inc.
Covers subject to change.
RATED T TEEN
SB
VIZ media
www.viz.com

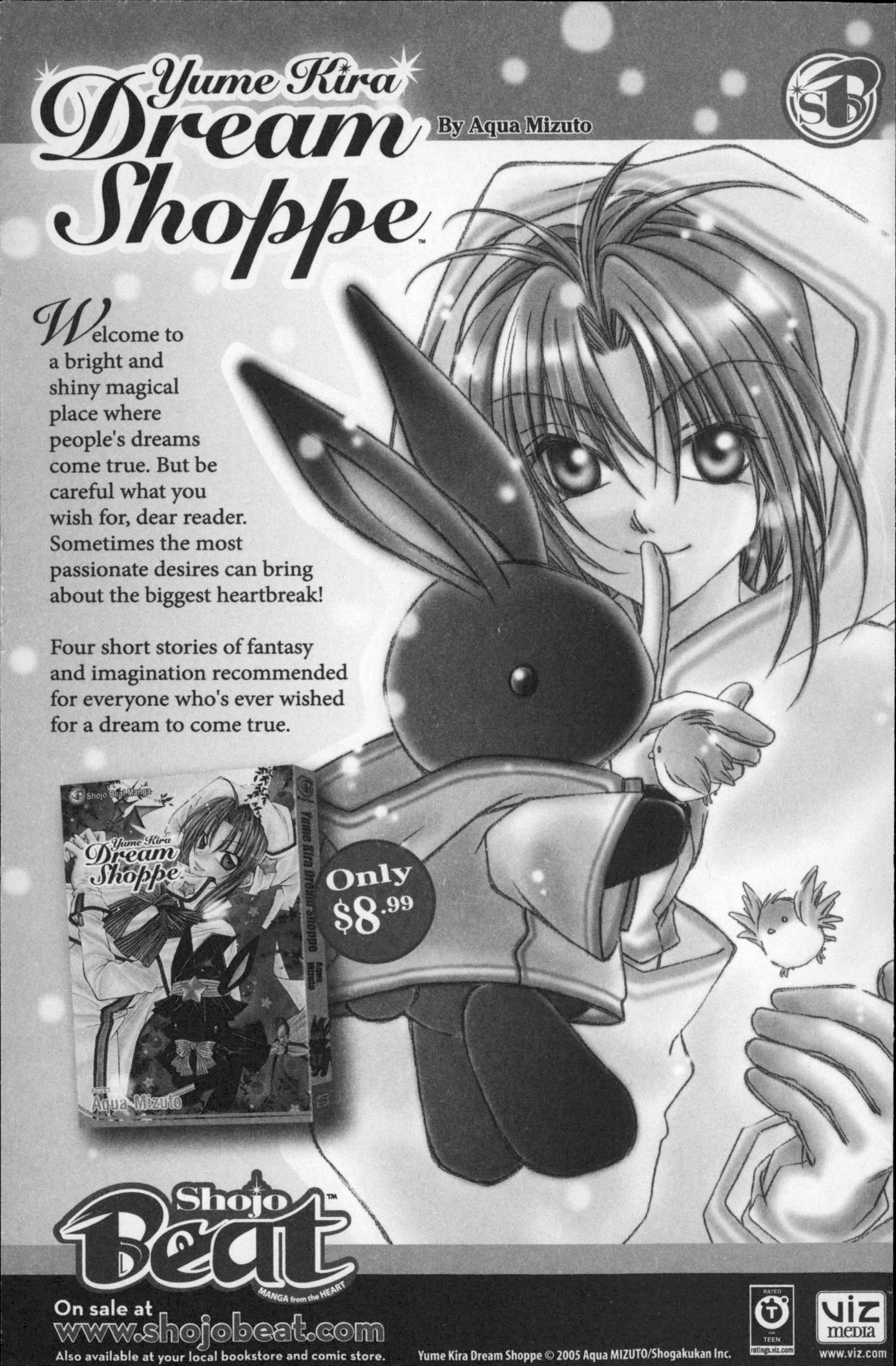

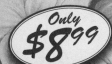
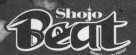

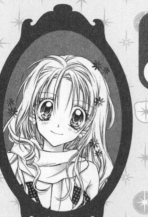
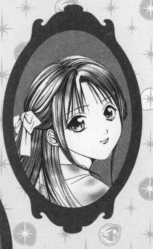

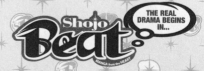